Jimmy Carter

BOOKS BY VICTOR LASKY

Seeds of Treason
with Ralph De Toledano
JFK: The Man and the Myth
The Ugly Russian
Robert F. Kennedy: The Myth and the Man
Say, Didn't You Used to Be George Murphy?
with George Murphy
Arthur J. Goldberg: The Old & the New
It Didn't Start with Watergate
Jimmy Carter: The Man and the Myth

Jimmy Carter
THE MAN
&THE MYTH

VICTOR LASKY

RICHARD MAREK PUBLISHERS
NEW YORK

Library of Congress Cataloging in Publication Data

Lasky, Victor.
  Jimmy Carter, the man and the myth.

  Bibliography: p.
  Includes index.
  1. Carter, Jimmy, 1924–   2. Presidents—United States—Biography.   3. Presidents—United States—Election—1976.   I. Title.
E873.L37   973.926'092'4 [B]   79-625
ISBN 0-399-90042-X

To my wife,
Patricia Pratt Lasky

CONTENTS

JIMMY CARTER
The Man and the Myth

1
PROLOGUE

HE IS, UNDOUBTEDLY, THE MOST AMAZING MAN EVER TO BE-
come President of the United States. And he is, undoubtedly, one
of the more inept. Rarely in the history of the Republic has there
been an occupant of the Oval Office who demonstrated so quickly
an inability to conduct even the simplest affairs of state. And rarely
has there been a Chief Executive who has aroused so much
concern among friends and foes alike. He is perceived both at
home and abroad as a politician of limited and uncertain talents, a
well-meaning man whose power derives far more from the office
he lucked into than the qualities of personal leadership he has
been able to exert. It is difficult to think of any other American
President of whom, after a relatively short period in office, so
many people were saying, "Just why in heaven's name is he doing
the things he's doing?" Or, "Does he know what he's doing?"

It can be argued, perhaps, that Jimmy Carter was not entirely at
fault. He arrived at the White House when Congress was almost
arrogantly assertive of its own powers; and when the American
people themselves had begun to regard all levels of government
with suspicion, if not downright hostility. Which, of course, was a
legacy of Watergate. Thus, President Carter, who rode into office

because of that scandal, was also its victim. And still another irony lay in the fact that as his standings in the opinion polls plummeted, "the perspective with which Americans view Watergate"—as a *Time* essay put it—had altered. "Nixon's foreign policy accomplishments—China, SALT, the Middle East, and the rest—look pretty good against the developing Democratic record." Whatever else may have been said of Nixon, his admirers and his detractors viewed him as The President. With Carter, however, there was a growing feeling in the nation that the man who occupied the Oval Office did not exactly occupy the presidency.

Into his second year in office, Carter retreated with his Administration to the wilderness at Camp David for what was widely billed as a searching self-analysis, emerging with the big news that Anne Wexler, a Democratic activist, would be taking over some of Midge Costanza's duties as liaison with "special interest" groups. And Midge, who had reveled in her close proximity to the Oval Office, soon found herself consigned to a basement office in the White House, later to be unceremoniously booted out.

But was that all there was on the mountaintop? No, press secretary Jody Powell said later. The President had "read the riot act" to his Cabinet members and chief advisers. For one thing, there was too much "intramural squabbling and bickering." And too much of it was getting into the press. Carter then told his troops he wanted them to act like a team. From now on, he said, the Administration would speak with one voice.

This was a far cry from those halcyon days when Carter had given his Cabinet members full freedom to run their departments in their own way. His was going to be an "open administration." This, of course, was meant to be the exact opposite of how the Cabinet supposedly operated under Nixon. Carter got so carried away with trying not to act like Nixon that, at his first Cabinet meeting, he announced he was considering opening such sessions to press coverage. Even more stunned than the correspondents were the Cabinet members, who argued they could hardly express themselves freely to the President under such circumstances. Carter had second thoughts, and the idea was soon forgotten.

The Administration continued to babble with many voices—the disarray most notably affecting foreign policy, as Secretary of State

Cyrus Vance took issue with national security adviser Zbigniew Brzezinski on how to handle the Russians. Meanwhile, the Ambassador to the United Nations, Andrew Young, was making his own foreign policy, declaring among other incredible things that the Soviet-backed Cubans constituted a "stabilizing force" in Africa. It was as if *The Gong Show* were being taped in Washington.

And once again, the Leader of the Free World sought to bring things under control. He called in all of his top foreign policy advisers and told them to be more self-disciplined in their public comments. And then he felt compelled to tell the American people that "I'm the President, I make the decisions."

But at times, it was difficult to understand what those decisions amounted to. For, as Senator Barry Goldwater noted in another context, Carter "has the bad habit of taking both sides of a question the same day." So low had Carter's credibility sunk that at one point he was forced to defend his honesty against charges by Fidel Castro that he had lied.

No wonder then that, on top of his other problems, neither supporters nor opponents were able to take Jimmy Carter seriously. The feeling that he was a one-term President swept across the land. Except, as some Washington wits phrased it, "When does his first term begin?"

But, for better or worse, it had begun. It began with a series of public relations gestures which, for a time, added considerably to the President's popularity. There was the walk down Pennsylvania Avenue on Inauguration Day, an entire nation watching enthralled as television relayed images of the nation's new leader and his wife walking unafraid to the White House. Then came other symbolic gestures aimed at presenting a President as just one of the people, just like you and me. There were the informal state dinners, fireside chats, telephone exchanges with ordinary citizens, town meetings in small communities, with the President spending the night at the modest homes of local supporters. And no one could say that the man from Plains, Georgia, was putting on airs just because he was forced to fly on that well-appointed Air Force One. Why, he made sure he was photographed carrying his own luggage.

It was as if the 1976 campaign had never ended. Now, however, everything was geared to the selling of a President, if not a candidate, with the headquarters appropriately transferred from Atlanta to 1600 Pennsylvania Avenue. And for the first six months or so everything seemed to be coming up magnolias for the new President, who was enjoying extremely high popularity ratings. We were told, for example, that the Chief Executive was considering policy and signing bills to the strains of Puccini, Wagner, Rachmaninoff, and Amy Carter's violin. Moreover, he was reading passages from a Spanish-language Bible every night. And for his first fireside chat he wore a cardigan sweater. The playing of "Hail to the Chief," it was emphasized, was sharply curtailed. The imperial presidency of Franklin Delano Roosevelt and his successors was no more. Or so it was advertised.

And then the dam burst. The President's best friend, Bert Lance, was forced to resign as Budget Director, suddenly rendering the President as visibly vulnerable. From then on, everything seemed to go downhill. Little the President did seemed to go right. Even with a Congress dominated by members of his own party, the President found it impossible to get things done. And in far-off Australia at the end of the first year, *The Brisbane Mail* summed it all up by observing, "An ineffective symbolic activist is . . . the most disastrous combination you could imagine in the America of 1977."

Into his second year in office, the questions concerning Carter continued. In fact, they took on new urgency. The economy continued to falter. During the first quarter, inflation devoured the dollar at the annual rate of 10 percent. Then came the most boring and pointless presidential journey in U.S. history, this one to several countries, including Brazil, whose leaders let it be known they hadn't invited the Leader of the Free World in the first place. He had actually invited himself.

After which came the extraordinary neutron bomb decision, for which there was no historical comparison in this or any other republic of literate men. But, the President argued, his decision was made out of antinuclear moralism. Within days, however, he turned around to overrule the Nuclear Regulatory Commission in order to send 7.6 tons of enriched uranium to India, the only nation actually to divert atomic materials into the proliferation of nuclear weapons. Of course, as a candidate, Carter had complained, "When India exploded its so-called 'peaceful' nuclear device, the U.S. made no public expression of disapproval." And he further noted that we actually "rewarded" India with further nuclear materials. Now he himself was "rewarding" India, and he failed to see any inconsistency between his words as a candidate and as President.

Nevertheless, the President did concede that he had too often appeared "fuzzy." Senator Henry M. Jackson had another word for it. This powerful Democrat from the state of Washington said publicly that the President was afflicted by "abulia," a Bill Buckley-type word meaning an abnormal inability to act or to make decisions.

At first, Carter's problems with Congress were chalked up to inexperience. Leaders openly complained that the President was throwing too much at them, that his liaison work was faulty, and that he failed to understand the need for compromise. But, they said confidently, he would learn.

As the months passed, the leaders began to wonder when the learning process would begin. House Democratic Whip John Brademas openly questioned the competency of the Carter Administration. He blamed the President's advisers for permitting him to become embroiled in too many difficult foreign policy questions while not involving him in domestic questions that were snowballing out of control.

All of which was reflected in a Lou Harris poll in April 1978, showing that the President's public approval rating had fallen to 33 percent—worse than the lowest figures of Presidents Kennedy, Johnson, and Ford, and a mere seven percent better than Richard Nixon's Watergate low. The perception of an inept leader in the Oval Office was sinking in deeply among the populace. Returning from several "town meetings" with his California constituents during the Easter recess, first-term Democratic Congressman Leon Panetta told *The Washington Post*, "Last year it was a question of inexperience. The question now is whether the President has the capacity needed for leadership."

Confirmation of this trend came again from Lou Harris, whose polling showed that two out of three Americans questioned Carter's ability to do the job. A June 1978 survey showed that 64 percent of those contacted felt that, although the President was well intentioned, "at times you begin to wonder if he had the basic competence to do the job." The turnabout in Carter's standings was dramatic. In July 1977, he was given a 64-to-31 positive rating on the question of restoring public confidence in government. A year later, he got a 63-to-30 negative mark. "In just twelve months," commented Harris, "there has been a total flip-flop in confidence in the President's capacity to provide the kind of leadership he promised during his 1976 campaign. In the end, people are likely to judge any President on the basis of what they think of him as an individual, what they think of his record as a national leader, and whether they have confidence in his leadership. President Carter is in real trouble on all counts right now."

Comments abroad were equally disheartening. *The Economist* of London led one week's issue with a worried article about what it called Carter's "insouciant presidency." America's friends, it said, must hope that "the giddy slide" in his fortunes was coming to an end. And, focusing on Carter's handling of neutron weapons, the respected *Financial Times* in London contended, "The Europeans must now recognize President Carter as an erratic, if not unreliable, partner." Even friends in the domestic media voiced trepidation about Carter's fitful handling of international affairs. "Is anybody in charge?" asked columnist James Reston in *The New York Times*.

And the President's curious conduct in the contretemps involving the dismissal of David Marston, the youthful U.S. Attorney who had been probing Democratic corruption in Philadelphia, evoked memories of Watergate—what with obvious White House deception and allegations of "cover-up." This, of course, was a President who had ridden into office on a white horse, telling an eager electorate he would never lie to them or act in any way like such predecessors as Lyndon Johnson and Richard Nixon.

At the same time, Carter failed to do anything about the buffoon and low comedy images projected by brother Billy, or his sister Ruth Stapleton, who converted smut magazine tycoon Larry Flynt to Born-Again Christianity.

And the antics of Hamilton Jordan didn't help much, either. Jordan, who in everything but title was the President's chief of staff, acted strictly from Dogpatch. First, there was an episode involving the Egyptian Ambassador's wife. Then the White House was forced to issue a lengthy document, practically a White Paper, attempting to refute allegations by *The Washington Post*'s Rudy Maxa that Jordan, fresh from the pyramids, had spat a drink down the blouse of a female in a Foggy Bottom bar.

This was an Administration whose leader had come to power using such remarkable phrases as "Why not the best?" and the necessity for "a government as good as its people," etc. It was an Administration whose leader had campaigned mainly on style but little substance—a style that appeared to be the absence of style. As Professor John P. Roche, a onetime LBJ speechwriter, noted, he was a leader who was a "genius at maintaining a blurred image: Every promise he made came with three footnotes." About the only thing that came through clearly in his 1976 campaign was that he was a loner, the "Outsider sent by God to clean out the Washington stables." In fact, he disliked Washington so much he proposed to live there. And it worked. The Outsider became the Insider. And very little worked. Even Carter's much-vaunted success in putting through the Panama Canal treaties was nearly botched. Instead of a solid victory, a last-minute siege of amateurism made it appear to be a narrow escape from disaster.

Nagged by sagging polls and a bad press, the President finally turned to the man who helped put him in the White House in the first place—Gerald Rafshoon. An Atlanta ad man who had worked on every Carter campaign since 1966, Rafshoon was named Assistant to The President for Communications, with responsibility for "long-range" planning in bolstering the Presidential image. The Administration clearly felt underappreciated and had concluded that bad PR was the problem. "We could and should have done a better job in presenting to the American public what we were doing," explained Jody Powell.

The "magic touch" which "Jerry" had provided in the past just wasn't there in the White House—at least immediately. The appointment, announced May 18, 1978, did produce a selective return to "Hail to the Chief," which James J. Kilpatrick thought "a step in the right direction." But the columnist thought the President's rendition of "Salt Peanuts" at a Jazz Festival "purely painful."

Rafshoon flew with the President to Germany for the July 1978 economic summit. What he did there was little publicized; but there was one report that he had concentrated on making sure that the President was well covered by American television. When, for example, the President and Chancellor Schmidt were reviewing American and German troops, Rafshoon shooed away German officials in the cameras' way. "Madison Avenue nonsense," one official was heard to say. No, he was wrong; it was more like Peachtree Street, Atlanta.

As President of the United States, Carter was automatically treated with deference by the heads of government of the six other industrial democracies gathered in Bonn. But it was a deference given grudgingly by fellow politicians concerned that Carter's apparent weakness at home could lead to a still further weakening of the American position which, in turn, would affect their own economic situations. So, as Flora Lewis reported in *The New York Times*, the leaders of Germany, Japan, Italy, France, Canada, and Great Britain decided that, no matter their private doubts, it was essential "in the interest of all to bolster the American leader" and "that all would be hurt if the impression is spread that relations with Mr. Carter are poor."

Finally, in September 1978, President Carter got the major victory he had been so assiduously seeking. And, in so doing, he violated his own campaign arguments against "secret diplomacy." Be that as it may, the seeming accords reached at Camp David by Israel's Begin and Egypt's Sadat were trumpeted to the world as the beginning of a new era in Middle East diplomacy. For Carter, the rewards came immediately. Widely criticized for his ineffectiveness, the President had now become an instant architect of peace, hailed in the pages of *Newsweek* as "a formidable international horsetrader." And thanks to excellent stage management by Rafshoon, the President's stock rose for a time.

But the sad truth was that, in his jubilation, the President may have overplayed his hand. Two successive nights of television exposure with Begin and Sadat blurred the then-unrecognized imperfections of what was being hailed as the "Framework of Peace in the Middle East." And, in the months to come, Carter was to anguish publicly at his inability to complete quickly the labors begun at Camp David.

Still, the question remained: How did a little-known Georgia politician with no significant achievements and limited knowledge of Washington and the world succeed in convincing the American people that he was the man best qualified to assume the most important elective office they had to offer?

It apparently all began during the 1972 presidential campaign, when, in the midst of George McGovern's agony, it occurred to Carter and his Georgian advisers that he should, or at any rate could, be President. After all, if he wanted to remain in politics, he had no alternative: under Georgia law, he could not succeed himself in office as Governor, and he had little hope of winning Herman Talmadge's seat in the United States Senate. So why not run for the presidency? It is part of the Carter mythology that his resolve was bolstered when, as Governor, he was approached by various presidential aspirants and, with his steely eye, he decided they were a pretty grim lot, not much better qualified than he. As he put it in his autobiography *Why Not the Best?:* *

> I have always looked on the presidency of the United States with reverence and awe, and I still do. But recently I have begun to realize that the president is just a human being. I can almost remember when I began to change my mind and form this opinion.
>
> Before becoming governor, I had never met a president, although I once saw Harry Truman at a distance. . . . Then during 1971 and 1972, I met Richard Nixon, Spiro Agnew, George McGovern, Henry Jackson, Hubert Humphrey, Ed Muskie, George Wallace, Ronald Reagan, Nelson Rockefeller, and other presidential hopefuls, and I lost my feeling of awe about presidents. This is not meant as a criticism of them, but it is merely a simple statement of fact.

It is also a simple statement of fact that what motivated Carter in seeking the presidency was not any set of philosophical convictions but, rather, an Everest complex. He wanted to climb the world's highest mountain "because it's there." He had taken the measure of the other mountain climbers and decided he could beat them at their own game. The pursuit of power, therefore, was the reason,

---

*Pages 158-159.

and reason enough, for his choice of trade. Of course, as he
pursued his goal, he did take on some ideological luggage. But
exactly what was in those bags was difficult to fathom. A friendly
writer, Patrick Anderson, who followed him around in 1975 wrote
that Carter "shapes up as a fairly conventional liberal, but one
whose views take a conservative bounce now and then. He calls
himself a fiscal conservative, and he hammers away at the need for
Government cost-cutting, stressing that as Governor of Georgia he
practiced what he preached." As he moved from one primary state
to another, wrote Anderson, "Carter's pitch is more idealistic than
ideological." In effect, he was a born-again missionary whose
politics were based on love of man and truth. All he wanted to see,
he repeatedly said, was an America with a government "as
idealistic, as decent, as competent, as compassionate, as good as
its people." And, of course, he would never lie or duck an issue
just to be President.

As for the presidency, Carter didn't think it would be too
difficult. In fact, he thought it would be a lot of fun. "I like to run
things," he told an interviewer in Plains one quiet autumn
afternoon, "to be the one who makes decisions." Sure, he said,
there might be a few problems; but he never had any doubts about
his adequacy for the job. When he was Governor, he went on, he
used to wake up every morning overjoyed at the idea of facing new
problems. And he expected it to be the same when—he rarely said
"if"—he became President.

However, it wasn't the same when he became President. The
problems were there, all right; but it wasn't long before he began
wishing they would go away. And though he had promised during
the campaign he would stay at home his first year, he found it
necessary to take time out for foreign travels. The maiden trip
through seven nations in nine days was unprecedented for the
number of presidential gaffes. When Carter said into an open mike
in India that Secretary of State Cy Vance should send a "cold and
very blunt" letter about nuclear matters to India's Prime Minister
Desai, the London *Sun*'s headline ran: "OOPS: Jimmy's Adventures in Blunderland (cont.)." His celebration of human rights in
Poland and the hilarious translation gaffes at the Warsaw Airport
resulted in Poles telling Carter jokes. Then there were the mind-
numbing remarks about the Shah and the suggestion that a

Palestinian entity might be attached to Jordan *or Israel*. And so on and on, prompting columnist Joseph Kraft to note, "Branch Rickey, the great baseball magnate, once observed that 'luck is the residue of design.' Bad luck, by the same token, happens to people who don't know what they're doing."

That was not an overharsh judgment of the performance of the novice President. Jimmy Carter, who rode in promising efficiency and competence, just couldn't seem to get the federal government to work. On matters of substance, whether energy, taxes, or health care initiatives, his Administration continued in disarray, its spokesmen frequently unable to explain their own complex proposals. The Administration, in the words of Alan L. Otten of *The Wall Street Journal*, has been "spectacularly inept," with "the evidence of botched endeavors . . . everywhere."

And yet James Earl Carter, Jr., proved superlative in getting himself elected. That may well go down as his greatest achievement.

2

"POOR" BOY FROM PLAINS

"YOU KNOW," SAID REG MURPHY, "BACK IN 1976 I WAS INCAU-
tious enough to tell someone from *The Village Voice* that Jimmy
Carter was one of the three or four phoniest men I ever met. And
now two years later I see no reason to change my mind."

Murphy was an early observer of Carter, first as political editor
and later as editor of *The Atlanta Constitution*. Currently he is
editor and publisher of *The San Francisco Examiner,* where I
interviewed him.

Also back in 1976, Murphy predicted that Carter, because of his
ruthlessness, would win the presidential election. "He will win
. . . because he's more determined to win than anybody else," he
told *Newsweek*. "He will do what it takes to win: he will change
what views it takes for him to win. He will expand and expound on
any topic . . . and he will do it with what a lot of people take to be
grace and style and talent. . . . My problem is that I just don't
understand him as a leader. I don't think he has any human
warmth in him, and so I just can't imagine anybody being led by
him. I can imagine him sounding good to people for a day or two; I
can't imagine him sounding very good to them for four years. His
attitudes wear very thin very quickly. I also believe that leader-

ship demands more than just the cold-eyed ability to calculate where the votes are and that sort of thing, and I just don't think he has that."

These were tough words, indeed; and when asked about them one year after Jimmy Carter's inauguration as President, Murphy would say only, "Unfortunately, my analysis proved only too correct."

Of course, in Carter's defense, it could be argued that he was not the only politician who has at least occasionally resorted to verbal flimflam to win over specific audiences. But there is no doubt that Carter reached a new high in sending out mixed signals during his presidential campaign. Thus, while seeking support from the evangelicals with his born-again references, he made a direct appeal to the readers of *Playboy*, indulging in pulpit and locker-room language in one interview. This, needless to say, was the candidate who boasted about talking both to God and rock superstar Gregg Allman. His, at the very least, was a multifaceted personality, about whom Kris Kristofferson could well have been writing in the song which had the line, "He's a walking contradic-tion/ Partly truth and partly fiction."

"Partly truth and partly fiction" could well characterize the Southern, small-town, barefoot-poor boyhood portrait that Carter presented in his autobiography *Why Not the Best?* Carter made his family's economic situation sound worse than it really was during the 1930s. "My life on the farm during the Great Depression more nearly resembled farm life of fully 2,000 years ago than farm life today. . . . For years we used an outdoor privy in the back yard for sanitation and a hand pump for water supply." During the presidential primaries, he made it seem that he hailed from an area so primitive that Tobacco Road could have been considered paradise by comparison. "I come from one of the poorest parts of the country," he said in Florida. "In my county we don't have a doctor, we don't have a pharmacist, a dentist. . . ." Of course, what he didn't say was that the doctor, the pharmacist, the dentist, and modern hospital facilities were all down the road a piece in Americus.

And he would frequently remember the early period of his life as filled with the hard, hand-blistering labor of the average farm boy, leaving the impression that for the Carters times were tough indeed. Whenever he ran for office, he would repeatedly speak of his boyhood. "The thing that sticks in my mind the most about my boyhood is hard work," he said in 1970 while running for governor. ". . . . I worked this way until I went to the Naval Academy, shakin' peanuts, pickin' cotton, totin' water, hoein' cotton, puttin' out soda around corn, prunin' watermelons. My most vivid memory of my boyhood life is a long, hard day's work in the sun, in the fields. . . .." The headline in the Athens, Georgia, *Daily News* which carried the quotation read: CARTER REMEM-BERS HARD TIMES.

All of which says less about the facts of Carter's boyhood than his penchant for overstatement, a trait which was to cause him embarrassment on the campaign trail and as President. The truth is that while things were indeed tough for most of his neighbors, the Carters were comparatively well off. And while Carter has never really said they were poor, either in his autobiography or in his campaign oratory, the impression given by his writings and verbal recollections is that they were less than fortunate.

And nothing has more annoyed his mother, Mrs. Lillian Carter, than his misrepresentation of their status in Plains. "I know Jimmy writes about how poor we were," she once told Clyde Haberman of *The New York Post*, "but really we were never poor." Actually, she observed, the Carters lived in a fairly comfortable house, although "like all country people" in those days, they had no running water or electricity. "We didn't feel poor and we always had a car. We had the first radio in Plains. We had the first TV set."

On another occasion, she told an interviewer, "We didn't have much money, but we had everything we needed. Jimmy's book makes us sound so poor you want to get out a hat and take up a collection."

Though cash-poor, the Carters were land-rich, eventually accumulating several thousand acres of farm and woodland, raising peanuts and cotton. And by the standards of Plains and environs, they were as close to a patrician class as the community had, leading citizens in a society keenly aware of hierarchy. And the lowest of the low in that hierarchy were the blacks, dozens of whom worked on the Carter farm and purchased their vittles at the Carter commissary.

Jimmy Carter was brought up in a society dominated by racial segregation, one in which the "nigguhs" knew their place. And his father, James Earl Carter, Sr., made sure they knew their place. In his autobiography, Jimmy told a story indicating how the social rules operated. On the night of the second prizefight between Joe Louis and Max Schmeling, the Carters' black neighbors asked if they could listen to the fight on the Carters' battery-operated radio. As Carter noted, the fight had "heavy racial overtones" because Louis was "given a good chance to become the new black heavyweight champion of the world." The radio was propped up in the window of the Carter house, and everyone either sat or stood under a large mulberry tree nearby. Louis nearly killed his opponent in the first round, and, according to Carter, his father was "deeply disappointed."

Except for a polite "Thank you, Mister Earl," offered to Jimmy's father, the black neighbors didn't make a sound. "Then, our several dozen visitors filed across the dirt road, across the railroad track, and quietly entered a house about a hundred yards away out in the field. At that point, pandemonium broke loose inside that house, as our black neighbors shouted and yelled in celebration of the Louis victory. But all the curious, accepted proprieties of a racially segregated society had been carefully observed."

However, Jimmy's mother, Miz Lillian, differed with her husband on how blacks should be treated. A registered nurse, she took care of black families with no less compassion than she did whites. "I've been called a nigger-lover all my life," she said in 1976. "I have even had eggs thrown at me." In *Why Not the Best?* Carter summed up the difference between his parents: "He was quite conservative, and my mother was and is a liberal, but within our family we never thought about trying to define such labels."

But apparently even Miz Lillian can still give vent to racial outbursts, according to *The New York Times* correspondent James Wooten. After a black preacher from a nearby city made headlines by trying unsuccessfully to integrate the Plains Baptist Church on the eve of the 1976 presidential election, Miz Lillian, who was thought to have overcome her Dixie upbringing, snarled: "Somebody should have shot that nigger before he came on the lawn."*

---

*James Wooten, *Dasher: the Roots and the Rising of Jimmy Carter* (New York, Summit, 1978), p. 86.

With such a background, it is not surprising that Jimmy Carter waged a self-styled "redneck" campaign for Governor in 1970, indulging in blatant "seg-wooing," and then in his inaugural address proclaimed that "the time for racial discrimination is over." Consistency has never been Carter's strong suit.

An eighth-generation Georgian, whose ancestors—including cotton farmers, merchants, and Civil War soldiers—had lived in the southwestern region of Georgia for about 150 years, James Earl Carter, Jr., was born in the small town of Plains, in Sumter County, on October 1, 1924. His father, Mister Earl, had served in World War I as a first lieutenant in the Army. A fairly successful farmer, he was a recognized leader in the white community. Serving on the Sumter County School Board, he also taught Sunday School at the Baptist Church. He also served as one of the first directors of the local Rural Electrification Administration, and one year before his death in 1953 he was elected to the state legislature.

Carter's maternal forebears also had a great interest in politics. Miz Lillian's father, James Jackson Gordy, was active in Democratic affairs and, as a reward, the party named him postmaster in Richland, Georgia. "Jim Jack" as he was known, was also a great supporter and admirer of Thomas E. Watson, a fiery, nationally known Populist from southern Georgia who had polled a million votes in 1896 as the vice-presidential candidate of the national People's Party. It was an admiration which Gordy's daughter shares to this day. Miz Lillian still speaks of Watson with reverence, affection, and even love. Jimmy Carter, in a campaign speech, referred to Watson as a "great Populist Congressman," one whom his maternal grandfather had once served as a campaign manager.

As Professor Lawrence Goodwyn of Duke University has noted, this side of Carter's family "shared with Watson the conviction that credit merchants in the South, and the American banking system generally, were systematically exploiting the great mass of American farmers.

"On the other hand, Jimmy Carter's paternal forebears were credit merchants who, like their counterparts elsewhere in the South, managed to acquire title to much of the surrounding countryside. As such, from a Populist perspective, they were part of the problem, not part of the solution."

But Tom Watson was also something else. What Jimmy Carter did not say was that this "great Populist Congressman" was one of the crudest bigots ever to emerge on the Southern scene. For more than a generation, this embittered demagogue traded on the economic misery and discontent of the rural South, stirring up latent distrust of Catholics and Jews as aliens and enemies of "Christian America." Ironically, Watson had begun his political career, which eventually took him to the U.S. Senate, as a champion of Negro rights. But after losing two heated races for Congress, he turned against his Negro allies to become the leader of the drive to disenfranchise black people, a campaign that led to a tragic race riot in 1906.

Watson also edited a weekly hate periodical called *The Jeffersonian,* which had an enormous circulation throughout rural Georgia. In it, he took up the case of Leo Frank, a New York Jew who was on trial for the murder of a fourteen-year-old girl who had worked in an Atlanta pencil factory he managed. "Leo Frank was a typical young Jewish man of business, who lives for pleasure and runs after gentile girls," Watson wrote during the trial. "Every student of sociology knows that the black man's lust after the white woman is not much fiercer than the lust of the licentious Jew for the gentile."

After William Randolph Hearst took up the case, his numerous newspapers across the land lambasting "Georgia justice," Governor John M. Slaton commuted Frank's death sentence to life imprisonment, saying he did not believe Frank's guilt had been proved. For this, the Governor was denounced by Watson as "King of the Jews."

On August 16, 1915, a mob disarmed the guards at the Milledgeville Prison Farm, abducted Frank, took him to the outskirts of Marietta, and lynched him. And Tom Watson rejoiced in the lynching, which he called an "execution." He wrote:

In putting the Sodomite murderer to death, the Vigilance Committee has done what the Sheriff would have done if Slaton had not been made of the same mould as Benedict Arnold. JEW LIBERTINES TAKE NOTICE! Georgia is not for sale to rich criminals!

In his declining years, Watson became even more ferocious in his anti-Semitism. As his biographer C. Van Woodward wrote, ". . . if any mortal man may be credited (as no one man may rightly be) with releasing forces of human malice and ignorance and prejudice, which the Klan merely mobilized, that man was Thomas E. Watson."

And Thomas E. Watson was the man to whom Jimmy Carter paid tribute as a "great Populist."

Watson died in 1922, two years before Jimmy Carter was born. But as a boy, Jimmy heard a great deal of him because of Grandpa Jim Jack's relationship with the Sage of Hickory Hill. As Carter noted during the 1976 primary campaign, his grandfather had come up with the idea for Rural Free Mail Delivery. "It was passed, introduced by Tom Watson, our Congressman . . . so anyone who lives on a rural route can thank my grandfather. . . ." So great was Jim Jack's admiration for the Populist leader that when his youngest son—Jimmy's maternal uncle—was born, he named him Tom Watson Gordy. A pleased Watson wrote Jim Jack a note saying he hoped "that the infant who will bear my name through life will find the road onward and upward less rocky than it has been to his namesake."

Jimmy Carter has often proudly described himself as a "Populist." In an interview with *U.S. News & World Report* in September 1976, he said this meant he "derived my political support, my advice, and my concern directly from people themselves, not from powerful intermediaries or representatives of special interest groups." But he also made it clear during the presidential contest that his definition of "Populist" excluded appeals to racial bigotry. That, unfortunately, wasn't always true. In 1970, Carter made covert appeals to the darker instincts of Georgians. In his race for Governor, he solicited and received the endorsement of anti-black spokesmen. And, as President, he had no compunction about unloosing a campaign aimed at cutting into the effectiveness of what was widely described as the "Jewish lobby." Thus, during the 1978 debate on the President's proposal to sell warplanes simultaneously to Egypt, Israel, and Saudi Arabia, one of Carter's Senate supporters, Mike Gravel of Alaska, an outstanding liberal, assailed "Jewish influence" for seeking to persuade him and other Senators to cast a negative vote. Likewise,

George McGovern warned "Israel's most outspoken American advocates" against pressing their case.

Once Carter won on the plane issue—one of his few major victories—he cooled the White House-inspired rhetoric. Likewise, following his 1970 election as Governor, he turned to placating the blacks. He even arranged for the hanging of a portrait of Dr. Martin Luther King, Jr., in the State Capitol.

One thing Carter doesn't like is to be pushed around. And he claims to have inherited that spirit from his ancestors. "They were fighters, I mean actual fighters," he once told an interviewer. "My great-great-grandfather, my great-grandfather, and my grandfather had fights in which men were killed—you know, they killed their opponent or they [themselves] were killed in a fight. They were honest people, but they never have been willing to be pushed around."

"I was a little guy," Carter continued. "They called me 'Baby Dumplin'.' I don't know if you remember Dagwood, but he used to have a son and they called him 'Baby Dumplin'.' Daddy always told me to do the best I could and not let anybody push me around because I was small. I had a lot of fights. I kinda enjoyed the physical combat but I was real little for my age. When I graduated from high school I was five-foot three-inches tall. Then I grew all of a sudden. We're kinda late growers."

Some of Carter's strongest boyhood memories concern school and reading. When he was twelve, Miss Julia Coleman, a teacher at the all-white school Jimmy attended, opened his eyes to the wonders of literature. She urged him to read *War and Peace,* which, because of the title, he thought was about cowboys and Indians. Nevertheless, he read it and liked it. "I have always read three or four books a week," he said more recently.

He attended Plains High School, where he played basketball and attended "prom parties," those heavily chaperoned socials sponsored by the Baptist Church. "We'd spend the whole prom in the back seat of a car parked out in back of the church. It was just great. The chaperones didn't mind. You'd switch girls. They'd ring a bell every fifteen minutes, and we'd switch. At that time there wasn't any pairing off like there is now. My children can't believe it when I tell them about it."

In 1941, as a senior in high school, he took his first trip to New

York. His principal, Y.T. Sheffield, had arranged the trip for
Jimmy and several classmates to take in the World's Fair. Sheffield
had some Brooklyn friends who had written him to say he could
use their apartment while they were vacationing in Florida. The
apartment was near the Saint George Hotel in Brooklyn Heights.
"One night," according to Carter, "we got lost on the damn
subway. We missed the King [sic] George Hotel and went all the
way to the end of the subway and sat out there four or five hours
and then it came back. We didn't know what else to do so we just
stayed on it and we figured we'd eventually get to the King
George Hotel. We were so scared someone was going to steal our
money we walked around—all four of us—with our hand on our
hip pocket."

New York was the most exotic place young Carter had ever
visited, but aside from his subway adventure there is nothing on
the record to indicate how he felt, as a sixteen-year-old, about the
big, bustling metropolis occupied by people with strange accents.
At an early age, Jimmy had decided that traveling was for him. His
uncle Tom Watson Gordy, an enlisted man in the Navy, had
whetted his appetite for foreign climes by sending picture
postcards from various ports of call. Carter's autobiography tells of
his early decision to attend the U.S. Naval Academy. "Even as a
grammar school boy I read books about the Navy and Annapolis,"
he wrote. Without revealing his youthful age, he wrote the
Academy asking for the entrance requirements, practically memo-
rizing the catalogue when it arrived. He pondered long and hard
over whether such sins as "malocclusion of teeth" or "urine
retention" would bar his admission. "I was always ashamed to ask
whether that last clinging drop would block my entire naval
career!" he later wrote.

What was significant about all this is that Jimmy Carter had long
planned to enter Annapolis. But early admission to the Academy
was not to be. For one thing, the local Congressman, Stephen
Pace, could not swing the appointment. What with U.S. entry into
the war then raging in Europe almost a certainty, others were
doing their darndest to get their sons into military academies.
There was a long line, and Pace told Jimmy's father his son would
have to wait. Besides, the Congressman said, the boy needed
maturing and would do well to get some more of the schooling in

science and math he missed at Plains High. Pace, according to
Carter, was "a man whom my father had supported every two
years, both in hopes of obtaining my appointment to Annapolis
and also because our Congressman specialized in legislation
concerning peanuts—our major crop." In years to come, Carter
was to decry such obvious efforts at "purchasing" influence on the
part of others.

In 1941, at the age of seventeen, Jimmy Carter enrolled in
Georgia Southwestern College in nearby Americus. After one
year, he transferred to the Georgia Institute of Technology in
Atlanta—Georgia Tech—as a Naval ROTC student. The following
year, 1943, while most of Jimmy's buddies in Plains and environs
were being shipped off to military duty around the globe, Carter
wound up at Annapolis, his father's wooing of Congressman Pace
finally paying off. As Carter tells it, life at the Naval Academy was
not all that tough. "The academic requirements were stringent,
but in my opinion not so difficult as at Georgia Tech," he later
wrote. Classes were small and run competitively. The required
courses stressed engineering. Ironically, even in wartime, some
old traditions remained. The midshipmen "learned how to dance
from professional instructors—without girls. Fox trot, waltz,
samba, and rhumba were required subjects." He and his room-
mate used part of their earnings to purchase classical phonograph
records, and together with other midshipmen "we would argue for
hours about the relative quality of performance of orchestras and
concert soloists." It wasn't a bad life at all.

Carter graduated from Annapolis in 1946, finishing fifty-ninth in
a class of 820 without excessive grinding. The yearbook for his
class noted, "Studies never bothered Jimmy. In fact, the only
times he opened his books were when his classmates desired help
on problems. This lack of study did not, however, prevent him
from standing in the upper part of his class. . . ." By now, of
course, the war was over. And Carter started a two-year hitch of
sea duty. It wasn't the best of times. The postwar Navy was in bad
shape. Carter was assigned to a beat-up old battleship which had
been converted into an electronics and gunnery experimental
vessel. The work was interesting, but the duty was terrible. "I
became most disillusioned with the Navy, and the military in
general, and probably would have resigned had not I and all

Annapolis graduates been serving 'at the pleasure of the President.'"

In all, Carter served seven years in the Navy, two years on battleships and five on submarines, attaining the rank of lieutenant commander. The high point of his career was his service on the atomic energy submarine project under then Captain Hyman Rickover. Carter has told the story a thousand times of how when he acknowledged that he had not *always* done his best at Annapolis, Rickover demanded to know: "Why not?" Carter could not give an answer then, but the question eventually provided him with a title for his autobiography and a slogan for his presidential campaign. In one speech, Carter claimed that Rickover "has absolutely no tact—doesn't care for anything. As a matter of fact, all the time I worked for him he never said a decent word to me. However, he did change my life because he had one characteristic. . . . He would never accept mediocrity. . . ."

And while Carter has talked and written a great deal about Rickover, the actual period they worked together lasted slightly less than a year. In November 1952, Carter was assigned to Schenectady as senior officer of the precommissioning crew of *Seawolf*, one of the first atomic submarines then being built. During the day, he taught mathematics and reactor technology to the crew members; at night, he took graduate courses in nuclear physics at Union College for one semester. This, according to Carter, was "the finest Navy billet available to any officer of my rank." And, on the basis of these experiences, Jimmy Carter, during the 1976 presidential campaign, would describe himself as a *nuclear physicist*. Since he never received a degree, that was hardly a correct description. The appropriate term would have been *nuclear engineer*. Still, as *Atlanta Journal* political writer David Nordan wrote, "In Plains, Ga., a fellow who did graduate work in physics and ran a nuclear submarine is a nuclear physicist—whether a Ph.D. from MIT agrees with that or not."

Nevertheless, Jimmy Carter's penchant for hyperbole is striking, particularly in a man who had campaigned on a promise he would never ever make a misleading statement. Only a few weeks after he assumed the presidency, Carter visited the Pentagon to say hello to an enthusiastic throng of Defense Department employees. In the course of his impromptu remarks, he made reference to how he voluntarily "served in two wars." Perhaps so, technically. But in the late stages of World War II he was at Annapolis, cracking the books and learning how to tango. And during the Korean conflict, he was stationed on the East Coast, a married man, half a world away from the sounds of battle.

3
FROM NAVY MAN TO POLITICIAN

JIMMY CARTER ONCE REMARKED THAT HE THOUGHT THE U.S. Navy an unsatisfactory career because, at best, it could lead to being only Chief of Naval Operations. And that apparently wasn't good enough for the boy from Plains, Georgia. From the beginning, it was obvious that Jimmy did not derive any satisfaction from a naval career; what he termed his "lifetime commitment" began to falter. He had no particular love of the sea or any overwhelming desire to continue in the service of his country. And when his father died of cancer in 1953, he was confronted with a problem.

That problem was this: "Did I want to be the Chief of Naval Operations, and devote my whole life to that one narrowly defined career, which was a good one, or did I want to go back [to Plains] and build a more diverse life with a lot of friends, permanence, stability, in a community, in a relationship, in the life of a whole group of people?" Carter chose the latter, over the heated objections of his wife, Rosalynn, to whom Plains meant only one thing—proximity to strong-willed mother-in-law Miz Lillian.

Miz Lillian apparently was none too happy about the marriage of her oldest son to Rosalynn Smith, a pretty young thing who hailed from the area. For one thing, Miz Lillian had someone else in mind for Jimmy. Then, she felt Rosalynn was not good enough to marry a Carter, coming "from the wrong side of the tracks," according to Jimmy's cousin Hugh Carter. But on July 7, 1946, shortly after Jimmy was graduated from Annapolis, he married Rosalynn, and she began what she thought would be the long life of a Navy wife.

After seven years in the service, two of which were spent in idyllic Hawaii, James Earl Carter, Jr., resigned from the Navy. And in 1976, while being interviewed by Bill Moyers on the Public Broadcasting System, he looked back over the naval years and said, "Well, I would like, obviously in retrospect, to have been more with my father. I never thought he would die so young. But I've never regretted a day that I served in the Navy. That was an opportunity for me that paid off. I had a chance to travel extensively. I read and studied everything from, you know, music, drama, art, classical music, and so forth. I stretched my mind and had a great challenge, and I never had any regret for a single day that I spent in the Navy. I never regretted getting out a single day after I left."

In years to come, Carter was to describe his early life as a civilian as being most difficult. He moved his wife and three children into a newly built public housing project, rent $30 a month. For a few days, the family had lived with Carter's mother when they arrived in Plains. But as Miz Lillian later recalled, it was she who suggested they find another place to live "because no house is big enough for two women." Rosalynn later said moving was her idea, but she gave the same reason. Miz Lillian obviously was too much for Rosalynn.

As for the agribusiness he inherited from his father, Carter has repeatedly said that in his first year he turned a profit of less than $200. But the paper profit appeared to be misleading. According to Miz Lillian, the business actually had an uncollected $90,000 owed it that year. Jimmy's father, Mister Earl, hadn't died a poor man, either. He was said to have been worth well over a quarter of a million dollars when he passed away.* The Carter business, of

---

*Cousin Beedie and Cousin Hot: My Life with the Carter Family of Plains, Georgia, by Hugh Carter as told to Frances Spatz Leighton (Englewood Cliffs, N.J., Prentice-Hall, 1978), p. 91.

course, consisted of buying peanuts from local farmers and then selling them in bulk to large processors. By the early seventies, Carter Warehouses became one of Georgia's largest peanut wholesalers. And, in fact, so profitable did it become that eventually Jimmy was able to devote more of his time to outside pursuits.

From the beginning, Jimmy Carter was interested in politics. He noted, for example, that on the death of his father, local county leaders urged his mother to fill out the remaining year of his dad's legislative term as a state representative. But Miz Lillian said no, and they gave the seat to one of his father's close friends, who retained the post for eight or ten years. But, as Jimmy confessed, "I would not have challenged him for the seat, although I thought about it several times during the ensuing years." Which was an oblique way of saying that the thought had crossed his mind, but he let it pass. He had also thought about the State Senate, but that didn't appear to be much of a prize either. Such seats were rotated among three counties for two-year terms. That meant that no one could get much of a handle on the job. Election to the State Senate, therefore, was "of little consequence," Carter noted.

What Carter obviously was looking for was something of "consequence," something he could sink his teeth into, something that would make people sit up and take notice of Jimmy Carter. He bided his time, trying the organizational route in the meantime. "Although my efforts to establish a viable business were almost a full-time job," he said, "other opportunities arose for involvement in public affairs." In eight years, he became a deacon in the Plains Baptist Church; president of the state Certified Seed Organization; district governor of the Lions Club; chairman of the local Planning Commission; and a member of the local Library Board and Hospital Authority.

By now, too, Carter had begun to dabble in local politics. Because the Carters had long been one of the most prominent families in Plains, it was only natural that Jimmy would win a seat on the Sumter County School Board. "It seems hard to believe now," he later wrote, "but I was actually a member of the county school board for several months before it dawned on me that white children rode buses to their schools and black students still walked to theirs! I don't believe any black parent or teacher ever pointed out this quite obvious difference."

In this period, Carter was as segregationist as any of his neighbors. Though he was not a raging foe of integration, there is nothing in his six-year record on the school board to indicate he ever did anything to help implement the historic 1954 U.S. Supreme Court decision declaring segregated schools unconstitutional. When a group of white citizens protested the planned location of a black school near a white one, Carter—as chairman of the school board—proposed to relocate the black school. And he did not object to the practice of paying sick pay to white teachers but not their black counterparts. He also voted to use the surplus funds to give a raise to white teachers, but not to black teachers. Nevertheless, as he emphasizes in his autobiography, he did refuse to join the White Citizens Council, which called for massive resistance to the Supreme Court school decision. And when he offered a plan for school consolidation, which some perceived to be an integrationist ploy, he was defeated—the first political defeat he suffered. It was a defeat he characterized as a "stinging disappointment." But it did give Carter his first taste for political campaigning, which he has never lost.

Miz Lillian did notice a change in her son after his school board experience. "He seemed bored with business," she told James Wooten. "Oh, he worked just as hard as he ever had, but it just didn't seem quite so exciting to him as before. Besides, he and Rosalynn had done such a good job on it that it was beginning to almost take care of itself, you know. I could tell he was getting bored."

In the meantime, he and Rosalynn had built themselves a new house—one of the few in Plains ever designed by an architect. They had become the town's leading citizens. Frequently, they would drive to Americus to attend dances at the American Legion Hall, and they became friendly with Mr. and Mrs. John Pope of that city. (Pope was in the casket-manufacturing business.) Weekends, the four of them would drive wherever there were stock car races, for which Carter particularly had—and still has—a passion. And as head of the Lions Club, Carter directed a campaign for a public swimming pool project—whites only, of course—which eventually was built around the corner from his new house. All in all, it was a good life.

But it was not enough for the ex-Navy man. Carter now felt he was ready for bigger things. He had plans for his state and, presumably, the nation. The political bug was biting him. In 1962, just before his thirty-eighth birthday, he decided to seek the Democratic nomination for the Georgia Senate. Because of reapportionment, the Senate had become much more interesting. The rotation system had been ended; and a seat in the Senate now meant "substantive and continuing responsibilities." A visiting pastor, however, sought to persuade Carter to enter the ministry rather than the discredited profession of politics. But Carter responded, "How would you like to be the pastor of a church with 80,000 members?" The preacher, reported Carter, then conceded "it was possible to stay honest and at the same time minister to the needs of the 80,000 citizens of the 14th Senate District."

Carter's opponent was a prominent citizen of nearby Richland, Homer Moore, who, according to Carter, had the ardent support of "established politicians." With the help of family and close friends, Carter mounted what he described as "an amateurish, whirlwind campaign within the seven counties of the district. . . . My supporters were mostly young, and newcomers to politics." On Election Day, Carter visited as many polling places as possible. And what he saw going on in Georgetown, a small town on the Chattahoochee River, infuriated him. The local state legislator, the "dominant political boss in the county," was all but marking the voters' ballots for them. Carter protested, but to no avail.

Carter lost the primary by a few votes; but he knew that the votes cast in Quitman County were the deciding factor in his defeat. At the suggestion of an older cousin, Donald Carter, a newspaper publisher in Macon, Carter hired Atlanta lawyer Charles Kirbo to contest the primary. This Kirbo did successfully, proving to the satisfaction of a judge that the ballot boxes in Quitman County had indeed been stuffed with phony votes. Carter finally got his name on the ballot as the Democratic candidate, and was elected by 1,500 votes.

Arriving in the State Senate in January 1963, Carter made what later sometimes seemed to be an unfortunate pledge. In his exuberance, he promised to read every bill before he voted on it. But, as he quickly discovered, each session usually entailed several thousand bills and resolutions, surely excuse enough to water down his pledge. Instead, he took a speed-reading course, becoming "an expert on many unimportant subjects." Now thirty-eight years of age, he threw himself into his new life with enthusiasm. He was placed on the Appropriations and Agriculture Committees as well as the Educational Matters Committee (dealing with higher education) and, as such, sponsored several bills dealing with routine administrative matters such as student transportation at junior colleges.

Before long, many of his colleagues began to view him as a comer, mainly because he worked so hard. He would arrive early and stay late, five days a week instead of the usual four. And he rarely participated in the beer-drinking camaraderie usually engaged in by legislators happily away from their conservative rural constituencies.

In some Atlanta circles, Carter was considered a nitpicker. Reg Murphy, then political editor of *The Atlanta Constitution*, tells of first encountering Carter in a hall of the State Capitol shortly after he had been elected to the Senate. Carter was "waving a copy of *The Constitution*, explaining to me how a story we had in the paper was wrong and how we very rarely got things right in reporting on the State Senate. I think he believes there's a conspiracy in the newspaper business to get things wrong. You just dreaded to see Carter coming down the hallway in the legislative session because you never could talk about substantive issues for him wanting to point out little picayune comma faults in a story. My first reaction to Jimmy Carter was that there is a man who I never will get along with and who will never be humane enough to overlook the faults of anybody else."

Thus, Murphy captured the essence of Jimmy Carter. And one notes, in reading *Why Not the Best?*, that Carter did not seem to get any great personal satisfaction out of his two terms as a state senator. There is absolutely no mention of any pleasure he may have derived from the legislative give and take—or even friendship—other legislators have found rewarding. And he quotes Reinhold Niebuhr, his favorite theologian, as having defined politics as the sad art of establishing justice in a sinful world. It was a quotation he kept repeating all the way to the White House. The question, of course, was—and is—just how much Jimmy Carter was—and is—really affected by the desire to correct the world's evils.

One of the first speeches Carter delivered was in opposition to the notorious "30 Questions Test"—clever constitutional queries designed to confound black citizens seeking to vote. But the test was so outrageous that even the segregationist-minded legislature finally voted its abolition. Generally speaking, on issues involving race, Carter voted the way the folks back home wanted him to. Thus, in 1964, he voted for a state constitutional amendment aimed at preventing school integration. The amendment said simply, "Freedom from compulsory association at all levels of public education shall be preserved inviolate." Such "freedom of association" clauses constituted a common device to prevent what was then described as "mixing of the races" in the public school systems. But there was one problem with the amendment, Senator Leroy Johnson of Atlanta pointed out in the floor debate on June 15, 1964. Johnson, the first black member of the Georgia Senate since Reconstruction, argued it was unenforceable because the U.S. Supreme Court had already outlawed segregation in public schools. Nevertheless, Carter voted for the measure, which failed to carry. The next day, Carter voted for a move to reconsider the amendment. That, too, failed to carry.

Significantly, Carter has never made mention of this and other of his pro-segregation votes in the Georgia legislature. In his autobiography, for example, he avoids the subject by observing that "a hodgepodge of education laws" had evolved in Georgia over the years, a "situation . . . aggravated by the futile attempts to contrive laws which would circumvent the federal court rulings on racial integration." But he does not describe his own role in those "futile attempts."

According to state records later reported by *The St. Louis Post-Dispatch,* Carter also voted for a constitutional amendment that would have prevented the enactment of open accommodation and fair employment laws by counties in Georgia. The sponsor of the measure, Senator William Zorn of Jesup, was quoted in *The Atlanta Constitution* as saying his amendment was an attempt on the local level "to accomplish what Senator Talmadge and Senator

Russell are trying to do in Washington." And what the two solons from Georgia were trying to do in the nation's capitol that hot summer of 1964 was to block passage of the federal civil rights bill. Among other things, the bill that finally passed the Congress forbade discrimination in public accommodations and employment. But the Zorn bill, for which Carter voted, failed of passage by five votes.

Carter also voted against a bill sponsored by Senator Johnson to provide statewide tenure for teachers and other school personnel. The idea, said the black member from Atlanta, was to prevent arbitrary layoffs of black school personnel then taking place. The bill passed 29 to 14 without Carter's support.

But Carter did support two other bills introduced by Johnson to benefit blacks. One, seeking to abolish the practice of making separate lists of black and white taxpayers in the state, passed 33 to 9. Another for which Carter voted expanded Atlanta's city limits to include an all-black area, thereby increasing black voting strength in the metropolis.

It was at best a mixed record on civil rights, and appeared to conflict with Carter's oft-stated praise in 1976 of school integration and his characterization of the federal Civil Rights Act of 1964 as "the best thing that's happened to the South in my lifetime." And his record, as exhumed by *The Post-Dispatch*, also appeared to conflict with the reputation Carter had achieved among his former colleagues as having relatively liberal views, at least by the standards of the period. Even Leroy Johnson gave Carter high marks, if for no other reason than the fact the man from Plains— representing an extremely conservative constituency—was personally friendly. "He was one of the few people I could talk to," Johnson told *The Post-Dispatch* in 1976. "In 1963, it wasn't popular for a Southern white man to befriend a black man as it might be today. I think he went farther than the average white politician from south Georgia would have gone."

Civil rights leader Julian Bond, however, said Carter's civil rights votes in the Georgia Senate seemed to represent "the other side of the coin." Bond, now a State Senator himself, told *The Post-Dispatch* that "it may have been an attempt to placate his hometown constituency—or perhaps a true expression of his feelings. I think it paints him as not quite the civil rights advocate that he makes himself out to be."

One thing became obvious all through this period, however: Jimmy Carter was not interested in remaining a State Senator. At first, he had his sights on becoming his district's Congressman in Washington. The district was being represented by Howard "Bo" Callaway, the first Republican to be elected to Congress from Georgia since the days of Reconstruction. This was in 1964, the year that Barry Goldwater carried the state against President Lyndon Johnson. And Carter thought that Callaway's emergence as one of his state's more popular political figures was a fluke that he personally ought to rectify. After all, thought Carter, Callaway had ridden into office mainly on the coattails of the Republican Senator from Arizona. Moreover, he reasoned, in a non-presidential year like 1966, a strong Democratic candidate had an excellent chance of defeating Callaway in what was, after all, a traditionally Democratic district.

Callaway soon became aware of Carter's interest in replacing him in Washington. "Every time I would make a speech in Congress or release a statement," recalled Callaway recently, "I discovered that Senator Carter would respond in the local newspapers. It was obvious that Jimmy was out to unseat me." Callaway also had the feeling that Carter "resented" the enormous attention being given him by the Georgia media as one of the Grand Old Party's rising stars in the South. As Carter himself points out in his autobiography, "there was considerable conjecture about [Callaway's] being a future candidate for Governor or U.S. Senator." And Carter also noted that, in deciding to go after Callaway, he had a "not especially admirable" motivation—namely a "natural competitiveness" with Callaway. "He had graduated from West Point just about the same time I completed my work at Annapolis. When I was a state senator, one of my major projects was to secure a four-year college in southwest Georgia. As a member of the University System Board of Regents, Callaway tried unsuccessfully to block the college. He was leader of the Young Republicans, and in some ways I had become the leader among Georgia's Young Democrats. When we were around each other, both of us were somewhat tense."

Callaway, of course, can't speak for Carter; but, as he said recently, "I don't recall ever being tense on the few occasions I encountered him." And Callaway has a different view of the controversy over the four-year college. The school involved was Georgia Southwestern, the two-year institution which Jimmy had attended in Americus. The argument was over giving it a four-year status. "Like any other good local politician," says Callaway, "Carter was trying to get something for his constituents." Callaway, who also had roots in Americus, viewed the problem differently as chairman of the higher education committee of the Board of Regents. "We had limited funds and many other colleges to take care of. Moreover, the leading educators in Georgia were opposed to the four-year concept in Americus."

In the spring of 1966, Carter officially announced his candidacy for the Third District seat in the U.S. House of Representatives. And the Republican District Chairman said in response, "All we've got to do is hang Johnson on him."

Carter was ready for that one. "This is not 1964," he declared. "My name won't be under Lyndon B. Johnson on that ballot. It'll be under Richard B. Russell. I consider myself a conservative. I'm a Dick Russell Democrat." Senator Richard Russell of Georgia was, without question, the most popular politician of either party in that state. A strong advocate of national defense, he had impeccable conservative credentials—so conservative, in fact, he was considered anathema by the liberal wing of the Democratic Party. Among other things, Russell was ardently opposed to most civil rights legislation. So when Jimmy Carter publicly labeled himself a "Dick Russell Democrat," it could be considered coattail riding, 1966 style, in Georgia. The objective, needless to say, was to undercut Bo Callaway's conservative support.

From the moment he announced, Carter worked the district. Every day, he was out seeking votes by preaching the conservative principles of a "Dick Russell Democrat." Each night, he brought back home a list of names and addresses of the people he had met that day campaigning. And he, his wife Rosalynn, and his sister Gloria would laboriously type up individualized notes to each person he had met. Carter felt he was making headway against Callaway, who was still being considered the favorite.

Then the leading Democratic candidate for Governor, Ernest

Vandiver, suffered a mild heart attack and retired from the race. This was followed by an announcement by Bo Callaway that he would seek the governorship on the Republican ticket. The word was out that Callaway, young, attractive, and, like Carter, a wealthy graduate of one of the nation's military academies, had national ambitions, hoping after election as Governor to become a vice-presidential candidate in 1968, adding Southern balance to the national GOP ticket. Then, according to the reported scenario, Callaway hoped eight years later to get himself elected President of the United States, the first Southerner (LBJ was a self-proclaimed Westerner) in over a century.

The "natural competitiveness" with Callaway again asserted itself. So much so that Carter abruptly decided to give up what now appeared to be a sure seat in Congress for the governorship itself. On June 8, 1966, Carter announced his candidacy for the Democratic nomination for Governor. This time, however, he no longer considered himself a "Dick Russell Democrat" or a "conservative." Now, he announced, he distrusted political labels such as "conservative," "moderate," "liberal" or "middle-of-the-road." He said, "I believe I'm a more complicated person than that," adding that gubernatorial candidates should be "direct, truthful, and talk common sense." As Governor, he pledged, he would work for improvements in public education, mental health care, highways, and revisions in the state's tax structure. In his platform, Carter also stressed the use of surpluses and regular revenues to finance his various campaign promises. Many were thus led to believe there would be no increase in taxes. The "overriding issue" in the gubernatorial campaign, said Carter, "is whether Georgia shall achieve sufficient thrust in her forward progress to enter the orbit of the twenty-first century or whether our state shall falter and fall back into a fiery re-entry of the past."

Callaway, of course, had the Republican nomination sewed up. He had no real opposition. But to get the Democratic nomination, Carter faced considerable opposition. Other Democrats had heard the call; they included several segregationist candidates, the most prominent being Lester Maddox; and former Governor Ellis Arnall, considered the "great liberal hope" who was supported by party moderates and the powerful Atlanta newspapers. As a "new face," Carter did have a singular advantage. Comparatively youthful (he was forty-one that year), Carter, as a writer in *The Constitution* noted at the time, "has a quick wit about him and a quicker smile on a face that resembles John F. Kennedy's. . . ." The resemblance to the late President was occasionally startling to observers. Trim, fit, and with the same shock of hair, Carter would emphasize points with jabs of an open hand. And, like JFK, as another *Constitution* writer noted, "Carter's most active backers are among the young. Teenage girls apparently too young to vote have been leaving Carter headquarters in a near swooning condition."

Some Kennedy associates in Georgia did line up behind Carter. Robert Troutman, Jr., one of them, was described in *The Constitution* as "a wealthy, influential, long-time Democratic wheeler-dealer behind the political scenes, and was a big supporter and admirer of the late President Kennedy." At the 1960 Democratic Convention in Los Angeles, Troutman had masterminded John Kennedy's "Southern strategy" under Robert Kennedy's direction. The idea at the time was to undercut Lyndon Johnson's Southern support for the presidential nomination, a largely covert campaign aimed at labeling LBJ a "traitor to the South" who was largely responsible for civil rights legislation. Of course, the vagaries of politics being what they are, LBJ wound up on the ticket anyway—as JFK's vice-presidential running mate.

More directly involved in Carter's race were attorneys Charles Kirbo and Philip H. Alston, Jr. In charge of public relations was Parks Rusk, brother of Secretary of State Dean Rusk. Also on the team was a twenty-two-year-old youth named Hamilton Jordan, just graduated that spring from the University of Georgia, a political science major.

In his second month of campaigning, Carter became convinced the six-man contest for the nomination was actually a race between himself and former Governor Arnall. "And," Carter told *The Constitution*'s Sam Hopkins, "I don't think Arnall can get 51 percent of the primary votes. This means I would beat him in a runoff because he's about as popular in south Georgia as Lyndon B. Johnson." And LBJ was indeed far from popular in still largely rural south Georgia, largely because of his presidential record in behalf of civil rights and anti-poverty legislation.

Carter's major problem in the primary was to make himself

known around the state. "I was so unknown that some journalists labeled me, 'Jimmy Who?'" he later wrote. Lacking funds to put on a big television drive, Carter set up an extensive travel schedule aimed at shaking as many Georgian hands as possible. Meanwhile, whatever funds became available were to be put into a media campaign which was to stress these personal Carter qualities: Ability to win. Youth. Experience. Independence from the old political groups. Good moral character. Interest in the individual. Enthusiasm. Carter's family ties were also emphasized.

Saturday afternoons, regardless of where they might be, the family members would head back for Plains. "Jimmy wouldn't miss church and Sunday School," said Rosalynn Carter. "He's head of the Junior Department."

"Carter's role," a Georgia writer was later to write in 'The Nation,* "was to walk about, coat hooked over one shoulder, making liberal noises." But his main argument against Arnall was that he was antagonizing conservatives of the Vandiver and Maddox stripe. Only he, Carter insisted, could unify the party against Callaway. Arnall, he also implied, had not been all that good a governor. He said that the state constitution drawn up under Arnall was so bad that it had to be amended two hundred times. And he termed "ridiculous" Arnall's plans for financing new programs.

Mainly, Carter talked in generalities, rarely getting down to specifics. A likeable man he was, according to the political writers who met him at the time. There was, for example, his appearance at the Atlanta Press Club, about which Bruce Galphin wrote in *The Constitution:*

> For those who hadn't known Carter before, his appearance . . . was a startling experience. Here was a breed of politician new to Georgia's big contest: subdued, frank even about his deficiencies, refusing to torture the traditional whipping boys.
>
> When he got to talking about Milledgeville State Hospital, he said the plight of patients there made him choke up, and indeed his voice faltered and his face reddened a

---

*John Dennis, "Jimmy Carter's Fierce Campaign," *The Nation*, May 17, 1975.

shade. . . . He quoted Edmund Burke to the effect that
services should be centralized but power decentralized.
He spoke of a quest for excellence in state government,
and he said he wanted to invoke more of the public in the
affairs of government.

But some of the assets of Jimmy Carter the man may be
deficits for Jimmy Carter the political candidate. . . . He
admitted the unique problems of big cities were new to
him. He said he had been boning up on them in the past
few weeks, and you could believe he can learn fast. But it
was a deficiency, politically speaking, he shouldn't have
admitted.

He said Vietnam wasn't an issue in the Georgia governor's race—an honest position—but then went on to talk
about it, to admit it was complex and finally to confess, 'I
don't have any solution.' He would have done better to
stop after saying it wasn't an issue.

Then, on the eve of the primary, riots of racial origin erupted in
Atlanta, a city that had become known as one of the South's most
progressive in extending rights to blacks. What Carter had hoped
would be a two-man race suddenly turned into a three-way
contest. Lester Maddox, the Atlanta restaurateur who had closed
down his establishment rather than serve blacks, gained strength
with his get-tough statements. And Carter himself tried to catch
up with equally forceful remarks. When asked about the arrest of
black militant Stokely Carmichael, Carter said, "I think he should
have been arrested. Anyone who incites a riot should be. The
Atlanta police and mayor have handled the problem in a very
forceful way, and I believe law and order will now be restored in
our capital city." But it was all too late. Carter finished in the
primary a close third behind Maddox, who finished second to
Arnall.

But because Arnall did not get a majority, there was a runoff
election, as Carter had predicted. Only Carter was out of it. "Had
Carter made the runoff," the *U.S. News & World Report* reported
at the time, "there would have been a clear-cut test of sentiment
as between [Lyndon] Johnson and [Robert] Kennedy. Those close
to the Kennedy people said the plan was to present Arnall as a

'Johnson man.'" The race was now between Arnall and Lester Maddox. And, significantly, despite his later protestations of distaste for Maddox, Carter refused to endorse the more liberal Arnall. Maddox thus had clear sailing, easily winning the Democratic nomination for Governor.

Maddox faced Republican Bo Callaway in the general election. Liberal Democrats, who didn't want to support either candidate, organized a write-in vote for Arnall. In the end, Arnall received 60,000 votes, enough to prevent a clear majority for either Callaway or Maddox, though Callaway finished a fraction ahead of Maddox. This meant that the overwhelmingly Democratic legislature could decide the issue. With cousin Hugh Carter sitting in Jimmy's old seat in the State Senate, the legislature chose Maddox as the sixty-sixth Governor of Georgia. And when the vote was finally tallied, Governor-elect Maddox shouted with joy, "Praise the Lord."

Jimmy Carter was not that exultant. His pride was injured and his self-confidence shaken. He found himself in the depths of depression. He had given up a chance at a seat in Congress. He was deeply in debt. And he had lost twenty-two pounds in his desperate election effort. He had worked hard and had nothing to show for it.

Memories vary as to what occurred when Jimmy Carter returned to Plains following his defeat. That he took his failure badly is generally agreed. His mother, Miz Lillian, for example, has recalled that her Jimmy "cried like a baby." And Carter himself told Bill Moyers, using the awkward phrasing that sometimes creeps into his speech: "I was going through a state in my life then that was a very difficult one. I had run for governor and lost. Everything I did was not gratifying." And, in another interview with Sally Quinn, Carter amplified: "At that time, I wasn't getting any satisfaction out of any success, and when I had failures it was very upsetting. Even the smallest failures seemed like calamities to me. Life had no purpose."

It was at this time, according to his sister, faith healer and evangelist Ruth Stapleton, that Carter underwent a religious conversion that made him a "born-again" Christian. She had hurried to Plains from her home in Fayetteville, North Carolina, to be with her brother in his time of despair. They had gone for a long walk. And it was at "that moment of sitting out in that woods under the tree when Jimmy's whole life went before him, as he held his face up, the tears were just falling, and he said, 'Ruth, I don't know how I hesitated. I'll give up everything. I would rather have what you have than to even be President of the United States.'"

But, according to Carter, that's not exactly the way it happened. While walking in the woods with Ruth, she "asked me if I would give up anything for Christ, if I would give up my life and possessions—everything. I said I would. Then she asked me if I would be willing to give up politics. I thought a long time and had to admit that I would not." Not long afterward, the pastor of the Plains Baptist Church preached a sermon entitled, "If You Were Arrested for Being a Christian, Would There Be Any Evidence To Convict You?" And while Carter doesn't remember "a thing he said," he does remember that by the time the sermon was over, "My answer . . . was 'No.' I never had really committed myself totally to God. My Christian beliefs were superficial, based primarily on pride, and I'd never done much for other people. I was always thinking about myself."

That was the beginning of his "conversion experience." "It was not a profound stroke of miracle. It was not anything of the kind. It wasn't mysterious. It might have been the same kind of experience as millions of people who do become Christians in a deeply personal way." From then on James Earl Carter, Jr., described himself as a "born-again Christian."

In more recent years, President Carter has gone out of his way to deny rumors that he behaved as if he'd been through a traumatic experience following his 1966 defeat. The question was put straight to the President by Jack Anderson. The President said that the reports were "highly exaggerated." Of course, the reports were based largely on what his mother Miz Lillian and sister Ruth Stapleton had said concerning his post-primary behavior.

"People have let their imaginations run wild," the President went on. "I never did have any trauma or doubt my own ability after the '66 election. As a matter of fact, the day after the election, before I even left Atlanta to go home, I met with my key advisers, and we made plans that day for the governor's race in 1970. So there never was any doubt about my withdrawing from the political life or having a setback in my own ambitions. . . ."

And he could have added that shortly after his defeat he and Rosalynn went off by themselves for a week of relaxation in a friend's log cabin. Exactly nine months later, his only daughter, Amy, was born. The timing has long been the subject of jests by his friends.

In his autobiography, Carter wrote that he waited only a month after his defeat and then plunged into a grueling four-year campaign for the governorship of Georgia. "I remembered the admonition, 'You show me a good loser and I will show you a loser.'"

And he vowed never "to lose again."

4

THE 1970 PRIMARY CAMPAIGN

DESPITE HIS NEWFOUND COMMITMENT TO CHRIST, JAMES EARL Carter, Jr.'s, lust for political office dominated his every waking moment. For four years, from 1966 through 1970, as he later wrote, Carter "worked with more concentration and commitment than ever before in my life." He sought, for example, "to evolve a carefully considered political strategy to win the governor's race in 1970."

And, as we shall see, it was a strategy radically different from the one he had employed in his 1966 race.

For, as he had vowed, "I did not intend to lose again."

And that could conceivably mean that he would do almost anything—short of murder, of course—to win the keys to the white-columned Governor's Mansion in Atlanta.

And, as it turned out, Carter's campaign for the governorship was one of the roughest in Georgia's history, marked by appeals to racism, dirty tricks, laundered funds, lying, and hypocrisy. It was a campaign that was later to embarrass Jimmy in his race for the presidency. But not for long. Somehow he managed to convince the electorate in 1976 that he represented all the saintly virtues essential in the quintessential post-Watergate politician—honesty,

integrity, decency, and probity. Judgment was so nullified by
Watergate that Jimmy managed to pull it off. Much of the media,
too, wanted to root for someone who was palpably not Richard
Nixon; and Carter assured all and sundry he was not.

Adding to this illusion, needless to say, was Jimmy Carter's
religiosity. His situation was somewhat reminiscent of William
Jennings Bryan. "His evangelistic spirit," wrote one historian of
Bryan, "gave to every cause he advocated a religious fervor that
swept all doubts away." Carter has also been compared to Dwight
David Eisenhower. Both men mingled patriotic and religious
language; and both did nothing to discourage the conclusion that
there was a considerable moral distance between themselves and
those ordinary politicians down below.

But, unlike Ike, Carter devoted time and effort to his religious
pursuits. Following his spiritual rejuvenation at the hands of his
sister, Ruth Stapleton, he became a lay missionary. For some
months, he spent time "witnessing for Christ" in various parts of
Georgia and as far afield as Philadelphia, Boston, and New York.
And in between running his seed and other businesses, Carter was
also out politicking. In fact, he viewed his own political activity as
a form of ministry. And he was not above discussing his religious
beliefs and experiences while campaigning. When Billy Graham
was asked whether Carter wasn't "wearing his religion on his
sleeve" during the 1976 presidential contest, the noted evangelist
graciously remarked, "I don't believe it's on his sleeve; I believe
it's in his heart."

Carter had led a Billy Graham crusade in Sumter County and
later told a United Methodist General Conference that the noted
evangelist "had had a great impression and impact on my own
life." Nevertheless, they never were particularly close. And they
still aren't. Graham did not visit the White House in the early
Carter years, as he had in other Administrations.

No longer plagued by the doubts that had beset him following
his 1966 defeat, Jimmy Carter set about winning the governorship
in systematic, methodical fashion. That was his only goal. "There
was never the slightest hesitancy on my part about what to do," he
later wrote. "I thought I could run and win, and I never worried at
all about who else might be in the race against me." He had plenty
of time to concentrate on his goal because his younger brother,

Billy, had returned home from the Marine Corps to run the family business. Soon, Carter was receiving numerous invitations for speaking engagements. This was important in Carter's strategy since it would maintain the name recognition he had received in his 1966 campaign. Almost every night, therefore, Carter was off somewhere in the state making speeches. In May 1968, he was elected president of the Georgia Planning Association, thus giving him a new vehicle by which he could be seen and heard. Ultimately, Carter estimated, he delivered about 1,800 orations in that four-year period. And he figured that Rosalynn and he had personally shaken the hands of more than 600,000 Georgians— more than half the total number of voters in the state.

"By . . . 1968," according to Reg Murphy who was now editor of *The Atlanta Constitution,* "Jimmy Carter was running flat-out for Governor. Having been beaten as a liberal candidate for Governor in 1966, he had decided that he was going to run a very conservative political campaign in 1970 . . . and he showed up in every town in Georgia at that point, a relentless, hard-working, absolutely charming campaigner. I remember he used to say that he went into those little towns and he called on everybody except the sheriff, the banker, and the newspaperman. He didn't want any support from any of those guys. And that's the way he ran that campaign; he identified the sheriff and the banker and the newspaperman as the evil guys in town and did it very successfully. It was as good and skillful a campaign as I've ever seen run in the South."

Thus, in embryo, Carter provided a preview of his later campaign for the presidency. His formula was simply to run as an outsider railing against "the establishment" and the "political bosses and insiders" opposed to the interests of ordinary people. Likewise, another of his strengths appeared to be farsighted campaign planning. And he was not without outside assistance. He had "a superb group" of young volunteers, many of whom had been with him in 1966, working on analyzing the issues, preparing a campaign program, and studying voting results since 1952. "For each of the 159 Georgia counties, we prepared colored charts and graphs showing how the people there had voted in state and federal elections for all different kinds of candidates, emphasizing all kinds of issues. Since we knew the candidates and issues, it was instructive for us to compare the relative strengths of the candidates from one election to another. After a little study, the general impression of voter motivations in the individual counties began to form."

Two and a half years before the election, Jimmy Carter decided that the man he would have to beat in the Democratic primary of 1970 was Carl Sanders, the prestigious former Governor of Georgia who was seeking a political comeback. He thus began to size up his probable opponent, and in the following memorandum, written in March of 1968, he wrote down his characterization of Sanders in words and images which he would use again and again in speeches and statements to tear down the reputation of the popular former Governor:

> Some images to be projected regarding Carl Sanders
> . . . More liberal, has close connections with Ivan Allen
> [the liberal Mayor of Atlanta] and Atlanta establishment
> . . . refuses to let Georgia Democrats have a voice in the
> Democratic Party . . . Atlanta-oriented to the exclusion of
> other metro and rural areas . . . pretty boy . . . ignored
> prison reform opportunities . . . nouveau riche . . . re-
> fused to assist local school boards in school financing . . .
> excluded George Wallace from state . . .
> . . . You can see some of these are conflicting but right
> now we just need to collect all these rough ideas we can.
> Later we can start driving a wedge between me and
> him . . .
> . . . In Columbus last night Peter Zack Geer referred to
> Carl Sanders as Julian Bond's candidate . . .

Though there were to be other such memos written on yellow legal pads, this was the one that constituted the rough outline of what was to be Carter's winning plan for the governorship. As time passed, it was refined again and again. And some of the items Carter had planned to use against Sanders were dropped. For example, there was no point in bringing up Lieutenant Governor Peter Zack Geer's description of Sanders as "Julian Bond's candidate," since Geer eventually endorsed Sanders and even raised money for him. Julian Bond, meanwhile, wound up supporting neither Sanders nor Carter; but the image of the black civil rights leader supporting Sanders apparently was retained in Carter's mind. Bond, of course, considered Carter a "phony" and was to say so loud and often during Carter's bid for the presidency.

What finally determined Carter's strategy against Sanders was a statewide poll undertaken for him in the fall of 1969 by Washington-based William Hamilton, a Southern opinion specialist. Hamilton's interviewers talked with a select sampling of 800 Georgians. Sanders, who had served as Governor from 1963 to 1965, was given an overwhelming 84 percent favorable reaction for his state service. One in five voters rated him as "excellent." And as Hamilton noted in his report, "This is one of the best job ratings I have ever seen given a former Governor after three years out of office. . . . Even Leroy Collins, Florida's most popular Governor, did not have a job rating as good as Sanders. Even though Sanders appears to have a slight problem with his liberal image, he should be considered a very formidable opponent."

So formidable, in fact, that if the primary had been held in September 1969 Sanders would have pulled 53 percent of the vote against a large field of candidates, including Carter, who was good for only 21 percent of the vote. And this, despite the good showing Carter had made in 1966 and the strenuous campaigning he had done since, particularly on the chicken-and-peas civic club circuit. The Hamilton poll showed that all that yakking had not done him much good.

There was something else that showed up in the poll. "Both Sanders and Carter were seen as a little more liberal than the electorate," reported Hamilton. "This is more true of Sanders than it is of Carter." The pollster also noted that "twice as many voters were able to rate Sanders as were able to rate Carter. This, of course, suggests that Carter has a recognition problem."

"Of those voters who are aware of both men," Hamilton went on, "it is that group of populistic staunch segregationists who see both Carter and Sanders as being too liberal. This suggests that neither candidate has made strong inroads into this group which is 12 to 15 percent of the electorate. Sanders has the bigger problem because his past actions were better known to this group."

According to Hamilton's figures, 25 percent of the Georgia electorate had never even heard of Jimmy Carter; and only eleven out of every twenty Georgia Democrats had any opinion of him. Yet the pollster saw Carter's low recognition as an advantage in September 1969. "As he becomes better known over the next twelve months, he can emphasize a moderate conservative tone in his campaign and, therefore, put himself between Sanders and the bulk of the electorate." The pollster emphasized the fact that the Georgia electorate was not young, not black, and not poor. In fact, Carter's strongest supporters were white, between the ages of forty-five and fifty-nine, earned from $6,000 to $12,000 a year, liked George Wallace, and distrusted Atlanta "big shots." Hamilton's advice: "Carter should concentrate heavily on the working man, both the skilled and unskilled."

And this is exactly what Carter began to do. At the beginning, he had been pitching a centrist theme to such middle-class enclaves as the Civitan and Rotary clubs. But then, according to Bill Shipp, then political editor of *The Atlanta Constitution*, Carter's pollster convinced him that "the best route to the [Governor's] mansion on West Paces Ferry Road was a straight line to the right. . . . The grim-faced factory workers who brushed past Carter in the grey dawns of spring in 1970 found that by the following September Carter stood for everything they did, hated everything they did, lived and looked like they did."

Carter had no qualms about his sharp turn to the right. As his advertising adviser Gerald Rafshoon explained it to Shipp shortly after the election, "I want to emphasize that there's nothing in these polls that Jimmy Carter couldn't live with. He did not make himself over to suit the polls." According to Rafshoon, there was nothing wrong about "any smart leader" adjusting his rhetoric and ideology to cater to the electorate. "Sears would not go into a multimillion-dollar promotion without getting some research done on what the people want to buy."

Rafshoon, who had handled Carter's advertising in 1966, was and is one of the few non-Georgians among Carter's upper echelons. Born in Brooklyn, the son of an Air Force policeman, he went to the University of Texas, where he majored in journalism. Graduating in 1955, he did a three-month advertising stint at the Austin television station owned by Lyndon Johnson. Then, after three years in the Navy, Rafshoon worked for Twentieth Century Fox, eventually becoming the movie company's national advertising director in New York. In 1963, he moved to Atlanta to open his own agency.

In 1966, he worked on Carter's ill-fated campaign for the governorship. A few days after his defeat, Carter called Rafshoon and said, "Let's start next week. I'm running again."

Rafshoon thought that Carter could become Governor in 1970, if properly handled. And that he could provide the extra dimension needed for victory. In an interview published in the November 1969 issue of *Atlanta Magazine*, Rafshoon, who had worked for Bobby Kennedy in 1968, was quoted as saying that "the new politics" was what Carter excelled in. The Carter people, he went on, were "doing the other things well—precinct organizations and getting the troops out—but image is the new politics."

Image and hard work. As Carter later described his campaign:

We learned about scheduling, living off the land, and using maximum free news media coverage to supplement good paid advertising. . . . Neither we nor our staff workers stayed in hotels or motels for which we had to pay. We lived with supporters all over the state, and the late night visits did more than anything else to cement permanent friendships—and to let an effective exchange of information take place between campaign headquarters and people in the individual communities of Georgia. We personally visited the isolated country radio stations, many of which had to operate with a staff of only one or two persons. When we showed up at the station, they almost always welcomed a live or taped interview.

In his report to Carter, Hamilton had cautioned against undue pessimism. "While Sanders' favorable image is relatively high, no one has started shooting at him yet. And Carter has a chance to build his own favorable image among those who do not know him. On balance, Carter has a tough uphill fight but by no means impossible."

The pollster had only reinforced what Carter had already been thinking when he jotted down in his March 1968 memorandum: If Carter was to win the governorship, Carl Sanders had to be wiped out politically.

And Jimmy Carter set out to do precisely that, methodically and at times brutally.

For example, in probing for Sanders' weak spots, Hamilton had determined that twenty-seven percent of the undecided voters felt that the former Governor "has become too close to the Atlanta bigwigs. . . . About one-fifth of the undecided believed that Sanders had become too citified, nationally and Atlanta oriented."

From then on Sanders, the well-dressed, urbane attorney who had been a moderate Governor, became known as "Cufflinks Carl." A twenty-second television commercial, devised by Rafshoon, opened with a picture of a closed country club door. And these were the words that went with it: "This is the door to an exclusive country club, where the big-money boys play cards, drink cocktails, and raise money for their candidate—Carl Sanders. People like *us* aren't invited. We're busy working for a living. That's why our votes are going for Jimmy Carter . . . *our* kind of man, *our* kind of Governor."

From the very beginning, Carter made no bones about it. He was going to run against Sanders' wealth, even though—as it turned out—Carter may well have been more affluent than his adversary. And in addition to portraying Sanders as a "limousine liberal," Carter also began to publicly question whether "Cufflinks" had not misused his high office for personal financial gain. This he did in formally announcing his candidacy on April 3, 1970, in the Old Supreme Court room at the State Capitol. With Rosalynn and the children by his side, Carter told a group of several hundred supporters, "Georgians never again want a Governor who will use the tremendous power and prestige of the office for his personal wealth."

Carter looked boyish, even though he was several years older than Sanders. And he looked bashful, even though he said without hedging that he would "win the Democratic nomination and the election." Referring to his loss in 1966, Carter said, "I think the best man came in third." The "best man" now had new campaign pins—gold peanuts with "Carter" stamped on their grainy surfaces. And pretty girls handed out green-on-white bumper strips imploring voters to "Speak Out—Elect Jimmy Carter." An inquiring reporter asked if that wasn't a summons to the "silent majority" to whom President Nixon was then appealing for support. But a campaign associate preferred to talk about other things.

Peanuts became the unabashed symbol of the Carter campaign. "The symbol of the peanut represents what I stand for," he told supporters. "Working in the fields . . . going to church. Georgia accounts for one-third of this country's total peanut production, more than any other two states combined."

Jimmy Carter was off and running. Everywhere he went in the state, he hit hard on his pet campaign theme: "Carl Sanders used the Governor's chair to get rich." In Rome, Georgia, a week after his announcement, Carter poked his head into a spacious money vault at a bank and quipped, "Looks like Carl Sanders' basement." Later, at a press conference, Carter took another slap at Sanders' money. He also took the occasion to plug his old friend, Federal Judge Griffin Bell, for the Supreme Court. After that, Carter went out on the streets to be filmed for a television commercial. The director ordered the candidate to walk out of the Floyd County courthouse four times before the television crew got what it wanted—Jimmy Carter against a background of the American flag, budding dogwood, and a monument to the American Legion.

"Hold your shoulders up, Jimmy," a woman passerby advised while the candidate was performing.

Rosalynn, meanwhile, was working the stores, handing out Carter buttons and asking for support of "Jimmeh."

It was indeed a hectic schedule, with little time for sleep. But the Carters appeared to be loving the handshaking, fund-raising, picture-taking, and politicking. One longtime observer, who had spent a day and a half with the campaign, told Bill Shipp of *The Atlanta Constitution,* "Sanders may not have anything to worry about against Carter. If Carter maintains this pace, he'll have to retire from sheer exhaustion from the race by the end of July."

Generally, Sanders ran a more leisurely campaign, but one that reflected money, organization, and slick advertising. So confident was Sanders of victory that he did little stumping. Rather, he relied on such gimmicks as billboards, stating simply, "Carl ought to be elected Governor." The former Governor came through as an affluent, successful lawyer, which was exactly the image of his principal adversary that Carter was seeking to create among the electorate.

For the most part, Sanders deliberately ignored Carter's repeated taunts. Only late in the primary did the sniping about his "cufflinks" get to him. So gunshy did he become, Sanders told a Kiwanis Club, that he no longer wore long-sleeved shirts. He lifted his arm to show he wasn't wearing cufflinks or, for that matter, cuffs.

Carter's campaign was deliberately more rough-hewn, even to the point of using a far-from-flattering billboard picture of the candidate. The photograph, also used in his brochures, "made Jimmy look like an average working man," an adviser told Bill Shipp. "Our theme was, 'Isn't it time somebody spoke up for you?' You don't smile and beam when you say that." The slogan, of course, was clearly designed to appeal to the "little man" of Georgia. And Carter repeatedly contended that his campaign was based on "peanuts, pennies, and people" while Sanders' was based on "bucks, banks, and boondoggles."

Bill Shipp also described this television spot: "There's this guy, see, and he's wearing this yellow hard hat. And he comes crawling out of this manhole, and he looks up and, lo and behold, there's smiling Jimmy Carter. Carter's got his hand outstretched, and he wants to know what he can do to help the working man because he's a working man, too. Then some words flash on the screen, suggesting that you send money to Carter's campaign for Governor."

Other commercials showed Carter toiling in the fields of Plains, although with all the years he spent campaigning, it was difficult to believe he spent more than a few weeks, at most, down on his 2,500 acres, running a burgeoning business, let alone shoveling peanuts.

What, in retrospect, made Carter's bitter denunciations of Sanders' alleged support from moneyed groups all the more absurd was his own links with "big shots." From the beginning, Carter had wealthy supporters, mainly important Atlanta lawyers who early on had recognized his political potential and made certain he did not want for funds. And at least one banker, Thomas Bertram "Bert" Lance, was also part of this group of insiders. Carter, therefore, rarely had difficulty in raising "seed money" for his campaigning. Such early financing was easily arranged with several banks when Carter's affluent backers did the borrowing on their signatures alone.

By the summer of 1970, when it became clear that he could best Sanders in the primary, Carter began to receive even more contributions from individuals whom he had only in days past been berating as "special interests." One of his TV spots, in fact, showed a well-dressed Sanders boarding a Lear jet; the picture then flashing to a hand wearing huge cufflinks, presumably Sanders'; and then that hand was shown accepting a bucketful of cash from a prosperous-looking man.

In the closing days of the primary, Carter assailed Sanders at a press conference for having accepted large corporate contributions. But when Carter was asked whether he had been given similar corporate contributions, he conceded that that was the case, but he refused to specify the amounts and the names of his benefactors. More recently, on March 18, 1976, when asked about these 1970 contributions on NBC's *Tomorrow* show, Carter claimed that because there was no disclosure law in Georgia, "nobody ever made a report of contributors and we didn't maintain those records." If that were true, then Jimmy Carter would be probably the only politician alive who never kept such records.

But the facts appear to be otherwise. Phil Stanford, writing in *The Columbia Journalism Review,* reported that two accountants who had worked for Carter's campaign in 1970 had both told him that the campaign organization kept records of all contributions. One of them, Richard Harden, who had been named head of Georgia's massive Department of Human Resources while Carter was Governor, said that the contribution lists were kept by computer, and that monthly printouts of all contributors were sent to Carter's campaign managers.

There was nothing slipshod about the financial records kept by the Carter organization, according to David H. Gambrell, the Atlanta lawyer who acted as treasurer of the 1970 campaign. Gambrell told Nicholas M. Horrock of *The New York Times* that he had kept careful records of all contributions and expenditures that passed through the main Carter headquarters in Atlanta. And, according to Horrock, the Gambrell files plus the computerized list of supporters became the "nucleus" for the lists of potential contributors later put to good use during Carter's quest for the presidency.

Eventually, in the final weeks of the 1976 presidential campaign, the records which Carter had previously insisted did not exist were made public. They showed that a group of powerful Georgians—including bankers, lawyers, business executives, and contractors—had given Carter half the money he collected in a campaign in which he had run as a small farmer-businessman arrayed against what he had called the powerful "interests" in Atlanta.

Thus, it turned out that the very "interests" he had inveighed against so repeatedly were his chief supporters.

According to the documents belatedly made public by Carter, some 4,800 contributors had given him a total of about $690,000. An examination of the list by *The New York Times* showed that about 298 individuals or businesses made contributions ranging from $500 to $26,500, accounting for about half the total raised— an estimated $370,000.

The $26,500—the largest single contribution to the campaign— came from Anne Cox Chambers and her husband. Mrs. Chambers, chairperson of the Cox Broadcasting Company, got interested in Carter because of her lawyer, Charles Kirbo, the candidate's longtime confidante. An irony lay in the fact that the Cox organization owned Atlanta's two major newspapers as well as a radio and television station. And it was precisely those newspapers—*The Constitution* and *The Journal*—against which Carter had been campaigning as part of the Sanders-supporting media. Eventually, President Carter named Mrs. Chambers the U.S. Ambassador to Belgium.

The *Times'* survey showed that Carter received some $50,000 from persons directly involved in banking or the savings and loan industry. He also received substantial sums from bank directors whose primary enterprise was in some other business. And an estimated $70,000 came from people who did business with the state of Georgia or were subcontractors on state projects. About $60,000 came from the general business community—the Atlanta-based Delta Airlines; Coca-Cola; and textile, insurance, and retail sales organizations.

Still another $20,000 came from retail and wholesale liquor dealers, vending machine operators, a law enforcement association, a poultry group, and railroad interests. And what The *Times* described as "speculator real estate interests concerned about the location of new state roads and development trends" put up another $20,000.

Only one contribution came from the labor movement, normally the mainstay of most Democratic candidates. The Retail Clerks International Association gave $500.

Probably the most important member of Carter's inner circle, then and now, was Charles Kirbo, the conservative lawyer who first met the candidate in 1962 when Carter ran for the Georgia Senate and retained Kirbo to prove election fraud. Which apparently was the reason Kirbo was exempted from the savage attacks Carter had launched against other Georgia influence peddlers. It was only the "big shots" who backed his opponent whom Carter objected to so vigorously. That Kirbo was a "big shot" can be seen by a list of his clients. As a senior partner of King & Spalding, his clients included among others, the Coca-Cola Company, General Motors, and the Cox communications empire.

Carter's finance chairman was Philip Alston, Jr., senior partner of another Atlanta law firm, Alston, Miller & Gaines, whose clients included the Chrysler Corporation, the American Oil Company, Eastman Kodak, and E.I. duPont de Nemours & Co. Alston eventually wound up as the U.S. Ambassador to Australia under President Carter.

Carter's treasurer, of course, was David Gambrell, who was in a well-known Atlanta law firm. Gambrell's father, E. Smythe Gambrell, another early Carter backer, was also in a noted Atlanta law firm and was a major stockholder in Eastern Airlines. David Gambrell later said he and his father had contributed a total of about $4,500 to the Carter campaign.

And when Charles Kirbo declined the unexpired term of the late Senator Richard Russell, in 1971, Governor Carter named David Gambrell to the vacant seat. This gave rise to charges that Gambrell had "bought the seat" with his contributions to the Carter campaign. Gambrell termed the attack a "smear." As a candidate to succeed himself in the Senate, Gambrell was defeated by Samuel A. Nunn in the 1972 Democratic primary.

Another Carter contributor was William Gunter, a lawyer in a Gainesville firm that represented the Ralston Purina Company as well as major poultry producers. In 1972, Governor Carter appointed him to the Georgia Supreme Court.

James B. Langford, a Calhoun lawyer whose firm represented major textile interests in Georgia, was another major Carter supporter. Langford was a principal with Bert Lance in the ownership of the First National Bank of Calhoun. In 1974, along with two other men, Lance purchased the controlling interest of the Atlanta-based National Bank of Georgia, of which Lance became president. Following his election as President in November 1976, Carter's transition staff announced that his family's warehouse business owed $4.7 million to Lance's bank. The loans were described as routine business transactions. Routine or not, the arrangement still demonstrated that it was nice to have good friends in the banking business.

Probably the most interesting Carter "insider" was the colorful and unconventional businessman Erwin David Rabhan, a native of Savannah, who built a shaky and mysterious empire in the 1960s and early 1970s that included nursing homes in four states, a motion picture studio, a fish protein company, and a magazine for upper-class Atlanta blacks. But, according to a dispatch in *The New York Times* of December 3, 1976, filed from Atlanta by investigative reporter Horrock, this "close friend and supporter of President-elect Carter is the focal point of a wide-ranging federal investigation into alleged business fraud and accusations that money from organized crime was funneled into the business community here."

The dispatch also reported that since 1968 Rabhan had claimed an extremely close relationship with Carter, telling friends and associates, "Jimmy and I are so close we used to sleep in the same bed."

An accomplished small-aircraft pilot, Rabhan had often given Carter free rides in the early, crucial days of his gubernatorial campaign. Whether he had ever slept in the same bed is doubtful, according to Jody Powell. But the press secretary did concede that they had become extremely friendly as a result of traveling in the close quarters of the small plane which Rabhan had piloted. Powell also confirmed that Rabhan had kept in close touch with

Carter while he was Governor. So close, in fact, that in 1974, when his various business activities began to collapse, Rabhan gave up his Atlanta apartment and office to move into the Governor's Mansion, conducting his business from a basement office. Though Powell later insisted that Rabhan's stay at the mansion was only "two or three weeks" at the most, business associates across the country told Horrock that they had been able to reach Rabhan there with "regularity" for much of 1974.

Rabhan made much of his friendship with Carter, often displaying a portfolio of letters from him, including a letter of introduction typed on the stationery of the Governor of Georgia. In late 1973, Rabhan also had given Carter's youngest son, Jeff, then a twenty-year-old without a college degree, a job directing the rehabilitation of a vessel in Seattle. And, also according to Horrock, Rabhan had claimed that he was successful in persuading the Carters to arrange for a cosmetic facial operation for the boy.

In 1974, while apparently still living at the Governor's Mansion, Rabhan came under federal investigation in connection with several cases involving his collapsing business enterprises. And two years later, Rabhan was the subject of inquiries by federal grand juries in Atlanta and St. Louis; the FBI; the organized crime section of the Justice Department; the Internal Revenue Service; and the Securities and Exchange Commission. In addition, the Department of Housing and Urban Development as well as the Small Business Administration were investigating Rabhan's business relationships with their programs. According to Horrock, the various probes sought to determine whether Rabhan had misstated the values of certain properties to the SEC by inflating assets; whether funds were improperly handled in the operation of a federally insured nursing home in St. Louis; whether funds from this endeavor were siphoned to other operations; whether false statements were made to obtain mortgage financing; whether funds from organized crime in Atlanta were "laundered" through Rabhan; and whether he had attempted to evade taxes or file fraudulent returns.

At the height of these investigations in 1976, while Carter was fighting for the presidential nomination, Rabhan thought it the better part of wisdom to leave the country. He reportedly turned up in Tehran, where efforts by newsmen to contact him proved fruitless. And exactly what the status of the federal investigations has been more recently, now that his buddy is in the White House, is unknown. Rabhan seems to have dropped down into Orwell's memory hole. And there were few follow-ups on the part of the usually prying media.

Carter's associations with the powerful generally were little known in the Georgia of 1970. Which was why he was so successful in designing a campaign so markedly different from that of his principal adversary. Sanders, wrote Carter, "got almost all of the endorsements—from newspapers, judges, sheriffs, legislators, bankers, lawyers, and organized groups of all types. We made an issue of the big shots standing between him and the people, and eventually every endorsement (which he avidly sought) cost him votes in some fashion or other."

Carter hit hard at his opponent for his ties with Hubert H. Humphrey. The former Vice-President's role in promoting civil rights legislation, as far back as the 1948 Democratic Convention, had not been forgotten—or, in many quarters, forgiven. Not forgiven, either, was Sanders' well-publicized endorsement of the 1964 national Democratic ticket of LBJ and Humphrey in a year that Georgia voted for the GOP's Goldwater. Carter declared, "I don't think it's right for Governor Sanders to try and please a group of ultraliberals, particularly those in Washington."

Carter's people discovered that the "Count Me for Carl" buttons being distributed by the Sanders forces were actually recycled Humphrey buttons. This was even further proof of the linkage between Sanders and those "ultraliberals" in Washington, the Carter people happily pointed out all over Georgia. An embarrassed Sanders hastily ordered new buttons.

One Carter television commercial focused on a Sanders campaign button; when a rag was rubbed over it, Sanders' face turned into Humphrey's smiling countenance as a somber voice warned that Sanders was really a Humphrey Democrat!

So the war of nerves continued. Repeatedly, through the campaign, Carter claimed he had a "list" of occasions when Sanders, as Governor, had personally profited from public life. And Carter repeatedly told his audiences that the major issue of the campaign was "Sanders' integrity and how he got rich so fast."

When asked whether he had any evidence to back up his innuendoes, Carter said he would disclose specific charges at his convenience. And he denied that he had been conducting a "kill Sanders" campaign, as charged by one of his Republican rivals. "The only reports that I've been conducting a negative campaign," he said during a day of handshaking and public appearances in Athens, "came from one newspaper in the state of Georgia; that's *The Atlanta Constitution,* and some other misinformed editorial writers from certain papers that I won't mention, who picked it up and repeated it.

"I never made a speech criticizing anybody . . . ," he went on. "And I'm looking forward to meeting Sanders head-on in the campaign. I think his performance in office is a legitimate issue, but any comments I make on him or on his administration will be documented, will be responsible, very cautious, and very conservative."

But Carter kept hinting about dark charges involving Sanders. On June 10, Carter said he knew of "four or five" specific incidents in which Sanders had used "inside information" to line his pockets.

"It was a sufficient amount of money for the people to be concerned about it," he alleged, adding he had volunteers checking out reports of Sanders' past activities. "We have attorneys checking titles to property and partnership arrangements," he went on.

A week later, Carter kept up the refrain, telling a convention of the Georgia Association of Broadcasters he knew some interesting things about the sources of Sanders' wealth. Asked to elaborate on his accusation that Sanders had "used political influence to get rich," Carter declined, saying he preferred to wait until later in the campaign.

It was J.B. Stoner, of all people, who challenged Carter to put up or shut up. Stoner, an advocate of white supremacy also running for the Democratic nomination, wondered whether Carter was not "dragging a red herring across the road" in his effort to force Sanders to disclose his personal finances. He demanded that Carter "come out and say what it is" he knew about Sanders "or apologize."

Carter refused to rise to the challenge.

Then Carter announced he intended to hold a press conference at which he would explode a bombshell against Sanders. He said he would disclose material so damaging that Sanders would be forced to retire from the race. The next day, at Moultrie, Carter spoke for about three minutes, showing assembled newsmen a photograph of Sanders and Humphrey on the same platform. That, according to Carter, proved that Sanders was willing to sell out the interests of Georgians to the "ultraliberals." At the same time, Carter charged that Sanders, by favoring repeal of right-to-work laws, was selling out to "big unions."

Sanders had dispatched a trusted aide to obtain firsthand details of the "bombshell" that was supposed to drive him out of public life. The aide, who had flown to Moultrie, was enraged, particularly after one of Carter's grinning associates told him, "We changed our mind."

A reporter asked Carter when he intended to disclose what he had on Sanders. "I wish you fellows would quit bringing that up," the candidate grinned. But a Carter aide referred the newsman mysteriously to the Book of Revelations: ". . . If therefore thou shalt not watch, I will come on thee as a thief, and thou shalt not know what hour I will come upon thee."

What did that mean?

"You'll soon see," the aide replied.

Finally, at the tail end of the primary and after considerable needling from the media, Jimmy Carter released what he described as a "Carter proof packet" of his charges against Sanders. Boiled down, the documents involved a single allegation to the effect that Sanders had interceded with the Federal Communications Commission in an effort to gain television licenses for J.F. Fuqua, a prominent Atlanta businessman about whom there had never been a breath of scandal.

Sanders, who until then had been studiously ignoring his opponent, retorted that the charge was an "outright lie."

That led to a heated—and public—exchange of "Dear J.F." and "Dear Jimmy" letters on the subject. Fuqua said the allegation was "ridiculous." Which is exactly what it turned out to be. For Carter never offered any proof. Nor was any charge of illegality or personal gain on Sanders' part ever proved. And, significantly, Carter was not averse to accepting a $2,000 contribution from Fuqua after he had bested Sanders in the runoff.

Jimmy Carter had made a wild, unsubstantiated charge against his opponent, and he got away with it.

5

FROM STINK TANK TO GOVERNOR'S MANSION

THERE WERE OTHERS IN THE RACE FOR THE DEMOCRATIC NOMI-nation. They included Linda Jenness, a twenty-nine-year-old self-proclaimed admirer of Fidel Castro; Dr. McKee Hargrett, who described himself as a "Wallace-Maddox-Goldwater" Democrat; Jan Cox, a bearded former carpenter who came on as the "inner man" candidate; J.B. Stoner, the Savannah lawyer who believed Hitler had been too "moderate" toward the Jews; and C.B. King, an attorney and the first black ever to run for Governor in Georgia.

King, no relation to the late Martin Luther King, Jr., had been involved in numerous civil rights controversies over the years. Described by one political writer as having "the demeanor of an Oxford-educated African chief," King was extremely popular with Georgia's blacks. His entry into the race posed particular problems for Sanders, who had been hoping to win the primary without a runoff. But that would be unlikely if King drew any significant percentage of the black vote.

On the Republican side, Comptroller General James L. Bentley, a former Democrat, was battling Hal Suit, a popular television commentator, for the nomination.

All of which made for the "strangest, most complex and crowded gubernatorial contest in Georgia history," as Bill Shipp then reported in *The Constitution*.

And Lester Maddox, denied by the courts the privilege of succeeding himself as Governor, was running for lieutenant governor against five other official candidates and, as Shipp described it, "a host of unofficial enemies that include Communists, newspapers, militants, liberals, Nixon Republicans, Humphrey Democrats, and anybody else who happens to disagree with Maddox."

As the campaign progressed, Carter deliberately began to remold his image. Now, he proudly announced, he intended to campaign "as a local Georgia conservative Democrat. . . . I'm basically a redneck." And he vigorously denied that he had ever stated that the Supreme Court decisions on school integration and other issues were "morally and legally correct." A bare five days before primary day, he further emphasized his position by making a well-publicized visit to a lily-white "segregation academy." "You can rest assured," Carter told students at the school, organized to evade integration, "I'll do everything I can for private schools." And at a barbecue in south Georgia, he told supporters, "Don't let anybody, including the Atlanta newspapers, mislead you into criticizing private education. They need your support."

But a month earlier, Carter had been quoted in *The Atlanta Journal* as being opposed to spending "one dime of taxpayers' money" on "fly-by-night" private schools because there wasn't enough money and because state funding would menace the independence of such institutions.

In other words, on many issues Carter was not above taking both sides, a characteristic which became even more evident in his later race for the presidency. This was reflected in still another statement made during the 1970 campaign: "I expect to have particularly strong support from the people who voted for George Wallace for President and the ones who voted for Lester Maddox and excellent support among the leadership of the NAACP and Negro churchmen across the state."

As it turned out, Carter won only five percent of the urban black vote in the primary; but he got most of the hardhats and wool hats. All of which had been carefully planned by a group of advisers which included attorney Kirbo; campaign director Hamilton Jordan; media director Gerald Rafshoon; and press secretary Bill Pope, who had voted for Wallace in 1968. Despite any public disclaimers, wrote Bill Shipp shortly after the general election, "the four or five men who met nearly every Sunday during the campaign with Carter in Room 232 of the Quality Central Hotel to plot strategy say privately that 'the race question' was of inestimable importance in electing Carter." Race, Shipp concluded, was the "silent issue."

Carter was well aware of what he was doing. "You won't like my campaign," the candidate had warned one Atlanta black leader, "but you'll be proud of my record as Governor."

It was an unlovely campaign. Bill Pope, the press secretary, conceded some years later that he had run a "nigger campaign" for Carter against Sanders.

Sanders, in fact, had gotten hit from both sides on the race issue. First came the photograph showing Sanders receiving a "champagne shampoo" from a black basketball player—Bill Bridges. The picture had been taken in the dressing room of the Atlanta Hawks, of which Sanders was a part owner. It was the usual photo of a member of the team giving one of the owners the traditional treatment after a winning season. And it had been published in the sports section of *The Atlanta Journal*.

All of which was innocent enough. But then reproductions of the photo were incorporated in "fact sheets" which were mailed anonymously in the many thousands to white Baptist ministers, lawmen, barbershops, and filling stations across the state. Silly as it may sound in these days of greater racial enlightenment, the picture undoubtedly had a powerful effect on those groups of white voters, particularly in the smaller rural communities, who were likely to view with disapproval what was perceived to be Sanders' socializing with blacks. For, as Bill Shipp noted in *The Constitution*, "in the context of this political campaign, it was a dangerous smear that injected both race, alcohol, and high living" into an already heated contest.

Who was responsible? Political writer Steven Brill, in a *Harper's* article published during the 1976 campaign, flatly charged the Carter campaign with being responsible for the low-blow leaflet.* Brill quoted Ray Abernathy, who had been a vice-president of the Gerald Rafshoon Advertising Agency at the time, as saying, "We distributed that leaflet. It was prepared by Bill Pope, who was then Carter's press secretary." Abernathy also said that Hamilton Jordan, later Carter's White House chief of staff, was "directly involved in the mailing. He and Rafshoon masterminded it."

"It was something we joked about in the office," Abernathy told Phil Stanford of the Capitol Hill News Service. "At the time, it seemed like a hell of a lot of fun." The leaflet, he said, was part of a larger campaign operation jocularly referred to as the "stink tank."

"For instance," Abernathy went on, "during the runoff, the Sanders people started fighting back with their own brand of smut leaflets about Jimmy's mother being a member of CORE." Miz Lillian, of course, had served in India for two years as a volunteer in the Peace Corps, not CORE, the militant Congress of Racial Equality. According to Abernathy, the Sanders forces were flying the leaflets all over the state. "We found out which flights they were on, some people went to the airport to take delivery, and dumped them in the river."

Which raises the question as to whether Carter's "stink tank" had spies within Sanders' organization. Shades of Watergate!

In still another interview with George Lardner of *The Washington Post*, Abernathy again confirmed that the Carter campaign was behind the surreptitious mailing of the scurrilous leaflet. He said "it was mailed from Decatur under some spurious committee heading so it couldn't be tracked." Postage stamps were used in the mailings so there would be no meter number that could be traced. Abernathy's story was backed up by another former Rafshoon vice-president, Dorothy Wood, more recently part-owner of another Atlanta advertising agency. When asked whether she had ever seen the leaflets during the campaign, she said, "Oh, gosh, they were binding them in groups of several hundred or so in the [Rafshoon] office. I remember seeing several stacks of them. I had a fairly big office then, and I remember that they put several stacks of them in one corner of it for a few days."

*The Brill article, entitled "Jimmy Carter's Pathetic Lies," became a *cause célèbre* during the presidential campaign when it was published by *Harper's* in its March, 1976, edition.

Asked whether she recalled discussing the leaflet with anyone, she said, "Oh sure. We all talked about it with Gerry [Rafshoon] over a beer." And she said she also talked about it with Carter's son, Chip, then working on the campaign. "As I remember," she said, "he was shocked. But he was new to politics at the time."

Another Carter link to the low-blow leaflet was provided by Bill Shipp, then political editor of *The Constitution*. "Sure they did it," Shipp told reporter Phil Stanford. "I saw Bill Pope distributing the handbills at a Ku Klux Klan rally. I was with him."

Pope, of course, was Carter's press secretary and a close friend of Shipp. In the summer of 1970, they had both gone to a Klan rally to listen to a speech by the anti-Semitic, anti-black J.B. Stoner. The next morning, a Sunday, they both drove over to a country church to listen to Jimmy Carter.

Pope has disputed all of this. Interviewed years later by Stanford in Decatur, where he worked for U.S. Representative Elliot Levitas, Pope—a slight man with short-cropped white hair—denied having anything to do with the leaflet. Asked about Shipp's story that he had passed the anti-Sanders leaflet out at a Klan rally, Pope said he did "not recall passing out anything." He did concede he had attended the rally, "but all I did was to help Shipp get local color." Pope suggested that "Bill's memory must be faulty."

Faulty or not, Shipp had written about the event for *The Constitution* shortly after it occurred. The story, headlined "Stoner Visits Klan, Carter Gives Sermon," was published on July 27, 1970. Though Shipp did not name Pope, there are two references to the person Shipp says was Carter's press secretary. The pertinent one appears in the paragraphs dealing with the Klan rally at which Stoner spoke:

> A slightly-built fellow, his hat pulled down over his eyes, quietly circulated through the crowd passing out handbills.
>
> "I don't know what it is, but I bet it's good," said one Kluxer as he grabbed a sheet of paper. It was a photograph of Carl Sanders being doused with champagne by a Negro basketball player.
>
> The Carter sermon and the Stoner cross-burning were

miles apart—one on a sinister Saturday night, the other in the bright sunlight of a Sunday morning.

But a reporter who attended both said he could have sworn that a man sitting in the back of the church listening to Carter talk about the Golden Rule looked like the same man who stood at the edge of the light on Saturday night shouting his approval of J.B. Stoner's plan to drive the black man from the face of the land.

After the Brill article was published in *Harper's*, in March 1976, both Gerald Rafshoon and Ham Jordan denied having anything to do with the leaflets. However, Jody Powell, later Carter's White House press secretary, suggested it might have been done by an "overeager supporter" without the candidate's knowledge or approval.

This doesn't make sense to Reg Murphy, former editor of *The Constitution*. "Mr. Carter has been quoted as saying how he didn't know anything about the leaflet prior to its distribution. Technically, that might be true. But not philosophically. He obviously was operating on the basis of 'Don't tell me about it; but get the job done.' The fact is that Mr. Carter—even after he knew about the leaflet—never ordered his people to stop it. And he most certainly never apologized for it."

There were other "fact sheets." One told how Sanders had attended funeral services for Dr. Martin Luther King, Jr. Which, in fact, was true. As had most of the nation's leaders, among them Richard Nixon, Robert Kennedy, Eugene McCarthy, Hubert Humphrey, and Nelson Rockefeller. One person who did not attend was Jimmy Carter. Unlike Sanders, he didn't have the guts to pay his respects. Only later, in his presidential quest, was he to invoke Dr. King's name in his public litany of kindred spirits—and then only with selected audiences.

Other leaflets circulated by the Carterites claimed that Sanders, as Governor, had in the past kept George Wallace from speaking in Georgia. Which, in fact he had. And still another flyer contended that Sanders and State Representative Julian Bond, banned for a time from serving in the legislature because of anti-war statements, had a political alliance. Which was sheer non-sense. If anything, each man disliked the other. And, along with other black leaders like the Reverend Andrew Young, Hosea Williams, and Mrs. Martin Luther King, Bond was supporting the gubernatorial candidacy of black attorney C.B. King, not Sanders.

That these "fact sheets" had a devastating effect on the Sanders campaign was noted, after the election, by *Atlanta Magazine*. A Sanders worker in Cobb County called Atlanta headquarters to say, "They're killing us at Lockheed with the workers there. They're putting out slicks about Sanders keeping Wallace out of Georgia. The only way I know to fight slicks is with more slicks." And in a south Georgia county flooded with sheets about Sanders and Julian Bond, voters told a Sanders worker, "We like you all right, but we can't go along with this"—namely Sanders' alleged link with the black legislator. As *Atlanta Magazine* then noted, "Many white Georgians were frustrated enough to believe anything they read about purported alliances between blacks and politicians."

Another attack against Sanders came from something called the Black Concern Committee, which reportedly mailed 50,000 brochures to black barber shops, pool halls, funeral homes, and churches, falsely alleging that Sanders, while Governor from 1963 to 1967, had reneged on promises to make black appointments. The illustrated pamphlet even suggested that Sanders may have been responsible for the drowning of a black prisoner in a state prison camp in December 1966, and it went on to praise Governor Lester Maddox for having done more for blacks than had Sanders.

When asked about this smear at the time, Carter denied any involvement, saying that the issues must be adhered to. "In his eyes," wrote Bill Shipp, "they are, of course, his allegations that Sanders used the state Democratic Party as his private pipeline to wealth. Carter preaches party reform and government reform. But when he levels a serious charge, he has a habit of grinning, and one wonders why."

The scurrilous leaflets distributed covertly by Carter's "stink tank" operation take on new significance in the light of Watergate. As a former staffer on the Carter campaign said, "Some of the dirty tricks attributed to Carter's crowd make Donald Segretti's look like kid stuff." Hired by the Nixon forces to play pranks on the Democrats, Segretti landed in the slammer because he circulated a handful of childish leaflets attributing all kinds of bizarre conduct to several prominent Democrats including Governor Wallace and Senators Muskie, Jackson, and Humphrey. But no one in Carter's entourage was ever called to such account. And unlike Segretti, who personally apologized to those he had slandered, Carter's minions never had the decency to ask Sanders for forgiveness. Today, those minions are occupying high positions in Carter's White House, having easy access to and advising the man who had promised "a fair, compassionate, and loving" presidency.

Another 1970 dirty trick hatched in Carter's "stink tank," located at Rafshoon's agency, at 1422 West Peachtree Street in Atlanta, was the financing of some of the media advertising of C.B. King, the black gubernatorial candidate, in order to take black votes away from Sanders.

"I personally prepared all of King's radio ads while I was on Rafshoon's payroll and supervised the production," Ray Abernathy told Steve Brill. "And I helped channel money to the company Rafshoon used to pay for them. . . . I don't know if Jimmy knew about it, but everyone else did." The entire project cost about $7,000 or $8,000.

After the Brill article appeared, Jody Powell released a twenty-two-page rebuttal containing this response:

> Who did C.B. King's radio advertising? Ray Abernathy—but Abernathy had never worked on the Carter account. His work was directly with a C.B. King supporter, the spots were *not* paid for by the Carter campaign, nor did the Rafshoon agency place the spots. Neither Carter nor King was aware of even this amount of contact between the two campaigns. Both have denied knowledge of the incident. In point of fact, Carter, with more than 48 percent of the vote, would have received enough of King's support to have won without a runoff had King not been in the race.

It was an extraordinary statement. For it acknowledged that Abernathy, while working for the Rafshoon organization, then handling Carter's advertising, wrote and produced radio commercials for C.B. King. But, said the Powell statement, Abernathy was doing it on his own.

This, Abernathy told Phil Stanford, was nonsense. "I did it at the request of Rafshoon. He came to me and asked me to do it, and I did it because I knew I could cover myself. I wrote the spots, I recorded them. Our media buyer used plain white paper without a letterhead because we didn't want anyone to know who was behind it. I called several small advertising agencies and said we needed someone to place the ads. They wouldn't have to do any work, just collect their fifteen percent. I found one that was willing to do it, and we laundered the money through him."

It was obvious that someone was lying through his outsized molars. And at least one top-notch political writer decided to seek out the truth. Clark Hallas of *The Detroit News* flew to Atlanta and began checking black radio stations. Most of them, he discovered, had destroyed or misplaced their 1970 political advertising records. However, he found one, WAXP (at the time, station WERD), which had kept its receipts for the King ads. And they showed that the ads had been placed on behalf of Concerned Citizens for C.B. King by a small public relations agency headed by Jim Alford. Interviewed by Hallas, Alford confirmed that he had acted as an intermediary for Abernathy but that he "just assumed Abernathy was free-lancing" at the time. Meanwhile, the owner of the studio where the commercials were recorded told Hallas that Abernathy had asked to be personally billed for the session.

Concerning Jody Powell's claim that Abernathy had "never worked on the Carter account," Abernathy told Hallas, "I was actively involved in the campaign account from January to June 1970. After that, I had to pull off and pay attention to some commercial accounts which were suffering. Later, I was assigned to the King commercials. I was picked because we wanted to conceal it even from some of our own people who were working on the Carter campaign. I couldn't have done it on my own because, as a vice-president of the agency, I wasn't allowed to free-lance."

And, once again, Abernathy's story was backed up by Dorothy Wood, another former Rafshoon executive. "The C.B. King ads were laundered out of the Carter campaign," she said. "I don't know whose idea it was but many of us knew it was going on. I was kind of ashamed of it so I tried to know as little as possible."

"It was an obvious effort to take votes away from Sanders," she added.

Abernathy, who left the advertising agency in 1972 after a disagreement with Rafshoon, said he had kept silent about the "stink tank" operation for several years, but began changing his mind in the fall of 1975. This was after Carter's presidential campaign began rolling. "I felt guilty about it," he said.

He felt particularly guilty after a reporter for the "underground" *Atlanta Gazette* had approached him to ask about rumors of the Carter campaign's involvement in the anti-Sanders leaflets. "I lied to him," said Abernathy. "I decided that the next time I wouldn't." And he sent word to the Carter people through a friend, Bebe Smith, then working for Carter, that he did not intend to lie again. Smith, who left the Carter campaign in October 1975, confirmed Abernathy's story. When she informed both Rafshoon and Hamilton Jordan, she said, their response was "something like, 'Well, we knew it would come up some time. We'll deal with it when it does.'"

C.B. King, meanwhile, claimed he had no idea as to who placed his commercials. "There was no way we could have done it," he said, noting that during the final weeks of the campaign his organization hardly had enough money to pay the rent. Nor had he ever heard of any committee named Concerned Citizens for C.B. King, the name of the group which placed the ads.

"If Carter's people did it—and I have no personal evidence that they did—it wouldn't surprise me," King told Hallas. "I was politically naïve and I found out later that a lot of people used me for the wrong reasons.

"Carter is a highly opportunistic man. Regrettably, his face is a façade which reveals little of the inward person. His feet are not only made of clay, they're mired in it.

"When privately closeted with him during the campaign, he was very civil to me. But I remember that in public he would avoid me like the plague."

How much did Jimmy Carter know of these dirty tricks and when did he know it?

On September 13, 1970, during the runoff, Carl Sanders publicly charged that Carter had paid for the radio commercials. Specifically, he said, "In the last week before the primary, Carter paid for radio testimonials to be broadcast in behalf of Mr. King's candidacy. His slick ad agency wrote the commercials, produced them at an Atlanta recording studio, and paid for them."

All this Carter vehemently denied, contending he couldn't have paid for the commercials even if he had wanted to. "I had to cancel my radio and newspaper advertising because I didn't have enough money at the end to pay for them." And he attacked Sanders as a "desperate man," making "contrived and distorted" charges.

Years later, Dorothy Wood said, "I don't see how [Carter] couldn't have known" about the King commercials. "He had his finger on every aspect of the campaign."

Ray Abernathy, however, was not as certain about Carter's direct involvement, though he told Phil Gailey of *The Miami Herald* in early 1976 that he was "really disturbed by the Carter people's reaction to the story" of the King commercials. "The real issue," he said, "is not whether Jimmy Carter is a racist—I don't think he is—or whether he knew about some of these dirty tricks—I don't think he did, probably—but duplicity. That's the issue."

Throughout the campaign, Carter carried on a running battle with the Atlanta press, which was backing Sanders. And it got pretty rough at times, with Carter accusing *The Constitution*, particularly, of deliberately slanting the news and editorial comments against him. Of which he wrote, as follows, in his autobiography:

> My biggest problem and worst mistake involved one of the Atlanta newspapers. The editor . . . began to characterize me as an ignorant and bigoted redneck peanut farmer. Editorial cartoons showed me standing in the muck of racism while all other candidates disappeared into the sunrise of enlightenment . . .

The editor, of course, was Reg Murphy of *The Constitution*. And what Carter forgot to mention was the fact that *The Constitution*'s antipathy toward him actually began during the 1966 campaign. As Murphy more recently observed, "I know it has been pictured as a great personality clash between President Carter and me. But the fact is I wasn't working at *The Constitution* at the time. I had left in 1963 and was gone for three years."

Carter's original arguments were with "those old Southern liberals," Ralph McGill and Eugene Patterson, respectively the publisher and editor of *The Constitution*. And, according to Murphy, they couldn't abide "that little *pissant*," as McGill would call him. "But as far as I was concerned," continued Murphy, "I had nothing to do with those arguments. I was living in Philadelphia at the time."

Carter wrote what he himself later described as "an illtempered letter" attacking *The Constitution* and Reg Murphy. Using terms made popular the year before by Vice-President Spiro T. Agnew, Carter alleged that the newspaper was obviously biased, distorted the news, and misused the power of the press in order to mislead the people of Georgia.

When *The Constitution* refused to print the letter, Carter couldn't contain his anger. He bided his time. "When all the candidates were invited to address the annual convention of the Georgia Press Association," wrote Carter, "I used my time on the program to read the letter to all the state's editors."

Murphy particularly recalls the episode because his children were attending the breakfast at which Carter spoke. "It was a kind of uncomfortable moment for them—to have their father singled out at a meeting of the Georgia Press Association."

Carter seems to have mixed feelings about the utility of this performance. In his autobiography, he wrote that the letter proved to be "a mistaken and counterproductive action." But, in the previous paragraph, he conceded that the battle with *The Constitution* turned out to be a big plus "because it projected me into a position of prominence among the many candidates in the race."

And it probably won Carter a lot of votes. For to many Georgians, particularly in the rural areas, *The Constitution* represented the rich and powerful Atlanta establishment. And, knowing this, Carter calculatedly incurred the wrath of the big city press. "We loved all those scurrilous cartoons," Bill Shipp quoted Bill Pope, the Carter press aide, as saying. "We just didn't want it to stop."

Actually, Carter's appearance before the Georgia Press Association proved to be a disaster for another reason. For Carter also took the occasion to unleash one of the most preposterous allegations ever delivered against an opponent in recent memory. Carter told a hushed audience that he had positive proof that Carl Sanders had his eye on the U.S. Senate and, if elected, would not serve a full four years as Governor. As evidence, Carter pointed to the serial number on Sanders' airplane—62-72V—and said that the number had particular significance. Carter went on to explain that the "62" represented Sanders' election as Governor and the "72" suggested his interest in the Senate two years hence. The "V," according to Carter, stood for "victory."

Carter said he had checked with the Federal Aviation Administration and discovered that the aircraft number had been issued out of sequence, but he was unable to determine who had requested the special number.

Sanders, who had patiently listened to Carter allege that he had gotten rich while in office, apparently couldn't sit still for what he termed "this latest piece of nonsense."

"I'll get out of the Governor's race if he can prove I ordered a special number," said Sanders. "That serial number was on the airplane long before I leased it."

It wasn't a particularly good day for Carter. And, as Bob Cohn reported in *The Athens Herald*, "It was an exceptionally good day for Sanders, who appears to have Carter on the ropes, trying to punch himself out of the corner he backed into."

There was no doubt that Sanders looked good that day at the Georgia Press Association. He looked good particularly by comparison with Carter, who came through as a shrill, wild-swinging smear artist. In fact, Sanders now looked unbeatable. A poll taken of the editors and their wives gave Sanders a three-to-one margin over Carter in the Democratic primary, and a five-to-one edge over either of the two leading Republicans, Jimmy Bentley and Hal Suit, in the general election.

But this was late in June, and there were two months of hard campaigning ahead. And Sanders, resting on his laurels, continued to run what he called a "high road" campaign. A poll taken in his behalf shortly before the September primary date lulled him still further. It showed him taking 54 percent of the vote against the field. Which, of course, did not prove to be the case.

In the final analysis, what did Sanders in was the issue of race.

Carter played the issue for all it was worth; and it was worth plenty. For it helped propel him into the governorship and, thus, on the road to the White House.

It wasn't that Carter ever made any overtly racist remarks; that he never did. Nor did he ever say during the campaign that he was a segregationist; but he never disabused those who assumed that he was. What he did do most definitely was send out signals to the diehards that he was one of them. And he was clever about it. Thus, he came out strongly against the appointment of former Secretary of State Dean Rusk, admittedly "a fine person," to the faculty of the University of Georgia because, Carter said, the university "is not basically an international law school." Of course, in the back of many Georgians' minds was the knowledge that Rusk's daughter had married a black man.

More pointedly, however, Carter sought to tie himself to Lester Maddox, probably one of Georgia's most popular Governors but a segregationist. "All the policemen and firemen in the state are for me and Lester," he declared, after touring an Atlanta police station. "I'm not kidding," he reasserted. "You ask 'em." He also pledged to continue Lester's innovative "Little People's Day" at the Governor's Mansion. And, during the general election, Carter maintained that he was "very proud to be part of a party that is great enough to have men like Governor Maddox heading it up in Georgia." Previously, Carter had said he hoped "to measure up to his standards." And later Carter was quoted as praising Maddox as being "the very essence of what the Democratic Party stands for. He has compassion for the ordinary man."

Still, in an Atlanta radio phone-in show during the closing days of the primary, Carter denied being "an ultraconservative racist," as he claimed the Atlanta newspapers were "projecting" him. "I am basically conservative in my attitude toward government," he said. "As a businessman and farmer, I believe local government ought to be strengthened." And he made it perfectly clear that on other social issues he was as conservative as any one else in a state that had voted for George Wallace two years previously. Among other things, he was strongly opposed to the legalization of marijuana. "There are a lot of things that disturb me," he said. "Hippies in the Tenth Street area, for example. Wide-eyed young women who came to the big city for a modeling career, perhaps, now on dope. Atlanta, capital of the state, rapidly becoming the center of drug distribution for the whole Southeast."

From the beginning, Carter sought to figure out a way to link himself with George Wallace. One of the Alabama Governor's closest political allies was Marvin Griffin, who had once served as Governor of Georgia. Interviewed in 1976 by George Lardner of *The Washington Post,* Griffin recalled how in the summer of 1970 Carter visited him at his home in Bainbridge to explore ways of getting Wallace's support, finally hitting on the idea of promising—if elected—to invite the Alabamian to speak in Georgia. This would be in sharp contrast to Sanders who, as Governor, had twice blocked invitations to Wallace. A few days later, Carter issued an invitation to Wallace. In a speech before the Lions Club in Columbus, Carter said:

> I was a member of the Georgia Seedmen's Association. We rented a National Guard Armory and asked Governor Wallace to address us. At the last minute, Governor Sanders sent us word that he would not allow Governor Wallace to speak on Georgia state property. No matter whether we disagree with his political philosophy or not, I think it is incumbent on the next Governor to see that we have a free interchange of ideas with our sister state. I don't think it is right for Governor Sanders to try to please a group of ultraliberals, particularly those in Washington, when it means stifling communications with another state.

The Carter organization in Columbus then sought and, Griffin believes, obtained a mailing list of thousands of Wallace contributors in Georgia. A few days later, on September 1, 1970, Griffin met with Wallace in Atlanta. And, as Griffin recalled, the talk turned to Carter.

"Well," asked Wallace, "can you depend on him?"

"Damned if I know," replied Griffin.

Sanders, meanwhile, was boxed in. "Everybody knew what I was and what I stood for," he said shortly after his defeat. "I couldn't get out there on the streets in June and start waving my arms and saying, 'Hooray for George Wallace.' People knew me too well for that. It wouldn't have worked."

But it worked for Carter. As Sanders has since explained, "There's no question about the fact that he represented himself as one whom a Wallace voter should support because of the things he stood for, and, after the election, he took a completely opposite tack. Carter supposedly believed in the same principles Wallace did, whatever they were. He didn't define them."

Carter didn't need to. He just kept on appealing for endorsements from such conservative Democrats as S. Ernest Vandiver, who had served as Georgia's Governor from 1959 to 1963 and was best remembered for his decision to keep the state's public school system open in the wake of court rulings on desegregation. Vandiver, married to a niece of Senator Richard Russell, had supported Republican Bo Callaway in the 1966 gubernatorial race. In mid-August, Vandiver released a letter to Carter in which he said that he and his family had decided to support the candidate from Plains, whom he described as a man of "character and integrity."

The following year, Vandiver wasn't too sure about that description. Vandiver felt that Carter, then the Governor, had broken a promise to name him to the U. S. Senate following the death of Senator Russell. Instead, Carter appointed David Gambrell. And years later, in 1976, Vandiver conceded he had been "upset," recalling he had come out for Carter at a crucial time in the 1970 race.

"I think I made the difference," he said.

How much of a difference is hard to estimate. A poll of Wallace voters prior to the September 9 primary vote showed that many of them were confused, unable to determine which of the two major candidates for the Democratic nomination was the more conservative.

Carter wasn't hurt any when *The Atlanta Journal*, in a column by Steve Ball on June 8, 1970, reported that "it just may be that Carter's newly projected conservative credentials will get a boost in the form of an endorsement from onetime kingmaker and longtime leading segregationist Roy V. Harris of Augusta. . . . A Harris endorsement could help Carter solidify some of the conservative vote he's been seeking."

Harris was a powerful figure in the state. He was editor of *The Augusta Courier*, organizer of the White Citizens' Council, and had managed George Wallace's presidential campaigns in Georgia. One word from him and the state's Wallace vote would be Carter's. And Carter made every effort to get Harris to say the word.

Carter did extremely well in the primary election of September 9, but was unable to avoid the traditional runoff. Carter wound up with 48.6 percent of the vote, while Sanders took 37.7 percent. C. B. King, the black attorney, came in third with 8.8 percent. As it turned out, therefore, even had Sanders obtained most of King's presumably black vote, he could not have bested Carter.

As the results poured into his Atlanta headquarters at the Dinkler Plaza Hotel that long primary night, Carl Sanders appeared stunned. The man who had thought he would win hands down over that "clown" from Plains barely made the runoff. He could not believe that a man of his caliber and proven ability could be so thoroughly repudiated. Asked by a newsman if he could pinpoint the reasons for Carter's tremendous upset, Sanders said he felt he was "the victim of, at this point, a very cynical advertising campaign by my opponent to drive a wedge between me and the people. . . . His advertising claims I'm the rich boy and he's the poor, when the opposite is true. That he's for the working man and I'm not, when that, too, is completely false."

It was also obvious that Governor Maddox had also had a telling effect on the Democratic race to pick his successor as well as his own race for lieutenant governor. In every county where Maddox did well, Carter also did well. "The correlation," as one Sanders aide put it, "is amazing." It was obvious that Carter's catering to the Maddox-Wallace voters had paid off.

A "new" Sanders emerged from the ruins on Friday, September 11, appearing at a heavily attended press conference. The buttoned-up, slicked-down, super-cool ex-Governor had overnight metamorphosed into a tieless, coatless, loud, name-calling politician of the old school. Blazing away at Carter, he called his opponent a man "without conscience, integrity, or character," a "grinning chameleon who smeared me and my family all over Georgia," and one who "lied to deceive the people." Instead of being "my opponent," Carter had become a "smiling hypocrite," a man against God, old people, and the disabled.

That was just for starters. Sanders then described Carter as having a "nondescript" record when he served in the state Senate. "His fellow senators considered him an outspoken liberal from 1962 to 1966 and here he is today trying to pass himself to the people of Georgia as a conservative. There is nothing in Carter's record to show him to be a conservative or a legislative leader."

And he chided Carter for television spots that showed him working on his farm. "The last time Carter worked in the fields in the hot August sun was when his advertising agency took the pictures you see on television every day," he said.

Sanders said he had tried to follow the "high road" during the primary campaign but "Carter has cast the first stone." He indicated that he would no longer turn the other cheek and that he himself had a few stones. And he challenged Carter to a face-to-face televised debate "so the real Jimmy Carter can be known."

By contrast, a grinning and jubilant Carter derided Sanders for his sudden change in campaign tactics and for stripping down to his shirtsleeves to deliver campaign speeches. "I'm only thankful the runoff will be Wednesday before he completely disrobes and embarrasses everybody in Georgia," he said. And he declined the opportunity to debate Sanders on television, even though plans for such a statewide broadcast were in the works. Carter said he feared that Sanders would make "irresponsible charges" and "it takes several days to document the fact that they are not true."

Carter denied that he had promised to debate if Sanders would release his financial worth as the former Governor had finally done. "That's another of his unsubstantiated statements," said Carter. It apparently had been painful for Sanders to tell the people of Georgia that he was not the multimillionaire they thought he was. His financial statement disclosed his worth as amounting to only $685,000, probably less than was in Carter's coffers. "It was downright embarrassing for him not to be a millionaire," commented *Atlanta Magazine*. But, according to Carter, Sanders' public disclosure of his personal wealth came too late. "He should have made it two months ago," he said. "I'm still not going to debate him." And in a television appearance, he repeated charges that Sanders had used the office of Governor for private gain, saying at the same time he deplored what he said were Sanders' attempts to smear him. "But I'm going to win anyway," he added.

And again Carter lashed out at the press for allegedly being biased against him. He charged that Southeastern Newspapers, Inc., which published newspapers in Augusta, Athens, and Savannah, had refused to run two stories by its Atlanta correspondent Bob Cohn because, he claimed, they were favorable to him. But he poured most of his scorn on Atlanta's newspapers, again claiming they were unfairly trying to beat him. He said his supporters had told him of a "conspiracy" by the newspapers' owners, Cox Enterprises, to try to install Hal Suit, the Republican nominee in the November general election, so Cox could have his own television announcer in the Governor's office." Of course, as it turned out, there was no such "conspiracy." In fact, unbeknownst to the voters, the Carter campaign was being financed, in part, by the Cox interests, whose lawyer was none other than good ol' Charlie Kirbo, who was helping mastermind the Carter campaign.

Meanwhile, two teams of investigators descended on Carter's peanut farms to look over the housing of his black sharecroppers. One team came from *The Atlanta Journal*; the other from Sanders' campaign headquarters. Greeting the visitors was Billy Carter, the candidate's thirty-three-year-old brother, who chided, "You want to see the tenants we keep penned up or the ones we let out to pick peanuts?"

What the investigators discovered was not exactly pretty. They examined several dilapidated houses in which Carter's tenants lived. They were typical of the shacks in which impoverished blacks lived in the area. The shack in which Felton Shelton and his family lived, for example, had no water or inside bathroom. It had a leaking roof, rotten weatherboarding, and broken windows. Technically, the house was owned by Miz Lillian, whose heart went out to the impoverished on the Indian subcontinent. Shelton was something else, apparently not meriting any of the sympathy she felt for Hindu untouchables. For one thing, Shelton no longer worked the land, and he had been fired from the Carter warehouse. Now he was working for a neighbor across the road, and, as Billy and Jimmy said, he paid no rent.

Interviewed by newsmen, Mrs. Shelton said her husband had asked Jimmy Carter to put some sheeting around the outside of the house and some plywood on the inside, but was turned down by the gubernatorial candidate. "We were never told we had to live here," she added. "But we were never able to own anything of our own."

Countered Billy Carter, "It would suit my mother better if Shelton would move, but she gave him a television set and told him he could live there as long as he wanted rent free. My mother couldn't be expected to keep making repairs on a house when he isn't even working for us any more."

But the height of hyperbole came from the candidate when he commented on the televised reports on conditions of the "tenant houses" on his south Georgia farm lands. Jimmy Carter said the shacks "are better houses than the one I grew up in." Which, of course, was nonsense. He added, "I got a lot of requests around the state from people who would like to live in the tenant houses on my farm." Which also was nonsense.

Sanders sought to capitalize on all this. He accused Carter of being a "slaver" and a "slum landlord." And his organization distributed a leaflet throughout the state containing photographs of the housing for "working people" found on Carter's properties. The text quoted Carter as saying, "There are no shacks on my farms." The text, noting, "These pictures were taken on Sept. 15, 1970," then asked, "Isn't it time somebody spoke up for these people?"

Unfortunately for Sanders, this sort of material—accurate as it was—only played into Carter's hands. For it served further to convince the Wallace-Maddox supporters that "Jimmeh" was no flaming liberal whose heart bled for "nigruhs." In fact, "Jimmeh" was treating blacks like most white folks did in the rural Georgia of the period. Carter's seemingly heartfelt concern for the miserable conditions in which these blacks lived came only after he decided to try for the White House.

On Monday, September 14, Carter zipped over to Augusta, where he met with Roy Harris, the leader of Georgia's racist White Citizens Council and editor of the weekly *Augusta Courier*. They had what *The Constitution* referred to as a "secret confab." While some eighty "anxious supporters" twitched in their seats at a downtown restaurant, the candidate huddled in a car with Harris. What they said to each other was never fully disclosed.

"We just talked about politics in general and the election," Carter said later.

But Harris was not so uncommunicative. He told newsmen that he had voted for Carter in the primary and intended to do the same in the September 23 runoff election. He said he had ridden with Carter from his law office to a television station. "On the way," Harris said, "he asked me what I thought he should do, and I told him to just keep doing what he's doing."

Which helped explain, explained columnist Bill Shipp, why Carter couldn't debate Carl Sanders. He was too busy getting the support of Harris and others like him all that week. And, Shipp went on, "what a friend he's found in Roy, beloved by segs, mossbacks, and anti-eggheads throughout all the civilized Southland." As Shipp noted, Harris had most recently tried to prevent the appointment of former Secretary of State Rusk as a law professor. Carter, too, was opposed to the appointment.

After which Carter sought the endorsement of House Speaker George L. Smith, which he got, too. This "new friend" wrote Shipp, "typifies a Georgia legislator. You don't really need to say much more except that he uses the state airplane at our expense to commute between home in Swainsboro and lawmaking in Atlanta."

From there, Carter raced over "for a little set-to with those two giants of Southeast Georgia, Ralph Dawson of Ludowici and Sheriff Tom Poppell of McIntosh County." According to Shipp, Poppell ran his county "with an iron hand." And, he noted, "many fleeced tourists have some not-so-fond memories of being taken to the cleaners by the clip joints on U.S. 17 in the heart of Poppell County."

Ralph Dawson of Long County, wrote Shipp, "is known as a political boss. But he says he's not the boss— 'just a leader.' The land over which Dawson presides has done much to make Georgia nationally known. For a while, Ludowici, the county seat, was listed on nearly every tourist guide in the country—not for its flora and fauna, but for its sleight-of-hand traffic signal on U.S. 301 and traffic officers whose zeal is unmatched in the U.S."

However Bill Shipp may have felt, these endorsements, particularly that of Roy Harris, constituted a big plus for Carter.

Almost everywhere he went, Carter boasted of support from this "fine, patriotic Georgian." That is, until one day when he was asked by university students whether he would reappoint Harris to the State Board of Regents. Carter said he wouldn't.

"He called me from Atlanta the next day and apologized and wanted to take it all back," Harris said later. Then, after Carter clinched the governorship, "he called me and said he was not going to reappoint me to the board."

Though most of the pols who had supported George Wallace in 1968 by now had lined up behind Carter, Lester Maddox didn't quite trust the man from Plains. In fact, Maddox tried to keep him at arm's length. But it didn't work. Carter unabashedly embraced this outspoken advocate of segregation. "I am proud to be on the ticket with him," Carter proclaimed. "Despite reports we have heard, there has never been any difference between us in the primary." And he announced that Maddox had brought a "high standard of forthright expression and personal honesty to the Governor's office." Still Maddox kept his distance, counseling Carter to make good on his campaign promises. "When I put my money in a peanut machine," said the ex-restaurateur, "I don't expect to get bubble gum." Turning the other cheek, Carter replied, "I'm going to make every effort to include Governor Maddox in the planning stages of my program."

Carter easily won the runoff. He called it a "good and decent campaign, focused on the issues the people raised." But what were the issues? In a postmortem in his *Augusta Courier,* Roy Harris summed up the campaign as follows:

> The people who voted for Lester Maddox and Jimmy Carter had their minds on one thing; they were thinking about the race question. When the Negroes lined up with Carl Sanders and it became known that he was going to get at least 95 percent of their votes, and when he started denouncing me over the state as being a segregationist, the die was cast. The issue was in the open. There was but one real issue in the race in September. . . .

Having disposed of Sanders, Carter then turned his attention to the Republican candidate, Hal Suit, a personable TV newscaster and genuine war hero (he had lost a leg in World War II action). Though a newcomer to politics, Suit was no fool. He knew he had a tough fight ahead of him in the few weeks of the general election campaign. For one thing, he was underfinanced. And he was aware of the professional poll that was taken in October that showed he had little chance unless he could overcome Carter's commanding lead in south Georgia, an area described as "the power base of the state's most raucous political practitioners— Tom Watson, Eugene Talmadge, Herman Talmadge, and now, Lester Maddox." South Georgians had voted overwhelmingly for Wallace, the poll noted, adding that "Carter is winning nearly three-fourths of the potential Wallace vote, and the Carter-Wallace segment is apparently Carter's most dedicated and loyal source of support."

Carter continued to play to the Wallace-Maddox supporters by saying, for example, that he'd issue "shoot to kill orders" to the National Guard "as a last resort" to "protect innocent lives" in a riot. He told a Valdosta press conference that he had "always said I will not permit disruptions of our cities and on our college campuses." The memory of the Kent State shootings of student demonstrators still fresh, his opponent, Hal Suit, took a less belligerent stance. But on other issues, Suit found it "next to impossible" to pin Carter down. "Just look at this," said Suit more recently, waving a faded piece of paper. "This was Carter's platform. It's so vague he could have done almost anything when he got into office."

Carter took a dig at Suit for having invited both President Nixon and Vice-President Agnew to help him in the GOP campaign. "If this helps Suit, then it's a sad day for Georgia, when a national political leader can come into our state and tell us who to elect Governor," said Carter. And when asked about his running mate, Carter said he felt that Maddox "and I strengthen each other. . . . I think his being on the ballot helps me, and vice versa."

Maddox, irrepressible as ever, said the President was always welcome in Georgia, but he hoped Nixon would take time out to "visit a number of schools in the state that his administration has closed" in carrying out integration rulings. And Nixon did receive a warm welcome from a sizable crowd when he arrived in Savannah. Agnew flew in for a brief visit in Albany, offering a lukewarm endorsement of Suit and a ringing endorsement of Democratic Senator Richard Russell, who had just endorsed Carter and the entire Democratic ticket.

The momentum was still with Carter, and he and his aides knew it. Suit was still finding it difficult to raise big funds, though some money did come in as a result of the Nixon visit. Carter, meanwhile, had no such problems, particularly after the September runoff election, when contributions began pouring in from former Sanders supporters. One of the problems Carter did face, however, was that his volunteers appeared to be having difficulty maintaining their enthusiasm following the runoff against Sanders. So, in the closing days of the campaign, campaign coordinator Hamilton Jordan got on the phone to warn Carter's county chairmen that "the Atlanta power structure is up to something" in a last-ditch effort to elect Hal Suit.

"Hamilton knew the power structure wasn't up to anything," a Carter adviser told Bill Shipp. "He was just trying to scare those people so they wouldn't go to sleep on us."

The result was a near landslide for Carter and Maddox, who raised their arms together in victorious glee on election night. Carter received nearly 60 percent of the vote; Maddox did even better with 73 percent.

"The night he won," Ham Jordan later recalled, "I said, 'Well, Jimmy, I guess it's about time to start calling you Governor,' and he just shrugged and said, 'Well, whatever you want.' He didn't seem the least bit excited about it."

One reason may have been that he was exhausted. And once again he had lost considerable weight. And perhaps the rough tactics he had employed to gain victory troubled his conscience. For, according to friendly biographers Howard Norton and Bob Slosser, "Carter afterward told some of [his] friends that he 'felt bad' about his actions, and it was known that he had prayed for forgiveness for some of the things that he felt he had had to say and do to get himself elected. . . .

"It was unquestionably a campaign of expediency," they added. "And it worked. Carter confessed it all later—to friends and to the Lord."

Questioned about the campaign six years later during his presidential bid, Carter did not seem apologetic at all. For example, he told George Lardner, "If you ever find one instance in the 1970 campaign where I ever insinuated anything about race or tried to make people think I was a racist, you know I will admit it in the front porch of *The Washington Post* building in Washington."

And Lardner quoted a longtime Southern observer who professed a high regard for Carter as saying, "That's Jimmy. He's one of the most cocksure men I've ever encountered in public life. Unlike Lot's wife, he never casts his eye backward."

6
THE IMPERIAL GOVERNORSHIP

THE TELEVISED INAUGURATION OF JIMMY CARTER AS THE SEV-enty-sixth Governor of Georgia was the most elaborate and ostentatious ever conducted in that sovereign state. It was, as a subhead in the next day's *Constitution* described it, "Camelot Down South." And it set the tone for the next four years of the Carter administration.

The U.S. Navy Academy Band, whose appearance Carter had specifically requested, was flown down from Annapolis to open the ceremony on that brisk twelfth day of January 1971. The midshipmen were followed by an all-black choir singing the "Battle Hymn of the Republic," Abraham Lincoln's favorite hymn, which, legend had it, had been sung by Union forces when they burned down Atlanta. However, as one report noted, a lot of those in the audience who didn't hear the words thought the choir was singing "Glory, Glory to Old Georgia."

Several clergymen (including Carter's from Plains) then offered prayers. And as the bells of the Church of the Immaculate Conception pealed, Carter was administered the oath of office precisely at noon. A cannon boomed a nineteen-gun salute so thunderously that, as a dispatch had it, "the statue of General John

B. Gordon and his horse must have thought the Battle of Atlanta was on again."

Carter then delivered a twelve-minute speech on a red-white-and-blue platform specially constructed to hold 250 legislators and top Carter supporters. The platform had been built over the statue of Thomas E. Watson, which, as Hal Gulliver had previously noted in *The Constitution,* was a shame "because Watson would probably love to watch what's going on."

Most probably, Watson would have been confused. For here was Carter, one of his political descendants, indulging in what a report the next day described as "Kennedyesque rhetoric." Watson probably would have been more comfortable with Lester Maddox who, after being sworn in, told the crowd of some 5,000 of the inscription on the statue of the late Governor Eugene Talmadge. It read, he said, as follows: "I may surprise you, but I'll never deceive you." And Maddox added, "I don't see how I can surprise you any more, but I promise not to deceive you." Presumably, the newly sworn-in Governor was listening, for Carter was to use almost the same words in years to come while seeking the presidency.

The scene then shifted to the grounds of the new $2 million Governor's Mansion on West Paces Ferry Road, which Carter had voted against when he was a State Senator. Now he and his wife, Rosalynn, received thousands of friends, relatives, and other guests as they turned up to pay their respects to Georgia's new first family. About fifteen or twenty feet from them stood the Governor's mother, forming her own one-woman receiving line. Which seemed sort of peculiar to some of the guests. But, after all, it was Miz Lillian who, as almost everyone knew, always did things a bit differently. Only later was it disclosed by Jimmy's cousin, of all people, that Miz Lillian had planned to move into the mansion as Acting First Lady "because Rosalynn wasn't sophisticated or knowledgeable enough to handle it." Rosalynn, however, had other plans. She informed her mother-in-law in no uncertain terms she intended to run her own household and Miz Lillian could always "come and visit." A stunned Miz Lillian packed her bags and left.

Also in evidence at the Mansion was the Governor's beaming brother, Billy, who somehow managed to find for himself and his cohorts several six-packs of Pabst Blue Ribbon to while away the afternoon. After all, only punch, coffee, and sweet little cakes were to be served by the abstemious host, and that wasn't fit fare for good ol' boys from Plains. Billy had done his share to make the party a success. He had brought 300 pounds of peanuts from home and had put them in deep fat overnight. Guests were really munching on "Billy's nuts," served with white paper napkins that had "Inauguration 1971" imprinted in gold.

But the day wasn't over for Jimmy Carter. Dressed in white tie and tails, the new Populist Governor and his lady made appearances at four inaugural balls, each one of which was jam-packed. Guarded by Georgia Bureau of Investigation agents and state troopers, Carter danced with his wife at each of the invitation-only balls. At his final appearance, he said, "All I can say is you sure look like a different crowd of people than stood in the rain with me hoping this would come true."

However, not everyone had had a good time that day. The reason was *The Speech*, as it became known. Having taken the oath of office, Carter stunned the throng, including Lester Maddox, by declaring:

> I say to you quite frankly that the time for racial discrimination is over. Our people have already made this major and difficult decision. No poor, rural, weak, or black person should ever have to bear the additional burden of being deprived of the opportunity of an education, a job, or simple justice.

It was not the words themselves that were such a shock; it was that Carter was the one who delivered them. For was this not the same self-proclaimed "redneck" who just weeks before had waged a campaign with racist overtones? And was this not the man who had appealed to the supporters of Lester Maddox and George Wallace?

It most certainly was; but Jimmy Carter couldn't have cared less. He had gotten what he wanted—the governorship—and that was all that counted. And, by making *The Speech*, he had gotten something else—national attention. He was on the front page of *The New York Times* the next morning, and, across the country, editorials commented on this rising figure in what was now being called the New South. Thus, in the space of a few startling sentences pledging an end to discrimination, Carter was able to effectively separate himself from his own 1970 campaign. Now he had become, in the eyes of the national media at least, the symbol of a new moderation in the political life of the South.

And nowhere was that more apparent than in the surprising treatment accorded Carter by *Time* in its May 31, 1971, issue. In the cover story entitled "New Day A'Coming in the South," the fledgling Governor was described as "a South Georgia peanut farmer who is both product and destroyer of the old myths. Soft-voiced, assured, looking eerily like John Kennedy from certain angles, Carter is a man as contradictory as Georgia itself, but determined to resolve some of its paradoxes." * Actually, the *Time* piece was conceived as a roundup of all the racial moderates who had lately been elected to Southern governorships. They included Virginia's Linwood Holton; South Carolina's John West; Florida's Reubin Askew; and Arkansas' Dale Bumpers. And, unlike Carter, not one of them had relied on pseudo-segregationist symbolism to gain their victories.

Yet Carter was selected for *Time*'s in-depth reportage; and his portrait in full color, looking very much like the late John Kennedy, became the face on the cover. And the reason for this extraordinary treatment was the fact that, unlike the other newly elected Southern Governors, Carter succeeded an out-and-out segregationist. Thus, in the eyes of *Time*'s New York-based editors, he looked good by contrast. Which may well have been Jimmy Carter's most valuable asset. Another was his personality. There is no doubt that Jimmy wowed the rubes up in Rockefeller Center when he was invited for lunch by Time Inc.'s top executives prior to the publication of the cover story. He said all the right things. "It was the highest-level lunch I've ever seen," said one impressed observer. "That's usually reserved for someone

---

* Carter's resemblance to JFK, which his strategists assiduously cultivated, was to produce a surprising backlash. Early in the 1976 campaign, rumors spread across the land that Jimmy actually was the illegitimate son of JFK's father, Joseph P. Kennedy Sr.; that Miz Lillian had once been the elder Kennedy's secretary. Needless to say, the story was preposterous. From then on, however, references to the resemblance were discouraged.

like the Secretary of Defense or something." From then on, *Time's* top editors kept their eyes on Carter as a man to watch and encourage. *Time,* in its infinite collective wisdom, had decided to call an end to the Civil War and reunite the South with the rest of the Union.

"In the cover piece," Bruce Galphin noted in *Atlanta Magazine,* "Carter came off as Good Guy, but not Superliberal, and for that, he must have heaved a deep south Georgia sigh of relief. *Time's* heroes rarely get many votes in his part of the country." For, if the truth be known, Jimmy wasn't doing too well in the early months of his Administration. "If Jimmy Carter had to run for Governor again today," commented Bill Shipp in *The Constitution* four months after his inauguration, "he probably couldn't be re-elected. That is not a fact, of course. It is just a feeling. You get out in the state for a few days and listen to what people say. They say Jimmy promised this or that and he didn't do it. Some appointments didn't turn out as they had expected. People who had socked it to Carter's opponents six months ago now talk against Carter."

What was hurting Carter in some parts of the state, according to Shipp, was "the sudden national spotlight" on the Governor. "Hardly a week goes by that Carter is not being featured in some national magazine or on a national television program. . . . He's suddenly the liberal light in the Old South, a breath of fresh air, the voice of the New South. When *The New York Times* says so, it must be so. So everybody else in the business of disseminating news on a national scale grabs on and hails Carter."

"If you've got national political ambitions," Shipp went on, "this kind of thing can only help. But it can get out of hand at home. People in Georgia see Carter smiling at them from the pages of a national magazine and read about his liberalism in Dixie. They could've sworn that when they voted for him he was a friend of George Wallace and Roy Harris.

"Some of Carter's top admirers seem to recognize the problem. They, of course, are not interested in slowing down the Governor's national exposure. Even if politics were not a part of it, good publicity for Carter is good publicity for Georgia. . . . Carter is walking a tough path. While he is projecting a liberal image nationally, he still must practice just enough Georgia-brand demagoguery to keep the natives from getting so restless that his program will be wrecked."

At times, Carter did seek to slow down what Shipp had described as "his fast approach to the left wrought by the media." A classic example was the way he handled the case of First Lieutenant William L. Calley, Jr., who had been convicted by a military court of the premeditated murder of twenty-two South Vietnamese civilians at My Lai, a small hamlet about one hundred miles northeast of Saigon. When Calley was sentenced to life imprisonment, public reaction was emotional and sharply divided. Within hours, over 5,000 telegrams arrived at the White House, running 100 to 1 in favor of clemency.

After consulting with Democratic leaders, President Nixon ordered Calley released from the Fort Benning stockade and confined to his quarters on the base. When this was announced in the House of Representatives, there was a spontaneous round of applause on the floor. And, as Nixon later wrote in his memoirs, "Reaction was particularly strong and positive in the South. George Wallace, after a visit with Calley, said that I had done the right thing. Governor Jimmy Carter of Georgia said that I had made a wise decision." Two days later, Nixon announced he would personally review the Calley case before any final sentence was carried out. Later, Nixon changed his mind. He decided not to intervene. As it turned out, Calley was paroled by the Secretary of the Army three months after Nixon's resignation. As Nixon later commented, "I think most Americans understood that the My Lai massacre was not representative of our people, of the war we were fighting, or of our men who were fighting it; but from the time it first became public the whole tragic episode was used by the media and antiwar forces to chip away at our efforts to build public support for our Vietnam objectives and policies."

And this was exactly the way Governor Carter felt about the war generally and My Lai specifically. Only later, as he sought the presidency, would he characterize the war as "racist" and My Lai as one of its manifestations. But in his years as Governor, Carter fully backed President Nixon's handling of Vietnam. In fact, as a dispatch in *The New York Times* later put it, "Mr. Carter's support of the war was one of the most prolonged and persistent of any major political figure. He attempted to dissuade fellow Governors from condemning American involvement in the conflict and told journalists as late as 1974 that he favored continued Administration requests for more appropriations for the war."

Since the trial had taken place in their state, Calley's fate was of particular interest to Georgians, who overwhelmingly disapproved of the harsh punishment meted out to the young lieutenant. Amid the storm of protest, the Governor called a news conference. According to *The Constitution*, Carter disclosed he had directed his subordinates to switch all phone calls concerning the Calley case to him personally. He said he was impressed by the "responsible attitude taken by Georgians" on the case. And because of the "overwhelming unanimity of belief" expressed, he said he could assure American servicemen "they do have our complete backing."

Then Carter spoke of those "both within this country and without who would use these events to cheapen and shame the reputation of American servicemen and to shake the faith of Americans in their country." This was pretty much how Nixon felt about the matter. But Carter went the President one better. After describing Calley as a "scapegoat," the Governor proclaimed the following Monday to be "American Fighting Men's Day," asking the people of Georgia to display the American flag and to drive with their headlights on to show their "complete support for our servicemen, concern for our country, and rededication to the principles which have made our country great."

The statement sounded as if Carter was defending Calley and condemning his murder conviction. At least that's the way *The Arkansas Gazette* read it. Recalling "all the favorable publicity" he had garnered from his inaugural address, this liberal daily contended that "Carter was one of the first to leap to the lionization of Lt. Calley, the murderer of My Lai, after Calley's conviction. The Georgia Governor's performance in the Calley test was rather indicative, we fear, of his real character."

But more indicative of his real character was the way Carter desperately sought to change the meaning of "American Fighting Men's Day" five years later. Seeking the presidency in 1976, Carter bitterly assailed the war as immoral and one over which the American people had no direct control. Rather, it was their leaders who made the "decision to go into Vietnam and Cambodia and spend 50,000 American lives and 150 billion dollars. . . ." In Indianapolis, he expanded on this theme. Addressing a black church audience, Carter spoke of the daily spectacle on TV screens of American bombers flying out to "firebomb villages" and killing "every man, woman, and child in the village to save it."

"We did not think it was racist, but it was," said Carter.

Asked whether his remarks to the black audience represented an evolution in his thinking about the war, considering his 1971 statements, Carter said he had spoken about the "tinge of racism" in the war to general audiences in recent months. "It was obvious to me back in Calley's day that this was the case," he went on. "I never thought Calley was anything but guilty. I never felt any attitude toward Calley except abhorrence. And I thought he should be punished and still do. I never expressed any contrary opinion." But, at the time of Calley's trial, Carter felt "it was not right to equate what Calley did with what other American servicemen were doing in Vietnam."

"There was an attempt that was made by Calley's supporters— by some of the public officials who went down to Columbus [Ga.] to have massive demonstrations for Calley— that he was a typical serviceman, in what he did, which was appalling," Carter said. Moreover, the Calley trial had been a "departure from our nation's longstanding policy in military justice." In military trials in Germany after World War II, he went on, we "never punished the lieutenants to the exclusion of the captains and colonels and generals."

So, he concluded, "I don't see any incompatability at all in the statements."

Carter may well have felt that way about Calley and the war back in 1971, but he did not say so at the time. And when he called upon Americans to stand up for Our Boys in Vietnam— getting a tremendous amount of publicity in the process—Carter at no time ever explicitly or implicitly condemned Lieutenant Calley's actions. That was all to come later when political necessities made anti-Vietnam rhetoric obligatory. The 1971 statement, as Bill Shipp then noted, "was plainly calculated to show the folks who put him in office that he was the same old boy they voted for."

Carter clearly showed how he felt about Vietnam in June 1971, when he offered a resolution at a meeting of Democratic Governors in Omaha opposed to making the war an issue for the Democrats in the 1972 presidential contest. It was a move which, as Shipp reported on the front page of *The Constitution*, "could cause serious political trouble in the months ahead" for presidential hopefuls Ed Muskie and George McGovern, both of whom had "made it plain they intend to use the war as an issue" against Nixon. Carter "politicked for the resolution as if he were running for office again," reported Shipp. A watered-down version passed unanimously after Carter pointed out that Republican National Chairman Bob Dole already was seeking to make the war a GOP issue.

Still, the folks back home were beginning to wonder about what kind of Chief Executive they had elected. For one thing, Carter had early appointed a black man to the Pardons and Paroles Board.* And now there was talk the Governor intended to appoint another black as the new Superior Court Judge for Fulton County. "But," as Bill Shipp reported on April 16, 1971, "the word came down a few days ago that the new judge will be a white man." And Carter's "decision to go white undoubtedly has something to do with a fear that his image may turn so liberal that his statewide political support will go completely sour."

Carter's hesitance about hiring blacks for state jobs was noted by the Reverend J. C. Hope, president of the Georgia NAACP, who said in October 1972 that the Governor had made many public statements supporting "justice and equality for all people, but with very little results." During Carter's administration, "only token appointments of blacks in high level positions, if any, have been noted," Hope added. "The number of blacks have not significantly increased in lesser positions."

A year later, Carter was praised by *The Atlanta Journal* for what it termed his "straightforward stand against quota hiring within state government." An editorial described as "overzealous" efforts of the Department of Human Resources, which had been re-

---

* Even Governor Wallace, a man not known for racial moderation, had begun to appoint blacks to state positions. Another indication of the South's changing social climate was the naming of several blacks to his staff by Republican Senator Strom Thurmond of South Carolina, who in 1948 had run as the "Dixiecrat" candidate for President.

organized by Carter, to comply with federal equal employment guidelines. But Carter was opposed to such efforts, declaring, "We have not and we will not establish quotas or pass over better qualified individuals just to be able to say we are meeting a certain percentage goal." Such quotas, said Carter, constituted "reverse discrimination." Carter's position, needless to say, raised the hackles of black leaders.

The folks back home were also reassured by a string of Carter statements assailing various federal rulings affecting the South. The man who had been hailed as the leader of the New South now sounded very much like a leader of the Old South. "It's time for the federal government to quit kicking the South around," he said in May 1971. "The recent Supreme Court decision on busing singled out the South for the very restrictive part of their ruling, and they've let the rest of the nation have a different kind of freedom. I resent this very much. I don't want to see in the future any more laws passed by Congress or any more rulings by the Supreme Court that discriminate against the South."

In August, President Nixon announced his opposition to forced busing. In response, Governor Wallace reopened a school which had been closed by court order to achieve integration. Carter praised Wallace's defiance of the court and said that it provided the Nixon Administration with "an opportunity to demonstrate its sincerity" on the busing issue. Carter also said that Nixon should thank Wallace "for his timely assistance" and then get on with the job of "translating speeches and campaign promises into concrete action."

In September, Carter urged parents and public officials to protest Supreme Court rulings on "forced busing," predicting such efforts might ultimately have an effect on the high court. But he rejected a suggestion from Lieutenant Governor Maddox that he defy the law and go to jail if necessary to stop court-ordered busing. "I'm not in favor of Southern Governors going to jail and I'm not in favor of defiance of the law," Carter said.

In November, on the eve of the Southern Governors Conference in Atlanta, Carter reiterated his opposition to "massive school busing" and his support of neighborhood schools. He told newsmen he wanted all the potential Democratic presidential candidates as well as the party platform to take the same position. He said that he had questioned each of the potential candidates on where they stood; and he had found Senator Henry Jackson and Representative Wilbur Mills as acceptable presidential prospects in the South. But he granted Senators Edmund Muskie and Hubert Humphrey only provisional status, depending upon how well they came around against "discriminating" against the South on civil rights issues. As for George McGovern, he said, forget it. He didn't think he and the liberal South Dakotan were likely to think much alike anyway.

All of which left the liberal editors of *The Arkansas Gazette* aghast. Commenting on Carter's presidential choices, his "demagoguing" on My Lai and Calley, and his being "one of the first this year to turn tail before the 'busing' issue," *The Gazette* had this to say in an editorial titled "Scratch Carter:"

> There has been much talk about the "new breed of Southern Democratic governors" but we wish that wire services and columnists would keep a more up-to-date list on who is still qualified for the accolade.
>
> So far as we are concerned it is time to scratch Georgia's Governor Jimmy Carter from the "new breed" list, period. He is not even marginally qualified, on the record of his continuing performance in office. He made a good inaugural speech that got him top billing in Time magazine, but since then he has sounded more like John Bell Williams than the progressive Southerner he was supposed to be . . .

In early 1972, white parents in Augusta, Georgia, planned a one-day boycott to express opposition to the first phase of a forced busing plan. They wanted the state legislature to call on Congress to summon a constitutional convention to consider an anti-busing amendment. Carter agreed, asking the lawmakers to pass a resolution urging Congress "to call a convention for the purpose of proposing the following amendment to the Constitution of the United States: 'No student shall be assigned to nor compelled to attend any particular public school on account of race, religion, color, or national origin.'"

Carter said that if the legislature didn't pass such a resolution, he would support the one-day school boycott as a "last resort." He added, "The massive forced busing of students is the most serious threat to education I can remember." After the legislature passed the resolution, the boycott issue became moot.

Four years later, as a presidential candidate running not simply in one Southern state but in thirty primaries, Carter totally reversed his position. Interviewed in Madison, Wisconsin, one of the more liberal university cities, Carter stated, "I do not favor a constitutional amendment to prohibit busing. It would be divisive, it's an emotional issue, and I would hate more than anything in the world to see the legislatures in this country for the next eight years, particularly in the South, reopening the old wounds of the busing issue."

Carter's 1972 position did not go unnoticed in Little Rock, where *The Arkansas Gazette* compared the Georgian unfavorably with still another "in the new crop of highly publicized Southern Democratic Governors"—Florida's Reubin O'Donovan Askew, who "has emerged as a man of high principle and stout resolve, ready to meet the formidable busing issue squarely, even while Jimmy Carter has turned tail and fled before the segregationist outcry." Askew at the time was the only conspicuous Southern voice in favor of busing, not because he liked it but because it was important to obey the law and "meet racial discrimination head-on." This, *The Gazette* said, was "statesmanship in the best heritage of the Southern progressive. . . . As for Jimmy Carter, perhaps the most celebrated of the 'new' Southern governors, he met the 'busing' issue in a fashion that would compare favorably only with the performance of George Wallace."

By coincidence, the day the editorial appeared in Little Rock was the day Carter introduced Wallace to a joint session of the General Assembly in Atlanta. Calling Wallace "a personal friend of mine" whose voice "is being heard throughout the country," Carter told the Alabamian—to tremendous applause— "Many Governors now want you back in the party," meaning the

Democrats whom Wallace had forsaken in 1968 to run as an independent. Wallace, whose speech was boycotted by Georgia's black legislators, said the "real extremists" in the Democratic presidential race "are those who voted to bus your child, put us in a bind with foreign aid and welfare and advocated unilateral disarmament." He said his opponents "just got their hand caught in the cookie jar." Lester Maddox, presiding over the joint session, could hardly restrain himself in making an unabashed pitch for Wallace's national candidacy. "Tell it all, Mr. President," the Lieutenant Governor shouted.

Previously, in a speech before the Peace Officers Association of Georgia, Carter sounded like Wallace in describing how he dealt with racial disturbances, which he said had been frequent throughout the state since he had taken office. Just the other day, he told the lawmen, the police chief of the small town of Rossville had called to tell him, "Governor, I can stand here and see flames [from racial rioting] in the sky over Chattanooga, and I need some help." Carter told the chief that he would "have it as soon as I can get it to you." Carter then said that "the holocaust that had developed in Chattanooga was stopped at the state line because law enforcement officers at Fort Oglethorpe and Rossville and the smaller towns in that area knew full well that the state police and the Governor of their state stood behind them."

Carter said he had learned from experience that the way to deal with civil disturbance was to keep news coverage down and to seek to keep communications open between the factions. "If there's one thing you and I know about demonstrators, it's that what they want is to see themselves on television or read about themselves in the newspapers or hear about themselves on the radio. And I want you to help me . . . hold down local disturbances by minimizing publicity given to demonstrators who quite often come in from outside a community seeking only state and national publicity." [The "outside agitators" theme had often been sounded by George Wallace.]

The most highly publicized result of Carter's four years in office was his claim to have completely reorganized the state government, consolidating three hundred departments, boards, and agencies into twenty-two departments, thus saving the taxpayers $50 million a year. The issue is important mainly because, in his race for the highest office in the land, Carter invariably referred to this seemingly herculean accomplishment in pledging he would perform even bigger wonders in curtailing the bloated federal bureaucracy.

The idea of reorganization was not particularly new. In 1931, Governor Richard Russell had slashed the number of state agencies from 107 to eighteen. And Governors Vandiver and Sanders had also begun work in this area. Nevertheless, when Carter first proposed reorganization, he stirred up a hornet's nest. He discovered that the legislature, which had grown frisky under Maddox, was more independent than ever. Sanders' people, still in positions of authority, refused to forgive or forget what they believed to be "the dirtiest campaign in Georgia's history" waged against their man. And Lester Maddox was still shocked over Carter's having used him to get elected and then making that speech about the need to end racial discrimination.

As Lieutenant Governor, Maddox had considerable power over the organization and conduct of the State Senate. Consequently, Maddox was in a position to help or hurt the new Governor considerably. Which makes his story of his 1970 post-election meeting with the Governor-elect extremely meaningful as to what kind of man Jimmy Carter was in his moment of triumph. Having walked into Carter's office in a conciliatory mood (after all, he had outpolled Jimmy in the general election), Maddox said he was shocked when the Governor-elect told him, "If you ever oppose me on any issue, I'll meet you head-on and fight you with all the resources under my command and authority." The story was never disputed by Carter. In fact, it was indirectly confirmed by the manner in which the Governor dealt with the state's legislators. Carter apparently followed the nineteenth-century advice of Henry Adams: "You can't use tact with a congressman; you have to take a stick and hit him on the snout."

The combat between Carter and Maddox grew brutal. Maddox saw in the plans to reorganize the government a plot by Carter to set up a dictatorship. "There was a great deal of blood," Jody Powell said later. There was also blood spilled in the legislature. Apparently Carter had expected the legislature to vote on reorganization outright. When the lawmakers decided to debate the issue, Carter got angry. Why, the very idea that someone should disagree with him!

At the conclusion of the 1972 session, Carter called it the "worst" in the history of Georgia, terming the legislative deliberations "an absolute victory for every selfish interest and lobbyist that ever set foot in the capital." But by then, most of the pols had grown accustomed to Jimmy's temper. "We used to call him Jungle Jimmy," one of them told *The New York Times*. "There was no way of dealing with him when he went into his primitive state."

Very early in his administration, Carter's tantrums became proverbial. Reg Murphy, in a *Constitution* column entitled "Temper in High Places," told how the Governor lost his cool when a legislator came to visit with about twenty of his constituents. They had come, the lawmaker explained, to ask Carter not to veto a minor bill if it should pass both the House and the Senate.

Carter agreed he would honor the wishes of the delegation. But then he swung his attention to the legislator. "I won't be like you," he said. Then, to the embarrassment of all present, Carter denounced the legislator for having changed his mind on the Governor's reorganization plan. And for several minutes, he proceeded to describe the legislator's "poor qualities" to his hometown constituents. After which, according to Murphy, he "dismissed the group with another gracious burst of smiles."

Also according to Murphy, another legislator, this one representing an urban constituency, was greeted with an outburst when he met with the Governor for a discussion of taxes. "I'm not going to do any horsetrading on those tax bills," Carter told the astonished lawmaker. "We're going to pass them just like they are."

The legislator, who had been favorably disposed to Carter's tax program, concluded there was no point in continuing the conversation. So he took his leave.

Which explains why Carter found it so difficult to get the coöperation of the legislature for his various proposals. Temperamentally, he found it difficult to compromise. He had to have it his way or nothing at all. "If politics is the art of the possible," Murphy told *Newsweek* in July 1976, "Jimmy Carter won't get along with anybody in Washington, because he is a mean, hard-eyed sort of fellow who tolerates nobody who opposes him. The Governor just absolutely does not take challenges from anybody. I always figured that a man who would lower himself to get into a shouting match with Lester Maddox has a very low boiling point."

For a time, too, Carter complained about the scant attention given by the press to his program. In a speech before the Georgia Press Association in June 1971, he criticized the newspapers for "underestimating the importance of state government reorgan-ization."

"I am staking my whole reputation on this program," he said. But he said he shared the blame for lack of press interest. He conceded he had once attempted to bar news coverage of legislative reorganization committee hearings. He had changed his mind about secrecy in government. Now he was opposed to it.

Finally, the legislators were faced with the task of getting reorganization behind them so they could get on with the budget. Despite considerable opposition, reorganization was duly passed, albeit by bare margins.

But in the end, how successful was Carter's reorganization of the state government? Carter himself, while campaigning for the presidency, often told how he fought for his program, even "twisting some arms" to get it through. And, as a result, he said, 278 agencies and departments were abolished. "And not only did we make possible the savings of millions of dollars in administra-tive costs, we made the whole operation much more efficient and much more responsible to the needs of the people. I'm proud, really proud of that."

According to Ernest Davis, the now retired state auditor, the economic savings which Carter said had resulted from his restruc-turing of the government never appeared on his balance sheets. "I have personally not been able to identify any savings that resulted from reorganization per se." He said the claimed reduction of administrative costs was "strictly fiction." And when asked during the presidential campaign for figures to back up Carter's claim that as Governor he had slashed administrative costs by 50 percent, a Carter spokesman replied, "There are no such statistics available."

However, he suggested that reporters check with the Office of Planning and Budget in Atlanta. But Richard Cobb, the deputy director of OPB, said that he "did not have figures showing savings on administrative costs," noting that a 50 percent reduction in administrative costs "would be very difficult to substantiate."

Nor did Carter, as Governor, "eliminate" 278 agencies or anything near that. First, only sixty-six of the agencies involved were important enough to warrant funding. The remaining were study or ceremonial groups, none of which was important enough to warrant any type of budget. The Ty Cobb Baseball Commission was one. It hadn't functioned for many years, recalled M.W.H. Collins, former director of the University of Georgia's Institute of Government, who had worked on reorganization for Carter and other Governors. "They [the commissioners] were supposed to come up with a memorial for 'the world's greatest baseball player,' some sort of museum or something, but hell, there weren't enough people interested."

Still another agency was the almost moribund Superintendency of Naval Stores, which still required occasional consultations with the Turpentine Growers of America. "They were headquartered in Georgia, and one of the superintendent's jobs had been to check the quality of turpentine," said Collins. The Superintendency got axed without any great outcry.

"A lot of the 'elimination' was just regrouping," said Collins, more recently dean of American University's College of Public Affairs. "What he did was a rather radical reorganization. But the thing I frankly could never make Jimmy understand was that this wasn't the first time the state government had been radically reorganized. . . . We laid the groundwork under Vandiver and Sanders. . . . But, you know, a political leader wants to be first."

A more bitter critic was onetime Carter supporter Tom Murphy, speaker of the Georgia House of Representatives while Jimmy was Governor. Murphy, who had campaigned for Carter in both 1966 and 1970, broke with the Governor "when it became clear he just isn't the fellow he says he is. He's fooled a whole lot of people that way." As for reorganization, Murphy said that far from achieving "a revolution in state government," all Carter accomplished was "a cosmetic rearrangement of the furniture."

After investigating Carter's claimed accomplishments on state reorganization, George Lardner, Jr., wrote in *The Washington Post* in February 1976, "The notion that 278 state agencies were 'eliminated' is at best an overstatement." And Lardner quoted Carl Sanders as having said, "It was more show than substance. It appears that the state is having to grapple with rather serious problems that have developed in some major departments or bureaus as a result of it."

Carter's "favorite" reorganization showpiece was the sprawling Department of Human Resources, a conglomeration of all agencies relating to public health, welfare, and vocational rehabilitation. The Department, which Carter said as Governor he was "most interested [in] and most proud [of]," became a prime target of controversy. After examining the books of the department for the first full year of operation, the then state auditor, Ernest Davis, reported officially that the "inadequacy of control systems and confusion of records create a situation where theft or embezzlement is easily possible and would not be readily detected." Later, Davis said his investigations were initially unable to account for some $40 million. And Department officials acknowledged to *The Atlanta Constitution* that perhaps 45 percent of all Georgia welfare cases contained some error or fraud.

In 1975, one year after Carter left office, the Georgia legislature moved swiftly to repair the damage when it authorized his successor, the newly installed Governor George Busbee, to "undertake such reorganization of the Department of Human Resources" as "necessary to improve the management and administration of its function." This new mandate was effective through April 1, 1976, but Busbee discovered he needed even more time to revamp the bureaucratic monster. "When I took office," the Governor told a group of Georgia mayors in June 1976, "the Department of Human Resources was an organizational nightmare. The Department was under attack from both legislators and citizens for doing an inadequate job."

In the same speech, Busbee told of the distressing financial condition he had inherited from Carter. "It came as a shock last June to discover that the state's economy would not produce the revenues necessary to fund the fiscal year 1976 budget that had just been passed a couple of months before. It was necessary to summon our legislators back to Atlanta for the first budget-cutting special session in modern times." This was in the summer of 1975, when Carter was writing the autobiography in which he claimed to have left a $200 million state surplus. What *Why Not the Best?* did not disclose was that after Carter had been gone for six months, the Georgia legislature was called into special session to make $125 million in budget cuts to avoid a deficit.

In other words, Carter had so botched the state's budgeting system that Busbee found another mess to clean up. And no wonder. Carter hardly understood how the system worked, admitting in 1973 that "when I was campaigning for the [governorship] for four years, I kept making the speech about a zero-based budget. I didn't know what it meant, but it was a very attractive speech component, and after I realized I was elected, I realized I had to do something to carry out my promise."

Whatever else Carter's reorganization did, it did not slow down the growth of the state budget or the number of state employees. Under Carter, the budget grew from $1,071 billion in fiscal 1971 to $1,665 billion in fiscal 1974 (his last full year in office)—an increase of 58 percent. And, after six months of Carter's governorship, the state had 34,322 employees, who received $226,053,681 in pay. At the end of Carter's last full year in office, the Georgia Department of Audits and Accounts reported 39,298 employees, receiving $317,008,100. Thus, during his administration, the number of employees grew by 14.5 percent and the payroll by 40.2 percent. In those same years, the federal government added 6,000 new employees. In other words, Georgia added almost as many to the payroll. Clearly, the record does not support Carter's repeated claims to have halted the growth of Georgia government.

The blunt truth is that Carter's state reorganization proved to be something less than miraculous. Nevertheless, he made reorganization of the federal government a major theme in his presidential campaign. "I don't want anyone to vote for me as President this year unless you want me as President to completely reorganize the executive branch of the nation's government," he said in a speech on January 23, 1976. Later, he conceded he did not know how he was going to do it. "There's no way I can take off from campaigning to do a complete and definitive study of what the federal government is and what it's going to be three or four years in the future." But he insisted he did know that reorganization "only will mean more efficient, and not less expensive government."

There was to be one repercussion from Carter's gubernatorial battles on his cherished reorganization which was to prove decidedly embarrassing to Carter as President. And that had to do with an allegation by Carter that a prominent Georgia lawmaker had offered to vote for reorganization if he were given advance warnings of any state gambling raids in his home county.

The episode, said Carter, occurred in 1972. Six years later, as President, Carter gave videotaped testimony for a gambling conspiracy trial involving his old political foe, Georgia State Senator E. Culver Kidd. A federal jury in Macon, Georgia, listened to the testimony and then, the next day, voted in effect not to believe the President of the United States.

It was still another of those embarrassing moments for a President who had promised the American people he would never tell a lie.

And the extraordinary thing was that the story got minimal attention in the nation's press that April weekend. The jury's repudiation of a sitting President was not a fit subject for the network news. Had it been Richard Nixon, not Jimmy Carter, who had been disbelieved by a jury composed of citizens of his home state, the reverberations would still be felt.

Carter had taped his trial testimony at the Old Executive Office Building in Washington. The prosecution lawyers began the questioning.

"Would you please, sir, state for the record your full name?"

"James Earl Carter, Jr."

"And you are now the sitting President of the United States?"

"I am."

And then for fifty-one minutes the President was questioned about his allegation concerning Culver Kidd, a trusted lieutenant of Lester Maddox. As chairman of the Georgia Senate committee which held hearings on Carter's pet plans, "Captain Kidd," as he was known in the Carter camp, had held up reorganization.

President Carter's allegation was that Kidd, using R. Eugene Holley, then majority leader of the Senate, as an intermediary, had informed Carter that he was willing to drop his staunch opposition to reorganization "provided I would inform him prior to any gambling investigations or raids into Baldwin County." Carter said that he was "appalled with the proposition" and that the episode "made a vivid impression on me." And he added that he had discussed the episode with Hamilton Jordan, then his executive secretary, and Ray Pope, then head of the Georgia Bureau of Investigation (GBI).

But it wasn't until months later that the Governor did anything about the alleged bribery attempt. Late in 1972, he testified, he ordered the GBI, under a new director, to investigate gambling in Baldwin County "and Senator Kidd's possible involvement."

After the President's videotaped testimony was presented to the jury, Senator Kidd observed to reporters during a trial recess that it was strange that Carter had not ordered an investigation immediately. He said Carter's testimony was in error. "It didn't happen in the first place, and if it did, if he thought I was trying to bribe him, it was his job to call the state law enforcement people and have something done about it."

Senator Kidd could also have noted, which he didn't, that Richard Nixon's presidency was destroyed because, when he first heard of possible complicity of top aides in the Watergate coverup, he did not immediately call in the feds and demand that those aides be arrested. But here we had President Carter's own story of how he neglected to demand an investigation of an outright bribe offer for some months. As for the GBI investigation, apparently nothing came of it. It was only in December 1977, five years later, when the President was approached by a grand jury for details.

Under oath, Kidd flatly denied Carter's charges. And Holley's version of what had occurred also differed somewhat from Carter's. Testifying under a grant of immunity, Holley did concede he did have a conversation with Carter, but, he insisted, gambling per se had never been mentioned. What Kidd simply wanted was advance word of *any* investigation in his bailiwick by agents of the GBI. Which Holley thought was reasonable enough, testifying he was surprised when Carter said, "Tell Senator Kidd to go to the devil."

It took the jury three hours before reaching its verdict. Culver Kidd and a codefendant were found not guilty of charges that they had conspired to obstruct gambling laws while Jimmy Carter was Governor and lying about it to a grand jury.

"I feel wonderful," said Kidd after the verdict. And he accused the President of being "so vindictive" as to push for prosecution because of an old political animosity. "Justice triumphed," he said.

In the White House, the former Governor of Georgia grimly heard the news. To have a jury of Georgians decide in favor of Culver Kidd and against him was just another of the many bitter blows which befell Carter in the second year of his presidency.

7

DECIDING ON 1976

JIMMY CARTER HAD BEEN GOVERNOR FOR ABOUT A YEAR AND A half when he finally decided to run for President in 1976. This was shortly after the 1972 Democratic National Convention, which had produced Senators George McGovern and Thomas F. Eagleton as the party's nominees. Carter had, frankly, become bored with provincial politicking and arguing with the likes of Lieutenant Governor Lester Maddox and Senator E. Culver Kidd, "The Silver Fox of Milledgeville," who kept hurling roadblocks at every opportunity. There were occasions when Carter publicly lost his composure, responding to their vitriolic attacks with angry press conferences in Capitol hallways, once calling the legislature a "cancer." Having achieved a modicum of national prominence as a spokesman of the New South, Carter felt he was too big for this kind of nonsense.

Once he had decided to go for broke in 1976, there was a decided change in his attitude toward the governorship. Oh, he went through the motions of being the state's chief executive, but, as an associate, no longer on his staff, told *The New York Times,* "It was as though he was bored by the routine of the office. I don't mean he quit being Governor . . . but the demands in the office were just that for him: demands." After a while, however, there seemed to be a distinct absence of leadership in the Governor's office. The result was that, as one of Carter's old friends put it, "Lester Maddox just took over. I was very disappointed, even though I thought I knew what was happening."

Maddox, however, couldn't immediately understand what was happening. But he wasn't about to look a gift horse in the mouth. "Carter was a very hard man to deal with for a while," he later recalled, "but after a while, I didn't have to deal with him at all. Seemed like he just disappeared. He would veto this or veto that once every so often, but the last part of his term was very different from the first part." Maddox, who was already planning to run again for Governor, seized the opportunity to assert his newfound authority.

Exactly when the idea of running for the presidency planted itself in Carter's mind is difficult to pinpoint. But it began to germinate, at least, when a stream of aspirants to the job began passing through Atlanta on errands of state and politics in the early months of 1971. They were, of course, leading Democrats, and they had come to discuss the lay of the votes in 1972. No longer were the likes of Edmund Muskie, Birch Bayh, Henry Jackson, and Hubert Humphrey willing to write off the South. And all of them, plus George McGovern and Teddy Kennedy, had come a'calling at the Governor's Mansion on West Paces Ferry Road, usually spending the night. And invariably Carter's message was that Southerners would support a Democrat only if he campaigned among them and treated the South as part of the nation.

As Carter himself later recounted in his autobiography, there was something else on his mind as he played the gracious host to the high and mighty of the Democratic firmament. He came to feel that none of them was any smarter than he was. In fact, some of the presidential aspirants were far less impressive than the widespread coverage in the media made them out to be.

Moreover—something which he did not confide to the readers of *Why Not the Best?*—he found some of them surprisingly ill disciplined, particularly in their drinking habits. A few, indeed, had gotten sloppily drunk. Exactly who he never said. But it was a characteristic which made him wonder even more whether he—a man of temperance—was not better suited for national leadership than they. And late one night, after an evening of observing a would-be Leader of the Free World, Rosalynn said to her husband, as she recalled, "The boys and I think you'd be just as good a President as the Senator, and probably much better." The Governor did not argue the point. Instead, he laughed and said, "You and the boys are probably right, but we'll have to get Amy's opinion, too."

Few outside his inner circle were aware of Carter's innermost thoughts. Only obvious to outsiders was the fact that the Governor relished his new role as a new force in national Democratic politics. Bill Shipp, who had been closely observing Carter's first few months in office, noted in *The Constitution* that the Governor had been bitten by the National Bug—"a tiny creature that instills an insatiable desire in a public officeholder to wheel and deal on the national political scene."

Shipp was referring to Carter's appearance one early April morning on NBC's *Today* show. "What he said was a little hokey for home state consumption," Shipp noted. "But all in all, he did credit to himself and the state. At least, he didn't walk off the program when the subject of racial problems came up. He showed plainly that he wants to cut a proper figure for himself and his state on the national scene."

Indicating that he was much more interested in supporting a Democrat for President than his old friend, George Wallace, Carter told the nationwide audience, "I think one of the major factors obviously will be whether the Democrats select a candidate that will be acceptable to the South. . . . In the last two national elections, the Democratic candidates have written off the South. . . . I think Mr. Wallace two year ago was successful in Georgia because the Democratic candidates did not come there. We're basically a Democratic state."

On the basis of his *Today* performance, columnist Shipp thought Carter had a chance of making it big nationally. "Under exactly the right circumstances," he wrote, "he might emerge as the Democratic vice-presidential nominee. What is more likely, he might . . . become a kind of Dixie power broker for the Democrats."

And in that particular period, his becoming a power broker appeared more likely. The fact that presidential hopefuls had been streaming into Atlanta for visits with the Governor was well publicized. And, from the beginning, Carter made it perfectly clear that he was not about to endorse any of them. As he told *The Constitution* in April 1971, "I like to talk to them frankly about what Georgia needs and let them tell me frankly what their interests are. But I want to keep them at arm's length as far as any insinuated endorsement is concerned.

"I've told them all the same thing: If they're interested in my support, they've got to win the support of the Georgia people. So they're coming down here in a steady stream. I think it's good for Georgia."

Though he didn't have any "real preference" among the candidates, he said, "I think it would be between Muskie and Scoop Jackson and Humphrey as far as the ones I project as being acceptable to the people of Georgia. . . . I think these three would be the ones most likely to really campaign hard for the South." (Less than a year before, Carter had been wrapping Humphrey like an albatross around Carl Sanders' allegedly liberal neck.)

Completely unacceptable to the people of Georgia, according to Carter, were the more extreme liberal types, of whom at least one had successfully led the fight against the nomination to the Supreme Court of Judges Clement Haynsworth and G. Harrold Carswell. When both men were rejected for the High Court, President Nixon bitterly denounced the campaign against them, adding, "When all the hypocrisy is stripped away, the real issue was their philosophy of strict construction of the Constitution . . . and the fact that they had the misfortune of being born in the South."

This was the background for Carter's saying that such presidential hopefuls as Senators Birch Bayh, George McGovern, and Harold Hughes would not have "too much appeal to the Georgia people. . . . For instance, I think Bayh would have a hard time overcoming the fact that he took the lead in the fight over the Supreme Court nominations of Haynsworth and Carswell."

At a September luncheon of the Governor's Club, Carter announced that leading contenders for the Democratic nomination had pledged they would never again support "special legislation" singling out the South "for special rules and regulations concerning race or transportation or any other facet of American life," referring, of course, to civil rights and voting laws that provided for such special enforcement. Carter told forty-five business and professional men who had contributed at least $500 each to the Governor's Club that he had extracted that promise from Senators Humphrey, Jackson, and Muskie when they had visited him recently. "We want to be sure that never again do we see a situation develop that occurred in 1964 and 1968 where the chosen representatives of our party considered an active, open, aggressive campaign among those who live in the Deep South as a stigma on their nationwide reputation. I think we've already seen a change take place within the last few months when almost every single person who has been mentioned prominently as a potential presidential candidate has been down here to Georgia . . . to talk to me about the needs of the South and an end to discrimination against the South in the courts and in the Congress."

Later, in November, Carter added George Wallace to the list of possible candidates who had the potential for acceptance by Southern voters. He disclosed that he had urged the Alabama Governor to seek the Democratic nomination, but said he had offered no encouragement to Wallace or any other prospective candidate. And, as the Democratic National Convention approached, Carter was openly critical of those Democrats who had "prematurely" ruled out the possibility of a ticket with Wallace as the vice-presidential candidate. It was Carter's view that a ticket headed by liberal Hubert Humphrey with Wallace as the number-two man could conceivably lead the Democrats to victory over Richard Nixon.

There was increasing speculation in the media about the possibility that one of the new generation of moderate Southern governors—rather than Wallace—might be tapped for the number two spot. Wallace himself noted this in a speech to the Atlanta Press Club. He said that the image of the "New South moderate Governors" was largely "a figment of the press' imagination." He said the new Governors were saying the same things he and others had always said. "Go back ten years ago and see what they said then. Let some of them get a nomination to the United States Supreme Court and we'll find out how moderate they are when the press gets through with them."

"I don't think any of these folks that think they're going to get to be Vice-President are going to get it," Wallace said.

Quite obviously, Wallace had in mind Jimmy Carter and

Florida's Reubin Askew, both of whom were being touted as possible vice-presidential candidates. Asked if he'd be interested in running, Carter replied, "I don't know about that. It would depend on who the nominee was, the platform and what I've accomplished as Governor." And he again made it clear he most definitely would not be interested if the nominee was a Dixie-baiter like George McGovern, Birch Bayh, or John Lindsay, ultraliberals who hadn't yet "recognized that Southerners are just as enlightened, progressive, and free of discrimination as anyone in the nation."

But the big liberal press up North was having second thoughts about Carter. Almost overnight, Governor Askew's virtues as a leader of the New South were being trumpeted. And, for a time, it looked as if the Democratic powers that be, whoever they may have been, had decided to give the Floridian a closer look. Askew was named to give the keynote address at the Democratic National Convention in Miami Beach, the first host Governor in this century to be so selected for a role of high visibility normally reserved for young men of particular promise in the party. The feeling was that Askew might well wind up as the party's nominee for Vice-President.

A major piece on Askew—"Florida's 'Supersquare'—A Man to Watch"—was published in *The New York Times Magazine* of March 5, 1972. The author, Jon Nordheimer, the *Times'* correspondent in Atlanta, praised Askew as one of "the toughest, ablest, and most powerful Governors in Florida's history. In just one year, he has instituted sweeping reforms, broken the control of special interests in the Legislature, and quietly appointed more blacks to important, decision-making jobs in state and local government than any other Governor in Southern history."

Nordheimer, who had followed Carter's governorship closely, could not whip up similar enthusiasm for the man from Plains, even though "leadership" of the Southern moderates at first had been awarded Carter "on the strength of the attention he received from the national media" for his inaugural declaration that "the time for segregation is over."

"In view of his coziness with George Wallace and a string of antibusing measures he has penned," wrote Nordheimer, "it appears now that Carter meant to say segregation is legally dead, 'so let's forget it ever happened.' Moreover, Carter's performance in office has been weak. He has been unable to exercise strong leadership in his own state, much less the South, and his efforts to reorganize Georgia's government have been thwarted by a balky legislature and the connivance of Lester Maddox."

As the Democratic National Convention approached, it became obvious that George McGovern would probably emerge as the party's standard-bearer. For Carter, the thought was unbearable. It wasn't only because of the South Dakotan's liberal views on race. Perhaps even more important was McGovern's pronounced opposition to the war in Vietnam. And most Southerners, including Jimmy Carter, wholeheartedly supported the war against the Vietcong barbarians who sought to gobble up South Vietnam. In fact, they viewed McGovern as unpatriotic.

If McGovern should get the nomination, Carter predicted, the South would vote overwhelmingly for Richard Nixon. The same would happen if that other ultraliberal, Ted Kennedy of Massachusetts, would get the presidential nod. And Carter said he could not enthusiastically support either McGovern or Kennedy. At the same time, he did not see much chance of George Wallace being nominated, though he believed "Wallace can be a positive force in shaping the platform and selecting the nominee and can have a tremendous positive effect if he remains within the party." Which was what Carter said he intended to do—remain in the party.

On May 24, 1972, the day after McGovern won primaries in Oregon and Rhode Island, Carter told reporters, "We're going to stop him." Along with one of his top confidantes, lawyer Charles Kirbo, then the Carter-appointed Democratic State Chairman in Georgia, the Governor began to take soundings for what was publicly described as a stop-McGovern movement. Both Carter and Kirbo later disclosed they had pleaded with Democratic officials in twenty-five states for the ABM cause—Anybody But McGovern. Said Kirbo, "I'm in contact with Governors outside the South, and we're all in one accord. McGovern is not going to get that damn nomination." A McGovern nomination, he added, would be a "total disaster" for the party in the South. Keeping the Senator from the nomination was now a matter of "self-survival" for many Southern Democrats in local races.

A day later, Senator David Gambrell, whom Carter had appointed to fill out the term of the departed Richard Russell, proposed that the Governor try for the Democratic presidential nomination. He said that Carter would have a better chance of defeating President Nixon than George McGovern. In fact, he added, Governor Wallace "would come closer to beating Nixon" than McGovern. Asked if he would support Wallace if he were the Democratic nominee, Gambrell said, "I certainly would."

That same day, Carter unloosed another bitter attack on McGovern, accusing him of seeking to take control of various delegations through technical rule manipulations in states where he had "little or no voter support." Carter pointed out that "these rules were written by Senator McGovern." Carter also noted that he had compared notes on this situation with Taylor Hardin, Wallace's closest adviser, who had just been his house guest. Hardin and he had agreed, Carter said, that there was a "nationwide pattern" in the McGovern method of capturing delegates who should have been pledged to other candidates as a result of their primary victories. "In all primaries to date," said Carter, "McGovern runs a poor third in total votes . . . yet because of his use of the new 'McGovern Rules' his supporters are predicting a first ballot win in Miami."

While he did not detail plans for the "stop McGovern" movement he was said to be initiating, Carter did challenge the South Dakotan on a number of issues. "It is almost inconceivable to me that a man can be elected President who is known to favor forced busing of students, total and unrestricted amnesty for draft dodgers, legalized abortion on demand, $1,000 government handouts to every American, and a social spending program which would result in annual federal deficits in excess of $100 billion." On top of this, Carter charged, McGovern favored slashing the defense program by $30 billion and "seems to favor" immediate and unilateral withdrawal of all forces, "even abandoning our prisoners of war." And of extreme importance, McGovern alone of all the candidates refused to promise "equal treatment under the federal law for Southern states."

In early June, just before the showdown primary in California, Carter and Kirbo began to pull in their horns. Arriving in Houston for the National Governors Conference, Carter, described in a

New York Times dispatch as "the ostensible organizer of the campaign for a more conservative candidate," denied paternity of the movement to prevent McGovern's nomination. "I'm not heading any 'stop McGovern' movement," he told surprised reporters. All that had happened, he said, was that he had been "contacted by some Governors, senators, and party leaders about it." Which, of course, was somewhat at variance with the story Charlie Kirbo had been telling. Needless to say, Carter went on, some of McGovern's views were "completely unacceptable to the majority of voters in many of our states," but "there isn't much I can do except express my concern."

Carter also expressed his concern personally to McGovern when the Senator flew into Houston for a secret meeting with Democratic Governors. What he wanted from McGovern was what he later termed a "concession to the South," that is, a pledge by the South Dakotan to support changes in the Voting Rights Act that required special civil rights enforcement in six Southern states. But the way Carter asked the question was something else. Would you, Carter in effect asked McGovern, be in favor of applying civil rights enforcement equally across the country? And, without hesitation, McGovern said that, if elected President, he most certainly would be in favor of that. And Carter thought he had scored a major victory for the Southern position.

Except that McGovern's aide, Frank Mankiewicz, had been listening carefully to the colloquy. A lawyer, Mankiewicz realized his man had been "trapped" into taking a position at decided variance with that of the civil rights types who had backed the provision in the Voting Rights Act that took into account the historical pattern of discrimination in the South. After conferring with McGovern, as he recalls, either he or McGovern went up to Carter to straighten out the candidate's position. Thus, McGovern remained the only major Democratic contender who refused to promise Carter that, if elected President, he would see that the South obtained "equal treatment" under the law with the rest of the nation. And that, as Jimmy Carter seemed to be saying at the time, was unforgivable.

Which was still another reason why Carter finally decided to support Henry "Scoop" Jackson for the presidential nomination. Carter had come close to publicly endorsing the Washington

Senator in February 1972, when he said that Senator Russell had urged him to keep an eye on Jackson in the next presidential election. Russell had particularly admired Jackson because of his strong national security posture. A tough anti-Communist, Jackson—in Carter's eyes—had far more appeal in the South than George McGovern. Thus, despite the fact that McGovern had the nomination all but sewed up when convention time rolled around in the second week of July 1972, Jimmy Carter stood up in the vast Miami Beach convention hall to nominate Henry Jackson for President of the United States.

And no one was more surprised by these developments than George Wallace, who had been led to believe that Carter would support his presidential aspirations. Not only that but, according to Wallace, Carter also had promised to second his nomination at the convention. As it turned out, Carter reneged on his promises—something which Carter later denied.

Denial or not, the evidence appears to bolster Wallace's claim of betrayal. Among other things, the Alabamian noted Carter's appearance at a George Wallace Appreciation Day in Red Level, Alabama, in June 1972. This Carter does not deny, but his press spokesman Jody Powell said four years later that the Governor's appearance was "to help raise funds for Wallace's medical expenses" in the wake of the assassination attempt six weeks before. And Powell quoted—rather, misquoted—local press accounts, the local *Dothan Eagle*, as having stated—in Powell's words—that "Carter explicitly stated his visit was in no way an endorsement of Wallace and that his visit was solely for the purpose of joining them in wishing Wallace a speedy recovery."

What *The Dothan Eagle* actually said was this: "Although Carter stayed away from specifically endorsing Wallace, he emphasized forcibly many of the stands the Alabama Governor has taken in his bid for the Democratic presidential nomination." Furthermore, it was reported that the funds raised at the rally were not for medical expenses but for Wallace's presidential campaign.

The significant thing about all this is that neither a tape nor a text of Carter's speech was made available to the Georgia State Department of Archives and History, as was customary. This apparently was true of other speeches the Governor "made to groups in Mississippi, Alabama, rural Georgia, or places like that," according to one of the archivists. Obviously what Carter had been saying to so-called redneck audiences was not something he wanted enshrined in official records in Atlanta. Frank Daniel, a veteran archivist who traditionally prepared a volume of the complete public statements of Georgia Governors, told *Harper's* in 1976 that his efforts to compile the Carter volume had been "blocked by [Carter's] people. . . . They've only sent me the speeches they want to include."

One embarrassing document was sent to the archives. It was a letter to Mrs. Lena Mae Dempsey, who had written to the Governor complaining that he should have endorsed Wallace instead of Jackson at the Democratic Convention. The letter, dated August 4, 1972, read:

Dear Mrs. Dempsey:

I have never had anything but the highest praise for Governor Wallace. My support for Senator Jackson was based upon a personal request from our late Senator Richard Russell shortly before his death. I think you will find that Senator Jackson, Governor Wallace, and I are in close agreement on most issues.

Let me ask you to consider one other factor before I close. There are times when two men working toward the same end can accomplish more if they are not completely tied together. I think you will find that Governor Wallace understands that.

Please let me know when I can be of service to you or your children in Atlanta. I hope I have been able to give you a slightly better impression of me.

Sincerely,
Jimmy Carter

When the text of the letter was dug up by Steve Brill and published in *Harper's* nearly four years later, Jody Powell responded as follows:

The letter to Mrs. Dempsey was written by a staffer, never seen by Governor Carter, and did not accurately express his views. Several hundred letters each day often

were answered from the Governor's office by staffers;
inevitably, a few of these staff responses were not exactly
what the Governor would have written. Had the writer of
the article asked, he would have been told of the three-
letter-initial code used to identify staff letters.

The unfortunate choice of words by one staffer in one
letter is hardly a test of the national leadership ability or
the personal integrity of the Governor. . . .

It turned out Powell was right. In view of Carter's future plans,
it was indeed "the unfortunate choice of words by one staffer."
What Powell's response did not go on to say, however, was that
the "staffer" who wrote the letter was none other than Jody Powell
himself. And today Powell sits close to the Oval Office, speaking to
the world in President Carter's name. But, "unfortunate" or not,
Powell's 1972 choice of words pretty much reflected his boss' then
high regard for George Wallace, a regard which led Carter prior to
the national convention to recommend a Humphrey-Wallace
ticket as being acceptable to the South.

Of course, in 1976, while seeking the presidency, Carter
banished all past thoughts about Wallace from his mind and
indeed sought to banish them from the historic record. He went
around saying, "I never supported Wallace and never would."
Wallace, bound to a wheelchair because of wounds suffered in the
attempted assassination, but still feisty, called Carter a liar. That
he was hurt by Carter's efforts to expunge the record was obvious
to Elizabeth Drew, who interviewed the Alabamian for *The New
Yorker*. And Wallace, in a Howard Johnson motel room in High
Point, North Carolina, sought to set the record straight. Among
other things, he recalled how Carter, in his 1970 race for the
governorship, had kept invoking Wallace's name to his rural
Georgian audiences. "He went all over Georgia saying, 'I'll invite
Wallace to speak in this state.' Do you know that? He made a big
issue of it. If you go around and use a man's name in an emphatic
fashion— 'I'll *invite* him to come to this state'—Now, if you're not
for him when you say that, you're *misleading* people, aren't you?"

Also during the 1976 campaign, Carter vehemently denied that
he had pledged to endorse Wallace's 1972 candidacy if he came to
the convention with at least 300 delegates. As it turned out,

Wallace had won over 400 such votes. But, almost at the last moment, Carter decided to nominate "Scoop" Jackson.

Which was still on Wallace's mind four years later. While talking to Mrs. Drew, Wallace referred to a recent press clipping from Winston-Salem which discussed Carter talking about his religious beliefs. "I spent more time on my knees," Carter was quoted, "the four years I was Governor in the seclusion of a little private room off the Governor's office than I did in all the rest of my life put together, because I felt so heavily on my shoulders that the decisions I made might very well affect many, many people."

"That little room," commented Wallace, "where he said he spent all that time on his knees—that's where he made that little agreement with me that I wouldn't run delegates against his precinct delegates in Georgia, and he said he would support me, provided I got three hundred or more delegates, and we shook hands. I had no reason to doubt it—he had been so friendly, and used my name running for Governor. I went there with four hundred." But Carter got a better offer from Scoop Jackson—a chance to deliver the *nominating* speech for the Washington Senator. And he grabbed the opportunity for a televised moment in the national spotlight, forgetting—according to Wallace—his pledge to the Alabamian. "Maybe someday he'd like to take a polygraph test on that," said Wallace.

As Mrs. Drew reported, Wallace's bitterness was such that he couldn't get off the subject of Carter, the fellow Southerner who had used and then discarded him as if he were white trash. Wallace noted that the other candidates in the 1976 presidential primaries "don't owe me anything." They "didn't come to power in their states using my organization, my mailing list, and my name. I was very popular in Georgia. . . . But a man who rides your coattails, uses your organization. . . . He stayed with me as long as I was popular." Then Wallace seemed to be getting to what was really hurting. "They thought I was dying, that I was through with politics, that I'd be a vegetable the rest of my life, or I'd die . . . I wouldn't feel the way I do if he said, 'Yes, I supported Governor Wallace in those days. I didn't support everything he was for, but we were friends. But he understands I'm running for the presidency.' He has a right to run if he'd still be my friend. He has a right. I'm not the only one in my region. I'm the reason some of them are running—because I proved they could do well in other parts of the country."

On and on he went about Carter, despite Mrs. Drew's efforts to change the subject. He began imitating Carter: "I will never lie to you; I will never *misleeeeeeed* you." And he cited examples of Carter's *misleeeeeeeding* the American people in his 1976 rhetoric. "He can get out and shake hands and get on television," Wallace continued. "I can't do that. He was my friend when I was popular. He said he was for me when he thought I'd die. I don't mind the other ones, because they say what they think. Udall's a true liberal, and he's honest about it. Those other fellows criticize me, but they didn't use me. He talks about spending all that time on his *kneeeeees*. Well, I'm going to church tomorrow, but I don't go around talking about my religion."

And when Mrs. Drew started to leave, Wallace called after her, "He *yuuuused* me when I was popular." And then he said, "Look out for phonies, honey."

Like most such speeches, Carter's nomination of Scoop Jackson is hardly remembered. At times, it sounded as if he were touting John F. Kennedy, recalling those happy days when the Democratic Party "earned the trust and confidence of the American people in 1960 by nominating a man of compassion and courage." And he noted that "with the help of labor and with the help of farmers and the help of young and with the help of those filled with idealism and hope John Kennedy received his biggest majority in my home state of Georgia. . . ." Finally, Carter got around to Jackson, whom he described as "the man who wins elections because the people trust him and he trusts the people."

Carter made no deep impression during the tumultuous convention proceedings which produced George McGovern as the Democratic candidate for President. And, for that matter, neither did Reubin Askew, of whom so much had been expected. In his keynote address, the Florida Governor declared, "It is impossible to look upon this group without feeling that one has seen the face of America." But it was a face that most other Americans did not recognize. Because of the requirement that delegations "reasonably" reflect their constituencies by race, sex, and age, vast numbers of blacks, women, and youth had won convention seats. And it all made for an unruly spectacle on the tube. Ironically,

Jimmy Carter nearly didn't make it to the convention because a black college student came within fifteen votes of being elected as a delegate instead of Carter. This was because of the "democratization" of the Georgia party, which Carter had promised during the 1970 campaign, removing control from the Democratic bosses and returning it to the people. Thus, Carter almost became the first victim of his own reform.

The reform, however, did not satisfy Julian Bond, the black Georgia legislator who was nominated for Vice-President at the 1968 Democratic Convention. Along with his brother, Atlanta City Councilman James Bond, he "filed a challenge with the Credentials Committee of the Democratic National Convention against the Georgia delegates elected under a Carter-constructed system. We charged racial and sexual discrimination in the makeup of the Carter-led delegation. We won the challenge, and the compromise that resulted provided fair representation for Georgia voters."

Because of the "democratization" of the party nationally, brought on by new McGovern-sponsored rules, an extraordinary number of elected Democrats were excluded from the floor: 225 of the party's 255 Congressmen and the Democratic mayors of Philadelphia, Detroit, Boston, San Francisco, Los Angeles, and Chicago. "I think we may have lost Illinois tonight," Frank Mankiewicz said glumly after an elected delegation from that state was expelled from the convention floor by McGovern enthusiasts. Carter had lined himself behind the delegation headed by Chicago's Mayor Richard Daley. He voted to seat the Illinoisans. Four years later, the gesture paid off, with Daley throwing his strength behind Carter at a vital time.

The 1972 candidacy of Scoop Jackson never had a chance. He had fought valiantly against having his party, which he once served so industriously as national chairman, "destroy itself" by nominating McGovern. Toward this end, he had Jimmy Carter's full support. By 1976, however, Carter was singing a different tune about Jackson. Now they were rivals; and Jimmy was saying that he found Scoop's "exploitation" of the busing issue "disgusting." And he added, "As I've learned more about him, I don't feel so close to him any more." Of which Sanford Ungar had this to say in the July 1976 issue of *The Atlantic:* "The change of heart seems to date roughly from the fall of 1972, when Jimmy Carter decided he would like to try to become President himself."

And Carter appeared to have a change of heart about McGovern during the 1972 convention. The Sunday night before the convention officially opened, the Governor had dinner with his top aides at the Playboy Plaza Hotel. At that time, media aide Jerry Rafshoon asked whether Carter might not be interested in running for Vice-President. "Why not?" he replied. It would be good exposure for the future if he should decide to run for President.

Carter, moreover, felt he had something to offer McGovern. A poll had been taken by Bill Hamilton which indicated not very surprisingly that the South Dakotan would be more acceptable to the people of Georgia if Carter were his running mate. And, after all, John Kennedy hadn't done too badly by opting for the Southern strategy—that is, in selecting Lyndon Johnson for his ticket.

So Carter called Andrew Young and asked the Atlanta civil rights leader to talk to McGovern. "When my name was presented to McGovern," Carter later recalled, "there was some vile language used, and my name was immediately rejected, which was reported to me. I never tried any more to have my name put forward."

There is evidence, however, that Carter did prevail upon Julian Bond to intercede with McGovern in his behalf. Later, after a falling out between the two, Carter flatly denied having done so. And Bond rejoindered, "I did so twice, both before and after Eagleton, but now Carter lies and says it wasn't so."

A final effort to interest McGovern in the Georgia Governor was made with Carter's approval. Jerry Rafshoon, his media adviser, and Hamilton Jordan, his executive secretary at the time, went to McGovern headquarters at the Doral Hotel seeking to make the case. They finally managed to talk to *wunderkind* Pat Caddell, McGovern's round-faced pollster, then still a Harvard undergraduate at the age of twenty-two. "We spent about three minutes with Caddell," Rafshoon later recalled. "He said, 'Yeah, yeah, it looks good. Oh, yeah, I'm going to make a recommendation.' He said later he recommended a Southerner. I think he recommended Reubin Askew."

Caddell had indeed been pushing for a Southerner, and he had submitted Carter's name along with Askew's for consideration to McGovern. What killed Carter's chances, Caddell said later, was his nomination of Jackson—something that proved to be an inadvertent blessing. "If I had gotten him on the ticket, he would have gone down to an ignominious defeat with McGovern, and that would have been the end of Jimmy Carter. In a way, I saved Jimmy's political career."

And, though Caddell may have submitted Carter's name, it never came up in any of the vice-presidential calculations by McGovern's top aides. As for Askew, he had asked not to be considered. Only six names finally were taken seriously: Sargent Shriver, Boston Mayor Kevin White, Larry O'Brien, Wisconsin Governor Lucey, and Senators Abe Ribicoff and Tom Eagleton.

After considerable winnowing, Eagleton was selected. There was no great cheering from the ranks, however. But the Senator from Missouri seemed just right. Young, a Catholic, a city boy from St. Louis, he had been a former prosecutor with a liberal record, and, most important for McGovern, he had excellent connections with organized labor. Jimmy Carter, asked about McGovern's choice, said that he knew very little about Eagleton, but that he understood he was a fine man. "I hope he will fill some of the gaps in the McGovern support," said Carter. "I was hoping that Senator McGovern would pick someone to appeal to the Wallace voters, to the business community, and a man who insisted on an adequate defense."

All of which proved to be a revelation for both Rafshoon and Jordan. "I thought people were going to fall all over Jimmy at the convention," Jordan said later. "But he was just one of thirty or forty guys there." The fact that national politicians weren't taking Carter seriously also surprised Rafshoon. For Rafshoon had long had even bigger plans for the Governor. "From 1970 on," he told Kandy Stroud, "I figured he had as good a chance as anyone to be President. I knew he was capable of competing in the big leagues. . . . I was always cognizant of his national image. I knew he wouldn't just finish four years and go back to Plains. It would be a waste."

Rafshoon recalled walking back from the convention hall at 3:00 A.M. the night McGovern was nominated and saying to Jordan, "If those schmucks can do it, Jimmy can do it." That was when "we all decided to get together to start planning, but Peter Bourne jumped the gun on us and wrote him a memo."

Bourne, a British-born psychiatrist who had set up a drug rehabilitation program for Carter in Georgia, had also long been trumpeting the Governor's virtues to anyone who would listen. And one who listened was none other than Jimmy Carter. In July 1971, both of them had been in Washington, where Carter had testified before one of Senator Muskie's committees on intergovernmental relations. According to Bourne, Carter was surprised that Muskie was the Democratic front-runner at the time. "It surprised Carter because he was most unimpressed with Muskie, who just didn't strike him as that presidential," Bourne recalled. "He thought that if this guy can get to be President that it was not too farfetched for him." And Bourne agreed, asking Carter if he had ever thought about running himself. "No," replied Carter, "but if I ever do, I'd run the way I ran for the governorship, four years flat out." Bourne then assumed Carter was thinking about it.

A year later, in a July 25, 1972 memo, Bourne again raised the issue of Carter's running in 1976, so certain was the good doctor that McGovern—nominated only days before—was doomed to defeat. Bourne argued that reforms "as well as the climate in the country" had changed the control of the Democratic party. "The old politicians who think that once McGovern is defeated it will be politics as usual are dead wrong and do not understand the social forces at work in the country. . . . The people who will win the big prizes are going to be increasingly the people who are willing to take risks, particularly in terms of hazarding existing power bases. One can take moderate and compromise positions on issues and remain a successful, respected, secure politician, but one will not get the big apples." Four years later, Carter got the biggest apple of all precisely by fuzzing the issues.

Bourne looked over the field of potential Carter opponents and wrote off Ted Kennedy. "At this point, I do not think Kennedy will ever be President. He appears to have diminished ambition for national office, both because of the very real concern about assassination and the major problems in his personal life. Both he and his wife seem to be drifting from one emotional crisis to another, he has repeatedly handled stress poorly, and in fact has never been tested by a knock-down-drag-out campaign." But Bourne did believe that John D. (Jay) Rockefeller IV, then running for Governor of West Virginia, was "someone to watch." As it turned out, Rockefeller was beaten by the incumbent Republican Governor and remained generally unknown on the national scene. Kennedy, however, was to emerge as a potential threat to Carter when many dismayed Democrats began looking for an alternative to the Georgian during his first years as President.

Bourne said that one of the lessons of Miami was the fact that Carter was still not widely known outside his home state, reminding the Georgian that those who "knew anything about you identified you with three issues, your inauguration speech, your position on busing (mostly misinterpreted), and the 'Stop McGovern movement.'" Still, Carter had not hurt himself by seeking the vice-presidency, since he had not openly campaigned for the nomination. "However," Bourne wrote in his memo, "this was more by luck than anything else."

"Beginning two years from now," Bourne went on, "if you do not run for the Senate, you should capitalize on the image you have created particularly by such things as writing a book and go on a protracted nationwide speaking tour including fund-raising for the party. In that way you will develop a strong committed and obligated constituency throughout the country; you will also be able to capitalize on your greatest asset—your personal charm. The more people you can meet around the country during that year or so without overtly campaigning the stronger you will be when you are ready to go for real."

In retrospect, Bourne had written a brilliant memo. It was a scenario which Carter was to study and follow. And what seemed at the time hardly Carter's most important characteristic—namely, his "personal charm"—turned out in the long run to be one of the Georgian's major assets on his way to the White House.

The day Dr. Bourne sent his memo over to Carter was the very day that Senator Eagleton told a press conference in the Black Hills that he had been treated for mental illness. At first, McGovern took the attitude that he was "1,000 percent for Tom Eagleton." But, after a clamor developed, McGovern decided his support of his running mate was not quite 1,000 percent after all.

He permitted the new Democratic chairperson, Mrs. Jean West-wood, to say on *Meet the Press* that it would be "a noble thing" if the Missourian withdrew. On meeting Eagleton soon after, McGovern said, "Tom, believe me, I had no idea what she was going to say." And Eagleton replied, "Don't shit me, George." Eagleton had some support in the party. Jimmy Carter, for example, had sent a message to McGovern's headquarters urging that Eagleton be kept on the ticket "in the best interest of the party." But after his own shrewd fund-raiser Henry Kimelman reported to McGovern that campaign contributions had dried up, McGovern lost his indecisiveness and convinced Eagleton to do "the noble thing."

Following Eagleton's retirement from the ticket, McGovern scurried around seeking a replacement. But none of the top Democrats, including Muskie, was interested. Down in Atlanta, Julian Bond told *The Atlanta Constitution* that Governor Carter was under consideration. Bond, leader of Blacks for McGovern, said the subject had been broached by a "high-placed" McGovern aide. "He didn't mention anyone else but Carter, and I was noncommittal on the subject," Bond added. "I'd have to think about that for a while." Carter was quick to call the idea "utterly ridiculous." He said he was "not interested."

Eventually McGovern settled on Sargent Shriver, who fought valiantly for the ticket. But it was a lost cause. Meanwhile, aware that Nixon would sweep the South, Carter met with George Wallace in Birmingham, Alabama, to map out ways of saving state and local Democratic candidates. "We don't want to see our party destroyed," Carter said after the meeting. They had talked about ways of separating the national Democratic campaign from the state and local levels, he said.

Meanwhile, too, Carter met with his aides (though more secretly) to discuss a possible presidential run. Present at the Governor's Mansion were Jordan, Rafshoon, and an Atlanta lawyer, Landon Butler. "Yeah, I've thought about it," Carter said, after listening to their arguments. And when the meeting was over, Carter encouraged the younger men to continue. "It's an enormous undertaking," he said. "We've got to work at it. Think about it. And we've got to keep our mouths shut."

And while they kept their mouths shut, they wrote memos to

one another. One, from Rafshoon to Jordan, talked about creating a national image for Carter. "I believe that despite the accusations of back-sliding by the liberal press," he wrote, "that Jimmy's image in national circles and in the media has not changed much since inauguration. He is still the man who said the time for racial discrimination is over. . . . He still has a Kennedy smile." (And that smile was to become a national trademark four years later.) "What he does not have is much depth to his image. He is not as well known as many other big-name politicians in the U.S. and is not known for the heavyweight ideas and programs that he is capable of articulating."

But the major memo, consisting of over seventy pages, was largely prepared by Ham Jordan, then all of twenty-seven years of age. The document, dated November 4, 1972, the day before Nixon's landslide victory over McGovern, proved to be a veritable game plan to win the nomination in 1976. The assumption, of course, was that McGovern would be beaten big and the 1976 nomination would be up for grabs. As Jordan saw it, "a highly successful and concerned former Governor of Georgia and peanut farmer" had more than a good chance of satisfying the nation's "thirst for strong moral leadership"—a thirst which, Jordan predicted, "will grow in four more years of the Nixon Administration." The problem for Carter was how to capitalize on these trends. What he needed was a public persona. At the Democratic Convention, Jordan recalled, "I learned how naïve we all have been about national politics, particularly as it relates to you and your image. It was my feeling that because you had appeared on the cover of *Time* and had been the object of favorable national press, that you were in fact a 'national political figure.'" Instead, Carter had been merely "one of several bright and promising young Governors."

Then the Jordan memo discussed the Wallace problem. "The point that I would make here is that although another Wallace candidacy is unlikely," wrote Jordan, "and probably would be discouraged by his wife and friends, George Wallace today has every intention of running and winning in 1976 to prove himself and vindicate his philosophy."

"It is my guess," Jordan added, "that George Wallace resents you a little, as we used him effectively and beneficially in our campaign but refused to nominate him at the Democratic Convention. We should make every effort to court Wallace and gain his friendship and trust. If he cannot and does not choose to run in 1976, I doubt that he will sit it out. I would hope that you might gain his support if he saw in your candidacy an extension and continuation of his earlier efforts. This may be too much to hope for, but it is an opportunity that cannot be disregarded."

Thus, in what was then a confidential memo, Jordan acknowledged what Carter later persistently denied—the fact that Carter had used Wallace "effectively and beneficially" in his 1970 race.

Jordan next brought up the more troubling problem of Ted Kennedy. There was no doubt in Jordan's mind that Kennedy could easily win the nomination. But, because there was a great national desire for "strong moral leadership," he felt "it would be very difficult for Senator Kennedy to win a national election." And that was primarily due to the fact that "the unanswered questions of Chappaquiddick run contrary to this national desire for trust and morality in government." Though "time solves a lot of problems," he continued, "the memory of the Chappaquiddick incident is still fresh in the minds of a majority of American people . . ."

Also working against the Senator was a general "anti-Kennedy feeling," resulting from the fact that "in two decades of American politics, the Kennedy family has run over and alienated a lot of people."

Nevertheless, Jordan thought it wise that Carter face the possibility that Kennedy might decide to run in 1976, thus almost certainly becoming "the frontrunner and strong favorite." In that case, Carter should consider becoming Kennedy's running mate. Jordan's thinking was "that Kennedy probably would like to see someone from the South other than Wallace make a national effort. He knows that he cannot depend on the Southern states for any initial support for the nomination and would rather have someone like yourself to deal with than with George Wallace. . . . At any rate, I would place a high priority on an early meeting with Kennedy and a discussion on the future of the party and your intention to play an active role in the 1976 elections." (As it developed, Carter did not see Kennedy until the day he announced for President, December 12, 1974.)

As for Scoop Jackson, Carter was advised to stop sounding as if he were still promoting the Senator, even though they were compatible on most issues. In other words, Carter was to "be cautious to do nothing that might encourage him to run and make it plain that you have plans yourself."

But, Jordan urged, Carter should immediately proceed with a Rafshoon-directed program to obtain national press coverage. "Stories in *The New York Times* and *Washington Post* do not just happen, but have to be carefully planned and planted," he wrote. "The thrust of your national press effort should be that state government is working in Georgia and is solving the problems in meeting the needs of ordinary citizens. . . . I believe that you should attempt to develop the image of a highly successful and concerned former Governor of Georgia and peanut farmer living in a small rural town, speaking out on the pertinent issues of the day. Once your name begins to be mentioned in the national press, you will not lack for invitations and opportunities to speak in major groups and conventions . . ."

Jordan planned to compile a listing of regional and national political editors and columnists "who you know or need to know. You can find ample excuse for contacting them—writing them a note, complimenting them on an article or column and asking that they come to see you when convenient. Some people like Tom Wicker or Mrs. Katherine Graham are significant enough to spend an evening or a leisurely weekend with . . ." Other media types important to cultivate were James Reston and Max Frankel of *The New York Times;* Jack Nelson of the *Los Angeles Times;* David Broder of *The Washington Post;* columnists William S. White, William F. Buckley, Garry Wills, and Rowland Evans and Robert Novak; and magazine writers Marshall Frady, John Fischer, and Willie Morris.

"Like it or not," Jordan went on, "there exists an Eastern liberal news establishment which has tremendous influence. The views of this small group of opinion-makers in the papers they represent are noted and imitated by other columnists and newspapers throughout the country and the world. Their recognition and acceptance of your candidacy as a viable force with some chance of success could establish you as a serious contender worthy of financial support of major party contributors. They could have an equally adverse effect, dismissing your effort as being regional or an attempt to secure the second spot on the ticket.

"Fortunately, a disproportionate number of these opinion-makers are Southerners by birth and tradition and harbor a strong subconscious desire to see the South move beyond the George Wallace era and assert itself as a region and as a people in the mainstream of this country. It is my contention that they would be fascinated by the prospect of your candidacy and would treat it seriously through the first several primaries."

Then the memo called on Carter to begin a course of study appropriate for an aspirant to the highest elective office in the free world. Among other things, Jordan suggested that Carter immediately start reading such major newspapers as *The New York Times, The Washington Post,* and *The Wall Street Journal* every day. "Despite its liberal orientation," Jordan explained, *"The New York Times* is the best paper in the country and possibly the world. One cannot keep track of national politics or international affairs by simply reading *The Atlanta Constitution, Time,* and *Newsweek."*

Jordan also suggested that Carter ask former Secretary of State Rusk to begin "educating you on foreign affairs and to develop a continuing program which would include regular briefings, a reading list, and the establishment of a formal task force." Also, to make up for his lack of foreign policy experience, the proposal was made that Carter establish Georgia trade missions abroad "for the purpose of traveling to each of the continents of the world," meeting various foreign leaders. In other words, Carter was to use Georgia taxpayers' money for trips whose sole purpose was to advance his political ambitions.

And, thus, Jimmy Carter was to obtain a crash course in foreign affairs. But Dean Rusk eventually was dropped from the Carter faculty, tainted as he was by Vietnam and the disclosures in the illicitly released Pentagon Papers.

"Learn to speak from your prepared text," the Jordan memo went on. "I have heard Jody and Rafshoon both say that this is your only shortcoming as a candidate and that this skill can be easily developed through practice."

The Jordan memo also urged Carter to write a book. Which was what Carter eventually did, coming up with a campaign biography entitled *Why Not the Best?* Its self-adulation was noted in an otherwise friendly *Atlantic* piece by Garry Wills. "It seems not to have occurred to him that most candidates let *others* celebrate them," wrote the sage of Baltimore.

8

THE SECRET CAMPAIGN

THUS, WITHOUT ANY PUBLIC ANNOUNCEMENT, JIMMY CARTER launched a campaign to win the highest office in the land. It was, of course, to be a secret endeavor, one in which only a handful of advisers, including wife Rosalynn, were to participate. The reason for secrecy was obvious. Premature disclosure of his plans, he felt quite properly, would only result in his being laughed out of the state. Jimmy Carter for President? How ridiculous could you get?

Moreover, there was the McGovern problem. The problem for Carter was how to go through the motions of supporting the Democratic presidential candidate without wasting too much energy. And this did not sit too well with Atlanta attorney Bob Patrick, McGovern's Georgia campaign manager. "I was irritated at the time that he [Carter] didn't do more," Patrick said later, "but I think he was right in retrospect."

According to Patrick, Carter had told him two months before the election "that we were going to lose by a landslide." But another reason Carter refused to get too close to McGovern was that he feared harming the Democratic primary chances of his ally, David Gambrell, whom he had appointed to fill out the late Senator Russell's term. As it turned out, Gambrell was beaten by a little-known state representative, then thirty-four years old, Sam Nunn, who went on to trounce the Republican candidate in the general election.

Toward the end of the campaign, McGovern sought desperately to obtain George Wallace's endorsement. And, according to Patrick, the Democratic nominee entertained "real hope right to the bitter end" that the Alabamian would bail out his failing candidacy against President Nixon. But it was not to be. Jean Westwood, the McGovern-appointed chairlady of the Democratic National Committee, traveled to Montgomery for a soul-searching session with the Governor. But Wallace wasn't biting. Then Patrick approached Carter about interceding with Wallace in McGovern's behalf. And word came back that "it's all Governor West [of South Carolina] and I can do to keep him from endorsing Nixon." Carter, however, did announce he would vote for McGovern, but he stopped short of urging others to do so.

Carter, as Patrick later noted, proved to be "most prophetic." Nixon took Georgia with 75 percent of the popular vote. (Four years later, Carter took the state with 67 percent.) In all, Nixon carried forty-nine states; only Massachusetts and the District of Columbia went to McGovern.

And Carter couldn't have cared less. The question for Carter now was how to further involve himself in national Democratic affairs without revealing his hand. His first major move was to work with others for the termination of McGovern's control of the party. To this end, he sought the removal of the outspoken Jean Westwood as head of the National Committee. "I think we have to establish a moderate tone for the national party and bring back those disaffected by the 1972 presidential election," said Carter. Which was another way of saying that the McGovernites had to be swept out of party headquarters in Washington. At a December meeting of Democratic Governors in St. Louis, Carter voted with a narrow majority to dump Westwood and replace her with Robert Strauss of Texas, the former national treasurer beloved by most party regulars. Among those who unsuccessfully opposed Strauss was the then Governor of Ohio, John Gilligan, who said that to elect the Texan "may among other things represent a return from the dead of John Connally." After which, Carter's pal Charlie

Kirbo, as Georgia state chairman, lobbied for Strauss and voted for him at the National Committee meeting in Washington.

Strauss had first met Carter earlier in the year when he called on the Governor in Atlanta to pay his respects. They had commiserated with each other about the possibility of a McGovern nomination, which they agreed would be a disaster for the party. Carter then caught Strauss' eye at Miami Beach when he nominated Scoop Jackson for the presidency. After the convention, on a plane returning to Washington, Strauss commiserated with then House Majority Leader Thomas P. "Tip" O'Neill about the forthcoming McGovern debacle. And, according to John Osborne of *The New Republic,* Strauss recommended two measures to repair the inevitable damage to the party: his installation as National Chairman and the eventual recruitment of Carter to campaign around the country for local, state and congressional party candidates. This apparently was the first time O'Neill had ever heard Carter mentioned in a serious way, according to a spokesman. And O'Neill thought it a good idea.

Of course, neither Strauss nor O'Neill knew that Jimmy Carter had decided to go national. And this involved the necessity of Carter's separating himself "from Georgia's Stone Age image," as Steve Brill was later to phrase it in a *Harper's* article which was to arouse Carter's ire. To this end, Carter sought a return to his image as the tough, no-nonsense Governor who had declared that the time for racial discrimination was over. On January 15, 1973, he proclaimed a day in honor of Dr. Martin Luther King, Jr. But his "most endearingly symbolic liberal act," as Brill put it, was the placing of a portrait of the assassinated civil rights leader (along with those of two other black Georgians) in the State Capitol on February 17, 1974— "seventeen months after he knew he was running for President as an enlightened Southerner." After all, he had little to lose; he couldn't run for re-election anyway.

Meanwhile, Carter sought to signal Democrats nationally that, even though his state had gone 75 percent for Nixon, he personally viewed the President with distress. In fact, two days before he was to attend Nixon's second inaugural as the representative of his state, Carter let loose with a savage attack at the President. He said that of the Presidents he could remember, he admired Truman most and Nixon least. "Nixon's character is becoming more evident now that the election is over," Carter said. "He's becoming a recluse." The following day, Republican leader Armstrong Smith reminded his fellow Georgian Senators that Carter was going to attend the inauguration. "I think it is rather ill mannered for the Governor of a state who is going to attend such an event to announce how he feels on the eve of his departure," said Smith. His resolution commending Nixon on his second inauguration passed without a dissenting vote.

Perhaps it was a coincidence—though Carter didn't think so—that when he, his family, and friends arrived in Washington for the Nixon inaugural on January 20, 1973, they discovered that they had no overnight accommodations. Cousin Hugh Carter was later to write about how just two seats had been set aside for the Georgia party. They were, of course, used by Jimmy and Rosalynn, while the others were provided with a limousine tour of the city. Seated in the stands outside the U.S. Capitol on that brisk day, the Governor and his lady watched Nixon being sworn in. And they heard the President signal his plan to liquidate the domestic programs of liberal administrations with a paraphrase of John Kennedy's most memorable line, "Let each of us ask, not just what will government do for me, but what I can do for myself."

All in all, Carter said later, it was a "most impressive" occasion. Little did he know that even then a series of events was occurring behind the scenes which would lead to the unmaking of a President. That evening, by coincidence, the Carters attended a cocktail party and then a dinner at the Watergate complex. The service was inordinately slow and the Carters were forced to leave without eating in order to attend one of the five inaugural balls. All Carter could remember was an enormous crowd shouting "Four More Years!" when a beaming President and Mrs. Nixon arrived. By midnight, the Carters and their guests were aboard their plane returning to Atlanta. Four years later, the Carters were to host their own inaugural balls in Washington.

It was four years devoted almost entirely to campaigning for the grand prize. Being Governor now became a secondary proposition. Not that it didn't have certain immediate advantages. For one thing, Carter was able to arrange a lucrative contract for Jerry

Rafshoon, to promote Georgia tourism, industrial development, international trade, and the state as a location for motion pictures. Later, Carter was to deny he had "pressured anyone with regard to any state contract except to express my desire that they be awarded solely on the basis of merit." And, of course, everyone in Atlanta knew how able Rafshoon was, particularly as Jimmy Carter's media adviser. The contract, which totalled $750,000 a year, of which $108,000 was Rafshoon's fee, was first awarded in 1973 and renewed for several years thereafter.

The contract raised few hackles at the time, since even Carter's strongest critics, and he had many by then, conceded it was a traditional part of the Governor's "perks." What the critics did not know, however, was Rafshoon's secret role as a top-level adviser for Carter's presidential ambitions. Had they learned of that role, the critics probably would have felt that Carter and Rafshoon had taken leave of their senses.

The critics did come out in the open when it was disclosed that the Governor had earmarked $210,000 of the state's emergency funds for the removal of tree stumps from Lake Blackshear near his Sumter County homestead and the construction of a swimming pool in Plains. The expenditures had aroused the ire of State Representative James H. (Sloppy) Floyd who said, among other things, "I don't know whether building a swimming pool is an emergency or not." Floyd, chairman of the Georgia House Appropriations Committee, had previously accused Carter of "playing politics" by authorizing emergency expenditures sought by the Governor's cousin Hugh Carter. This time, however, Carter hit back, terming the $210,000 "a relatively tiny investment" and condemning critics of the Sumter County projects as coming from "a few ill-informed people in north Georgia," a direct slap at Floyd. Carter maintained he had tried to get the tree stumps removed from Lake Blackshear since 1965.

"I've never called a Governor a liar in my life," responded Floyd, "but if the statements are true that were printed this morning, then the Governor is a liar. . . . This is the third year that he has been Governor and he has submitted three proposed budgets, and in none of these proposed budgets has the Governor ever recommended the removal of stumps from Lake Blackshear.

I wonder why he would say he has been trying to get stumps removed since 1965, since he has not even made a budget request for it."

Being called a "liar" by the likes of Sloppy Floyd did not sit too well with a politician who had begun to go national. The only consolation was that the heated argument never got any media attention outside of Georgia. And, even in Georgia, it was quickly forgotten.

Less than a month after Nixon's second inaugural, Carter turned up in Washington to deliver what in retrospect was his first major speech for the presidency. But few at the National Press Club that day in early February 1973 could envision the slight figure up on the rostrum as much more than a one-term Georgia Governor who, if he got the breaks, could conceivably wind up in the United States Senate. However, Andrew Young, much more attuned to Georgia politics, figured what was going on. Sitting at the head table, the newly elected Congressman from Atlanta passed a note to Peter Bourne which read, "I'll be damned if he isn't running for President."

Carter's subject for discussion was the then current hassle between Capitol Hill and the White House over President Nixon's impoundment of funds already appropriated by Congress. The irony, which apparently was lost on Carter, was that he himself was having problems of his own in Atlanta battling the legislative branch of his state government. But that didn't stop Carter from assailing Nixon for not getting along with Congress; in fact, seeking to dominate both houses. And he blamed both the Congress and his fellow Governors for permitting the President to seize control of federal spending. (Five years later, in a public relations gesture to demonstrate he was presidential, Carter was to veto what he termed an unwieldy defense budget.)

In addition to attacking the Administration's fiscal policy broadside, Carter accused Nixon of running a "federal government by crisis and surprise," where decisions were made "in secrecy and consultations are few." Again the irony was lost on Carter; for he, too, was being accused in Atlanta of springing surprises on the state legislature.

As a Governor, Carter went on, he resented the fact that he had no lines of communication with the White House or the people who decided what federal programs were to be cut. "Final decisions," he contended, "are made by the Ehrlichmans, the Haldemans, and the Ashes. I don't know them and I have no access to them. Neither, unfortunately, do most of our Congressmen."

(Carter kept up a steady refrain on how the Nixon Administration refused to consult with him on its drastic cost-cutting plans. So much so, that *The Constitution* began to refer to him as "one of the most vocal anti-Nixon Governors." In April 1973, the White House held a top-level briefing for the nation's Governors, and forty-seven of them showed up. But not Carter, a fact noted at a press briefing by presidential spokesman Ron Ziegler. Observing that Carter had complained because he couldn't get an audience with White House officials, Ziegler said, "Those who say that the loudest do not avail themselves of the opportunity." With a smile, Ziegler added that Carter had said "he had business in his state and went home." Stung to the quick, Carter had spokesman Jody Powell say, "The insinuations by the President's press aide were, in my opinion, unjustified and uncalled for.")

In essence, what Carter called for at the Press Club was more federal funds for Georgia. He did not like White House cutbacks on agricultural spending, poverty programs, and housing subsidies. Yet he divined the "mood of the people" to be "one of basic conservatism" which he was all for. How he reconciled his demand for increased federal programs with that mood he did not say. But he did say that "conservatism does not mean racism. It does not mean stubborn resistance to change. It does not mean callousness or unconcern about our fellow human beings. . . . I predict that we shall see an emergence of what might be called benevolent conservatism. There are many conservative people who care."

Thus, for the moment at least, Jimmy Carter appeared to have emerged as a "benevolent conservative." But it was a description of his ideological bent he would rarely use again. The reason, simply enough, was that neither conservatives nor liberals understood what he was talking about. Not that it really mattered. For Carter's speech at the National Press Club obtained a minimum of attention.

But the astonishing thing, in retrospect, was that this man— hawkish in his views on Vietnam, believing that "detente has been pushed too far," favoring right-to-work laws, supporting the death penalty, opposing federal aid to New York City, favoring abolition of corporate income tax, opposing forced busing—would later be accorded liberal benedictions. William vanden Heuvel, a major supporter of Robert F. Kennedy, for example, would tout Carter in 1976 as "someone who has stood with us on the right side in every fight that's been important to us over the last two decades." Which, of course, was sheer nonsense.

Also overlooked by most liberals was Carter's support of Vice-President Spiro T. Agnew in the latter's final days of government. In fact, three weeks before Agnew resigned the second-highest office in the land in October 1973, Carter phoned him. As the Governor recounted it at a press conference the next day, September 20, "I told him that I hope that he would remain in office. I hoped he would not resign under pressure. And I told him there were a lot of Democratic Governors and a lot of citizens in the states and in the nation that I thought would be disappointed if he resigned at this time. And he thanked me for my comments."

"I have said earlier," Carter added, "maybe too quickly, that I thought he was completely innocent. I don't have any way to know that, but I know him and I think he's been abused unnecessarily and too early in the press . . . and I don't think he's received adequate support from the President."

When the Atlanta-based reporters expressed surprise at his comments, Carter explained that he had become a friend of Agnew when the latter took over federal-state liaison under the Nixon Administration's revenue sharing program. "As a matter of fact, he and I have been very close," he added.

Carter had also sided with Nixon in the latter's opposition to publication of the Pentagon Papers. In fact, Carter went much further than the President in discussing with Senator Muskie—as *The Constitution* reported on July 9, 1971— "the possibility of enactment of federal legislation that would make newspapers criminally liable for publication of classified material that affects the nation's security." Muskie had called Carter to discuss, among other things, the attitude of Southerners toward publication by *The New York Times* of the Pentagon documents. And Carter said he thought "direct quotations from classified documents" and even certain declassified materials should be prohibited by law. Such "direct quotations," Carter noted, could give other nations the key to U.S. secret codes, even if the codes not used in the documents were not now in use. And he said he had also told Muskie that some means had to be found to assure other nations that their communications with the U.S. government would not be made public. Carter also proposed that a special classification be affixed to certain documents that should never be disclosed. "Say, if the President of France told the President of the United States that he thought the President of Mexico was a ----, then I don't think that should be made public, not even forty years from now," Carter said he told Muskie. But, Carter said he also favored a review procedure which would constantly declassify material that was no longer of a sensitive nature. (In contrast, Lester Maddox took the opposite point of view. "If *The New York Times*," said the Lieutenant Governor, "has information about our involvement in the Vietnamese war which proves that our political leaders have not been honest with the people, then it is treason by America's political leaders and the people should be told the truth.")

All of which seems clear enough. Jimmy Carter, as Governor, took a position during the furor over the Pentagon Papers which was not much different from that expressed by the Nixon Administration. As a presidential candidate, Carter completely changed his position—refusing, however, to acknowledge any such somersault.

On the eve of the 1976 Democratic Convention in New York, James Hoge, editor of *The Chicago Sun-Times*, questioned Carter on *Meet the Press* as follows:

"At the time of the disclosure of the Pentagon Papers, you counseled that there ought to be laws enforcing criminal liability against the press for publishing classified information and, indeed, some unclassified information. My question is, if that was so, under certain circumstances, what would check the government's penchant to overclassify information to protect its own reputation rather than to protect the national security?"

"I don't believe that is an accurate statement of my position now or ever in the past," replied Carter.

"Well," said Hoge, "it is from *The Atlanta Constitution*."

"I understand that," Carter went on. "My preference is that the press be open. I personally feel that the Pentagon Papers should have been revealed by *The New York Times*, and I would do everything I could to protect the right of the press to conceal its sources of information, and let the responsibility of the press be its major check on how it acted as it deals with sensitive material or with matters that might affect our own country."

Of course, Carter managed to evade commenting on what had been attributed to him in *The Constitution*. The man who promised he would never lie to the American people didn't exactly tell the truth. And he got away with it.

As he got away with accepting gifts from major corporations in his state—even though, later, he was vociferous in his condemnation of such practices. Mainly, he benefited from the largesse provided by Georgia's major corporations—Lockheed Aircraft and the Coca-Cola Company. Among other goodies, both giant companies provided the Governor use of their executive jets even though the state provided him with travel funds and aircraft. Carter's record, therefore, was in striking contrast to what he himself later claimed ought to be public policy. Thus, in his presentation to the platform committee of the Democratic Party in 1976, Carter urged that "absolutely no gifts of value should ever again be permitted to a public official. A report of all minor personal gifts should be made public." And two years previously, he was quoted in *The Constitution* as having said that some people who had been elected Governor "enjoy the prerogatives of the office to travel around, go to conventions, play golf, or whatever they choose," implying that Carter personally disapproved of such activities.

But Carter never made public all the occasions that he utilized planes and other corporate facilities during his tour as Governor. Only later were the facts unearthed by Nicholas Horrock of *The New York Times*. In his investigative report, published April 1, 1976, Horrock noted that "the use of corporate executive aircraft by public officials raises questions of whether the companies providing the flights can obtain favoritism from the officials they carry as passengers. Only last year, Governor Marvin Mandel of Maryland came under widespread criticism for taking trips on private corporate aircraft."

In his autobiography, Carter records how in 1972 he and his

wife visited Recife, the capital city of Pernambuco in Brazil, where "we helped to arrange for an annual exchange of private citizens between the two states." But he did not mention that his three-week trip to five Latin American countries had been arranged by Lockheed, which provided him with one of its plush Jetstars. Nor did he reveal that he used the trip to promote sales for the debt-ridden aerospace firm, which later became the target of numerous investigations on charges of having bribed foreign officials as part of its aircraft sales techniques. All of which was confirmed by Jody Powell when interviewed in 1976 by Alexander Cockburn and James Ridgeway of *The Village Voice*. Conceding that Lockheed had paid for "the major portion" of the Carter trip, Powell said, "One of the reasons we were down there was to sell Lockheed airplanes." Apparently Powell became annoyed by the thrust of the interview, which he concluded by uttering the memorable words "Up yours!"

In a handwritten letter dated May 5, 1972, later exhumed by *The Voice*, Carter wrote to thank Lockheed vice-president R.D. Roche for "one of the finest experiences of my life . . . being with you on the trip to Central and South America." Carter said that "in addition to the remarkable performance, luxury, and convenience of the Jetstar, the opportunity to learn more about Lockheed was extremely important to me."

"It was obvious," Carter gushed, "in my discussions with the leaders of the five nations—presidents, ministers of defense, and many others that the C-130 Hercules is an airplane which is universally admired and appreciated. . . . I have carried this message of admiration to our own national leaders in the State Department, Defense Department, and the Congress, and will continue to do so. In my opinion, our government and its agencies should marshal its efforts to help all of our friends throughout the world to buy and to use this plane because of its obvious quality and because it is such a fine example of a contribution to both effective defense and peacetime usefulness."

Largely because his work in behalf of one of the giants of the industrial-military complex was conducted behind the scenes, Carter managed to escape the kind of liberal opprobrium that was leveled against the Senator from Washington, Scoop Jackson, who also defended the interests of his state's major industry. For years, he was unfairly called "the Senator from Boeing," a canard which did not set too well in his pursuit of the presidency.

On November 26, 1972, Carter wrote another thank-you letter to Marie and Lucian Whittle, of the Brunswick Pulp and Paper Company—a large Georgia concern. Along with Boo and Charlie Kirbo, Nancy and Ham Jordan, Nan and Jody Powell, and three other couples, the Carters had weekended at the company's luxurious hunting lodge at Cabin Bluff. The Governor and his party obviously had had a good time. For as Carter wrote to the Whittles, "You have given me and my family one of the finest experiences of our lives." Of course, this was the second such experience that year. ". . . The guides were also very patient with us—and successful. Our turkeys and Rosalynn's first quail are sources of great pride.

"Perhaps of even more importance was getting to know you, Lucian, and to learn more about Georgia's most important single industry. You are a fine spokesman for Georgia's forests and their potential, and your company could not have a better representative. . . ."

Carter, as *The Voice* later reported, was to return to the freeloading joys of Cabin Bluff a few more times.

How often Carter utilized Coca-Cola planes has never been fully estimated. But that he was a frequent user of the company's facilities on trips to several Governors' Conferences as well as on flights to Washington is beyond dispute. Not that there was anything unusual about Georgia Governors relying on Coke planes for their travels. But none of them had ever taken such a holier-than-thou attitude about the practice until Jimmy came along. That is, until it turned out that he did not practice what he preached.

The Coke connection had another great advantage. On his increasing number of trips overseas, ostensibly to drum up business for Georgia, Carter relied on a worldwide network of Coca-Cola executives to pick him up at airports, drive him around, and make appointments for him with the local head of state. In fact, Carter would soon be calling the soft-drink company "my own State Department." As Carter quickly learned, the company constituted a mighty empire abroad. The sun never set on Coke.

Someone once estimated that around the world fifty billion bottles of the brown-colored liquid were consumed daily, enough Coke to float a light cruiser. Head of the Atlanta-based operation was J. Paul Austin, who at first was no great admirer of Carter. In fact, Austin had openly supported Carl Sanders in the 1970 gubernatorial contest. Still, both men had a mutual friend, Charlie Kirbo, who was counsel to the Coca-Cola Company. And, after the election was over, Carter would call Austin at his Atlanta headquarters for advice, and the friendship blossomed. So much so that, during the 1976 presidential campaign, Austin co-hosted an important luncheon for Carter and a group of prominent businessmen at New York's "21" restaurant. And, after the election, Austin soon became known as something of an unofficial emissary for Carter whenever he traveled abroad. It was a relationship which Austin sought to downplay, perhaps because of the more publicized friendship between former President Nixon and PepsiCo chairman Donald M. Kendall. Their two companies had long been rivals. It was a rivalry which Adlai Stevenson had once called "the ice cold war."

By now, too, Carter was also making use of his connection with *Time*. As he was preparing for the obligatory visit to Israel, the magazine's bureau chief in Atlanta, Jim Bell, offered to communicate with his opposite number in Jerusalem so that the Governor would be able to pick up some quick expertise in Middle East problems. As the story was told in *Parade*, Carter and his sidekick Ham Jordan, on their arrival in the Holy Land, were invited by the *Time* man to dine with some Israeli journalists. During the dinner, the two Georgians listened eagerly and bewilderedly to the journalists vigorously arguing among themselves about local situations of which Carter and Jordan knew practically nothing. After dinner, Carter shook hands all around and smiled at the journalists, "I hope y'all win." Then he effusively thanked his host and hostess "for the local cuisine."

The dinner, as *Parade* noted, consisted of Chinese food.

Carter later conceded that much of his travel abroad was designed to help him brush up on foreign affairs in preparation for his presidential pursuit. And in his pursuit of such knowledge, Carter got one of those lucky breaks which at times made him think he was destiny's child. He was invited to join the Trilateral

Commission shortly after it was organized in 1973 by David Rockefeller, chairman of the Chase Manhattan Bank, in order to study problems of common interest to the United States, Western Europe, and Japan. Rockefeller had first met Carter in November 1971, when the Governor flew to New York just to have lunch with the banker in the Board of Directors Dining Room of the Chase Bank. Lockheed, incidentally, provided one of its Jetstars for the round trip.

Exactly what was discussed at the luncheon was never made public. But it apparently had a deep effect on Rockefeller. For when he and Zbigniew Brzezinski, the Trilateralists' first director, were casting around for a non-Establishment type, particularly from the South, to join their élite group, they invited Carter. "It was a close thing between Carter and Reubin Askew of Florida," Brzezinski later told *London Sunday Times* correspondent Peter Pringle, "but we were impressed that Carter had opened up trade offices for the state of Georgia in Brussels and Tokyo. That seemed to fit perfectly into the concept of the Trilateral."

Carter, who was to campaign for the presidency as an "outsider," was only too happy to join this newly formed group of "insiders." As Gerald Rafshoon said later, the invitation was "one of the most fortunate accidents of the early campaign and critical to building support where it counted." For Carter was now rubbing shoulders with the likes of Hedley Donovan, editor-in-chief of Time, Inc.; Arthur B. Taylor, president of CBS; Leonard Woodcock, president of the United Auto Workers; Alden Clausen, president of the Bank of America—and, of course, the insiders' Godfather, David Rockefeller.

The Polish-born Brzezinski was to David Rockefeller what the German-born Kissinger was to Nelson Rockefeller. In many ways, the two foreign policy advisers were like peas in a pod, though for years they were rivals for eminence in the tiny, incestuous world of big thinking in foreign affairs. Henry, of course, had moved on to bigger and better things. From Nixon's National Security Adviser, he had become Secretary of State. Eclipsed by Kissinger, Brzezinski had jockeyed himself into running the Rockefeller-financed Trilateral Commission and was biding his time. His time came soon enough, even though he apparently did not meet with the approval of Hamilton Jordan, who frankly did not like "insiders." In fact, Jordan had been impolitic enough to tell Robert Scheer of *Playboy* prior to the election that if Cyrus Vance were named Secretary of State and Brzezinski head of National Security in the Carter Administration—as had been widely rumored— "then I would say we failed, and I'd quit. But that's not going to happen."

But that's exactly what happened, much to Jordan's discomfiture. But he didn't quit. And at least sixteen other top-level executives of the Carter Administration were drawn from the cozy Trilateral membership, including Harold Brown, as Secretary of Defense; W. Michael Blumenthal, Secretary of the Treasury; Paul C. Warnke, Director of the U.S. Arms Control and Disarmament Agency; Elliot L. Richardson, U.S. Ambassador at Large with Responsibility for U.N. Law of the Sea Conference; Gerard C. Smith, U.S. Ambassador at Large for Non-proliferation Matters; Robert R. Bowie, Deputy to the Director of Central Intelligence; and Andrew Young, U.S. Ambassador to the United Nations. Previously, he had selected Walter F. Mondale to be Vice-President, another ascendant politician tapped by Rockefeller. So the Trilateralists were more than well represented in the Carter Administration, giving rise to the thesis in both right-wing and left-wing circles that some sort of dark conspiracy was involved. What actually took place was that the "insiders" once again ended up running the country, an old story. Even Nixon, who so distrusted the "Harvards," found himself surrounded by the same kind.

In addition to becoming knowledgeable in foreign affairs, the Carter game plan called for, in Rafshoon's words, his emergence "as a leader in the Democratic Party and someone involved in bringing it back." The question was how to get Carter into the national arena without making his overriding ambition public, lest he quickly be laughed out of political life. The opportunity presented itself in March 1973 when the newly installed Democratic National Chairman, Bob Strauss, came to Atlanta for a speech. Invited over to the Governor's Mansion, Strauss discussed politics with Carter and Charlie Kirbo. And it was then that either Carter or Kirbo, or both, noted that Carter's term would end the following year and that the Governor was interested in doing something for the party. Why, exclaimed Strauss, he had something in mind. He needed a fresh name for the letterhead of the national 1974 Democratic Campaign Committee. Would the Governor be interested in becoming chairman? The job would entail traveling around the country at National Committee expense, speaking for Democratic candidates at every level. That's exactly what he had in mind, said Carter.

To Strauss, the assignment he had offered Carter was a generally routine and thankless one, a "nothing job." But Carter thought otherwise. The night the appointment was announced, Carter had a small party in his office to celebrate. Carter also celebrated when Strauss agreed to permit Ham Jordan to work at the DNC for a while. Carter had told Strauss it would be "good experience for the boy, being as how he didn't know much about national politics and all," the chairman recalled later. "Hell, I didn't think much about it, didn't think much about it at all."

So Jordan quietly resigned as Carter's executive secretary, slipped out of Atlanta, and wound up in Washington as staff director. No one really paid any attention to the episode. The feeling in Atlanta was that the stocky, twenty-eight-year-old Jordan had decided to leave the Carter Administration early for greener pastures elsewhere. In politics, it happens all the time. Only when it became known that Carter himself had been named committee chairman were questions asked. "Who the hell knew what was going on back then," said state Senator Hugh Gills, a longtime Carter foe. "I mean everybody knew Jimmy was an ambitious man, but the White House, never. Somebody said he might be looking for a vice-presidential nomination, but everybody laughed at that. A Senate seat maybe, that's what we figured."

But the only Senate seat that would have been available was occupied by Herman Talmadge and for a time Carter thought of contesting "Hummon" for the post, but decided against it in mid-1971 after soundings taken among the electorate indicated Carter would be trounced in a primary fight. And the reason was, as a pollster told him some years later, that Carter had an "unfavorable image" in his own state. "In fact," wrote Georgia editor Millard Grimes, "most Georgians in 1974 believed that Carter would have had real trouble winning re-election to the governorship if he could have succeeded himself." The first of

Carter's political setbacks was the failure of his handpicked senatorial candidate, David Gambrell, to win election against a little-known state representative. Another defeat which unmasked Carter's weakness occurred in 1974, when Carter picked Bert Lance as his heir-apparent. A banker, Lance had been transformed into a political figure when Carter named him the state's highway director. Although he was a Carter protégé and far outspent his opponents in the Governor's race, Lance emerged in third place, with only 17 percent of the vote. And, according to newsman Grimes, the blame for these Carter setbacks could be pinned on "the widespread suspicion among the people that Carter had hoodwinked them."

But it was in connection with Lance's gubernatorial campaign that Carter became involved in a questionable scheme whose disclosure led Lester Maddox to describe it as Jimmy Carter's "own little Watergate." Carter had told the Atlanta press that he had commissioned a poll to obtain public reactions toward highway routes for a new interstate highway which was slated to cut through the city. But what he had failed to mention was the fact that he and Georgia Democratic Chairman Charlie Kirbo had also agreed in secret to "piggyback" onto the poll a series of questions which also tested the public's feelings about Carter (there were as many questions about him as there were about the highway) and about gubernatorial candidates Bert Lance, Lester Maddox, David Gambrell, and George Busbee.

Public reaction became so vehement after the "piggybacking" was exposed by *The Constitution* that Carter was forced to concede he had authorized an unusual arrangement whereby the polls had been paid for by both state and Democratic funds. At first, Carter forgot and then re-remembered the costs. Terming the results a secret, he then released them, acknowledging he had not mentioned the poll to the State Department of Transportation. The firm he used happened to be the same one which had traditionally done his political polling and was at the same time also doing a survey for Bert Lance.

All of Lance's gubernatorial opponents in the primary leaped at the issue. Maddox, whose political power had been assessed, said that the tandem polls constituted "improper use" of party and state funds. The Lieutenant Governor noted that the state was paying $5,500 for a poll worth about $4,000. And he questioned whether the Democratic Party would have paid anything for the political portion of the poll had the newspaper exposé not appeared. "It wasn't planned for the party to pay anything until Carter got caught with his hand in the cookie jar," said Maddox. "It's just one of his many Watergates."

Also attacking the Governor was former U.S. Senator Gambrell, by now on the outs with Carter. "I would say that, at the present time, the credibility of the Democratic Party is destroyed by this incident," said Gambrell. "My reaction is that the political part of the poll is on behalf of the Lance people, and they are trying to determine whether a Maddox candidacy or a Gambrell candidacy would be the biggest threat to Lance."

A somewhat chastened Kirbo maintained that the poll "came about in an innocent and unwise way." Carter's closest confidante, who operated out of an office in the State Capitol, said the decision to have the poll done jointly was "arrived at in a casual manner when" both he and Carter "were supposed to be thinking more clearly."

And Lance, also embarrassed, said he had nothing to do with any of it. "I did not have any input into it, did not suggest that it be done. If I had been asked, I would have said it shouldn't be done."

The 1974 gubernatorial primary was, as usual, a heated one. Most of the Democratic candidates concentrated their fury on Lance, "the Governor's pal." Gambrell, for example, lashed out at the burly banker, citing his nearly $1 million campaign fund and declaring that "big spending in politics is nothing but a temptation to corrupting influence."

But Lance had his defenders. One, the Reverend Martin Luther King, Sr., declared that Bert would "make the best Governor." At a luncheon in Atlanta, the pastor of the Ebenezer Baptist Church said, "I've checked him out every way I know, and he's clean. He's clean. I checked him as a businessman; I checked him as a family man; I checked him as a church man, and I checked him as a man of honesty and integrity." Despite the accolade, Bert went down to defeat only to emerge several years later in Washington where Jimmy Carter—by now President— also vouched for Lance's honesty and integrity.

Later in 1973, Carter called a press conference to say he was flying to Washington to straighten out the farmers' (and his own) peanut subsidies with the Department of Agriculture. He neglected to note he was planning to spend much of his time campaigning for Virginia gubernatorial candidate Henry Howell, who was running a Populist campaign. Identifying himself as a former Virginia resident, Carter told voters that the issue in the Old Dominion was the contest between "the special interests who have long dominated Southern politics—the banks, corporations, insurance companies, and power and telephone people—and the people who demand their own right to . . . control their own government." And, referring to Watergate, Carter said, "What has happened in Washington is a direct result of secrecy in government. . . ." Howell couldn't have been happier; but in a few days he went on to lose to Republican Mills E. Godwin.

By now, Carter was spending more and more time out of Atlanta, forsaking routine gubernatorial duties. But Hamilton Jordan, the Governor's right-hand man on the DNC's campaign committee, denied that Carter might be using the powerful 1974 position as a launching pad into future political ventures of his own. "The Governor," said Jordan, ". . . is approaching this thing more as a technician; he's not using this as a vehicle for running around the country making speeches." And Carter himself denied national ambitions. He said he hoped to get potential presidential candidates "to forego any preoccupation with 1976 and to get by 1974."

Wherever he went, he kept saying how he was trying to get potential candidates for the presidential nomination to put off their campaigning until after the 1974 midterm elections. "I've really had some run-ins with Mondale," he told a small group in Lebanon, New Hampshire, in the spring of 1974. He was referring, of course, to Senator Walter F. Mondale, the Minnesota Democrat, who was already stumping the country in quest of the big prize. Asked about his own plans, Carter said, "I don't know what I'll do in '76. I'm not interested in running for Congress or the Senate. I might pick a candidate I like for President and work with him. Or else I might strive for a place on the '76 ticket myself."

Carter, of course, was well aware of what he wanted to do in '76. And to that end, he was stepping up appearances around the country, speaking for candidates and developing contacts. In Rochester, New York, for example, he helped Vice-Mayor Margaret "Midge" Costanza in her unsuccessful race against the popular GOP Congressman Barber Conable; and two years later won her support for his presidential campaign. Costanza seconded his nomination at Madison Square Garden, and after his election she became a top presidential aide until she was toppled in an internal White House struggle.

Wherever Carter went, Jody Powell went, too, developing a card file of priceless political contacts. Though the DNC paid all travel expenses, Carter and his aides usually stayed as the houseguests of the Democrats they were meeting. They did this not because they wanted to save money but because, as one Carter aide told Martin Schram, "It helped to build the close personal relationships—the family-type relationships—that are so important when you are later asking people to give of themselves and bust their humps for you." In many ways, Carter was emulating the techniques used by Richard Nixon in 1966 to build a grass-roots base for his successful 1968 bid for the GOP presidential nomination. Except that Nixon, then a New York lawyer with questionable political prospects, had to hire his own staff and raise money from friends to finance his tireless travels on the "chicken-and-peas" campaign circuit, where he picked up invaluable IOUs from the numerous candidates on whose behalf he appeared.

Carter had something else going for him. Ham Jordan was acting as his eyes and ears inside the Democratic National Committee, reporting regularly to "the boss" on what was going on in Washington. And plenty was going on. For by now, Watergate was undermining an Administration which had been re-elected by the greatest vote in American history. The Democrats knew they had the opportunity of a lifetime to make big gains in the 1974 elections. And they were finally in the position to deliver the coup de grace to a President who had successfully won the support of a "New Majority," consisting largely of disaffected Democrats. At first, however, Carter appeared to be ambivalent about Watergate. When it first began to unravel in the spring of 1973, he warned his party against exploiting the scandal. He said it would be "a mistake to manipulate Watergate in an overly partisan manner." And at a Democratic Governors' conference, Carter introduced a resolution for national prayer, including prayers for Nixon. But the Governors, more interested in embarrassing the President than in praying for him, tabled the resolution. Not long after that, Carter had a change of heart about Watergate. A day rarely passed when he wasn't sounding off on the subject.

By now, too, Strauss had a pretty good idea of what Carter was really up to. The young Georgia Governor whom the party chairman had believed to be nothing more than an attractive Southern moderate who wanted to help the party was in business for himself. For much to his amazement, Strauss discovered that the soft-spoken Jimmy actually was running for President while heading the Democratic Campaign Committee. And Strauss came upon this knowledge in a singular way.

The facts are in dispute. All that can be confirmed is that Ham Jordan left in or on his desk a copy of his then still secret memorandum advising Carter how to win the presidential nomination. Somehow or other, it came to the attention of Strauss' man at the DNC, Robert Keefe, the party's executive director. "Early on," Keefe told Martin Schram, "some people left some things around that they should not have left. I found them on my table." And Keefe passed the intelligence on to Strauss. How the information got to his "table" he did not say. But later on, at the Carter White House, two stories circulated, according to John Osborne. One was that Keefe happened to notice the memorandum on Jordan's desk and showed it to Strauss. Both men, after having a good laugh at the very notion of Jimmy Carter for President, kidded Jordan about it. The other version was that Keefe, in Jordan's absence, "sneaked his way through a notebook on Jordan's desk," reporting the essence of what he had read to Strauss. "In this version," wrote Osborne, "Keefe and Strauss laughed at the notions all right, but never mentioned Keefe's spying to Jordan." Spying? Why, that's difficult to believe in an organization whose headquarters at the Watergate had recently been victimized by such tactics. Nevertheless, according to Osborne, Jordan learned about it from other people and kidded about it with Strauss only after the party chairman was admitted to Carter's inner circle following the 1976 election.

But for a long time, the plain-speaking Strauss, whose taste in presidential aspirants ran to the Jackson, Humphrey, and fellow

Texan Lloyd Bentsen type, in that order of preference, was decidedly underwhelmed by Carter. For one thing, it had become painfully obvious to Strauss that Carter was taking full advantage of the job he had given him to generate publicity for himself. His occasional unorthodox utterances, moreover, irritated the party chairman. As when, at a Democratic Governors' conference in the spring of 1974, Carter publicly voiced his concern that, unless Nixon resigned, his Watergate problems would "seriously distort the political process" by causing the defeat of "a lot of deserving Republicans." Even more astonishing to the party faithful was Carter's contention that the Democrats might not be prepared for the added responsibility that enlarged congressional majorities would bring. Strauss could hardly believe his ears; and a close associate told Bob Shogan of *The Los Angeles Times* that the party chairman considered Carter to be "the village idiot."

About the same time, Carter was quoted in *People* magazine as saying, "The longer [Nixon] stays in office, the better it is for the Democrats and the worse it is for the country and the Republicans." Carter also described himself as "a Nixon hater from way back." The magazine also quoted Carter as saying that Nixon would never resign but would be impeached.

Carter's virulence did not sit too well with the folks back home who had so overwhelmingly voted for Nixon and who felt in large measure that Watergate was being blown out of all legitimate proportion by an Eastern media which had long been out to "get" the President.

The result was a retraction of sorts by Carter. In a statement released by Jody Powell, Carter said he did not have "any personal animosity toward Mr. Nixon. . . . Neither do I wish to prejudge the guilt or innocence of anyone accused of a crime prior to legal determination of guilt based on the evidence. My offhand personal comments about Mr. Nixon came during a general conversation which I incorrectly assumed was not for publication. . . ."

Though he did not wish "to prejudge the guilt or innocence of anyone" involved in Watergate, Carter did precisely that on a *Meet the Press* panel on the eve of the June 1974 opening of the National Governors Conference in Seattle. "I personally feel the President is guilty and that the recent evidence would prove it," he said. Again Carter said he did not believe Nixon would resign but would be forced out of office by impeachment.

But Nixon did resign. And Carter still couldn't suppress the off-the-record "hate" he felt toward Nixon. He firmly rejected proposals that Nixon be granted legal immunity from future prosecutions in the Watergate affair. The courts, he said, were "the proper place to resolve any future questions of guilt or punishment of the President." And he faulted Nixon for failing to "show any evidence of penitence or admission of any wrongdoing on his part." But he "was not surprised," he said. "One of the characteristics President Nixon has always exhibited is the inability to admit any mistakes on his own part." (It was, of course, a characteristic not peculiar to Nixon. As President, Carter was to demonstrate an abundance of that trait.) However, Carter did credit Nixon with doing "the right thing to spare the nation the ordeal of going through the impeachment process."

Carter also expressed full confidence in Gerald Ford, about to be sworn in as Nixon's successor. He said that, as a result of meetings on the energy crisis and other matters, he had gotten to know Ford "very well." And, he added, "he's a good man, and I think he has the confidence of the American people. He certainly has mine." Of course, politics being what they are, Carter was soon to change his mind about Ford.

And one of the things which helped him change his mind, he said, was Ford's energy policy. It was a policy, "if it can be described as a policy, designed to enrich the corporate interests at the expense of the American people." Which was exactly what Carter said about Nixon's energy policy. Except that Carter suggested that the oil companies which had contributed heavily to Nixon's re-election had "commitments" permitting them to reap large profits. Under close questioning, Carter stopped short of accusing the companies of manufacturing the energy crisis or of accusing Nixon of an outright deal with them. "I don't think it's a plot," he said, "but I do think the oil companies are using a worldwide shortage to make unconscionable profits."

Which, of course, was a case of having his cake and eating it too. This was a technique Carter employed on other matters. As when he accused President Nixon of bowing to pressure from major airlines in refusing to approve direct flights to Europe from the Atlanta airport. In an Atlanta radio talk show, the Governor suggested presidential aide John Connally's membership on the Pan Am board as a possible contributing factor to the White House position. Then he appeared to soften his charge. "I don't say there's any skulduggery involved. I don't say that it's illegal pressure or something I don't understand. If I were with TWA, I'd be doing the same thing."

In other jibes at Nixon, Carter scored the President's "slapstick handling" of the energy crisis and criticized Administration fiscal policies which, he said, had failed to prevent devaluation of the dollar. Yet, Carter announced with pride that dollar devaluation would soon bring foreign business into Georgia.

After the outbreak of the Yom Kippur war in October 1973, the Arabs invoked an oil embargo, and again Governor Carter warned that special interests, whom he did not name, were seeking to take advantage of the energy crisis. But all through the crisis, while thousands of small gas stations were going out of business for lack of product to sell, one two-pump station in Plains, Georgia, was doing very well indeed. That was the one owned by the Governor's brother, the then not-so-well-known Billy Carter, who somehow managed to keep his station "alive"—and very profitable—with emergency gasoline shipments of up to 25,000 gallons a month. And the man Billy Carter credits with having "kept me alive" with gasoline supplies was none other than Lewis C. Spruill, who was appointed chief of Georgia's Energy Office by then Governor Carter. One of Spruill's employees at the Energy Office was the Governor's son, Chip Carter.

Billy Carter willingly acknowledged receiving the emergency gasoline. Interviewed by investigative reporters Patrick Tyler and Charles Thompson, Billy Carter did acknowledge some puzzlement about his good fortune in receiving a good deal more gasoline than he otherwise would have been entitled to. "Hell," he told them, "if I've done anything illegal, I wouldn't try to hide it, I'd brag about it." In their dispatch, published in *The St. Petersburg Times* on February 26, 1978, Tyler and Thompson established that Billy Carter—thanks to his good friends in Atlanta—had obtained a windfall. And in his column of July 22, 1978, Jack Anderson described the situation in these words: "The fumes of a Georgia fuel scandal have wafted from Billy Carter's gas station in Plains to the doorstep of Jimmy Carter's White House. The odor simply won't go away."

9

STARTING ON THE LEFT FOOT

WHEN WORD BEGAN TO LEAK OUT ABOUT JIMMY CARTER'S ULTI-
mate ambition, Reg Murphy could hardly believe it. The editor of
The Atlanta Constitution took to his typewriter and rapped out a
column which was published on July 10, 1974. "And," as he said
more recently, "I wrote one of the more famous headlines of our
times." Which it most certainly was. It read, "Jimmy Carter's
Running for WHAT?" Murphy now thinks it was "the most stupid
headline that has ever been written." But at the time, it made
sense. The column itself read, in part, as follows:

> Governor Carter's timing was just right. The state
> needed a good bellylaugh and Carter obliged by announ-
> cing he would run for president. It needed a followup
> chuckle, and Carter was helpful again. He claimed to be
> leaving office as one of the most popular governors in
> recent history. He said he was leaving office with a high
> rating from the people. His own pollster, William
> Hamilton of Washington, may not have found that funny.
> Hamilton just found that Carter has a higher unfavorable

rating in Georgia than Lieutenant Governor Maddox by seven points.

Carter said he had been building national political strength by helping Congressmen and Senators campaign this summer. . . . What the Governor carefully didn't mention was that everybody in the Governor's race in Georgia now is running to keep from being associated with him.

Thinking over the nation's trials to be endured in the next few months, we concluded Carter could be helpful to our sense of humor for the next year by continuing to run.

Next month, tell them how well the reorganization program works, Governor. Explain to them how efficient the Department of Human Resources has become. (On second thought, that's not funny. It's pathetic.)

Tell us how 35 percent of your former voters now give you a negative rating, and explain that it was just a coincidence that the pollsters found that result. . . .

Wait a minute. Maybe the Governor didn't mean his announcement as a joke.

He can't go back home to run for the Sumter County Commission. They tend to elect practical folks down there. . . .

He can't run for Congress. Those folks in the district like Governor Wallace, who once believed he had a promise from Carter to second his nomination at the 1972 Democratic National Convention.

Incredible as it sounds, Carter may not have intended to give us all a laugh.

Oh, well, he succeeded in being comical whether he intended it or not.

Murphy still sticks by the body of his commentary. When he wrote it, he felt he had good cause. After all, Carter had been a "lousy" Governor, a poor administrator. He didn't save any money nor did he run an efficient shop. But he has so rewritten the record books that, Murphy believes, Carter began to believe he was a capable administrator. Yet few Georgia legislators who watched Carter in action believe that. "Which was why," says Murphy, "I couldn't believe he was running for President, and I certainly didn't believe anybody would take him seriously."

Amazingly, one person who was taking Carter seriously was Dr. Hunter S. Thompson, the High Priest of Gonzo Journalism. Representing *Rolling Stone*, Thompson had turned up in Georgia in May 1974 in the company of Senator Edward Kennedy to attend a Law Day ceremony honoring Dean Rusk. The ceremony was to take place at the University of Georgia in Athens. But, first, everyone assembled at the Governor's Mansion. This was where Thompson met Carter. And, according to the beer-guzzling journalist, Kennedy was in somewhat of a snit. Only later did Thompson learn that "Carter had waited until the last minute—just before I got to the mansion—to advise Kennedy that a sudden change in his own plans made it impossible for him to lend Teddy his plane for the trip to Athens." Which, he added, "was the reason for the tension I half-noticed when I got to the mansion." Kennedy's aides had been forced to get on the phone to locate the Secret Service in order to get two cars out to the mansion. "By the time they arrived, it was obvious that we would not get to Athens in time for the unveiling of Rusk's portrait—which was fine with me, but Kennedy was scheduled to speak and he was very unhappy."

Throughout the ceremony honoring Rusk, Thompson made frequent trips out to the parking lot, where he had a quart of Wild Turkey stashed in the trunk of a Secret Service car. But when Carter began speaking, he said things that so startled Thompson that he forsook the bottle for his tape recorder. And one of those things was this: "I'm not qualified to talk to you about law, because in addition to being a peanut farmer, I'm an engineer and nuclear physicist, not a lawyer. . . . But I read a lot and I listen a lot. One of the sources of my understanding about the proper application of criminal justice and the system of equities is from Reinhold Niebuhr. The other source of my understanding about what's right and wrong in this society is from a friend of mine, a poet named Bob Dylan. Listening to his records about 'The Lonesome Death of Hattie Carroll' and 'Like a Rolling Stone' and 'The Times They Are A-Changin','' I've learned to appreciate the dynamism of change in a modern society. I grew up as a landowner's son. But I don't think I ever realized the proper interrelationship between the landowner and those who worked on a farm until I heard Dylan's record, 'I Ain't Gonna Work on Maggie's Farm No More.' So I come here speaking to you today about your subject with a base for my information founded on Reinhold Niebuhr and Bob Dylan."

Hunter Thompson could hardly believe his ears. This was jargon right out of the pages of *Rolling Stone* itself. "What the hell did I just hear?" he asked two Kennedy aides. One of them replied, "He said his top two advisers are Bob Dylan and Reinhold Niebuhr."

And then Carter went on to talk about judges who took bribes in return for reduced prison sentences, lawyers who deliberately cheated illiterate blacks, and cops who abused people's rights with something called a "consent search warrant."

"I had lunch this week with the members of the Judicial Selection Committee," said Carter, "and they were talking about a consent search warrant. I said I didn't know what a consent search warrant was. They said, 'Well, that's when two policemen go to a house. One of them goes to the front door and knocks on it, and the other one runs around to the back door and yells 'Come in.'"

It was, wrote Thompson, "the heaviest and most eloquent thing I have ever heard from the mouth of a politician. It was the voice of an angry agrarian populist, extremely precise in its judgments and laced with some of the most original, brilliant and occasionally bizarre political metaphors anybody in that room will ever be likely to hear. . . . I had already decided, by then, that I liked Jimmy Carter—but I had no idea that he'd made up his mind, a few months earlier, to run for the presidency in 1976. And if he had told me his little secret that day on the plane back to Atlanta, I'm not sure I'd have taken him seriously. . . . But if he had told me and if I had taken him seriously, I would probably have said that he could have my vote, for no other reason except the speech I'd just heard."

But, as columnist Vic Gold was later to observe, it was a speech which, if "delivered by Hubert Humphrey before a Minnesota bar group, would leave Thompson retching. But in dealing with the New Left press, Carter benefits from low prior expectations. This fits into [Ben] Wattenberg's Red-neck Chic thesis. Disenchanted with the political hero-images and crusades of the 1960s, Thompson and other New Journalists are now strangely drawn to a Southern Baptist who says 'Eye-talian' (a slip for which Jerry Ford would be mercilessly ridiculed) and owns a wool-hat brother who explains that pronunciation by telling newsmen, "Shit, it took us eighteen years just to learn to say 'colored.'"

Thompson got to talk with Carter on several other occasions. And he got to know him fairly well. One interview, fully taped, took place in Plains and lasted for six hours. The tape is liberally sprinkled with what Thompson described as "my own twisted comments about 'rotten fascist bastards . . . who peddle their asses all over Washington,' and 'these goddamn brainless fools who refuse to serve liquor in the Atlanta airport on Sunday.'" Apparently, Carter took it all in good spirit, for he never seemed to complain. Which may have prompted Thompson to note that "he is one of the most intelligent politicians I've ever met, and also one of the strangest." Strange in that Carter was one of those "people who talk about their feeling for Jesus"—in short, a "Jesus freak," a type around whom Thompson has "never felt comfortable."

Apparently, Carter felt comfortable around Hunter Thompson. For, as Thompson wrote, "Both Carter and his wife have always been amazingly tolerant of my behavior, and on one or two occasions they have had to deal with me in a noticeably bent condition. I have always been careful not to commit any felonies right in front of them, but other than that I have never made much of an effort to adjust my behavior around Jimmy Carter or anyone else in his family. . . ."

All of which proved somewhat puzzling to Robert Scheer, a free-lance journalist who interviewed Carter at length for a fateful feature in *Playboy*. Noting that Carter often sounded "like an evangelist," Scheer wondered how come he associated "with people so different from you in lifestyle and beliefs. Your publicized friendship with journalist Hunter Thompson, who makes no secret of his affinity for drugs and other craziness, is a good example." And Carter responded with some vigor:

> Well . . . I'm not a packaged article that you can put in a little box and say, 'Here's a Southern Baptist, an ignorant Georgia peanut farmer who doesn't have the right to enjoy music, who has no flexibility in his mind, who can't understand the sensitivities of an interpersonal relationship. He's gotta be predictable. He's gotta be for Calley and for the war. He's gotta be a liar. He's gotta be a racist.'
>
> You know, that's the sort of stereotype people tend to assume, and I hope it doesn't apply to me. And I don't see any mystery about having a friendship with Hunter Thompson. I guess it's something that's part of my character and it becomes a curiosity for those who see some mystery about someone of my background being elected President. I'm just a human being like everybody else. . . .

Scheer also asked how Carter's well-publicized relationship with Bob Dylan came about. It came about, said Carter, because of his sons' admiration for the poet of the Counterculture. They had been greatly influenced by Dylan in their attitudes toward civil rights, criminal justice, and the Vietnam war. "So when I read Dylan was going on tour again, I wrote him a little personal note and asked him to come visit me at the Governor's Mansion. I think he checked with Phil Walden of Capricorn Records and Bill Graham to find out what kind of guy *is* this, and he was assured I didn't want to use him, I was just interested in his music."

Dylan came one night, and they talked about "his music and about changing times and pent-up emotions in young people." They also discussed Israel. "But that's my only contact with Bob Dylan, that night."

Actually their meeting that night was not all that personal. The Governor had arranged a post-concert reception at the Mansion. Much to the surprise of Phil Walden, president of Capricorn Records, Dylan did show up. The party lasted until about two in the morning, without the appearance of another of the guests of honor, Gregg Allman. However, the rock star finally did turn up at the Mansion at four in the morning, apparently a bit stoned. Carter, who didn't seem to mind, sat around talking with Allman until nearly dawn. As Allman later commented, the Governor of Georgia was "really far-out."

Carter, discussing both Allman and Dylan, told Sally Quinn of *The Washington Post,* "I care for these people, and I respect them. They are performers who lead strange lives as viewed from the eyes of a peanut farmer. They are strange kids, and yet they look on me with love. There's a closeness I feel to these young people." And whenever he spoke before young people, Carter would express affection for the music of his "good friend," Bob Dylan. Which came as a surprise to the folksinger who, after all, had only met the Governor once. Another popular singer who had a similar experience was John Denver. Denver had flown to Atlanta so as to be able to spend some time with Carter on a Georgia-to-California flight. It was not to be. For nearly four hours, Denver waited to talk to the candidate. Only when the plane was about to land was he summoned before the presence. After ten minutes of conversation, Carter got off the plane, walked to a microphone and told a crowd of supporters that he had just flown in with his "good friend," John Denver.

"Far out," said the singer.

Jimmy Carter's introduction into this strange world came about through his friendship with Walden, the rock impresario whom Carter had once called "my one-man campaign organization." Walden, whose Macon, Georgia, firm became the largest independent recording company in the world, thanks to the Allman Brothers, had once told a woman friend he had two ultimate ambitions: "become the Governor of Georgia or control the President." That was shortly before he met a man with even greater ambitions, Jimmy Carter.

"At first blush," wrote Robert Sam Anson in *New Times,* "it is difficult to imagine a more unlikely relationship than that between the non-drinking, born-again Christian candidate for president and the hard-drinking, non-believing, drug-taking proprietor of Capricorn Records . . ."

They had first met in 1973 when Carter, as Governor, made a trip through Georgia. Stopping off in Macon, he visited the

Capricorn offices at the behest of one of his special aides. At first, Walden was "apprehensive," he later said, "because I thought it was just window dressing. But then I was surprised by his knowledge of our industry and his perceptive questions. There wasn't anything patronizing about him." The friendship blossomed. They kept in touch, often by phone. A year or so later, Carter agreed to be the guest of honor at an Allman Brothers concert in Atlanta. And, later, as part of his legislative package, Carter introduced a tough law prohibiting tape piracy, a major concern in the music industry. All of which, as Anson noted, benefited Phil Walden.

Illicit narcotics, of course, were part and parcel of the drug culture. But that didn't seem to concern Carter, whose friendship with Walden grew even closer. And it survived even when Walden's top star, Gregg Allman, became involved in a nasty drug scandal. To beat an almost certain jail term, Allman had turned state's evidence and testified against his valet and friend, who had provided him with drugs. The friend received fifteen years, and *The Macon Telegraph* condemned the government's decision to "let the real culprit go scot-free." The "real culprit," as far as most Maconites were concerned, was Allman. The sentence sent tremors through Capricorn Records; and Walden issued strict orders to all his employees, banning drugs from the premises. The word was out that the feds were out to nail Walden. "I hear the rumors, just like everybody," he told Anson. "I know there are a lot of people in this town who would like to pull me down, who would like to embarrass Jimmy Carter, but let them. There is nothing I have to hide."

Asked whether any of this was likely to affect his presidential race, Jimmy Carter claimed to be unaware of any drug investigation. And he stuck by Walden, who by now was one of his confidantes. In fact, Walden was among the first to be told of Carter's secret presidential ambitions. Walden offered to do whatever he could to help. And help he did to an incredible degree. For Walden was to raise enormous amounts of money at precisely the right times. "If it hadn't been for Phil," a former Carter staffer told Anson, "Carter would have been dead. We were just about through when Phil came along. Phil made everything possible. . . . Jimmy owes Phil an enormous debt."

There were those around Carter who sensed possible danger in the Capricorn Connection. Ham Jordan, for one, felt the scandals besetting the music industry could well tarnish the virtuous image which his man was seeking to project in the Watergate era. Watergate itself had come to a head with the resignation of President Nixon. And Carter was determined to make trust and integrity his major rallying cries to the electorate.

There were many other potential candidates making soundings across the country. It may have been early, but the Democrats smelled victory in 1976. There was considerable talk that Ted Kennedy could have the nomination just for the asking. Kennedy did play around with the idea for a while. Ironically, it was Watergate which helped do him in. For in the wake of that scandal, several publications, including *The Boston Globe* and the Sunday magazine of *The New York Times,* published belated, in-depth accounts suggesting that the Massachusetts Senator had not been fully responsive about Chappaquiddick. Finally, on September 23, 1974, Kennedy removed himself from presidential contention. He called the decision not to run "firm, final, and unconditional," adding there were "absolutely no circumstances" that would alter the decision. He was speaking out now "in order to ease the apprehensions within my family about the possibility of my candidacy, as well as to clarify the situation within my party."

The decision threw the race within the Democratic Party wide open. For a time, it appeared to confuse Carter and the people around him. For they had been operating on the assumption of a Kennedy candidacy. In fact, a month before Kennedy's surprise announcement, Jordan had written still another confidential memorandum in which he urged Carter to make it perfectly clear, in his forthcoming announcement of candidacy, that "you are totally committed to the race and will run against anyone anywhere; you will run against Wallace in the South and Kennedy in New England."

Strangely, Carter and his aides had mixed emotions about Kennedy's withdrawal. By remaining in the race, they had figured, Kennedy would frighten off other possible contenders. Now everyone would be getting into the act, particularly Democrats of liberal persuasion. But this, too, turned out to be a blessing in disguise. For it would give Carter the golden opportunity to separate himself from the others by picturing himself as a moderate with appeal to both sides of the ideological spectrum.

In his August 1974 memo, Jordan also emphasized the importance of Carter's presenting himself as a reasonable alternative to George Wallace, who despite his infirmity still was considered the most powerful Southern contender for 1976. The idea was to head off other "New South" Governors whom the media had been discussing as presidential prospects, most notably Florida's Askew, whose dislike of Carter was no secret, and Arkansas' Dale Bumpers, then contesting J. William Fulbright for his Senate seat. And one way for Carter to appear to the rest of the nation as a battler for a progressive "New South," Jordan wrote, was to lend a hand in defeating Lester Maddox's bid to return to the Georgia governorship. That would mean supporting George Busbee, who had edged out Carter's gubernatorial choice, Bert Lance, for second place in the primary. "If there's a runoff," warned Jordan, "you can be sure that David Broder and other nationally prominent columnists and reporters will be through here to cover [it]. I think it is critically important that the national press know you are working quietly and effectively behind the scenes to defeat Maddox. When it is all over, hopefully the news stories will read that the progressive administration of Jimmy Carter and his political organization in Georgia were major factors in Lester Maddox's defeat."

That Carter had to be persuaded to work "quietly and effectively behind the scenes" against Maddox, in order to project a national image, was most revelatory. For obviously, at the time, Carter had lost all interest in parochial Georgia politics, particularly after his buddy Bert Lance lost his race. And the alternative to Maddox, George Busbee, was not exactly palatable. For one thing, Busbee was almost as much a political enemy as was Maddox. From the start, Busbee had made it clear he was no admirer of Carter's much-vaunted reorganization scheme.

Maddox, of course, was defeated; and the new Governor, Busbee, soon let it be known that he had inherited a mess from Carter. But Carter turned the other cheek, knowing full well that Georgia politics rarely made the front pages of the nation's major newspapers. In fact, the only time most non-Georgians knew about his state's reorganization was when Carter brought it up on his far-flung travels as one of his remarkable achievements. But, by now, he was adding a fillip wherever he went. Typical was a luncheon he had with a group of newsmen in Los Angeles on October 28, 1974. Then, as Kenneth Reich reported in *The Los Angeles Times,* "a relatively little-known Governor from a Southern state . . . calmly announced, 'I'm running for President of the United States. I do not intend to lose.'"

The newsmen were startled. For a comparative political unknown to state flatly he would be the next President seemed the height of absurdity. One startled luncheon guest asked the obvious question: "How do you plan to become known, to establish your viability as a candidate?"

"I'm going to defeat George Wallace in the Florida primary," he replied. That primary, of course, was then more than sixteen months away. Otherwise, according to Reich, most of the newsmen who had listened to Carter were not overimpressed.

Nor was Representative Thomas P. O'Neill impressed when Jimmy Carter talked to him shortly after the November 1974 Congressional elections. The then House Majority Leader recalled how the Georgia Governor walked into his office on Capitol Hill and declared, "I'm going to be the next President." As a Bostonian used to a certain amount of blarney, Tip did not seem overwhelmed by the news. But Carter continued, "I know you're supporting Teddy Kennedy, but he's not going to run. Hubert Humphrey will make a lot of noise, but in the end he won't run, either. Jackson won't get off the ground. The man I've been running against—Mondale—just announced he's withdrawing."*

Walter F. "Fritz" Mondale had indeed taken himself out of the race. After spending nearly a year probing his presidential prospects, the Minnesota Senator decided the hell with it. "Basically," he announced, "I found I did not have the overwhelming desire to be President which is essential for the kind of campaign that is required." Moreover, he said, the idea of spending another whole year "sleeping in Holiday Inns" appalled him.

But there were others who quickly filled the vacuum left by the

---

* So confident was Carter about his prospects that, in early 1975, he visited the Mayor of Plains to discuss the need for a new zoning ordinance in town. Carter feared that once he became President tacky souvenir shops and motels would spring up all over the place.

departures of Kennedy and Mondale. They didn't mind "sleeping in Holiday Inns" or doing whatever else had to be done to win the biggest political prize their nation had to offer. Eventually, the list of potentials consisted of at least a dozen would-be saviors of mankind. Among them were eight liberals: Representative Morris K. Udall of Arizona; former Governor Terry Sanford of North Carolina; former Senator Fred R. Harris of Oklahoma; Governor Milton J. Shapp of Pennsylvania; Senator Birch Bayh of Indiana; R. Sargent Shriver, former Peace Corps director and George McGovern's 1972 running mate; Senator Frank Church of Idaho; and Governor Edmund G. Brown, Jr., of California. Two middle-of-the-road prospects were Senators Jackson of Washington and Lloyd Bentsen of Texas. On their right was Governor George Wallace, no longer strident on race but still seeking to "send a message" to Washington on other issues. In time, Wallace was to accuse Carter of stealing his Populist thunder. But, by then, it was too late.

On December 12, 1974, at the National Press Club in Washington, James Earl Carter, Jr.— "please call me Jimmy"—formally announced his candidacy to a less than enthusiastic audience. His wasn't even the first hat in the ring; "Mo" Udall had already declared his candidacy in Bedford, New Hampshire, a piece of news that didn't set off fireworks, either. But Carter's speech that day was particularly significant in that it set the tone of his forthcoming campaign. Referring to the discontent many felt in the wake of Vietnam and the disclosures of Watergate, Carter said, "It is time for us to reaffirm and to strengthen our ethical and spiritual and political beliefs." And he concluded, "It is now time to stop to ask ourselves the question which my last commanding officer, Admiral Hyman Rickover, asked me and every other young naval officer who serves or has served in an atomic submarine.

"For our nation—for all of us—that question is, 'Why not the best?'"

That night, in Atlanta, Carter told a rally of about 2,000 friends and supporters at the Civic Center, "I have to tell you with complete candor that being elected President of the United States is not the most important thing in my life. There are many other things that I would not do to be President. I would not tell a lie; I would not mislead the American people; I would not avoid taking a stand on a controversial issue which is important to our country or the world. And I would not betray your trust." And after completing his formal remarks, Carter returned to the microphone to say, "There is one thing I forgot to say and that is: I intend to win; I intend to be your next President."

But, outside Atlanta, Carter's announcement was greeted with smiles among the cognoscenti. After all, who could take an ex-Georgia Governor with zero ratings in the public-identification polls seriously? "Forbidden by Georgia law to succeed himself," *Newsweek* reported, "Carter is to leave office in January, and there are skeptics who wonder openly if his presidential bid isn't a last ego trip before an inevitable retirement to peanut farming."

In announcing, Carter also pledged to run in every primary—a pledge he was to keep, except for West Virginia. There he bowed to the state's favorite son, Robert Byrd, feeling he eventually would get the Senator's delegates—which he did. The decision to run everywhere was based on his plan to win the nomination in the primaries. Thus, he got out earlier and stayed out longer than the opposition—250 days in 1975 alone. As he once told his sister Ruth, "Honey, I can either will myself to sleep until 10:30 A.M. and get my ass beat, or I can will myself to get up at 6:00 A.M. and become President." And he put the whole family to work. Like him, Rosalynn hit the road, along with two grown sons and their wives; a third junior Carter worked in Atlanta headquarters; while Miz Lillian, back in Plains, babysat with daughter Amy.

Thus, while other potential candidates occupied themselves with general "explorations" of candidacy, the Carter team—and it already was in place—was at work. And working hard. For as Carter had written in a letter mailed to a list of prospective contributors, "The person who works hardest usually wins. Nobody will work harder than I will." But few national observers took either Carter or his letter very seriously—at first. As Robert Walters was later to point out in *National Journal*, most of them still regarded Carter "as a weak and frivolous candidate who was not to be taken seriously by either his fellow contenders or the voters."

Still being taken seriously, despite the fact that he had taken himself out of the race, was Ted Kennedy. "The guess here," wrote James Reston in *The New York Times,* "is that [the party elders] will probably turn to Mr. Kennedy in the end." And Kandy Stroud wrote a cover piece for *New York* which publisher Clay Felker personally entitled "Is Teddy Running? Are You Kidding . . . Do Birds Sing in the Morning?" And this, despite the fact that Carter had personally told Ms. Stroud that he had had a two-hour talk with Kennedy and the Senator had "reaffirmed that his withdrawal from the race is irrevocable. I believe him."

But, however they might have felt about Kennedy, few in the media believed that Jimmy Carter was of presidential quality. As Dick Tuck, the Democratic prankster-turned-journalist, was later to note in *Playboy,* "Jimmy Carter will get a little run for his money, but I can't help but think that to most people he looks more like a kid in a bus station with his name pinned on his sweater on his way to a summer camp than a President on his way to the White House. . . ." By this time, Kennedy indeed appeared out of the running. It was Tuck's guess in early 1976 that a ticket comprised of Governor Hugh Carey of New York and Senator Adlai Stevenson of Illinois would eventually make it into the White House. Hugh Carey! Such was the level of political prognostication during the 1976 presidential contest.

Carter, however, was scoring points with some members of the writing fraternity. Patrick Anderson, fresh from writing Watergate figure Jeb Stuart Magruder's bestselling *mea culpa,* was persuaded by Peter Bourne to meet and travel with Carter. The result was a panegyric, published just before the primaries in *The New York Times Magazine,* that couldn't have been better for Carter's image had Jody Powell written it himself. Entitled "Peanut Farmer for President," the article said: Personally, Carter is a soft-spoken, thoughtful, likable man, an introspective man who enjoys the songs of Bob Dylan, the poems of Dylan Thomas, and the writing of James Agee, William Faulkner, John McPhee, and Reinhold Niebuhr. Yet this slightly built, seemingly shy man is also one of the most driven, relentless, downright stubborn political campaigners who ever came out of the South. He stubbornly defied segregation in his home town of Plains; he stubbornly overcame overwhelming odds to become Governor of Georgia, and now he is just as stubbornly running for President."

Beginning in January 1975, when his term as Governor ended,

Carter was on the road five or six days a week. Thus, his being out of office proved to be a decided asset, not the disadvantage some had believed. For no longer did he have to pay attention to official duties at inconvenient moments while campaigning. Quietly, moreover, Carter was making progress—at first barely perceptible to the big media types in New York and Washington. After he had made three trips to California, for example, *The Los Angeles Times* reported on March 20, 1975 that "there are signs his presidential candidacy is beginning to make some headway . . . [he] appears to be effectively articulating a moral tone for his campaign that visibly impresses many of the people he meets." It was a moral tone which sounded particularly persuasive during the era of Watergate when public cynicism was so prevalent. Carter kept hitting hard on the theme he was not one of those "Washington politicians." And he emphasized his lack of identification with the Eastern Establishment by headquartering his campaign organization in Atlanta.

Another of Carter's assets was his unusual number of identities, each one of which enabled him to reach out to different groups. He was a farmer, a businessman, a former naval officer, a nuclear engineer, a former legislator and Governor, a Southerner, a Baptist and a born-again Christian. Carter himself has told the story of how, visiting the home of a woman musician in Ohio, he made a beeline for the harpsichord in her living room. The woman was entranced when Carter told her that he had studied at Annapolis to recordings of Wanda Landowska's harpsichord playing. The woman and her family became early volunteers in the Carter campaign.

Carter had other unique cultural tastes. Talking with Sally Quinn, after *The Washington Post* had decided to take him seriously, Carter told that newspaper's premiere interviewer that his favorite spectator sport was stock car racing; so much so that he "used to study different cars. I have records of automobile engines that I listen to." Different strokes for different folks!

Of course, as he later told *Playboy*, Carter had also developed an affection for "the country-music folks in Georgia, as well as the Atlanta Symphony Orchestra," thus covering all bases in the music world. "The first large contribution I got—$1,000—was from Robert Shaw, the music director of the Orchestra. We've been over at the Grand Ole Opry a few times and gotten to know people like Chubby Jackson and Tom T. Hall." But his most important contact remained Capricorn's Phil Walden. For there came a time, in the fall of 1975, when Carter appealed to the music impresario for help. Unless he could raise $50,000 in a hurry, Carter told Walden, he would have to quit running. Walden quickly arranged a concert in Providence, Rhode Island, featuring two of his groups, the Allman Brothers and Grinderswitch. With federal matching funds, the concert resulted in nearly $100,000, putting the Carter campaign back in business. More concerts followed, plus a very successful telethon, all of which raised some $400,000 (doubled after the federal funds were added) for Carter's coffers when it was needed the most. "Had it not been for rock and roll," commented Bob Anson in *New Times,* "especially the unique, hard-driving sound of Gregg Allman, Jimmy Carter might well be down in Plains today, worrying about nothing so much as this fall's peanut crop."

There was an additional benefit from Carter's association with the rock people. He was able to garner some badly needed publicity among the young from the concerts and his well-heralded meetings with rock performers. Even after Capricorn came upon hard times, in the wake of the drug scandals, Carter did not forsake Walden. The candidate turned up at the annual Capricorn Barbecue and Summer Games, wearing a T-shirt bearing that legend. Some of Carter's aides were appalled. "We ought to have someone check out these birds before the FBI does it for us," Anson quoted a senior adviser as saying.

Another of Carter's advantages in 1975 was his pledge to do battle with George Wallace in the Florida primary. In fact, Carter implored other candidates to stay out of the race so he could engage the Alabamian in a one-on-one contest. The liberal contenders and, for a time, Scoop Jackson, assented. They had no reason to believe they could fare well in a state which had long been a Wallace stronghold. Moreover, they felt that a Southerner had a chance at humiliating Wallace, a decided bonus for all concerned. Long after the Florida primary, Mo Udall rued his decision to remain out of the fray. He told Jules Witcover that Governor Askew had "said the election was decided when I decided not to go into Florida. . . . Clearly, I could have pulled enough votes away from Carter to give Wallace the win." And that most certainly would have stopped the Carter juggernaut. But Mo's supporters had come to him to say the Carter people had convinced them it was essential to beat Wallace. It sounded like a good idea. "It not only made very good sense to me," said Udall, "avoiding the swamp that is Florida, the immense amount of money and time you would have to plow into it, but I didn't think that the party was really going to nominate Jimmy Carter."

Reubin Askew had never made any secret of his antagonism toward Carter. Reportedly the liberal Governor felt Carter had doublecrossed him in failing to back him for the chairmanship of the Southern Governors Conference. Instead, Carter had supported the more conservative Dolph Briscoe of Texas, who had also been endorsed by Wallace. Thus, when pressures were put on him to back Carter as the alternative to Wallace, Askew took no position. And, later, Askew gave public support to Scoop Jackson's presidential bid in the Florida primary.

In that primary, Carter won the important support of fellow Trilateralist Leonard Woodcock, president of the United Automobile Workers, and such prestigious fund-raisers as Max Palevsky and Harold Willens. Anything to eliminate Wallace, they thought, even supporting a comparative unknown.

Perhaps Carter's most important catch at the time was Andrew Young, the black Congressman from Atlanta and strong voice in the civil rights movement. Young, who didn't particularly like Carter (he had not supported him for Governor in 1970), liked Wallace a lot less. Thus, he became the first prominent Georgia political figure to endorse Carter, and he was to campaign vigorously· among Florida's blacks. Also joining up was the Reverend Martin Luther King, Sr., father of the slain civil rights leader. King, a lifelong registered Republican, had been won over when his son's portrait had been hung in the State Capitol.

One prominent black leader refused to be persuaded. Asked by an intermediary to endorse Carter as a reasonable alternative to Wallace, State Senator Julian Bond replied, "Fuck him! I'm going to run myself."

"We didn't care much," Ham Jordan said later. "We had Andy

and we had 'Daddy' King. We knew that that meant we'd get Coretta [the younger King's widow]. We didn't much care what the great Senator Bond had to say about things."

Beating Wallace in Florida was a major part of Carter's strategy. The idea was to demonstrate to Democrats elsewhere that he could take the South from Wallace. A moderate Southerner like himself, he argued, could restore the solid South to the party. Thus, Carter made thirty-five separate visits to the Sunshine State prior to the primary.

But Carter was also spending a tremendous amount of time in Iowa, addressing hundreds of small groups and organizing carefully. Iowa, in Carter's estimation, had become important because its precinct caucuses constituted the first definitive step in the nation's presidential delegate selection process. George McGovern had scored his first media impact with a modest showing there back in 1972. Carter thought he could do better. "At that point," Jody Powell said later, "*The Des Moines Register* became more important than *The Washington Post*. The only coverage you get at that stage is local. We might not have known much about anything else, but we did know local media."

And it was to convince *The Register* of their man's strength in Iowa that Carter's people indulged in the kind of political tricks that had given some of Nixon's advance men a bad name. What had happened was this: the state Democratic Party, aware of media interest in Iowa as the first state to pick delegates in 1976, arranged to hold a large Jefferson-Jackson Day fund-raising affair at Iowa State University. All the candidates, including Carter, were invited to speak.

When *The Register* announced it would poll all those attending the dinner, Tim Kraft, Carter's Iowa coordinator, who later became a top White House aide, sought to pack the hall. For those unwilling to pay fifty dollars a couple for a chicken dinner, Kraft advised paying two dollars to sit in the balcony. And in a memo, Kraft suggested that "one probably could drift down from the balcony onto the floor and vote"—even though this was against the procedures set up by *The Register*. A number of Carterites, not entitled to vote, did infiltrate, appropriating ballots along with the chicken dinners. And the result was that Carter bagged 23 percent of the vote, almost twice that received by the undeclared Hubert

Humphrey. Bayh came in with 10 percent; with everybody else an also-ran.

Thus, as a result of a tiny but padded vote, Carter overnight became a man to watch in the presidential sweepstakes. "Carter Appears to Hold a Solid Lead in Iowa as the Campaign's First Test Approaches," said a headline in *The New York Times*. The story by R.W. Apple, Jr., told how Carter "appears to have taken a surprising but solid lead" in Iowa's delegate race. "Whether he can maintain his early lead here when the contest switches from opinion leaders to rank-and-file voters is unclear." Obviously, Carter had seized the media advantage from the other declared candidates—Udall, Bayh, Fred Harris, and Sargent Shriver.

The *Register* tabulation sent a scare into the camps of Carter's opponents. And for several months thereafter, the Democratic hopefuls crisscrossed the frozen cornland by auto, plane, and camper. Like Carter, they stood in subzero weather outside factory gates grasping outstretched hands. And they flooded the mails with thousands of pieces of literature as well as saturating the airwaves with radio and TV spots. The prize hardly seemed worth the gargantuan effort: Iowa would pick only forty-seven delegates out of the total of 3,008 who would select the nominee at the national convention. But, as a curtain raiser, the Iowa precinct caucuses—as Jimmy Carter well knew—could give one candidate a publicity break of enormous proportions and a jump on his rivals.

So what happened when all the votes were counted? Of some 45,000 Democrats who voted in several thousand precinct caucuses throughout Iowa, the biggest bloc—over 37 percent—went to "uncommitted," a fact generally lost in most media reports the next day. But what came through loud and clear was that Jimmy Carter had come through with 27.6 percent of the vote, twice as many as obtained by his closest rival, Birch Bayh of Indiana. But, more important, Jimmy Carter had achieved a media victory. Roger Mudd had named him the "clear winner" on *The CBS Evening News*, adding that "no amount of badmouthing by the others can lessen the importance of Jimmy Carter's finish." And all this at a time when the Gallup Poll showed Carter with only a 5 percent national standing, behind six other candidates.

How did Carter do it? In the first place, he campaigned longest and hardest of all the candidates ("I'm Jimmy Carter and I'm going to be your next President"). Along with members of his family, his organization was reinforced by volunteers and out-of-state supporters. But, most of all, he knew how to appeal to the Iowa voter, presenting himself as a plainspoken peanut farmer and small businessman who wanted to straighten things out in Washington. Exploiting the fact that he had never been a member of Congress or the federal bureaucracy, Carter began a typical speech, "I'm not from Washington." Applause. "I'm not a lawyer." Applause. "I think this is the time for someone outside of Washington of about my age. . . ." Laughter.

Carter was also aided in Iowa by his extraordinary ability to be on both sides of controversial issues. One such was the inflammatory question of abortion. The Iowa Catholic Conference sent out a newsletter suggesting that Carter would support a constitutional amendment against abortion. The fact was the Georgian was on record as having opposed such an amendment, but he managed to fuzz the issue by saying he would favor a "national statute" limiting abortion. Also, he had told one young "pro-life" woman at one precinct meeting that he could possibly back some other, unspecified type of anti-abortion amendment. His ambiguous stance won him the support of Right-to-Lifers. In heavily Catholic Carroll County, for example, he overwhelmed the only Catholic candidate, Sargent Shriver, by 47 percent to 3 percent. Columnists Evans and Novak subsequently reported that Shriver's Iowa chairman, Don O'Brien, had desperately sought to stem the tide by convincing Monsignor Frank Brady of Sioux City that Carter was trying to work both sides of the street. Checking Atlanta, the Monsignor was shocked to learn that Carter had indeed been opposed to an anti-abortion constitutional amendment. But, by then, it was too late. And Carter couldn't have cared less. He had gotten what he wanted, and that was all that mattered. Carter's handling of the abortion issue in Iowa was a harbinger of things to come. Deliberate ambiguity became the order of the day.

But there was nothing ambiguous about how Jimmy felt about the grand old man of Democratic politics—Hubert Humphrey. In the flush of his Iowa victory, Carter took a potshot at the Minnesotan, then cogitating whether to enter the primaries for still another try for the presidency. Carter stressed Humphrey's age (sixty-four) and his "reputation as a loser."

The second caucus test came in Mississippi. And here Wallace was the front-runner. Carter was hoping to surprise the pundits, but it proved to be no contest. Wallace ran away with 44 percent of the vote; while Carter got 14 percent; Shriver 12 percent; and Bentsen 1.6 percent. When Carter heard the news in Vermont, his aide Greg Schneiders sought to console him. After all, said Schneiders, Mississippi wasn't all that important.

"I know," said Carter, "but I hate to lose anything."

However, Carter went on to win minor victories in Oklahoma and Maine. The fact that they were victories gave him a certain momentum and helped to create still more interest in his candidacy. Contributions began to pick up. And Carter needed all the money he could lay his hands on. For he had made fairly heavy expenditures of manpower and funds in the early going, spending $2 million on his gamble to show well in the early contests. And this included his first major battle—the nation's first and best-publicized primary, in New Hampshire. Carter was ready. He had been visiting the Granite State for over a year. And he had something else going for him—a planeload of Georgians who knocked on doors in Manchester and elsewhere, distributing bags of peanuts and pleading for votes for "Jimmeh." The "peanut brigade," as they were to be called, was a far cry from the groups of volunteers usually making the rounds for more liberal candidates. Fred Harris, for example, had attracted a motley crew of "far-outs" who, tromping through the snow, probably lost votes for the self-styled Populist.

Again Carter had everything going his way. As in Iowa, he was running against a liberal pack, dominating the moderate to conservative spectrum. And he wasn't hurt any when his old foe Lester Maddox showed up in New Hampshire proclaiming his intention to expose Carter as a "radical liberal." Said Lester, "He's two-faced, he's the biggest phony I've ever known, and I just hope to God the American people find out before it's too late." Carter's more liberal opponents thought likewise; but they found it difficult to draw a bead on the Georgian. Udall, for example, complained to reporters that he found it difficult to understand how Carter managed to obtain labor support. For, after all, he refused "to fight for the union shop." And Birch Bayh, in radio ads, asked, "How can a man who is a former Governor and has been going around the country running for President say he isn't a politician?"

But that was Carter's line, and he was scoring with it. To voters disillusioned by Vietnam and Watergate, he also presented himself as a man of utmost integrity, someone whom they could trust. "You know," he said in his standard stump speech, "if we could just have a government as good and as honest and as decent and as competent and as compassionate and as filled with love as are the American people, that would be a wonderful thing—and I believe we can, don't you?" And he would conclude, "If I ever lie to you, if I ever mislead you, if I ever avoid a controversial issue, then don't vote for me, because I won't be worthy of your vote if I'm not worthy of your trust." Of course, as later events were to dramatically illustrate, all of this jargon was vapid nonsense. But, at the time, Carter cornered the trust market. And, according to his pollster, Pat Caddell, "the trust thing" was what ultimately won him the nomination. For without it, "he couldn't have made it," Caddell told Jim Wooten. "He was the only one who could have used it as the basic thrust of a presidential campaign. Most people would really rather trust other people than distrust them, except in politics; most people have a reason to distrust most candidates. Jimmy was a stranger in town. They had no reason to distrust him, and he didn't give them one."

Dave Broder, one of the more astute political observers, had been among the first columnists to evaluate Carter's talk of love and trust. In a column, headlined "Love Is Sweeping the Country," Broder noted that the Georgian was the first presidential candidate since William Wintergreen who talked about bringing love to the White House. And William Wintergreen was a character in the Pulitzer prize-winning musical *Of Thee I Sing*.

According to Broder, there was "genius" in Carter's discernment "that, after the spiritual travails of the past decade, voters are ready to listen to someone who can talk, without visible embarrassment, of something as simple and basic as love." But Broder was not all that awestruck. For behind all of Carter's mawkish phraseology, there lurked—wrote Broder— "a thoroughly tough, opportunist politician, who comes into almost any competition with his elbows out."

And, despite his repeated insistence that he would never lie, the suspicion arose that he wasn't always telling the truth. Thus, during the New Hampshire primary, he sat one afternoon with a reporter in a Manchester restaurant. The reporter wanted to know about Carter's meeting with William Loeb, the conservative publisher of *The Manchester Union-Leader*. Loeb, of course, was the *bête noire* of liberal Democrats. The fact that Carter had a friendly session with him had raised a few eyebrows.

"When you met with Loeb, did you make some sort of deal?" the reporter asked. Carter said there had been no deal. "But you did meet with him, didn't you?" the reporter persisted. "Yes," said Carter, but the meeting had nothing to do with politics. "No politics?" the reporter continued. "That's hard to believe." At which point Carter got so angry that the vein in his right temple began to throb.

"Listen," he whispered, "I'm not a liar. You get that in your head. I'm not a liar." Raising himself from the table, Jimmy Carter strode out of the restaurant.

Three weeks before the New Hampshire vote, Broder disclosed that back in 1971 then Governor Carter had written a letter to the National Right-to-Work Committee, an organization opposed to the repeal of Section 14(b) of the Taft-Hartley Act, which permitted states to bar union-shop contracts. In his letter, on official stationery, Carter wrote, "I stated during my campaign that I was not in favor of doing away with the right-to-work law, and that is a position I still maintain." During his 1970 campaign, of course, Carter had warned that his opponent, Carl Sanders, intended to repeal Georgia's right-to-work law, thus opening up the state to what was viewed as forced unionization.

But, as the White House beckoned, Carter's position sounded a bit different. Except he insisted it wasn't. "My position now is the same as in 1970, when I was running for Governor. I told the labor representatives from Georgia that any time the repeal of the right-to-work law could be passed by the legislature, then I would sign it. That has always been my position since 1970. I would do the same as President."

That was not always his position. And that was pointed out in the closing weeks of the New Hampshire primary. But the revelation did little good. Jimmy Carter ran well among trade unionists. When the final results were in, Carter had won a plurality of the vote (almost 30 percent), with 24 percent going to Udall, 16 percent to Bayh, 11 percent to Harris, and 9 percent to Shriver. By splitting the liberal vote four ways, Carter's foes gave him what appeared to be a clear-cut victory. The fact that 60 percent of the state's voters had voted for the four more "liberal" candidates was ignored by the media. Instead, Walter Cronkite proclaimed the results had given Carter "a commanding head start in the race," and Roger Mudd declared Carter's victory "substantial." The following week, *Newsweek* declared him the "unqualified winner." And his picture appeared on the covers of both *Time* and *Newsweek*. On the inside pages, he received 2,630 lines of coverage, while Udall, who came in second, wound up with 96 lines. During the week following New Hampshire, Carter received three times the television news coverage of his major rivals and four times as much front page newspaper coverage.

All this was analyzed in a paper delivered the following year by Professor Thomas E. Patterson of Syracuse University before the American Political Science Association. In the paper, Patterson discussed the press handling of the 1976 presidential primaries, concluding that "only the winner in a state seemed important" to the media. "No matter how close the voting, the headlines and most of the coverage went to the winner, and he alone. . . . Moreover, the press showed little hesitancy in projecting the results of a single primary." The result, therefore, was an exaggerated picture of a candidate's national standing, one that the press itself had helped to create.

As a result of New Hampshire, Jimmy Carter was well on his way. He clearly had the momentum and the psychological advantage. But he was also acquiring the problems of the front-runner.

On the very day Carter was winning the New Hampshire primary, Broder reported that after a meeting of Democratic Governors in Washington "there was a spontaneous outpouring of misgivings about Carter." When asked about published reports of his former colleagues' coolness, Carter acted with icy disdain. "I'm not depending on a few Governors to put me in office," he said. "I'm not running for chairman of the Governors Conference."

At the same time, he and his record were coming under increasingly hostile examination. Questions were raised about his claimed liberal credentials. But the candidate was braced for the expected onslaught. "The only way to avoid that kind of attack," Carter shrugged, "is to lose."

And, as Jimmy Carter once pledged, he did not intend to lose.

10
THE 1976 PRIMARIES

JAMES EARL CARTER JR.— "I PREFER TO BE CALLED JIMMY"— had until then generally led a charmed life in the national media. After being anointed by *Time* as the star of a cover article on the "New South," Carter for five years rarely felt the stings of antagonistic prose. But now, as he moved into the forefront of the Democratic battle for the presidential nomination, Carter began to feel the heat.

First came a column by Rowland Evans and Robert Novak alleging that Carter had failed his own "candor" standards on any number of issues. For example, he had claimed to have "worked hard" on a voluntary school busing plan for Atlanta and was proud of it. "But," commented the columnists, "nobody in Atlanta, either with the school board or the NAACP, remembers Governor Carter working on the plan 'hard' or otherwise. He did sit in on one NAACP school board negotiating session as an observer, objecting to any busing in Atlanta. 'For him to claim that he did anything to help a settlement, is an outright lie,' one black leader told us." *Esquire*, which also looked into the matter, elaborated, ". . . the feeling at the time was that Carter shrewdly avoided any identification with the whole business until it had been settled and seemed okay." Within days of the Evans and Novak column accusing him of misrepresenting his role in Atlanta's school desegregation, Carter responded on *Meet the Press* with what he said was a letter from the city's integration leaders attesting to his role. But, as Joe Kraft noted in a column describing Carter as "the media candidate," the Georgian "seemed to me to be on the defensive" in responding to various charges on the NBC broadcast.

Evans and Novak had also quoted Carter as having said on November 30, 1975, "I've been a member of Common Cause for a long time, and participated in the evolution of the ideas that led to the [federal election] law." But the facts were that it was his wife, Rosalynn, who had joined the liberal group late in Carter's governorship, and there was no record of Carter himself ever participating in election reform.

Also on November 30, Carter had explained his 1972 nomination speech for Senator Jackson as follows: "I've known Scoop since I was working under Admiral Rickover on the atomic submarine program and he was a junior member of Congress involved with atomic energy, so I don't have any apology to make about a long-standing friendship with Scoop."

Jackson, however, had no such memory. According to the columnists, the Senator was certain he had not met Carter until he ran for Governor in 1970. "Furthermore," they reported, "nuclear officials doubt a Navy lieutenant in operations would have had much contact with a member of the Joint Atomic Energy Committee or, for that matter, with Rickover."

When told what Jackson had said, Carter recalled reminiscing about the "old days with Scoop" with the late Senator Richard B. Russell over breakfast in 1970. But a former Russell intimate said, "Carter has greatly exaggerated his relations with Senator Russell," adding that Carter had leaked Russell's alleged deathbed wish that he be elected Governor. "I know that to be a lie," the Russell man said.

"Actually," commented Evans and Novak, "'fibbing' better describes falsely claiming credit—common among candidates, who usually have more than a little Baron Munchausen in them. But Carter is the anti-Washington, anti-government, anti-lawyer candidate telling audiences, 'I'll never lie to you' and setting post-

Watergate standards of honesty. Against that pledge, old enemies in Georgia use the words 'lie' and 'liar' with disturbing frequency to describe him."

Even *Time,* his major supporter in the national media, questioned Carter's penchant for hyperbole. The magazine's Marshall Loeb and Stanley Cloud asked the candidate about why he had been listing, among others, Wilbur Cohen, former Secretary of Health, Education, and Welfare, and George Ball, former Undersecretary of State, as people he consulted regularly on public policy, when, in fact, he had never even sought their advice. Carter conceded he had made an "inadvertent error" in overstating the relationship. He had asked both men if he could consult them, but thus far neither he nor his staff had done so. After this minor embarrassment became known, Carter carefully refrained from again mentioning their names as advisers.

About the same time, *The Village Voice* published an article entitled "The Riddle of Jimmy Carter," in which James Ridgeway and Alexander Cockburn alleged, among other things, that the man who now was courting the liberals and "doves" had advocated a court-martial for Commander Lloyd M. Bucher shortly after the captain of the electronic spy ship *U.S.S. Pueblo* had surrendered to the North Koreans. Carter, they claimed, had stated that Bucher should have fought the North Koreans to the death and gone down with all guns blazing.

As a candidate who vowed never to tell lies, stated that he was not really a politician, and exuded confidence occasionally bordering on arrogance, Jimmy Carter necessarily invited close examination. At first, he insisted he welcomed such probing. In fact, he said, it was good for him and good for the country. "If I can't stand the scrutiny," he said, "I don't deserve to be President." But when questions actually were raised about his record or seemingly contradictory views, the candidate could hardly contain his annoyance. His dislike of the media soon became obvious. "To have this concentrated attention on myself and the other candidates by the press at this early stage is really extraordinary," Carter told Jules Witcover in late January 1976. He didn't think that the press should be so demanding of "final answers on complicated questions at the early stage of a campaign. . . . No matter how demanding people might be, it would be a very serious violation of my word of honor if I pretended to know those answers." Thus, as Witcover noted, even a refusal to give a plain answer to a plain question was converted by Carter into an act of political morality.

But Carter and his associates nearly became unglued when they learned that *Harper's* was soon to come out with an investigative report titled "Jimmy Carter's Pathetic Lies." Written by Steven Brill, twenty-five, a free-lancer out of Yale Law School who was once an assistant to former New York Mayor John V. Lindsay, the article was an indictment of the former Georgia Governor, members of his staff, and some of the means they employed to seek the nomination. "This is the paradox of Jimmy Carter," wrote Brill. "His is the most sincerely insincere, politically antipolitical, and slickly unslick campaign of the year. Using an image that is a hybrid of honest, simple Abe Lincoln and charming, idealistic John Kennedy, he has packaged himself to take the idol-seekers for a long ride. . . . The tantalizing promises Carter is making are potentially more disillusioning than the myths he is floating about his past record. They are vague enough to please everyone—for now—and Carter hypnotizes his audience with them so effectively that most seem to go away convinced that all his pledges will materialize about four hours after his inauguration."

In an effort to head off any political damage, Carter met with his top aides in Atlanta several weeks before the magazine was due to hit the newsstands. Powell had obtained a copy of the article by calling *Harper's* to ask for an advance text. "I explained that the text of the article would not become generally available for about three weeks, and asked Powell not to distribute copies of it," Lewis H. Lapham, the magazine's editor, later wrote. "Yes, sir, [Powell] said, on my word of honor. That was Friday afternoon. I hadn't yet read in *Time* magazine that Powell had been expelled from the Air Force Academy for cheating on a history examination, and I did not yet appreciate his indifference to the meaning of language."

On the following Monday, February 2, Powell distributed photocopies of the article to reporters friendly to Carter. "At the same time," reported Lapham, "he bruited it about that Brill had flunked out of Yale Law School, that his article had been commissioned by Birch Bayh, and that the ADA had refused to publish his study of Jackson because of its incompetence." Actually, all of the allegations were untrue. Americans for Democratic Action, for example, did publish Brill's twenty-one-page report on Jackson, which contended that on many issues of domestic policy the Washington Senator frequently was on the conservative side.*

"Also on Monday," continued Lapham, "I received the first of several telephone calls from citizens of Georgia representing themselves as longtime readers of *Harper's,* a journal that they previously had esteemed for its integrity. With robotlike precision they denounced Brill's article as 'garbage.' The mail reflected the same uniformity. The letters were so strikingly similar that Brill took the trouble to make a random call to one of the correspondents, a man by the name of Tom Beard who had assumed the character of a subscriber interested in literature. He answered the phone at Carter headquarters in Atlanta."

On Tuesday, February 3, Carter began telling the television cameras that Brill's article had been "widely distributed" and that it was "very, very vicious . . . full of outright untruths . . . the most remarkable piece of fiction I've ever read." Of course, the only copies of the article that at that time had been distributed were those circulated by Jody Powell. The response was predictable. Jack Germond of *The Washington Star* termed the article "but the latest round in what has become a liberal assault on Carter perhaps unmatched in harshness and intensity in any presidential campaign of the postwar period." And *Time,* still going great guns for Jimmy, quoted a "Washington-based political correspondent" as describing Brill as "a hit man . . . the liberal enforcer." And down in Florida, Rosalynn Carter also described Steve Brill as "the liberal hit man," claiming he "was hired by the ABC group (Anybody But Carter)" to defame her husband. "The article is all false," she went on. "Brill said we removed things from the archives. But when Jimmy was elected we turned over all our records to the archives. The archivist even called us and said he wished everybody could be as thorough as Jimmy." And as late

---

*Brill's article on Jackson may have been "incompetent" according to Powell, but Carter's volunteers handed out copies by the hundreds in the closing days of the Florida primary, claiming that it was the work of a careful, sober, accurate, and truthful reporter.

as March 10, Howard K. Smith on ABC News referred to the *Harper's* article as part of a "publicity gang-up" against Carter.

"The slander," wrote Lapham in his "Easy Chair" column, "had been repeated often enough over a long enough period of time (roughly three weeks) to endow it with the solidity of cliché. The issue had been transferred from Carter's record to his critics, and by overcoming the latter Carter appeared to have redeemed the former."

At the same time, Lapham charged that Brill was the victim of "character assassination" unloosed by the Carterites. "The managers of the campaign to discredit Brill went about their work with an eagerness reminiscent of the tactics used by the Nixon Administration," he wrote. And he went on to accuse *Time* of having delivered a "malicious broadside" against Brill as part of a plot to elect Carter President. Lapham also made note of *Time's* advertisement promoting its election coverage and featuring Carter sitting in a rocking chair. It looked, wrote Lapham, "very much like an ad for Jimmy Carter." Which it most certainly did. And it appeared in magazines across the country: in *People, Forbes, Harper's, Atlantic, Psychology Today, New Times, Sports Illustrated,* and other journals. One media expert, writing for *MORE,* estimated the cost of the space as worth about $100,000, and "the publicity value cannot be calculated."

But *Time's* Henry Anatole Grunwald, normally the calmest of managing editors, shot off an angry missive to *Harper's*, calling "Lapham's general description of how this [Brill] story was supposedly handled at *Time* . . . so absurd as to defy comment," and denying that *Time* had "endorsed Carter or any other candidate." Yet there can be little argument about the fact that *Time's* stories on Carter constituted more or less straight puffery. "Now that he is a real challenger," *Time* said in a major profile, "Carter is being asked to pass sterner tests than other candidates. He has been accused of fudging the issues. He has been charged with telling little white lies—and indeed he has occasionally exaggerated past accomplishments—along with some big ones. But he seems mostly to be faulted for advancing himself at the expense of others. . . ." (*Time,* however, did not explain those "little white lies," exaggerations, and "big ones.")

Time added: "The most difficult of all the candidates to

categorize, Carter is liberal on some issues, moderate to conservative on others. At a time when many in his audiences want simple answers, he recognizes that issues are complicated—and sometimes gives complex or even confusing answers. But, more often, his positions are clear."

Another publication given to puffery about Carter was *The National Enquirer*, the nation's most widely read weekly tabloid. And one main reason was the Georgian's professed belief in flying saucers. All of which was made clear to members of *The Enquirer*'s Washington bureau. As Inette Miller-Conte, a former *Time* correspondent, put it, "Nothing unfavorable about Jimmy Carter was going to be published in *The Enquirer*." Only favorable material. Thus, on April 13, 1976, six stories covering two pages were devoted to Carter. They included an analysis of his handwriting, three "top psychiatrists" explaining "The Secret of His Astonishing Appeal," and a "truth detector" test that revealed the Georgian as "The Honest Man Who'll Never Lie to the American Public." A week later, another article appeared, entitled, "Gov. Carter's Wife: Jimmy and I Lived in a Haunted House for Five Years."

But the *pièce de résistance* was published on June 8, 1976. In inch-tall letters, the front page announced "JIMMY CARTER: THE NIGHT I SAW A UFO. . . . If Elected I'll Make All the Govt's UFO Information Public." And the future President was quoted, "I am convinced that UFO's exist because I've seen one."

This, actually, was an old story. Carter's claim to have personally observed an Unidentified Flying Object was made in 1973. This was three years after he had the close encounter in Leary, Georgia, where he had been campaigning before the Lions Club. Later, he claimed to have spotted the UFO thirty degrees above the horizon; and that ten or twelve others saw the "shiny and saucer-shaped" object with him. But no one in Leary who had been with the future President at the time of the supposed sighting has any memory of it, according to Tom Tiede of Newspaper Enterprise Association. And the Mayor of the town, Stanley Shephard, wondered why any extraterrestrial visitors would be interested in observing Leary, Georgia, in the first place. "All we got here to see," he said, "is that dust coming from the peanut processing plant." And Herman Balliatt, Lions Club secretary in 1970, said Carter himself was the closest thing to a local UFO: "Those days, nobody knew who the hell he was."*

During the primaries, one of the positions Carter was not too clear about was his tax program. But he kept promising a more detailed analysis of what he proposed. Basically, however, he called for the elimination of most tax deductions, which, in turn, would permit a general lowering of tax withholding rates. Asked at a Boston forum whether he also favored the elimination of tax deductions for home mortgages, a refuge for millions of home-owners, Carter said it "would be among those that I would like to do away with."

A *Boston Globe* reporter, Robert L. Turner, phoned the other Democratic candidates for comment. And they all expressed shock that Carter would single out homeowners for such action. Scoop Jackson, for example, said that without the deduction "millions of middle-income people would be forced to sell their homes. . . . The mortgage interest deduction is one of the few tax advantages that the average family gets." Pennsylvania Governor Milton Shapp thought "it would be disastrous for the housing industry" and would raise mortgage interest payments 30 to 40 percent. And Mo Udall said he believed the controversy "could be a sleeper issue."

That's exactly what Carter feared. He knew he had blundered. But, instead of backtracking, he took the offensive. In effect, he branded his critics as unpatriotic. How, otherwise, can one interpret his somewhat incoherent remarks in Boston's Faneuil Hall? "I don't believe," he said, "that the nation appreciates personal animosities and attacks among candidates hoping to be President of the American people." Such attacks, he went on, "won't hurt me, but I'm afraid it might hurt the country. . . . One of the things that concerns the people . . . is the bickering, squabbling, hatred, and animosities, and blame handed back and forth in our great nation's capital in Washington. This is not good

---

*As President, Carter seemed to have lost interest in UFOs. And, according to *New York* magazine, "the White House staff hasn't been eager to talk about the President's belief in flying saucers," going so far as to deny *Time*'s report that Carter had seen *Close Encounters of the Third Kind* several times. All that the President's men would admit was that he had seen the film once at Camp David. The *Enquirer*, believing he had reneged on a pledge to make public all UFO information in U.S. files, ran this headline on May 27, 1978: "Carter Broke His Promise on UFO's."

for our country. I want to be the next President of this country. I expect to be the next President. But that doesn't mean that I have to take my political success from personal hatred [and] attacks on the character and ability of my opponents. . . . [The people] have got enough judgment, enough common sense, and know me well enough so that these attacks will hurt the ones who make the attacks."

Carter's opponents were dumbfounded by the outburst. All they had done was to criticize—and quite legitimately—one of his seeming gaffes. It was, after all, a hard-fought political contest. Now they were being accused of indulging in cheap politics at the nation's expense. No wonder, then, that a Udall aide was quoted at the time as saying he would rather vote for Gerald Ford than support Carter. "Carter's so damn slick," he said. "What monopoly does he have on goodness? To me, he's dangerous." And Alan Baron, press secretary to George McGovern, had this to say: "By saying that he would never tell a lie, Carter decided for himself that that's going to be his standard. Well, fine, let's hold him to it." By now, too, mutterings arose from within the Democratic National Committee about how its top echelons had been "snookered" by the soft-spoken, ever-smiling Georgian. Chairman Bob Strauss, who had unwittingly opened the door for Carter's candidacy, was said to be aghast at the progress he was making. For Strauss had other candidates in mind, politicians more in the traditional mold. That there were "some strains" between Strauss and Carter during this period was no secret.

And while Carter assumed an above-the-battle posture in the Massachusetts primary, Jody Powell was sticking it to his boss' rivals. Typical was his remark while having drinks with newsmen in a Boston bar: "Wait until we get Udall on the fact he didn't come out for impeachment until three days before Nixon resigned." This from the press secretary of a candidate who had just sounded off against such attacks. The question was indeed raised by a caller to a radio talk show on which Udall was the guest. "The reason I waited," replied Udall, "was because I knew if Nixon was going to be impeached, I was going to have to be a member of the jury, and I wanted to wait until he had time to defend himself. I thought it was important we get Nixon out, but to do this the right way. I was trying to be a responsible member of the jury."

Off mike, the talk show host said the Carter people were "vicious." He couldn't "pinpoint it, but they're like the Sun Myung Moon people. They're dangerous. They smile a lot, but behind that façade, they're mean."

"Yeah," Udall responded, "all the Southern Governors detest him."

Meanwhile, Jackson was coming on strong in Massachusetts. And he was touching most ethnic bases, scoring particularly among the Jews, who considered him the Senate's foremost defender of Israel. Also, at a time when a federal judge had ordered an unpopular busing plan for Boston's school districts, the Senator took out full-page newspaper ads, proclaiming, "I am against forced busing."

"I'm getting kind of nervous about Massachusetts," pollster Pat Caddell told Carter the night before the vote. "Jackson's really coming on."

"I can't believe that," Carter replied. "That defies everything I know about politics. . . ."

Carter was hoping that the momentum from Iowa and New Hampshire would carry him to victory in the Bay State. It was not to be. Instead, Senator Jackson emerged as the big winner, with nearly 23 percent of the vote. Udall came in second with 18 percent. Wallace was one point behind Udall with 17 percent. Carter came in an embarrassing fourth with 14 percent.

Returning from Boston, correspondent Kandy Stroud ran into Vince Clephas, a top communications aide to Bob Strauss, walking through National Airport. Clephas said the Democratic National Chairman was "delighted" with Jackson's victory. "We finally got rid of Carter. He can't roll 'em up now. The bloom's off the rose. Now, four candidates will come to the convention with an equally divided vote, and the convention will nominate a regular. Not Carter. He's not a regular."

Nevertheless, the fact that Jackson had won a primary much larger than New Hampshire's with 23 percent of the vote was generally dismissed by the media. And the reason was, as Paul Weaver later wrote in *The New York Times Magazine*, that reporters generally did not like Jackson. Whereas Carter's vote in New Hampshire was considered a "substantial victory," giving him "a commanding head start," Jackson's vote in a state seven times as large was viewed as only "a strong finish" that "scrambled the race." In effect, the media decided that Carter's 23,000 votes were far more significant than Jackson's 163,000.

Nevertheless, Carter was disconsolate. As a matter of fact, according to pollster Caddell, he "was really off balance and upset by Massachusetts." He felt one of the reasons he had done so badly in Massachusetts was that *The Boston Globe* had been out to get him and, for that purpose, had pursued the home-mortgage issue far beyond its true news value. "That's my favorite news-paper," he remarked, "and Lester Maddox is my favorite politi-cian." Thus, in the week between the Massachusetts and Florida primaries, he was unusually snappish with the press. "I'll be glad to repeat myself again—or else you can play your tape back to yourself," Carter growled at a reporter in Florida. On another occasion, he snapped, "Do you want to stop talking so I can give you my answer or do you want to go ahead and ask a second question as well?"

Adding to his irritability was Scoop Jackson, who had entered the Florida primary in the face of Carter's desire to go one-on-one with George Wallace. Wallace had indeed been Carter's main target until Jackson's surprise victory in Massachusetts. He had, in fact, sent out a fund-raising newsletter which read, "Please help us win a victory in Florida and allow the Democratic Party to choose its presidential candidate in an arena free of demagoguery. . . . I need your help now to end once and for all the threat Wallace represents to our country." It was, apparently, a threat that Carter had not fully recognized in 1970 when, in running for Governor, he had latched on to Wallace's coattails.

The newsletter, however, was mainly for out-of-state consump-tion. Within Florida, Carter played the game differently. Instead of attacking Wallace, Carter questioned his credentials as a realistic candidate, suggesting repeatedly that while he did not disagree too much with the Alabamian's "message," Wallace had no chance of becoming President. In Carter, however, Souther-ners had a chance of "sending them a President." That "message," plus Wallace's obvious wheelchair infirmities, was to help to decide the issue in Carter's favor.

Now, in the closing days of the Florida primary, Jackson had suddenly become a problem for Carter. According to a report in

Time, Scoop had made a deal with Hubert Humphrey whereby the Minnesotan would help out—he let Jackson use a tape of a laudatory old Humphrey speech in Florida radio commercials—if Scoop would support Humphrey in the event his candidacy collapsed. "That arrangement," reported Richard Reeves in *New York*, "made for some interesting doings in Florida, where Carter was going to clobber Wallace, perhaps finishing him off for good, until Jackson suddenly decided to go all out to try to cut Carter's vote. So, given a choice, old liberals Humphrey and Jackson preferred the survival of Wallace, who threatens the country more than he threatens them, to the survival of Carter, who threatens them more than he threatens the country."

Scoop had come into the Sunshine State bearing tidings of Carter's home-mortgage snafu. The Senator placed newspaper ads, asking, "Can Floridians afford the Carter tax reform?" And Jackson was also scoring among the heavily Jewish areas in Miami Beach. Along with Daniel Patrick Moynihan, who had declared for his candidacy, the Senator moved through pro-Israel constituencies like a hot knife through cream cheese. Carter tried to compete. Speaking at a Jewish center, he told of his trip to Israel and his talk with Golda Meir. His words about the Holy Land were as strong as those of Jackson. But, wearing a yarmulke, he "looks like 'Jimmy,' chief of the Mouseketeers," reported correspondent Martin Schram. "He comes off like grits at a seder."

All efforts at civility were disappearing in those closing days. At press conferences and interviews, Carter charged that he had lost in Massachusetts because Jackson had run a racist campaign. "I'm not in favor of mandatory busing," he said in Orlando, "but to run my campaign on an anti-busing issue is contrary to my basic nature. If I have to win by appealing to a basically negative, emotional issue which has connotations of racism, I don't intend to do it, myself. I don't want to win that kind of race." Oh, he continued, he wasn't meaning to suggest that Jackson was a racist. "I didn't say Senator Jackson was a racist," he said. "I didn't say he wasn't, but I don't think he is a racist. He exploited an issue that has racist connotations." Elsewhere, he said, "To build a campaign on an issue that has already created disharmony, and sometimes even bloodshed, is to me the wrong approach to politics. I wouldn't do it. But Senator Jackson did. . . ." And on and on. It was obvious that Jimmy Carter, who had been preaching love and trust, was now losing his cool.

And after new Jackson ads had accused him of threatening national security by his advocacy of cuts in defense spending, Carter said, "I can't sit back and have one of my opponents deliberately and consistently make false statements about me. . . . He's been in Congress for thirty-five years. He's not a dishonest man, he's not a bad man, but he wants to be President so bad he's departed from his normal truthfulness."

But, most of all, Carter stressed that only he could knock out Wallace. And this was most essential to the Georgian's game plan. If he could not beat the Alabamian in the South, then he could not expect to be accepted as a "real" candidate anywhere else. Carter began to breathe easier when early returns indicated he would be a big winner. The final returns showed him the winner, but not by as big a margin as he had hoped. Carter wound up with 34 percent of the vote; Wallace, 31 percent; Jackson, 24 percent; and Milton Shapp with 2 percent. But it was enough to re-establish Carter as the front-runner—a born-again front-runner.

And it was obvious Wallace was finished. But, as Ray Jenkins, the editorial page editor of *The Alabama Journal*, a longtime critic of Wallace, noted, "If Wallace had been well, he would have won Florida . . . and Carter would have been the one who was finished. . . . The only real difference between Wallace and Carter is fifteen years. They both started out in politics as opportunists with slight liberal inclinations. The only way for Wallace to get elected Governor in 1962 was as a segregationist, but that made it impossible for him to command real nationwide support. By the time Carter became Governor of Georgia in 1970, the Civil Rights Act and the Voting Rights Act had made it possible to get elected in the South without mortgaging your future to the rednecks. The person Jimmy Carter has to thank is not George Wallace—it's Lyndon Johnson."

Meanwhile, Joe Kraft thought the Florida results showed "that the country is gradually nursing itself back to political health," but that Carter's chances were only so-so. Kraft felt there were enough uncommitted delegates shaping up "for an outsider such as Hubert Humphrey." (Outsider? Why, that was what Jimmy Carter claimed to be. Humphrey, according to the Georgian, was one of those "insiders" who had messed things up in Washington.) On his return to Georgetown from Orlando, Kraft foresaw "a fluid period with a lot of wheeling and dealing just before or during the convention itself, perhaps to the benefit of Senator Hubert Humphrey." A few days later Kraft asked, "Is America ready for a Christian President from the South?" Clearly Kraft was not. He felt the religious approach "heightens qualities apt to cloud Carter's prospects as the primary parade moves into more hotly contested industrial states." Kraft obviously was getting concerned about Carter: "He is overconfident and stakes out claims—such as reforming the federal goverment—which he can't back up." But he now conceded Carter could get 800 delegates, which "would at least make him a prime candidate for Vice-President."

A week after Florida, Carter again scored heavily against Wallace in Illinois. He won 48 percent of the vote to Wallace's 28 percent. Sargent Shriver polled just 16 percent and was finished as a candidate. Chicago's Mayor Richard Daley was impressed. And he said so: "His was a campaign that some respect must be paid to." In a short time, Carter had covered all bases. He made a particular effort in black communities. And it paid off. In Illinois, he received 47 percent of the black vote. And he also did well among the God-fearing folk who inhabited the rural areas down-state. In this, his own well-advertised religiosity did him no harm. But he also had his younger sister Ruth Carter Stapleton to thank. A professional faith healer, she had achieved a modicum of fame as a practitioner of what she called "inner healing." A striking blue-eyed blonde, given to wearing eye shadow, gold rings in her pierced ears, and modish clothes, Ruth Stapleton campaigned hard for her brother. Among other things, she sent out a form letter to a long list, selling her brother on the basis of his "deep personal commitment to Jesus Christ and his will to serve Him in whatever capacity he finds himself." In her opinion, she wrote, "one of Jimmy's greatest qualifications" was that as President he would be able to "render spiritual leadership." And she concluded:

> As one who knows the importance of Christ in your personal life and who I'm sure wants our nation to be under His blessings and guidance—please pray for

Jimmy. . . . On Tuesday, March 16, the Illinois Primary
will be held. Please call your friends and neighbors to go
with you and cast your vote for Jimmy . . . and for his
delegates in your particular Congressional District.

Sincerely in Christ,
Ruth Carter Stapleton

It was an unusual letter to say the least. For it brought a
candidate's religion right smack into the realm of politics. Until
then, that was supposed to be a definite no-no. John F. Kennedy,
for example, had been forced to swear on a stack of Bibles that his
Roman Catholicism would have no bearing on how he would
govern the nation. But times were indeed a' changin'. Sixteen
years later, a candidate had emerged who deliberately thrust his
theological beliefs into his electioneering. It was a subject that
troubled most commentators. And it was brought up on *Meet the
Press* on the eve of the Democratic Convention in New York.
Carter was asked whether religion might not become an issue in
the general campaign, "considering that some people have expressed uneasiness about what it would mean to have in the White
House a Southern Baptist, a 'born again Christian,' a man who is
not hesitant to talk about his religious views in public."

Carter responded by noting that Harry Truman was a Baptist
"and I think he was able to exemplify a compatability between
deep religious beliefs and also public service." The only problem
with this was that President Truman had rarely, if ever, discussed
his religion.

Carter did concede that the question of his religion had created
some problems. "I have never initiated any issue about religion,
but I generally try to answer the questions frankly. And it was a
hard thing for me to decide . . . whether to respond truthfully
about my own religious beliefs or try to avoid that issue. I finally
decided to respond truthfully, because I think the American
people ought to know it." That a man who promised never to lie to
the American people would have difficulty responding truthfully
concerning his religion was somewhat eye-opening.

While Carter may not have "initiated" any discussion of his
religion, he did little to dissuade questions on the subject. In fact,
in certain areas of the country, he seemed to welcome such

questions. They obviously weren't doing him any harm in the so-called Bible Belt. In North Carolina, for example, where he was pitted one-on-one against Wallace, Carter spent a great deal of his time talking about the very personal nature of his Southern Baptist beliefs. Asked why he had responded in such intimate detail, whereas in the past he had given short replies about how religion was separate from politics, Carter declared:

> The questioner wanted to know if I was going to disavow my religion . . . in order to get votes around the country. This question had come up several times before and I would try to give a brief answer like yes or no or that's the way I feel. . . . [The] question was coming up with increasing frequency, so I thought for once and for all with all the reporters present I would answer the question a little more completely and have it over with. And there was no surge of questioning of me by the news media until after Richard Reeves wrote an article about me in *New York* magazine, ascribing my political success to a spiritual desire on the part of the American people that I was meeting. I have never known how to assess the impact of one reporter's writings upon another reporter's, but apparently that article had a great deal of effect on the interest of other reporters in that subject.

The Reeves article, he could have added, also had a great deal of influence on selling Carter to scoffers, particularly the trendies who read *New York*. For Reeves, formerly of *The New York Times*, had developed a deserved reputation as one of the more perceptive observers of the political scene. At first, Reeves conceded, he hadn't taken Carter seriously. When, in the process of courting the press in early 1975, Carter "invited me to breakfast," wrote Reeves, ". . . I didn't pay any attention. I thought he was wasting his time (and mine) and I can't remember a word he said."

But then Reeves began to take notice. "A man does not come from where he did to within reaching distance of the presidency without establishing, prima facie, that he is one sharp country politician," Reeves noted. And his impression now was that Carter was "head and shoulders above most of the politicians I've seen in recent years—a brilliant politician who may have a feel for a kind of post-ideological leadership of a media nation." Yet, at the same time, Reeves conceded that Carter was a "phony," adding "he's a politician, an actor, a salesman. What I like is that the product he's peddling is one of the most interesting I've seen in a long time. He's a Southern populist free of the race anchor, something of a 1976 Huey Long outgrowing his origins and repackaging the salable points of his life and public record."

"And," admired Reeves, "he is an absolute master at using the same facts to give different impressions to different audiences." Thus, when he spoke before a group of young lawyers in Miami, he was asked about his repeated assertions that he was not a lawyer, suggesting that somehow lawyers were part of the American problem. "I had to turn what seemed to be a disadvantage into an advantage," he replied. "Had I been a lawyer, I'd be bragging about it."

As Reeves also noted, Carter invariably would tailor his litany of American heroes— "George Washington, Thomas Jefferson"— depending on the kind of group he was addressing. In New Hampshire, for example, he usually included Martin Luther King; in Florida, he usually did not. And David Broder, after following him in Wisconsin, observed that Carter had told a white audience that he was opposed to forced busing while omitting reference to that question in a somewhat similar speech to a black group.

None of which obviously did Carter any harm in North Carolina. He took the Tarheel State with 54 percent of the vote. Wallace, who obtained 35 percent, was virtually eliminated as a viable presidential candidate. And he knew it. Carter knew it, too, though he graciously acknowledged that Wallace was "a very courageous, tough, persistent campaigner." From now on, Carter was to moderate his criticism of the Alabamian. Wallace had served his purpose by providing a convenient foil. But he could still be useful in Carter's drive for the nomination and, later, the presidency itself.

Still, Wallace kept on campaigning in Wisconsin, even though he had sadly conceded, "I guess you could say that Arthur Bremer messed me up politically with that gun." In an interview with *The New York Times*, he spoke of his problem with the voters, a problem which Jimmy Carter did not face: "All they see is the spokes on my wheelchair. The television catches everyone. You've got a man standing up saying, 'Big Government is eating you up.' And you got a man in a wheelchair, all humped over, saying the same thing. It's hard to beat." When Wallace showed up in Madison, he was greeted by a group of University of Wisconsin students wearing masks of Arthur Bremer, the man convicted of shooting Wallace, and chanting, "Free Artie Bremer, give him another chance; he should have shot him in the head, instead he shot him in the pants." Previously, these champions of compassion had heckled Carter, throwing peanuts at him. And Senator Jackson was greeted with paper airplanes labeled "Boeing" and "SST," while being spat upon and heckled.

Carter himself showed a mean streak when he again lashed out at Hubert Humphrey. Carter had not done well in Virginia, where he got only 30 percent of the vote in the state's caucuses. Sixty-two percent of the vote went for "Uncommitted," which was generally interpreted as a vote for the still-undeclared Humphrey. And, in spite of Carter's efforts to win them over, uncommitted delegates at state conventions in Oklahoma and South Carolina remained uncommitted. In Washington, meanwhile, Humphrey claimed there may have been "racism" behind some of the criticism leveled against federal programs, though he specifically denied he was attacking Carter.

Not assuaged, Carter accused Humphrey of being "devious," saying the Minnesotan had taken a "departure from rationality . . . from the truth." Once again, he charged Humphrey with being a "loser." Unable to contain himself, Carter said Humphrey would probably want to stay out of the race because of unresolved questions concerning unreported campaign contributions from the late Howard Hughes, about the conviction of his 1970 senatorial campaign manager for accepting an illegal campaign contribution, and "how old he is—things like that."

Carter also got testy about Julian Bond, who had come to Wisconsin to campaign for Udall. This was rather embarrassing to Carter because, after all, the celebrated black legislator was from Georgia. And Bond was warning blacks to be wary of the smiling Georgian who sang their hymns. Asked about him, all Carter would say was that Bond wanted to be Vice-President and he knew he could not do so on a Carter ticket. But there was much more to it, and Carter knew it. Bond believed Carter to be a "liar" and said so. There was, for example, Carter's denial of Bond's claim that Carter had asked him in 1972 to suggest to McGovern that he choose the then Governor as his running mate. And at another point in the campaign, Carter boasted that his administration in Georgia had passed a fair housing bill that was tougher than the federal law.

"Well," Bond said later, "I had missed only four days in eleven years in the legislature and I'd never heard of this state fair housing act. I checked with the Senate and was told we didn't have such a law. I asked some reporters to check out Carter's story, but they never did."

Finally, on April 6, Carter won a narrow victory over Udall in Wisconsin—so narrow that the news media had prematurely declared the lanky Arizonan the winner. Typical was the first edition of *The Milwaukee Sentinel* whose Dewey-eyed 1948 headline said, "Carter Upset by Udall." After it became clear that it was actually Carter who had won by 37 percent to Udall's 36, a broadly smiling Carter held the newspaper over his head, Truman-style. That picture, appearing in hundreds of front pages within hours, "obliterated that disaster in New York," commented Pat Caddell.

At first, New York did appear to be a "disaster" for Carter. The primary results there showed Jackson taking 38 percent of the vote; Udall, 25.5 percent; while Carter was buried deep in fourth place with just 12.8 percent—beaten even by uncommitted slates which statewide took 23.7 percent. But since the news media were now playing up Carter's comeback in Wisconsin, the New York results took second place in the press coverage that followed. And Jackson was infuriated, blaming the networks particularly for downplaying New York. As evidence, he cited the fact that two of the nationwide broadcasts emanated from Milwaukee.

Jackson's big win in the second-largest state in the union was immediately downgraded by the commentators. Lesley Stahl of CBS News declared that his victory did not give him "momentum," while her colleague, Roger Mudd, observed that the Senator's winning coalition was "peculiar to New York." Writing in *Public Opinion*, Professor Michael J. Robinson of Catholic

University reported, "In 1976, New Hampshire cast a total of 82,381 Democratic votes and on the day following the election, received 2,100 seconds of total news time on the three commercial networks. Six weeks later, New York cast 3,746,414 Democratic votes and the following day received only 560 seconds on the three shows combined. In proportionate terms each Democratic vote in New Hampshire received 170 times as much network news time as each Democratic vote in New York. Media reality—television reality—implied that a victory in New Hampshire totally overwhelmed a victory in New York."

It may very well be the case, Professor Robinson concluded, that Senator Jackson was the candidate mainly "victimized" by what he dubbed "the hoopla imperative"—the inherent need of television for spectacle. For in the six early primary states where Jackson had been a contestant, Robinson noted, he had actually beaten Carter by over 300,000 votes. But that's not the way it came out on the tube.

Carter's dramatic "victory" in Wisconsin temporarily overshadowed a flap created by his remark about "ethnic purity." The remark had been published in *The New York Daily News* and was in response to a question put to the candidate by that paper's chief political writer, Sam Roberts. The question had to do with how Carter felt about low-income scatter-site housing in the suburbs. And Carter replied, "My next-door neighbor is black. It hasn't hurt us—provided you give people the freedom to decide for themselves where to live. But to artificially inject another racial group in a community? I see nothing wrong with ethnic purity being maintained. I would not force a racial integration of a neighborhood by government action. But I would not permit discrimination against a family moving into the neighborhood."

The seemingly offhand remark was published on page 134 of the Sunday edition of *The Daily News*. But within days it became a front-page story in most major newspapers and was featured on all three television networks. What happened was this: a CBS official in New York spotted the comment and asked Ed Rabel, traveling with Carter, to question him about it. This the correspondent did in Indianapolis on the very day of the New York and Wisconsin primaries.

"What did you mean by ethnic purity?" asked Rabel.

"I have nothing against a community that's made up of people who are Polish, Czechoslovakians, French-Canadians, or blacks who are trying to maintain the ethnic purity of their neighborhood," said Carter. "This is a natural inclination on the part of the people. . . . I've never, though, condoned any sort of discrimination against, say, a black family or other family from moving into that neighborhood. But I don't think government ought to deliberately break down an ethnically oriented community deliberately by injecting into it a member of another race. To me, this is contrary to the best interests of the community."

The questioning continued in other cities, and Carter became increasingly irritable. He blamed the media for "trying to make something out of it, and there's nothing to be made out of it." Still, Carter sought to explain what he meant by "ethnic purity." Elaborating, he warned of "black intrusion" into white neighborhoods and of "injecting into [a community] a member of another race" or "a diametrically opposite kind of family" or a "different kind of person."

All of which continued to astonish the correspondents following Carter on the primary trail. One of them, the tough ABC correspondent Sam Donaldson, cornered the candidate in Pittsburgh. He asked whether "such terms as 'ethnic purity' and 'alien group'" weren't "almost Hitlerian?" Carter tensed, but he controlled himself. He repeated what he had been saying, leaving out the inflammatory phrases and concluding, "If anyone derived from my statement the connotation that I have an inclination toward racism, then I would resent that because it's certainly not true."

It took several days before Carter realized he was in serious trouble. His foremost supporter in the black community, Congressman Andrew Young of Atlanta, was absolutely distraught. For, after all, his own credibility was at stake. "A lot of people who said, 'You can't trust a Southerner' are going to say, 'See, I told you so.'" Young added that he didn't think Carter fully "understood the loaded connotations of the words" he had been using. "I can't defend him on this. It will be an issue in Pennsylvania." And he urged Carter to apologize.

Which is what Carter finally did. Arriving in Philadelphia on April 8, Carter told newsmen that he had talked to black leaders around the country and had decided to clarify his controversial remarks. "I think most of the problem has been caused by my ill-chosen *agreement* to use the words 'ethnic purity.'" he said, implying that he had not originally thought up the phrase, which he had, but that someone else had. "I think that was a very serious mistake on my part. I think it should have been the words 'ethnic character' or 'ethnic heritage,' and I think that unanimously my black supporters with whom I discussed this question agree that my position is the correct one. . . . I do want to apologize to all those who have been concerned about the unfortunate use of the term 'ethnic purity.' I don't think there are any ethnically pure neighborhoods in the country, but in response to a question and without adequate thought on my part, I used a phrase that was unfortunate. . . . I was careless in the words I used. . . . I have apologized for it. It was an improper choice of words."

Minutes after he apologized, Carter arrived at the offices of *The Philadelphia Inquirer* for an interview. He appeared "particularly subdued," according to reporter Larry Eichel, who wrote the story of the interview. "I make my mistakes," he said, "and I try to correct them as best I can after they're made."

On the subject of "ethnic purity," a phrase he now disavowed, Carter said he would not force an all-white suburban township to allow construction of a federally funded low-income housing project if township residents were opposed. "If they don't want federal program money," he said, "I would not make them take it, that's right. That goes beyond my concept of what the federal government ought to do. . . . I feel that way."

At the same time, Carter said that he—unlike Ronald Reagan, George Wallace, and other presidential candidates in search of the anti-Washington vote—was not opposed to having a strong federal government. "In the first place," he said, "I don't ever say that government's too big. I have never said that. I do talk about efficiency. There's a distinction between the two. . . . I'm not afraid of government. My government in Georgia, as has been widely published by Udall and Jackson, grew considerably while I was Governor, but I guarantee that it was infinitely more efficient and economical and simpler in structure than it was when I took over. And that's the way I intend to approach it as President."

Despite his apology over "ethnic purity," the controversy continued. The following Tuesday, April 13, Jimmy Carter appeared with the Reverend Martin Luther King, Sr.—Daddy King—at a noon rally in a downtown Atlanta park. Said the father of the slain civil rights leader, "I have a forgiving heart. So, Governor, I'm with you all the way." The two men embraced before the cameras. His spirits thus refreshed, Carter flew off to Philadelphia, accompanied by black state leaders. In the City of Brotherly Love, he told newsmen that while he had apologized for using the word "purity," he still felt strongly in favor of preserving "ethnic" neighborhoods. Asked about the other expressions he had used, such as black "intrusion" and "alien groups," Carter maintained that "those phrases were taken out of context." And, let's get off the subject, please.

Still, some critics were insisting that what Carter had done was make a cleverly veiled appeal to Wallace supporters, now looking for a place to roost in the face of their hero's political demise. One of the critics, Dr. Ethel Allen, a black surgeon who headed the Ford for President campaign in Philadelphia, told Kandy Stroud that the "ethnic purity" statement was a "brilliant" political move. "He calculated the timing of that statement to get the Wallace vote in Texas, Missouri, and Georgia, and it's paying off handsomely. It made him an instant household word, and it didn't antagonize the Ku Klux Klan, the White Citizens Council, or the American Nazi Party. He didn't lose points with them by apologizing, because he had already said it."

"He didn't lose points with blacks," Dr. Allen went on, "because blacks can forgive a man who's religious sooner than they can forgive a man who's not close to God. That's why they didn't turn off when they saw the pictures of Daddy King embracing him, like they did when they saw Sammy Davis, Jr., hugging Nixon. He's astutely assayed the mood of the country. People are looking for God and honesty in the post-Watergate era. . . ."

The "ethnic purity" flap proved to be no problem for Carter in Pennsylvania. Carter took 37.2 percent of the vote; Jackson, 24.7; Udall, 18.8; Wallace, 11. Carter said the results had put his candidacy "in good shape to get a first-ballot victory." Still worried about Humphrey, however, he warned that the party "might be committing political suicide" if it did not abide by the results of the primaries in picking a standard-bearer.

All through Pennsylvania, Carter's rivals had made much of the demonstrable fact that the Georgian was fuzzy on the issues. The criticism was beginning to get to Carter. For Carter took the position that there was no need to go into excessive detail on any of the programs he espoused. Once he got to the White House, he insisted, he would become more specific. Still, his aides had become concerned at the criticism. Jerry Rafshoon, his media specialist, responded to the vagueness charge by adding the line "Jimmy Carter on the issue of . . ." at the beginning of the very television commercials which were being criticized for fuzziness.

Nationally, the criticism persisted. Joe Kraft, in a widely noted column, also took issue with Carter's religious posture by saying, "He looks on himself as a vessel of God, asks to be taken on faith, and is ungracious with those he has defeated. . . . Carter tends to take his initials too seriously."

At Pat Caddell's urging, the Carter team had brought on a new speechwriter, Robert Shrum, to assist in "sharpening up the image" and make the candidate look "more liberal." In a memo, the pollster described Shrum as an "excellent, brilliant writer, who can pull together ideas and statements for the Governor and who has good political sense. Someone who knows how to capitalize on opportunities and also how to avoid disaster. . . ."

Shrum's background was that of a very liberal wordsman, who had penned many an oration for candidates like John V. Lindsay, Edmund Muskie, and George McGovern. In fact, he left a job as staff director of McGovern's Select Committee on Nutrition when he agreed to join the Carter team as the number-one speechwriter. When he told McGovern he was leaving, Shrum said he was doing so because "I think Carter's for real." It didn't take Shrum too long before he felt otherwise. Nine days later, Shrum decided to quit because he had come to believe Carter was "a dangerous man," who believed in little else than in getting to the White House. Not only was he fuzzy, but he was *deliberately* fuzzy on issues. And in a letter to Carter, Shrum wrote:

> You say you wish to keep your options open. Within reason that is understandable. But an election is the only option people have. After carefully reflecting on what I

have seen and heard here, I do not know what you would do as President. I share the perception that simple measures will not answer our problems; but it seems to me that your issues strategy is not a response to that complexity, but an attempt to conceal your true positions. I am not sure what you truly believe in, other than yourself. I have examined my reactions closely. I have attempted to justify a different conclusion. But I cannot rationalize one. Therefore, I must resign.

At their first meeting, Carter "smiled a lot," Shrum recalled, "a very warm and genuine smile." But after Shrum had signed on, "I never saw him smile in private unless there was someone there he wanted to impress." There was very little visible emotion in Carter, just a granite hardness. "Carter is a man of iron control," Shrum concluded. "[It] is pervasive, constant, unremitting." And the candidate imposed his "iron control" on his own life, giving up tennis for the campaign, for example, because he was afraid it would seem too frivolous. Aides confided to Shrum that Carter was a "loner [who] doesn't like to hear things he disagrees with."

Shrum's disillusionment had begun almost immediately. He had flown to Atlanta from Cambridge, Massachusetts, where he had been lecturing at the Kennedy Institute of Politics at Harvard. This was at the time when the "ethnic purity" flap was at its height. Carter was meeting with Shrum when the candidate learned that the black Mayor of Atlanta, Maynard Jackson, was asking "for one last thing" before he would endorse Carter. According to Shrum, Carter angrily told an aide, "Jackson can kiss my ass, and you tell him that. I'm through calling him." Of course, Shrum had heard such hardnosed comments before in private political sessions. And the Watergate tapes showed that such jargon was not unfamiliar even within the Oval Office itself. But, as Jules Witcover noted, Carter's "out-front religiosity had prepared him for a somewhat less descriptive response."

And Shrum was definitely not prepared for what he claimed was Carter's response to a suggestion he make still another statement on the thorny Mideast situation. He quoted Carter as saying: "We have to be cautious. We don't want to offend anybody. . . . I don't want any more statements on the Middle East or Lebanon.

Jackson has all the Jews anyway. It doesn't matter how far I go. I don't get over four percent of the Jewish vote anyway, so forget it. We get the Christians." Shrum, however, considered the remark politically pragmatic, not anti-Semitic. Still, its disclosure sent a shock wave of concern throughout the American Jewish community.

At the same meeting, Carter said he planned to tell a group of trucking executives who were potential contributors that he was with them in opposing the diversion of highway trust funds to mass transit. When aide Stu Eizenstat reminded the candidate he was on record in favor of the diversion, Carter replied, "All right, maybe that's what I've said, but I think all this mass transit isn't a good idea. I don't see why highway users should pay for subways. I think that money should be used for highways."

The next day, Shrum prepared a statement proposing additional black lung benefits for miners after thirty years. But Carter vetoed it that night on the campaign plane, explaining that the mine safety provisions were "too controversial and expensive." Moreover, Carter said, they "would offend the operators. And why should I do this for Arnold Miller [president of the United Mine Workers] if he won't come out and endorse me?" Besides, he added, "I don't think the benefits should be automatic. They *chose* to be miners."

In interviews and in an article he wrote for *New Times,* Shrum gave other cases in which he felt Carter had deliberately been fuzzing issues. Most important was the candidate's posture toward the defense budget. Though Carter had publicly pledged to slash allocations by five to seven percent, Shrum said he was ordered not to make any references to specific cuts because former Deputy Defense Secretary Paul Nitze had advised Carter the budget might have to be raised $20 or $30 billion.

Shrum said he was appalled by Jody Powell's reply when he asked the press secretary how much reorganization in Georgia had saved the state. "We say $30 million," said Powell, "but no one really knows how much it saved or cost. It depends on how you calculate it."

Powell had also warned Shrum not to go too hard on the "ethnic purity" issue because "we don't want to lose white votes." And Shrum said that fund-raiser Morris Dees had told him that the statement which the media had described as a gaffe had "helped more than it hurt." Which pretty much bore out the analysis that Dr. Allen had given Kandy Stroud.

Also causing Shrum concern was Carter's vetoing of a TV spot assailing Philadelphia Mayor Frank Rizzo, a Henry Jackson supporter, for his previous support of President Nixon. "We don't want to offend the Nixon voters," Shrum quoted Carter as saying.

On the Friday before the Pennsylvania primary, Shrum nearly became unglued by a discussion he had with Carter aboard the campaign plane. Shrum had urged the candidate to consider asking the Congress to override a veto of a child-care bill by President Ford. Carter said he would have vetoed the bill, too, had he been President, as too costly and restrictive. "If I was Governor of Georgia," Carter went on, "I wouldn't accept the federal money under these standards. I'd close down the program first." And then, turning to Shrum, he said, "I suppose your ex-boss [McGovern] thinks the bill is just great."

In Philadelphia the day before the primary, Shrum attended a meeting with other staffers who discussed the task forces which Carter had assembled to report on various issues. "Jimmy doesn't take these guys seriously," one of the aides said. "He wants their names, but he doesn't like other stars around him. He's the star, and he wants people to carry out his ideas."

And that did it for Shrum. The very last thing he did before quitting was prepare a victory statement for Carter to use following the Pennsylvania primary. "I reread it when I finished it," he told Jules Witcover. "I decided that it was good, and that I didn't believe it." For he had reluctantly come to the conclusion that the man who so desperately wanted to become President of the United States was little more than a liar and a deceiver. "What made it hard was to listen to the stump speech, 'I will never lie to you; I will never mislead you,' said with fervor and passion, and seeing that people believe it."

The Carter people were clearly upset when Shrum went public with his damning accusations. Jody Powell, for one, accused Shrum of being "childish and hurtful" and suggested that the young writer had come under a great deal of pressure from liberals, including McGovern aide Alan Baron, who had seen Shrum in Philadelphia during this period of agitation. Andrew

Young was much more sanguine about it all. He was prepared to concede that while most of Shrum's facts were correct he was wrong in his conclusions. "I can believe 85 to 90 percent of what he said—except I would give it a different interpretation. . . . If someone wanted to hang around here and do a real hatchet job and prove I was really callous and Machiavellian, they could probably do it. The only way to let off tensions in a campaign—you got to express them to somebody. I don't want to go home and take it out on my wife. I mean, you need an inner circle you can express to." (Which, incidentally, was exactly the explanation offered by the Nixon people for some of the stuff recorded on the White House tapes. The President's comments within the inner circle were not to be taken too seriously.)

"I don't feel inclined to comment on this young man's statement," a visibly angry Carter said in Terre Haute, Indiana. "He obviously wrote the letter for the news media. . . . I'm not a liar and I don't make any statements in private contrary to what I make in public." A few hours later, Carter calmed down. "I have nothing but admiration for Mr. Shrum," he said, adding that he "has never been on our payroll." That was technically true. Because Shrum had neglected to fill out the requisite tax form, he was never paid for his nine days with Jimmy Carter. The episode, needless to say, provided still another example of how the "never lie, never mislead" candidate played with the truth.

Discussing the contretemps several months later, Carter told Robert Scheer of *Playboy,* "Shrum dreamed up eight or ten conversations that never took place and nobody in the press ever asked me if they had occurred. The press just assumed that they had. I never talked to Shrum in private except for maybe a couple of minutes. If he had told the truth, if I had said all the things he claimed I had said, I wouldn't vote for *myself.* When a poll came out early in the primaries that said I had a small proportion of the Jewish vote, I said, 'Well, this is really a disappointment to me— we've worked so hard with the Jewish voters. But my pro-Israel stand won't change, even if I don't get a single vote; I guess we'll have to depend on non-Jews to put me in office.' But Shrum treated it as if it were some sort of racial disavowal of Jews. Well, that is a kind of sleazy twisting of a conversation."

Queried about Carter's statement, Shrum declared, "I was pretty surprised at it. It's not true that the conversations never took place. I believe he doesn't believe he tells untruths about anything." It was a very perceptive analysis of the man who claimed he would never lie to the American people.

11
LOCKING IT UP
BEFORE THE CONVENTION

FOR THE MOST PART, THE SHRUM AFFAIR—WHATEVER IT MAY have revealed about a leading candidate for the presidency—was quickly forgotten. The media, though momentarily interested, failed to follow up. Events considered of greater political significance were taking place. Carter's breakthrough in Pennsylvania, for example, had virtually eliminated Scoop Jackson. Carter was now so far ahead that Hubert Humphrey, whose ranking in the polls was still high, was discouraged from seeking actively to stop him.

Over nationwide television, the doughty Minnesotan threw in the towel. "One thing I don't need at this stage of my life is to be ridiculous." But he conceded there was always the possibility of a miracle—a deadlocked convention which might turn to him. "I shall not seek it," said Humphrey. "I shall not search for it. I shall not scramble for it." He paused. "But, I'm around."

Campaigning in Texas when he heard the news, Carter was particularly ungracious. He would have liked for Humphrey to stay in the race, he said, so he could give him a "beating." Which was a rather strange comment coming from a man who had been moaning across the land about the possibility of Humphrey entering the fray and, with the aid of unnamed political bosses, picking up all the marbles.

Confidante Charles Kirbo had thirsted even more openly for a New Jersey primary battle with Humphrey. He wanted Humphrey bloodied up before the convention, just in case Carter fell short of the nomination on the first ballot. A Carter-Humphrey battle might have been nasty, the Atlanta lawyer conceded. "I don't know if we could have brought it out," said Kirbo on the New Jersey battle that never developed, "but there are a lot of damn negatives on Humphrey—all those unpaid bills from his 1968 campaign, all that milk money stuff." In other words, a little smearing would have been in order.

The primaries went on, however; and now all that stood in the way of Carter and the nomination was the eleventh-hour entry of two fresh challengers—Senator Frank Church of Idaho and Governor Edmund G. "Jerry" Brown of California. And much to Carter's surprise, the two newcomers began handing him defeats. Church took Nebraska, beating Carter by one percentage point. But probably more important was what Jerry Brown was doing to the Georgian in Maryland. There, the Californian conducted a whirlwind campaign which attracted considerable attention. He also won the support of the powerful state Democratic machine headed by Governor Marvin Mandel. Mandel had never really forgiven Carter for reneging on his pledge to support him for the 1971 chairmanship of the National Governors Conference; nor did he forget Carter's proposal to the Governors that they go easy on Nixon during Watergate. Mandel, of course, was having well-publicized difficulties with the feds, having been indicted, among other charges, for bribery. When Carter finally noted that the Governor had "expressed disapproval of my candidacy," he added sarcastically, "So far I've been able to overcome that devastating blow in the primaries."

Carter took the offensive, labeling Brown the candidate of "powerful political bosses and machine politicians." Brown responded, "I don't call it a machine. I call it a new generation of politics." Mandel and cohorts a new generation of politics? But Brown was getting away with it, primarily because he was exciting and a new generation on campuses in Maryland and elsewhere. The word had spread that the youthful former Jesuit seminarian was into Zen and had refused to live in a Taj Mahal-like Governor's Mansion and instead slept on a mattress, but no bed, in a modest Sacramento apartment.

Columnist Vic Gold received a letter from his daughter Paige reporting that in a Tulane straw poll Jerry Brown led the field after only a month's campaigning. Why? Because he was "young, new" and "he gave up that mansion." As Gold noted, "The PR power of a single gesture . . . can outdo millions spent in political advertising and promotion."

Sensing trouble, Carter assumed the role of the underdog, claiming he was behind in the polls because he hadn't had the time to concentrate on Maryland. But the polls showed something else, an increasing awareness that Carter was soft on issues. Carter responded, with considerable exaggeration, that he had position papers "on every conceivable issue."

Meanwhile, Brown was hammering away at the accomplishments Carter claimed as Governor. Reorganization in Georgia, Brown noted, had resulted in an increase in the number of state employees. And he termed Carter's much-vaunted zero-based budgeting "a form of consumer fraud in the political arena."

Carter insisted that reorganization of the federal bureaucracy was necessary. He would reduce the number of governmental agencies and bureaus from 1,900 or so to just 200, giving no examples. And he even carried this message into the Maryland suburbs of the nation's capital, heavily populated by people who work in the federal bureaucracy. The message obviously wasn't selling. Carter quickly changed his spiel. At a press conference on Capitol Hill, he told amazed newsmen, "I'm not anti-Washington.

Of which Jerry Brown was heard to say, "I don't say I'm against Washington until I get there; and then say I like Washington."

Brown could also have been referring to Carter's well-publicized foray into the Georgetown-Chevy Chase establishment and what he had once called its "non-elected professional politicians." In late February, Carter had told a *New York Times* reporter that the Washington dinner party crowd feared "that someone who is not their candidate might actually become the next President. . . . They can hurt me by propping up someone like Frank Church for a while, or somebody else, but I don't think they can decide who the nominee will be." It was a dislike of the affluent liberal set matched only by that of Richard Nixon.

Yet the night before his big victory in Illinois, the populist from Plains, Georgia, turned up at the Georgetown home of liberal columnist Clayton Fritchey to demonstrate that he knew which fork to pick up when the salad was served. The candidate had been supplied with thumbnail rundowns on each of the influential guests, including former Defense Secretary Clark Clifford, CBS commentator Eric Sevareid, *Washington Post* publisher Katherine Graham (who invited Carter to lunch at her home to meet her editors and reporters), Common Cause leader John Gardner, British Ambassador Sir Peter Ramsbotham, former Xerox chairman Sol Linowitz and retired columnist Joseph Alsop. ("Not much liked by the other guests," the poop sheet noted. "Be as tough on him as he is on you.") Alsop did ask some questions about national defense; and Jimmy couldn't have been nicer. At the same time, Carter got his new message across. "I am *not* an anti-Washington candidate," he insisted.

Meanwhile, Dr. Peter Bourne, who had worked with Governor Carter on drug problems in Atlanta, had moved to Georgetown, where he played host to Jimmy whenever he came to town. Along with his wife, Mary King, Bourne for a time represented Carter's major Washington beachhead. They spent most of their time explaining to the natives that, no, Carter did not walk barefoot. Besides, they insisted to doubters, Jimmy was a real liberal. And he was hip—into Bob Dylan, the Allman brothers, and stuff like that there.

Carter's flip-flop on Georgetown, however, made it increasingly apparent that consistency was never one of Jimmy's strong suits.

Nor, for that matter, the truth.

Thus, the day after he was endorsed by Birch Bayh, Carter boasted that he had "never gone to anyone yet and asked them to endorse me." But, in pulling out of the race, Bayh stated that Carter had phoned him the previous week and had specifically asked for his help. Asked about this seeming contradiction, Carter explained, "My point was that I have never depended on endorsements to put me in office," adding that while, yes, he had asked for Bayh's help, he had never asked for his endorsement.

Meanwhile, Brown was drawing huge crowds wherever he went in the Free State. It was obvious that Carter was up against something totally new in the way of opponents. For the California Governor was insisting he was the real "outsider" in the race. And, at a news conference, Carter cleverly described Brown as "the new me." And "the new me" was hitting hard at Carter. Appearing on *Face the Nation,* Brown declared:

> I think one of the issues this campaign is going to develop is about where is the real Jimmy Carter—there's the smile, but what's the person behind that? When at the very time he says he's not seeking endorsements, he's on the telephone to the president of the United Auto Workers and Birch Bayh, trying to get the endorsements. . . . I think that is a very interesting issue because of the inherent inconsistency and discrepancy between what appears to be and what is. When someone says the other candidate is seeking endorsements, and I'm not, and in fact he is, I think people ought to look at that because that's a test of credibility of the whole campaign.

The attack on his credibility stung Carter, as did the final results. Brown received 49 percent of the vote; Carter, 37. That night, Brown exulted at his Baltimore headquarters, "The nomination is still open." And a despondent Carter responded, "There's no way to win all of them."

Almost as humiliating was the outcome that night in Michigan, where Carter had counted on a big win against Udall. After all, he had the support of the 700,000-strong United Auto Workers and black Detroit Mayor Coleman Young. But the Arizona Congressman had decided not to permit Carter, whom he considered a dissembler, to get a free ride to the nomination. He played hardball, particularly criticizing Carter's fuzziness on the issues.

Wherever he went in the heavily unionized state, Udall assailed Carter on right-to-work, welfare reform, and his late conversion to the Humphrey-Hawkins full employment bill. And Udall approved the showing of a half-minute TV spot which showed two cartoon faces of Carter, smiling and frowning at each other, as narrator Cliff Robertson read conflicting Carter statements on such issues as Humphrey-Hawkins, divestiture by oil companies, and national health insurance. The spot ended, "Does all this sound confusing? Vote for a man who means what he says."

It was, as Martin Schram reported, "negative advertising at its best—biting and effective." And perfectly legitimate. But it infuriated the Carter forces. Their response came soon enough. On May 14, before a group of black Baptist ministers, Mayor Young thundered, "I am asking you to make a choice between a man from Georgia who fights to let you in his church and a man from Arizona whose church won't even let you in the back door." It was probably the most bigoted remark of the campaign, one aimed at a candidate's religion—in this case, Mormonism. That it was particularly unfair lay in the fact that Udall claimed to have left the church because of its policies of racial exclusion. The other irony was that, though Carter claimed to have opposed the barring of blacks from his own church in Plains, he continued to attend its services.

Asked to repudiate Mayor Young's remarks, Carter flatly refused. He said he would only consider doing so if Udall himself would "apologize for all the misleading statements he has made against me." He also accused Udall of having attacked him "on religious grounds" in New Hampshire. Since no reporter could remember any such attack, Jody Powell was asked about it. An embarrassed press secretary was forced to concede that while Udall personally had never said anything about Carter's religious beliefs, it had "been a fairly consistent theme" among Udall's campaign workers. Once again the candidate who said he would never lie or mislead was caught in a lie. But the episode was quickly forgotten as the results came pouring in from Maryland, where Carter lost big, and Michigan, where he nearly lost. Carter won the Wolverine State by less than one percent—43.5 to 43.2 percent. It was, as pollster Caddell later said, "the worst night of the campaign." For Carter came close to losing two primaries at a time when he was supposed to be pulling away from the pack.

Carter had another bad night in Oregon. There, the primary results showed Frank Church winning with 34.6 percent of the vote. Carter came in second with 27.4 percent. A remarkable showing was made by Jerry Brown who, having entered the race at the last minute, took 23.3 percent of the tallies, all on write-ins. But Carter's run-everywhere strategy again paid off. He won easily in three border states: Tennessee, Arkansas, and Kentucky. And these victories, reported earlier on the East Coast, camouflaged his bitter disappointment in the Beaver State. What was happening in the late primaries was that voters had begun to perceive the front-running Carter as an "in" member of the very political establishment he had so effectively criticized. Carter and his aides had failed to foresee that the two late starters, Brown and Church, would appeal to the public as refreshing newcomers and underdogs. And his opponents were winning the votes of those who were suspicious of his Southern origin or the depth of his commitment to liberal programs, unions, or Israel.

Carter was at the New York Sheraton Hotel listening to the Oregon returns when he was asked about a statement made earlier in the day by Ted Kennedy. The Senator, in New York to receive the National Father of the Year Award, had told reporters that Carter was being "intentionally indefinite and imprecise" on many issues, and—according to *The New York Times*—he "hedged" on whether he was part of a "stop-Carter" movement. *The Chicago Sun-Times*, meanwhile, quoted "sources close to Mr. Kennedy" as saying he was annoyed by Carter's apparent lack of commitment to various issues, and that Kennedy's recent hints he might run for President or as a vice-presidential candidate with Humphrey were meant to spur Carter into being more specific.

In Carter's suite, watching the returns with him and his staff, was David Nordan, political editor of *The Atlanta Journal*. "A hint of anger" flashed in Carter's eyes, Nordan reported, when told of Kennedy's remarks. "I'm glad I don't have to depend on Kennedy . . . to put me in office," he said. "I don't have to kiss his ass."

Asked about the remark, Carter said he didn't "remember the details" of the talk he had had with correspondent Nordan. However, had he known his remarks were destined for publication, he said he "would have expressed" himself differently.

Meanwhile, Carter accused his critics (unidentified) in the stop-Carter movement of seeking to prevent "the people of this country from regaining control of their government. They want to preserve the status quo, to preserve politics as usual, to maintain at all costs their own entrenched, unresponsive, bankrupt, irresponsible political power."

These were harsh words, indeed, a name-calling attack on his critics. The following day, the paragraph was dropped from the text of the candidate's basic speech. And these words were added: "Our campaign has not been perfect. In retrospect, more time might have been given to this state or that issue. Sometimes in the heat of political combat, harsh words are spoken or overstatements made."

Hours later, in Youngstown, Ohio, Carter accused Udall of using advertisements that were "personally vituperative" and thus lowering the tone of the campaign debate. Udall countered by denying his campaign was using negative, anti-Carter ads. "We are simply asking Carter to be specific on the issues," the Arizonan said.

All of which did not go unnoticed by some in the media. For some time, the boys on the Carter bus had been wondering what had happened to the nice little Georgian who would do anything within reason to get some space or broadcast time. Now Jimmy Carter had become increasingly testy with reporters, so much so that a few had begun to write about the situation. Typical was a story written for *The Boston Globe* by political reporter Curtis Wilkie: "Jimmy Carter's phenomenal rise has been fashioned around the politics of love, but behind his façade of smiles is a cold, tough, driven, complex character. It is a side that is showing itself more frequently these days as the struggle for the Democratic presidential nomination intensifies, manifested in harsh attacks on his rivals, sarcastic asides, acrimonious press conferences, and flashes of anger." Wilkie described a press conference in Peoria, Illinois, at which Carter said he would dispose of questions from the national press and then "turn to the more substantive questions from the local press." And in Madison, Wisconsin, when reporters sought an unequivocal answer on whether he would use grain to negotiate with the Russians, a bristling Carter finally said, "I've answered that three times, and if you don't understand it, then I apologize to you." He refused to answer another question on the subject.

James M. Perry, another highly respected political journalist, wrote in *The National Observer*, "The more I see Carter, the more I wonder about this kind of behavior. He is a very tough fellow, he seems to nurse grudges, and he tends to lash out at people who criticize him, even when their intentions are purely honorable. He even sounds different now. When I first heard him—I wrote about him and said he was a serious candidate for the nomination in May 1975—he was soft-spoken, almost gentle. Not any more. His voice is much louder now, he bites off his words. What had been self-confidence now seems to be cockiness, even arrogance."

Writing in *The Atlantic*, Sanford Ungar noted that Carter showed "an unusually detailed interest in the inner workings of the press, more so than any presidential candidate since John F. Kennedy. He is familiar with deadlines, and understands the difference between what will make news in a small town and what on the national level. He has his own list of 'enemies' in the press, believes that some of the negative articles about him are motivated by pure maliciousness, and forgives very slowly, if ever, for any coverage that he considers unfair."

What Evans and Novak described as "a vein of vindictiveness in the man most likely to be the next President of the United States" was uncovered in Cleveland on May 31 when a "beaming" Carter greeted with delight the news that Senator McGovern had fired two young political aides. And, according to the columnists, there could be little doubt that Carter was behind the "Memorial Day mini-massacre." The dismissals of McGovern aides Alan Baron and Jack Quinn "cannot make the slightest difference to Carter's highly probable nomination," Evans and Novak noted. "What matters is that the incident tends to support claims by Carter's old enemies back in Georgia that his admirable intelligence, discipline, and dedication are accompanied by vindictiveness extraordinary even for a politician."

Both Baron and Quinn had been identified in a *New York Times* article as being leaders of a "loose and shifting alliance" of Democrats opposed to Carter's nomination. The article quoted Baron as saying, "A lot of our people see Carter as a positive evil, surrounded by a staff committed to no ideals, like Haldeman and Ehrlichman." That night, McGovern phoned Baron in Cleveland, where he was assisting Udall in the primary race. The Senator reported there was a "fire storm" of protests against the participation of his aides in the stop-Carter coalition. The next day, both aides were back in Washington, and they were fired. When Baron said he would have to go public on this, McGovern said (according to Baron), "Do it, Alan. Personally, I think that Carter is a dangerous man." Previously, about the time of the Iowa caucuses, McGovern had volunteered that Carter was "our Nixon."

McGovern took a different tack, however, in announcing the dismissals. He said he had requested the resignations of Baron and Quinn despite what he termed Carter's role in a "destructive" stop-McGovern movement in 1972. "I want no part of any such effort in 1976," the South Dakota Senator said. "In 1972, a large number of politicians, including Governor Carter, engaged in a desperate effort to deny me the presidential nomination even after all the primaries were over and I had secured nearly 1,500 delegates. That was a destructive, exhausting effort that set the stage for the overwhelming Democratic defeat in the general election." The fact that he had endorsed Udall "does not mean that I will permit my office to become involved in an anybody-but-Carter movement."

In their statement, Baron and Quinn declared, "It is regrettable that Governor Carter and his supporters have found our dissent and our principles so dangerous that they felt compelled to bring this pressure."

Praising McGovern for his decision, Carter said, "It's important for a United States Senator to have good, sound political judgment, and perhaps Senator McGovern decided that these two staff members don't have sound judgment politically."

The fact that Carter nurses grudges was made clear to Julian Bond, alone among Atlanta's black leaders in resisting Carter's siren song in 1976. Bond preferred Mo Udall and ran as a delegate for the Arizonan in the Georgia primary. He was clobbered by a Carter supporter. According to Bond, a black friend who was in

Carter's hotel suite told him how Carter and his closest aides yelled and slapped each other on the back when word came of Bond's defeat—the only election he had lost since he won a seat in the Georgia House in 1965.

"Liberal Democrats find comparisons between Carter and Nixon frightening," commented Patrick J. Buchanan, the former Nixon speechwriter. "This writer does not. A certain toughness, deviousness, flexibility and capacity for maneuver are not attributes to be disparaged in a chief executive. Indeed, it is the hidden attributes of Jimmy Carter—rather than the public persona—that convince me that stop-Carter crowds will be no more successful in Madison Square Garden than was the stop-Nixon coalition in Miami Beach."

By now, Jimmy Carter had a new speechwriter. He was Patrick Anderson, who had written the panegyric for *The New York Times Magazine*, entitled "Peanut Farmer for President." Anderson had also written several novels, the latest of which was a thriller, *The President's Mistress*, which was vaguely based on the mysterious death of a young socialite who had been having an affair with the late President Kennedy. (And after serving for a time with the newly elected President Carter, and being let go for unexplained reasons, Anderson came up with a new novel, *First Family*, in which a fictional President is depicted as having an affair with his comely secretary.)

Anderson was brought on as Carter's principal speechwriter after Bob Shrum had quit in a huff. His main job was to counteract what Jody Powell and Pat Caddell felt was becoming a major problem—the feeling of voters that Jimmy was unclear on the issues. Al Hunt, in a major *Wall Street Journal* editorial page piece, "The Vagueness Behind the Smile," discussed what he described as "a disturbing side of Mr. Carter's phenomenal political rise: A willingness to substitute symbolism for substance. This characterizes his approach to a number of issues, and gives rise to the impression that he isn't eager to let voters know where he stands."

As Hunt noted, serious questions about Carter's willingness to deal with the tough issues had been raised by Bob Shrum, who concluded from his brief experience with Carter that "the only thing I am sure he believes in is himself." Shrum, for example, related that prior to issuing a major economic statement, Carter had stated, "I hope it doesn't commit me too much." On another occasion, according to Shrum, Carter said of policy statements generally, "We have to be cautious. We don't want to offend anybody." And Shrum quoted a top Carter aide as saying the candidate didn't like to discuss the specifics of issues because he was afraid he "might make a mistake."

"On a case-by-case basis," commented Hunt, "the Carter people may have adequate answers for most of Shrum's charges. And there's a thin line between desirable flexibility and undesirable obfuscation. But taken as a whole the Shrum memorandum is consistent with a conclusion one reaches from close analysis of the candidate's speeches and campaign style: Jimmy Carter seems much more preoccupied with getting to the White House than with what he hopes to achieve after he gets there."

"Until recently," Hunt also wrote, "Carter was just another candidate in a crowded field; he had little obligation back then to articulate a set of policy positions. But now that he's finished off most of his opponents and has emerged as the likely nominee, he faces tougher standards. Voters are entitled to know in some detail where Carter stands on the issues."

In responding to Common Cause's request that the candidates set forth their budgetary priorities, Carter responded that he favored increased spending for most of the programs dear to Democratic hearts, such as health, education, manpower, and social services, and that savings somehow could be found by cutting Pentagon waste and by general government reorganization. But at no time did Carter give any clues to the emphasis he would give to any of these priorities. "To say," said Hunt, "that his answers are about as responsive as other candidates' is beside the point; none of the others is likely to be the nominee."

Nor was he responsive on tax policy. Throughout the primaries and into the general election campaign itself, Carter relied heavily on the manipulation of symbols. Terming the tax system "a disgrace to the human race," he promised to substitute one that was progressive, simple, treated all income alike, and avoided double-taxation. But he never provided details, repeatedly promising to do so in the course of the campaign. Finally, he conceded he couldn't come up with specifics until a year after he took office.

As a result of the heat he took during the Massachusetts and Florida primaries for suggesting the elimination of the home mortgage interest deduction, his tax positions—as Al Hunt reported—became even more "muddled." Originally, Carter had proposed to end the deduction because, he said, it favored wealthier individuals. But at a press conference some weeks later, he denied ever proposing to end this tax preference and said he actually might want to increase it.

And whenever he addressed a well-heeled audience—as he did at a $125-a-plate dinner in Beverly Hills—he would invariably omit his usual indictment of the U.S. tax system as "a disgrace to the human race." Instead, he would concentrate on what seemed to be his main issue—governmental reorganization. In the late primaries, Carter appeared to be extraordinarily defensive. Meeting with Jewish community leaders in Los Angeles, he volunteered that he had been told of "a great deal of concern . . . by Jewish leaders about my beliefs" as a Southern Baptist. "I ask you to learn about my faith before you permit it to cause you any concern." He assured them that "I worship the same God you worship."

On foreign policy, Carter was also vague. A supposedly definitive address on the subject, Hunt wrote, "consisted mostly of bromide, and clichés." Half of the speech attacked Henry Kissinger for being too soft on the Russians, and the other half attacked Daniel Patrick Moynihan for being too hard on the Third World. And consider how he sidestepped a major question of Middle East policy. During the New York primary, he declared, "it would not be wise at this time to supply strike weapons to Egypt, despite that nation's recent signs of friendship for the United States." But, as Hunt noted, nobody was talking about giving strike weapons to Egypt. At issue was whether the U.S. should provide Egypt with six transport planes; and Carter failed to express an opinion about that.

Then Carter's propensity for hyperbole was demonstrated when he said, "When I go into an embassy in South America or Central America or Europe and see sitting as our ambassador, our representative there, a bloated, ignorant, rich major contributor to a presidential campaign who can't even speak the language of the country in which he serves, and who knows even less about our own country and our consciousness and our ideals and our motivations, it's an insult to me and to the people of America and to the people of that country."

As Eugene J. McCarthy, himself a presidential candidate in 1976 as an independent, later noted, "Certainly it would be an insult if true. But a check on the eleven countries included in the trip on which Carter supposedly based these comments found that there was no ambassador who was bloated or ignorant, as Carter reported; that all but three of the eleven were career diplomats, rather than political appointees; and that of the three political appointees, two could speak the language of the country, and the third was learning it."

On *Face the Nation* over the CBS network on March 14, 1976, columnist Bob Novak interrogated Carter about this subject.

NOVAK: Governor, when you are asked on the campaign trail about foreign policy, I noticed that you always make a criticism and get a great deal of applause for it, that one of the things wrong with our foreign policy is that whenever you walk into an embassy and see, quote, a fat, bloated, ignorant, rich major contributor to Nixon, who can't even speak the language of the country in which he serves, you think that's part of what's wrong with our foreign policy.

Governor, can you name one such fat, ignorant, bloated ambassador who can't speak the language?

CARTER: No; I wouldn't want to name any.

NOVAK: Well, can you name one, though? You make the accusation all over. There are only four ambassadors, Governor, who gave contributions to Mr. Nixon. Are there any of them that fit that category?

CARTER: Well, I wouldn't want to name names, but the point that I'm making is, and I don't do it every time I make a foreign policy speech—

NOVAK: Pretty nearly.

CARTER: Every now and then I do, but not often. When I've been in foreign countries, and go into the embassies, it's obvious from talking to the people in the countries, and talking to the ambassadors, that they are not qualified to be diplomats for this country. They are all appointed as a political payoff. The point I make is that whether they are actually fat or thin, that they are appointed because there are political interrelationships and not because of quality. . . .

NOVAK: Governor, your credibility has been challenged by your critics and by some people in the press. . . . [T]here are only four people who are now serving as ambassadors who gave money to Nixon. Three of them know the language of the country that they work in, and one of them is taking language training. Isn't that bordering on demagoguery when you make a statement about these kind of, quote, fat bloated, ignorant ambassadors?

CARTER: Well, I don't believe so. . . .

NOVAK: Are you going to continue to use that formulation and get applause from it?

CARTER: I may or may not.

ED RABEL: Governor, there is something else you do on the campaign trail. In front of some audiences, you tick off the names of great Americans like Thomas Jefferson, Abraham Lincoln, Martin Luther King, Jr. And I've noticed, though, in front of some all-white audiences you omit the name of Martin Luther King. Now, do you do that intentionally, or have you just forgotten his name?

CARTER: No. As a matter of fact, when you . . . asked me that on the plane the other day, it had not been a deliberate thing. What I ordinarily do, if the audience does have black people in it, I always do include Martin Luther King's name, even if there is only two or three black people in the whole audience. But since that was pointed out to me, I have very carefully included Dr. Martin Luther King, Jr.'s, name, and I am going to continue to do it.

RABEL: Did you do it intentionally before?

CARTER: No; it wasn't. Except that I always intentionally put Martin Luther King's name in if there were black people in the audience, because he was a great American.

RABEL: Why did you leave it out when they were all white?

CARTER: Well, it was not a deliberate thing, and it won't be done any more. . . .

In the end, none of Carter's hyperbole, obfuscations, ill-tempered outbursts, and cliché-ridden speeches seemed to matter. Neither did the late-primary successes scored by Jerry Brown and Frank Church. For it all came down to the crucial Ohio primary; and the reason Ohio was crucial was because the old king-maker Richard J. Daley said it was. On the day of the vote, the Mayor of Chicago made it clear he was not overconcerned about who would win California and New Jersey, whose primaries were taking place that same day. (As it turned out, Jerry Brown took both those states.) Meeting City Hall reporters on the morning of Tuesday, June 8, Daley announced he had just spoken with Carter by telephone. "I said, 'Hello, Jim,' and we had a talk." Then, for the first time, Daley spoke as if he finally had decided that Carter was his man. "He started out months ago and entered into every contest in every state and he won 'em and he lost 'em, and, by God, you have to admire a guy like that." The old pol particularly admired a guy who was on the verge of sewing up the nomination.

A reporter asked Daley whether it wasn't possible for Humphrey to be drafted at the National Convention. And "da may-er," who had never liked Hubert, flared, "Who said that he's the man now who should be knighted on a white horse to walk him into the Convention? I don't think anybody should be so honored, no matter who he is. And I don't think they will."

And that pretty much ended Humphrey's chances.

Returning to Carter's virtues, Daley said, "This man has fought in every primary. He's got something we need more of. He's got a religious tone in what he says, and maybe we should have a little more religion in the entire community. The man talks about true values. Why shouldn't we be sold on him? All of us recognize the violent and filthy movies, and the newspapers with all the mistresses on the first page stripped down to the waist! What are the kids going to do in the society that sees that around?"

And while Carter lost California and New Jersey, he did

extremely well in Ohio, obtaining 52.2 percent of the vote compared to Udall's 21 and Church's 13.9. Carter, it turned out, had made sudden inroads into votes considered Udall's—liberal, affluent Democrats. And his Buckeye supporters included one-half of the voters who had voted for McGovern in 1972, as well as one-half of the Democrats who had defected to vote for Nixon that year. According to a *New York Times-CBS* survey made as voters left the polls, major factors in Carter's victory were his personal qualities, a bandwagon psychology, and the limited appeal of his opponents.

Once Daley had declared that the Ohio primary would be definitive, it hardly seemed to matter that on that same Tuesday in June Jerry Brown was winning his sixth straight primary against Carter, and the largest plurality (1.6 million votes) ever recorded in a single contested presidential primary.

The next morning, Daley made it official. "The ball game is over," His Honor told newsmen. The ball game was over, too, for George Wallace. The Alabamian had phoned Carter at 2:00 A.M. to bury the hatchet. "All I asked him," Wallace said, "is that he would promise, if elected President, he would use all the resources at his command to try to make all the people of this country one of the finest Presidents we've ever had." And Carter replied, "George, I'll make you the best President this country ever had." Which, even in the flush of victory, was quite a statement. Quickly, other contenders capitulated. Jackson freed his delegates to Carter, while Udall and Church pretty much acknowledged the race was over. Humphrey scuttled the anybody-but-Carter movement with his own hand. "Governor Carter," the Happy Warrior said a bit cheerlessly, "is virtually certain to be our party's nominee." Later, in a more introspective mood, Humphrey recalled the pain of failure and defeat, running into debt and having to beg people for money to pay campaign debts. "Now Mr. Carter comes along and he gets it. I have stood in some admiration for his splendid organization, and somewhat envious that he could say so little and get so much. . . ."

The resistance, even from liberal activists opposed to Carter, had virtually collapsed. In retrospect, Udall supporter Mark Shields said later, the resistance had ended too soon. "What I really underestimated this year," he told *The New York Times*, "was the consuming desire of Democratic activists to win the White House. A lot more people than I imagined must have law partners they want to stash away in the Interstate Commerce Commission."

Only Jerry Brown remained an active candidate. But he was tilting at windmills. Said he, "These Nervous Nellies who have joined the Carter bandwagon, I think, misread the public pulse." And then he accused Carter of "all of a sudden doing a flip-flop" because he had accepted endorsements from the likes of Wallace and Daley. "Jimmy Carter," he challenged, "wherever you are, I'm looking for you. I want to debate you."

Jimmy ignored the Californian. He had other things to do. Like getting some rest. He figured he had made over two thousand speeches in the past sixteen and a half months, "and I'm tired." But not too tired to begin thinking of a running mate. And his image problems. *Time*'s Stanley Cloud, who had covered Carter for months, summed it up thus: "Another problem for Carter—and one that will probably persist as the Republicans zero in on him—has been his reputation as a steel-hard, ambitious man for whom winning is the highest value. The description is by no means complete, but there is some truth in it. Carter is a man of striking contradictions. He tirelessly invokes love but can be a tough political infighter. He speaks movingly of the need to help the poor and downtrodden, but he suggests that the solution is to change government organization and programs. One of his great strengths is that he can appeal to a broad cross section of the American people; but he faces the danger that when he details his positions, many who supported him will feel that they were misled. In particular, conservatives may feel deceived when they discover his basic liberalism, which borders on populism."

The fact was, however, that much of the public still considered Carter a conservative. According to *The New York Times-CBS* poll, perception of the Georgian as right of center rose from 10 percent in February 1976 to 52 percent in April. And Gallup poll figures showed that 52 percent of Carter's supporters claimed they were on the right of the political spectrum, 26 percent on the left, 11 percent in the middle. As Professor Jeffrey Hart noted of these figures, "This is surely an extraordinary moment in political history, when the concrete commitments of the candidate are so at variance with his actual voter support."

Another question for Carter was the future of Bob Strauss. There had been published reports that, to win the support of liberal Democrats, Carter had pledged to dump the DNC chairman as soon as his term expired at Convention time. In fact, Bob Shrum had quoted Carter as saying, "If we can't remove Strauss, I'll be a pretty pathetic nominee." But now, on the eve of the Convention, Carter spoke cordially on the phone with Strauss. And Strauss spent two days with the nation's Governors meeting in Hershey, Pennsylvania, to make sure that the Democrats among them supported Carter for President. In the end, twenty-nine of thirty Democratic Governors in attendance fell into line. Only Louisiana's Edwin W. Edwards dissented. A colorful and independent Cajun, Edwards said he intended to continue his support of Jerry Brown "as long as he wants to play Don Quixote." He felt no regional pressure to back Carter, the Lousiana Governor added, because, "Nobody I know views Carter as a traditional Southerner or as a spokesman for Southern beliefs."

Otherwise, under Strauss' watchful gaze, the gathering of Democratic Governors constituted a love feast. Maryland's Marvin Mandel, who had backed Brown while accusing Carter of being a welsher and a covert Nixonite, introduced a resolution hailing him as a man who had proved that he could "heal the divisions of the past" within the party. Recognizing the inevitability of Carter's nomination and hungry for control of the White House, even the Georgian's harshest critics went along. Typical of the change in sentiment was Patrick J. Lucey of Wisconsin, who had privately voiced concern about the depth of Carter's commitment on issues. A key element in his conversion, said Lucey, was the article by Hunter S. Thompson, supporting Carter, which had been published in *Rolling Stone*.

Other conversions were taking place. Thus, after Carter read a carefully crafted speech before the Foreign Policy Association in New York, James Reston of *The New York Times* and the unofficial bishop of The Establishment, baptized Carter on foreign policy. This was the columnist who, incidentally, had been referring to Carter as "Wee Jimmy." It was a tribute to "Wee Jimmy" that after his Waldorf-Astoria speech on June 23, Reston was writing about "Governor Carter." In his speech, Carter cited differences with the "lone ranger" approach of Secretary of State Kissinger. But, as Reston noted, "The important thing about the Governor's latest speech is not that he differed with so many of Kissinger's policies but agreed with so many of them."

But Reston was still telling "Wee Jimmy" what to do, for instance, in selecting a running mate. "If he chooses Henry Jackson of the State of Washington, for example, or any of the other extremists of his party, he is obviously going to be in trouble." Being in trouble meant, of course, incurring the wrath of James Reston.

Jackson, who learned with no little surprise that he had been baptized an extremist, was not averse to being considered Carter's number-two man. And though his name was being touted as one of the people under consideration, the fact was that Carter had early on eliminated him as a possibility. Nevertheless, when Carter arrived in New York for the Convention he did meet with Jackson, as he did with others, already out of contention, Adlai Stevenson, Jr., and Peter Rodino. But it was all show, no substance. Still, it gave a news-hungry media something to chew over.

New York City had been chosen as the site of the Democratic National Convention largely "by default," according to Bob Strauss. The site-selection process had narrowed down to a choice between Gotham and Los Angeles. But Jerry Brown didn't seem overly enthusiastic about having the Convention in California. The Governor had let it be known that he didn't like the idea of a bunch of fat-cat Democrats hanging around luxury hotels, suggesting they consider sleeping in church basements instead. Rhode Island Governor Philip Noel, a member of the site committee, bitterly assailed Brown. "He accuses us of going to fancy parties—this dude who grew up in a Governor's mansion while my mother was hitting a press in a jewelry factory. . . . The little bastard doesn't have a full seabag." And Strauss chimed in about "that little bastard—I couldn't trust him. Who would go someplace where Jerry Brown controls the National Guard? I had visions of riots and him sitting on a mattress and refusing to call out troops."

There were no riots in New York. The proceedings at Madison Square Garden turned out to be more coronation than confrontation. Outnumbering the delegates two to one, the representatives of the fourth estate combed the hotels and buttonholed Democrats on the jammed Convention floor, desperate for some hint of controversy. But there wasn't any. The predicted women's revolt fizzled, the usually raucous Bella Abzug deciding decorum might better assist her chances of obtaining a U.S Senate seat in New York. The more militant blacks, led by Ronald Dellums, whose name was placed in symbolic nomination for the vice-presidency to remind the delegates they were still alive, decided to give Carter the benefit of the doubt and eschew inflammatory rhetoric. The anti-abortionists got in a few licks, but the impressive control exercised by the Carter forces over the Convention machinery minimized their impact. The same forces made certain that Governor Brown remained holed up in the about-to-be-shuttered McAlpin Hotel on West Thirty-third Street, a once-grand hostelry turned fleabag, forsaken by the rest of the California delegation. The fear was that Brown would somehow manage to get to the podium and thus spark a movement for himself as Carter's running mate. And this both Bob Strauss and Charlie Kirbo were pledged to prevent at all costs. They were to prove eminently successful. And for good reason. For at this most Carterized of conventions, Jerry Brown was the major pariah—"that little bastard" who refused almost to the end to bend the knee. And he was treated as such. Yet only six weeks before, as Bill Buckley had noted, Brown had come to New York for a fund-raiser and was introduced to a salon full of fashionable people with the statement: "We all know that 62 percent of the Democrats in this country are anti-Carter." Where were these Democrats now? In line to pay Carter homage.

The image of the 1976 Democratic Convention presented to the American people via television was that of Middle America itself, in its best bib and tucker. It was the Rotary Club luncheon, the Ladies Auxiliary tea, and the Holiday Inn reception all rolled into one. Rarely had there been a national political gathering at which God was so often invoked or one in which so many speakers closed their remarks with a "God bless you." Gone was the McGovernite rabble which had so dominated TV coverage four years previously at the Miami Beach Convention. Gone were the bare feet, dirty jeans, tangled hair, obscenities, and freakish shirts. Whatever pot was smoked was smoked out of camera range. The geeks and freaks were forced to remain outside the Garden, their demonstrations effectively swallowed up by the masses of humanity jamming the sidewalks of New York.

Even the late-night partying seemed strangely constrained. One exception was the madcap affair sponsored by *Rolling Stone,* the rock magazine whose publisher Jann Wenner had invited four hundred of his closest friends to have "supper with the Jimmy Carter campaign staff." Martin Nolan, of *The Boston Globe,* saw it as an effort by *Rolling Stone* to become "the *Osservatore Romano* of the Carter Administration." To Wenner's chagrin, however, Dick Tuck had printed a copy of the invitation in *Reliable Source,* the occasional paper the political prankster published at national conventions. As a consequence, thousands showed up at Automation House on East 68th Street, and the police had to be called to maintain order outside. The doors were closed, and late-arriving guests were unable to gain admittance. Among those anxious to break bread with the Carter team were Lauren Bacall, Ben Bradlee, Chevy Chase, Carl Bernstein, and Warren Beatty. Others who showed up included Sam Brown, a veteran of the 1968 Eugene McCarthy campaign, and Senator Gary Hart, a member of the 1972 McGovern team. Jane Fonda was there with her husband, Tom Hayden. The Chicago Seven alumnus had recently disclosed that his "close friends" who were working for Carter had told him he's "one hundred times more liberal than he appears to be." And, in the words of Senator Hart, "The Kennedy-McCarthy-McGovern wing is still very much alive, but it's inside the party now." But not all those on the left were that sanguine about Carter. Stewart Mott, the millionaire bankroller of liberal causes, announced he intended to work on congressional campaigns, not the presidential. Would he support Carter? "Probably. But now I'm hibernating. Now there are no issues. Nothing bothers me about Carter but nothing inspires me, either."

And further south that night, at the exclusive "21" Club, Barbara Walters sat with Gerald Rafshoon, Carter's media specialist. "We won because we understand the mood of the country," he said. "We won because we knew enough to enter every campaign. We ran a balls-out campaign. . . . Sure we call Jimmy 'Jimmy.'

Will we call him 'Mr. President' when he moves into the White House? I don't know. Are you supposed to? . . .

"There are five of us who are running the campaign. We're the same five who are going to run things after the nomination. The Washington Democrats organizing for Carter are doing it on their own. . . . You know who we were worried about when we started the campaign? Birch Bayh. We thought he'd take all the liberals. Then when we saw him in New Hampshire, we knew we had it.

"No, we weren't worried about Humphrey.

"Jerry Brown is going to run in 1980. I don't like the guy. I don't know what he stands for.

"Ford? We'll beat his ass.

"I've never been in this restaurant except for tonight and once before when Bob Strauss took me here. Who are these people here tonight? Punch Sulzberger, publisher of *The New York Times?* Ben Bradlee? Dorothy Schiff? Where? Walter Cronkite. Sure, they're important. But they don't make an election. How do I feel about all these people in one room? Let's just say I'm 'whelmed.'"

All in all, the Convention was *The Jimmy Carter Show,* and the show stuck to the script. *The National Review* recalled that not too long before, Democrats were warning how the Republic was being wrecked by what they called "the imperial presidency." In fact, the party's historian laureate, Arthur Schlesinger, Jr., even assembled a book with that for the title. "What they meant by 'the Imperial Presidency,'" noted *NR,* "was Richard M. Nixon, whose scalp they were after—and got—for the high crime and misdemeanor of blocking hungry Democrats from access to the joys of incumbency. Although most Democrats promptly forgot the phrase as soon as they got rid of Nixon, Jimmy Carter seems to have taken it at face value. He has assumed the Imperial Presidency even before getting elected to it. Certainly this Madison Square Garden show was more like an imperial coronation than like political conventions as we used to know them. Besides the ceremonies, its only serious function was to proclaim the monarch and to do his will with respect to such trifles as program and Crown Prince."

The selection of the latter was about the only real suspense during the Convention proceedings, and that was overdone. "If no one else noticed the similarity between Carter's performance and Richard Nixon's in choosing Gerald Ford, let me be the first to point it out," wrote Benjamin Stein in *The Wall Street Journal*. But Nixon had done it with more finesse. Peter Rodino, who had been on Carter's well-advertised original list, confided to Carter that he feared a recurrence of glaucoma. The New Jersey Congressman asked Jimmy to simply say that he had dropped out of the vice-presidential sweepstakes and not mention the reason. So Carter blabbed about it at a news conference, embarrassing Rodino no end.

Originally, Carter was believed to have favored John Glenn, the astronaut-turned-Senator, as his running mate. But then questions were raised about the Ohioan's use of income tax shelters. And Carter confirmed that an accounting firm retained by his campaign organization had scrutinized Glenn's tax returns. "I am sure there was no detrimental aspect to the way that Senator Glenn's income tax returns were approached," Carter told newsmen in New York. He said the accountants found the Senator's use of tax shelters "perfectly proper" and "I can tell you he paid an awful lot of taxes." Carter also said that Glenn had actually used a "very conservative approach" to protecting his income from taxation.

"He could have cut corners, but he did not."

Of course, Carter had been vigorously campaigning against the U.S. tax system as "a disgrace to the human race" and had been particularly critical of the fat cats who took advantage of loopholes in the tax codes.

But, as it later turned out, Jimmy Carter himself took advantage of the very same type of loopholes he was condemning. And even more significant was the fact that Carter did not pay "an awful lot of taxes," as did Glenn, in using those loopholes. In fact, questions were raised in the second year of his presidency as to whether Carter hadn't engaged in misrepresentations in order to fleece Uncle Sam of his just due.

What finally did Glenn in was his keynote speech on Monday night. Singularly uninspiring, it contrasted badly with the oratorical flourishes of Congresswoman Barbara Jordan of Texas. And America's astronaut-hero saw his vice-presidential hopes fizzle there on the launching pad. Jordan had made such a big impression across the country that there was an immediate boomlet in her behalf as Carter's running mate. It was true that the black Congresswoman had been on the candidate's original list of such potentials. But that was largely a charade. And everyone, including Jordan, knew it. Now, when people like the Reverend Jesse Jackson were demanding her consideration, Carter's aides let it be known that it wasn't good politics having two Southerners on the same ticket. But there was something else involved. Representative Jordan had been quoted as confessing she didn't "know enough about Governor Carter to develop any impression about this man." She was reduced to attesting, "I believe that Governor Carter is telling the truth when he says he can run on the Democratic platform, that he will do the things the platform calls for to be done." And her hesitance about giving full endorsement to her party's candidate was what was to do in Jordan in her later quest for a cabinet position in the Carter Administration.

On Tuesday, the word was that Muskie had become the front-runner, primarily because of his Catholicism, a fact which would have given Carter an added reach into that 27 percent of the electorate which viewed a born-again Baptist with a rural Southern accent with suspicion. Moreover, despite a voting record which would pass muster with the ADA, Muskie was a familiar and reassuring figure to millions, a man of broad experience and great recognition. But Muskie, because of Glenn's mediocre performance, decided he had to deliver a stem-winder and, as Carter watched on the tube, he launched into a shouting diatribe, his arms and elbows flapping. The raging Muskie, dressed in a white suit and wearing aviator glasses, startled Carter, who had expected one of those quiet, statesmanlike performances. And that, plus reports of Muskie's legendary hair-trigger temper, meant the end of his hopes.

Which left Walter Mondale, who had been the first choice of *The New York Times*, back when Carter was beneath the notice of the gray lady of West Forty-third Street. Besides, as a loyal Minnesotan, Mondale had sought to keep Humphrey's hopes alive deep into the primaries. And there had been a time when Mondale had felt, he said, "There is no way on earth people can take the Vice-President of the United States seriously." But this time "Fritz" was viewing the vice-presidency more solemnly. In fact, he was working on his acceptance speech even before he got the call from his fellow Trilateralist.

"Did I wake you up?" Carter asked. "Would you like to run with me?"

"Governor," Mondale replied, "I'm deeply honored and thrilled."

Also thrilled was the liberal community, which had not viewed the interloping Georgian as one of them. But Mondale was everything the liberal Americans for Democratic Action might have hoped for. He was Carter's ultimate Valentine to the single group that, almost to the end, had refused to endorse the Georgian with enthusiasm. The Social Democrats USA, which in a previous incarnation had been the Socialist Party, fell in line. It endorsed the Carter-Mondale ticket, describing the Democratic platform as a commitment "to deal forthrightly . . . with America's most serious domestic problems." And AFL-CIO president George Meany, who had been cool toward Carter, called him to report that the eighty-five-member Executive Council had voted unanimously to support the ticket.

"You'll be very proud of me," Meany quoted Carter as responding.

Still, organized labor wasn't doing cartwheels over the Georgia Democrat. To the leaders of the AFL-CIO, Carter was no Kennedy, Johnson, or Humphrey. Secretary-treasurer Lane Kirkland, heir apparent to Meany, was quoted by *New Times* as telling a Democratic official, "We're realists. It doesn't make much difference between Ford and Carter. Carter is your typical, smiling, brilliant, backstabbing, bullshitting, Southern nut-cutter." But Mondale's selection did make a difference. As it did to Mo Udall. "I consider the selection of Senator Mondale a very wise choice, and I am delighted," said the Arizonan.

Also delighted, ironically, were the Republicans. For they had noted with more than passing interest Carter's efforts, ever since he had locked up the nomination, to consolidate his position with the previously dominant liberal wing of his party. Said Eddie Mahe, executive director of the Republican National Committee, "I'm delighted with the selection of Senator Mondale. Carter's trying to present himself as one kind of candidate, but every time push comes to shove, he comes down on the liberal side."

For example, Mondale was known in the Senate as "Mr. Busing." But the minister's son did not practice what he preached for others. True, he and his wife, both certified ultraliberals, had sent their three children to the largely black schools in the District of Columbia. But then they pulled them out because, they said, they weren't being trained properly for entrance into colleges. The children were then entered into such exclusive Washington institutions as the Georgetown Day and Sidwell Friends schools at a cost of about $8,000 a year in tuition fees. "You have to make a judgment about quality," said Mondale. But it was a judgment that none but the more affluent could make. And it was a judgment made by most liberals in the nation's capital, most of them vociferously preaching the benefits of integration for other people's children.

No wonder then that Mondale appeared somewhat uncomfortable when Jimmy Carter, in his acceptance speech, blasted away at the political and economic élite who, "when the public schools are inferior or torn by strife," send their children "to exclusive private schools."

Mondale always came up with reasons for failing to practice what he had so long preached. Asked, for instance, why he had moved from an integrating neighborhood in South Minneapolis to the lily-white Kenwood section of that midwest city, the Senator told *The New York Times* it was because his family needed a larger house. And, in that same interview, he made much of the fact that he was one of the few Senators who had moved into what he called Washington's "center city" and not its suburbs. But he forgot to mention that there were few blacks in the Cleveland Park section in which he lived. No wonder there are those who believe that hypocrisy has long been one of the primary exports of the capital city.

At a press conference announcing his choice of Mondale, Carter declared that since he had gotten to know the Senator personally he had "discerned a great compatibility between us on the major issues that face our nation and myself." And Mondale found Carter to be "an uncommon man, terribly gifted, committed, skilled, experienced, ready, but above all, a good man." He spoke, too, of the wonderfulness of "every word" of Carter's autobiography, *Why Not the Best?* Columnist Meg Greenfield described the syndrome as "the grovel factor," lamenting that even independent and self-respecting men such as Mondale often turn obsequious upon taking the number-two role.

The next day, on his way back to Plains, Carter lost his temper. First, he was annoyed because his chartered airline was kept waiting at LaGuardia Airport because of the press of Friday afternoon traffic. Then, during an impromptu press conference aboard the plane, he became irritated by the line of questioning. A reporter had asked whether he thought his acceptance speech was liberal or conservative.

"I think the speech not inadvertently shifted back and forth between the liberal and conservative," he replied. The waffle occasioned some giggles. And Carter went on to say his speech was "Populist" in tone.

"Are you saying you're a Populist?"

"Yes, I think so."

"How do you define Populism?"

"I'll let you define it," Carter replied. "How do you define liberalism? How do you define honesty or love? How do you define compassion or understanding?"

"Yes," said the reporter, seemingly unconcerned about Carter's increasing irritability, "but how do YOU define Populism?"

Carter's icy blue eyes glared at his inquisitor. "I don't want to be in a position where I have to define it," he snarled. With that, he disappeared into his closed-off quarters up front.

A few minutes later, Carter learned he had been photographed beside a gag poster, which had been taped on the bulkhead. The poster, showing Carter with the beard, long hair and white robes of Christ, had the legend "J.C. can save America." Angrily, the newly anointed Democratic nominee dispatched an aide to tear it down.

Meanwhile, asked by the *Village Voice* what Carter's failings might be as President, his media adviser Jerry Rafshoon said, "The failings might be that a lot of people who voted for him for their own reasons will be disappointed that he wasn't what they thought."

12

PREPARING FOR THE FALL CAMPAIGN

FORMER FIRST LADY PATRICIA NIXON WAS STILL AT LONG BEACH Hospital recovering from a stroke when a grinning Walter Mondale gripped the lectern at the Democratic National Convention. Sniffing out the mood of the crowd, the vice-presidential choice of what Jimmy Carter called the "party of compassion" ripped into Gerald R. Ford for having interrupted the prosecution of Richard M. Nixon. Using a line which had been dropped from Carter's speech, Mondale got his best reaction, an animal roar, when he said, "We have just lived through the greatest political scandal in American history and are now led by a President who pardoned the person who did it."

Next up was Jimmy Carter. "Our country," he said, "has lived through a time of torment. It is now a time for healing." Carter's idea of healing was to tear the scab off the Watergate wound, and remind his cheering audience that "big-shot crooks" were going free while "poor ones . . . go to jail."* Two years after Ford's

---

*In his acceptance speech, Carter claimed to be quoting Bob Dylan when referring to an America "busy being born, not busy dying." Which was not exactly what Dylan said in "It's All Right Ma (I'm Only Bleeding)." What he said in the song, used in the final scene of the movie *Easy Rider*, was "there is no sense in trying . . . he's not busy being born, he's busy dying."

pardon of his predecessor—done at great political cost and no personal gain—it still rankled the Nixon-haters. Mondale's reference to the pardon was not unexpected; vice-presidential candidates are expected to sling the mud. That's partly what they're for. Presidential candidates, however, are something else. They're expected to take the high road. Especially one who was constantly preaching compassion, love, and forgiveness.

"If there is any political juice left in that rotten old melon of Watergate," wrote Pat Buchanan, "you can bet that Carter and Mondale, the candidates of compassion and love, are just the boys to find it. Now, don't get them wrong. They are not against charity, just charity toward the Nixons. They are not against pardons, either. In fact, they plan to dole out about 5,000 pardons the first week they are in office—to the draft dodgers who ran away to Canada and Sweden when other, better young men went off to fight and die in Vietnam in what Jimmy Carter likes to call our 'racist' war. . . . Two years after the pardon, after the revelations of the sins of previous Presidents are laid alongside those of Nixon's men, it is clear that what the left was after, is after, is not justice, but Nixon. For eighteen months they had been mainlining it on Watergate. And the individual, no matter his name, who cut off the supply, who put them through cold turkey, would earn their eternal enmity. Ford, courageously, chose to be that man."

One of the sins of previous Presidents—John F. Kennedy and Lyndon B. Johnson—was their approval of the wiretapping, bugging, and surveillance of Dr. Martin Luther King, Jr. So, as Buchanan noted, it was appropriate for the Democratic Convention to pledge action on making the birthday of the late civil rights leader a national holiday. "One wonders what went through the mind of 'Daddy' King, delivering his benediction to a Convention which contained politicians and press who knew, and kept silent, during the '60s when the agencies of a Democratic Administration were gathering and distributing dirt on his murdered son." In retrospect, what two Democratic Presidents did to Dr. King was far worse than anything that occurred during Watergate. Carter and Mondale, however, were not going to bring that up, even though they spoke endlessly about the abuses of the FBI and the CIA—but nothing about the principal abusers,

John F. Kennedy and Lyndon B. Johnson. Nothing critical, that is. For, in his acceptance speech, Carter did refer ritually to Kennedy as "a brave young President" and to Johnson as "a great-hearted Texan." It was only later that Carter described the "great-hearted Texan" as a liar and a cheat.

Following his acceptance speech, Carter apparently had second thoughts about Watergate. In an interview with the Hearst Newspapers Task Force within a week after the Convention, Carter said he didn't "feel that it is completely advantageous to raise the question of Watergate. I would like to avoid that if possible. I have not yet discussed this matter with Senator Mondale. I did not know what was going to be in his speech and he did not raise the question. And I think it is a political mistake." He may not have discussed the matter with Mondale, but the fact remains that Mondale had sent the draft of his acceptance speech over to Carter's speechwriter, Pat Anderson, who in turn provided Mondale with the line on Watergate that was dropped from Carter's speech.

Of course, as it turned out, Watergate may well have been a deciding factor in the slim victory Carter eventually managed to squeeze out. The subject kept coming up all through the campaign. The idiocies attributed to Nixon's men kept returning to haunt Gerald Ford. Even Hollywood helped contribute to the Watergate-infected atmosphere. In the final two weeks before the November 2 election, Warner Brothers booked *All the President's Men* into six hundred theaters across the country. And a spokesman for the movie company branded as "ridiculous" any suggestion that the scheduling could be interpreted as a move to possibly embarrass the Republicans.

What could have embarrassed the Democrats was effectively squelched, however. And that was the fact that Carter's men, like Nixon's before them, had also conspired to electronically eavesdrop on the opposition candidates. The story was later disclosed in Richard Reeves' book *Convention,* and had it come out during the campaign it might well have cost Carter his election. This Reeves himself was to concede later.

According to Reeves, plans for a padlocked espionage room in the Carter Convention trailer at Madison Square Garden were drawn up as early as April, several months before the Convention.

The plans were originally approved by several of Hamilton Jordan's top aides, Rick Hutcheson, William Simon, and James Gammill, as a means of protecting their own communications system from disruption by opposing candidates. "We were paranoid about dirty tricks being played on us," said Gammill, the Convention coördinator. Assigned to assemble the protection equipment was an engineering researcher at the Georgia Institute of Technology named Ronald Pearl. The plan involved a "backup" radio communications system which would be put into operation should the Carter telephone lines at the Convention be sabotaged.

But, according to Pearl, Simon also asked him to put together a system whereby the Carter people would be able to monitor the private conversations of the opposing camps, as well as those of network producers and their correspondents. For, among other things, the Carter staff assumed that the networks would be tapping their phones. After all, the networks had been known to do such things at previous Conventions. In fact, the director of NBC's coverage at the New York Convention was the very woman who had pleaded *nolo contendere* to federal charges that she had placed a listening device inside a closed DNC meeting at the 1968 Chicago Convention. Fined $1,000 in U.S. District Court, the woman for a time was suspended by the network.

Pearl returned to the Carter camp with a plan for "monitoring" other peoples' conversations and, to this end, he was on the verge of purchasing over $30,000 in equipment from suppliers. Though he did not believe any illegality was involved, Pearl later said that he, along with Gammill, wondered whether such monitoring was "politically viable after Watergate."

Apparently, Bill Simon had no such fears, though the original plan to "bug" the opposition was dropped following the Ohio primary. "The nomination was locked up by then," said Gammill, "and the backup system just didn't seem cost-effective." Simon and Pearl flew to New York six days before the Convention to determine where the eavesdropping equipment would be installed. The main object now was to find out what ABC, CBS, and NBC were planning.

At this point, Carter's television adviser, Barry Jagoda, heard of the scheme. And he began to shout, "You must be crazy. Didn't you ever hear of Watergate? If somebody finds out, it'll destroy

Carter!" For two hours, Jagoda argued. "You're talking about bugging," he said. The others didn't see it that way. "Does Jordan know about this?" Jagoda finally asked. "Does Jimmy? Kill it, or I'm calling Hamilton right now."

"Okay," Gammill said. "We must have been crazy."

The resemblance to Watergate was indeed startling. Like Nixon's campaign aides, Carter's associates apparently on their own had decided on a caper which, if disclosed, would have proved most embarrassing to the Democratic candidate in the midst of the campaign. In Nixon's case, there was no pullback. Without the President's knowledge, the Watergate burglary team went into action in an effort to monitor the opposition's communications. And they got caught.

Fortunately for Carter, his boys never got themselves into the position of getting caught.

Not that the story wasn't known outside the Carter camp. Richard Reeves, for one, was aware of the details. And Dan Rather, in a CBS-TV interview with Reeves long after the election, noted that had "that astonishing disclosure" been made during the campaign, it "might have drastically affected the fortunes of Jimmy Carter."

And Reeves did not disagree, conceding that "just before the election, I had enough to go with a newspaper story."

"Sure you did," said Rather. "Now, why didn't you?"

"I wasn't working for a newspaper. I don't know my own motivation. But I thought then that it was conceivable that I had information to turn that election around."

"That if you exploded this story that the Carter people had a political surveillance system all set to go at the Democratic Convention—"

"The Ford people would have killed him."

"They would have killed him with it. The professional, personal political question that came in was what would I have done if I had the same information on Gerald Ford."

"What would you have done?"

"I—I honestly don't know the answer to that."

Several weeks after the Convention, Carter was embarrassed by the disclosure that his aides had paid off black ministers to "turn out the vote" in the California primary. A front-page investigative report in *The Los Angeles Times* of August 8, 1976, also disclosed that "up to $150,000 of the $3 million in federal matching funds Carter already has received" could not be accounted for. One influential minister, who received $2,000 to woo black support for the Georgian, was quoted, "I don't work for no damn politician for nothing."

Conceding the use of such "street money" was Paul Hemman, national Carter campaign administrator. "I guess when Jimmy stood in Maryland and said, 'I don't intend to deal with political hacks,' he was talking about not dealing with white hacks—not black ones," said Hemman, whose duties encompassed financial accounting for the entire campaign. "We had some white hustlers, too, but they were more sophisticated, more plugged into the system." He said they worked under the guise of consultants and free-lance professionals.

Of course, as *The Los Angeles Times* pointed out, the new federal election campaign law required written receipts for all campaign expenditures above $100 and the explicit reporting of such expenditures to the Federal Election Commission. Violations were punishable by a maximum fine of $10,000 and a maximum prison sentence of five years. The *Times* cited three cases in which the Carter campaign reports had listed expenditures as "advance travel" when the money was actually used for other purposes.

According to the story, there was something more than simply sloppy record keeping. The *Times* discovered that several black clergymen in the San Francisco Bay area had received payments of $1,000 to $2,000 from the Carter campaign with no indication of how the money was spent. One minister who supposedly was paid $1,000, according to the reports filed with the FEC, denied having received any money. Other ministers conceded they had received payments from the Carter campaign. While one Carter aide said he could produce written receipts for ninety percent of the money spent by the minority affairs division, Carter himself estimated that proper accounting was lacking for about $150,000 of his campaign expenditures. Another aide said the campaign might have to return $150,000 in matching funds obtained from the federal government because of this. All of which occasioned considerable scurrying around by Carter's people anxious not to be tarred with the Watergate brush.

The story that Mr. Clean's people had been behaving like machine ward heelers with federal funds may have been front-page news in Los Angeles, but it hardly caused a ripple in the big Eastern newspapers. *The New York Times*, for example, brought up the subject on page 13 of its August 9 issue. The headline and lead noted Carter's denial that he or any of his inner circle had known of or condoned the payments to the black clergymen. The *Times* then devoted the next four paragraphs to all of the eventful happenings in Plains, Georgia. First, there had been a fish fry, at which Carter played host. Then there had been Carter's meeting with Jerry Weintraub, a rock music impresario, about fund-raising concerts for the Democratic National Committee. Later, Carter greeted consumer advocate Ralph Nader, who was an overnight guest. Next there was a softball game with Nader, perspiring in one of his nondescript suit and ties, umpiring behind the plate. At that point came a gasoline-fumes explosion at Billy Carter's service station. And Billy had to be restrained from rushing into the danger area.

With all that out of the way, the *Times* dispatch got around to the little matter of those unreceipted expenditures. The story noted that "the use of what amounts to subcontractors, or neighborhood leaders, who are given 'walking around money,' is an established part of political life in some cities. . . ." And the story claimed that since Carter had seldom had the support of machines, his campaign "has seemed less tainted by such practices than some others." The others were not named.

Even more embarrassing was the disclosure shortly after the Convention that one of the members of Carter's inner circle—the candidate's pollster, strategist, and apologist—was on the payroll of the Royal Saudi Arabian Embassy for $80,000 a year. Pat Caddell's job was to provide poll answers to questions submitted by the Saudis and "personal consultations" to help them "employ the information" he gathered in their behalf. The deal was arranged, after months of dickering, five days after Carter won the New Hampshire primary.

The first to blow the lid off the Caddell affair was William Safire, later to win the Pulitzer prize for his series of columns in *The New York Times* on Bert Lance's financial shenanigans. In addition, Safire reported that Caddell was also receiving $80,000 a year from four oil companies. In return, Caddell provided the companies with four quarterly reports on American public opinion. Caddell insisted that he was performing an "educational function" in teaching Arabs about American attitudes. But, as Safire noted, the information could well have been purchased "to help lay the basis for Arab propaganda in America," which was why Caddell was required to register as a foreign agent with the Department of Justice.

Safire wrote he was "ready to believe" Caddell when he insisted that his $160,000 in oil money in no way influenced the questions posed or areas covered in his quarterly reports, also read by Jimmy Carter. "But," the columnist added, "is there no potential for abuse apparent? Carter's pollster says 'the confidentiality of my client situation' keeps him from revealing the thirty questions his Arab clients hired him to ask. Can you imagine the editorial roar of 'cover-up' if a Nixon aide used that excuse?"

Carter soon responded. "I don't have anything to conceal about it," said the newly minted presidential candidate, "and I don't think that because we have a contract with Mr. Caddell to do political polling that he should have to give up all his other subscribers where most of his income is derived. . . ." Caddell, said Carter, "does not fulfill a role in our campaign of establishing policy concerning the Middle East, or even the analysis of issues concerning the Middle East."

"As a matter of fact," Carter went on, "the person who is in charge of our issues analysis is Stuart Eizenstat, who happens to be Jewish and who I might say is a very strong proponent of a strong state of Israel. So I'm the ultimate one who makes decisions about the policy concerning international affairs and I do not see anything wrong or improper about Mr. Caddell serving Saudi Arabia or other nations in the Middle East."

The statement was dissected with dispatch by Bill Safire. The issue, Safire wrote, was not that Caddell "should have to give up all his other subscribers," as Carter had stated. "[The] conflict of interest is with one client, the foreign power that enforces the anti-Jewish boycott, which Mr. Carter's pollster signed up *after* the Carter bandwagon had begun to roll," wrote Safire. Moreover, Caddell was not going to go hungry without his Arab fee, as Carter suggested. The pollster's firm received "hundreds of thousands of dollars," in his own words, from the Carter campaign; and Caddell personally drew $1,500 a month as a consultant to Carter as well. "This is not an issue of making great financial sacrifice to come to work for a candidate. . . ." Safire went on. "This is greed, plain and simple, in the face of an obvious conflict of interest—and Mr. Carter's insistence that it is not 'wrong or improper' tells us what to expect in a Carter Administration."

As far as Carter's "some-of-my-best-analysts-are-Jewish response," Safire wrote, "this is what one expects now of Spiro Agnew. . . . The notion that Mr. Carter blithely presents of balancing one Jew against one Arab lobbyist on his staff—for him to then make Middle East decisions—is repugnant. He ought to be making his foreign policy on the basis of what is right and in the U.S. interest, with staffers providing facts, not representing other interests.

Caddell later was to become the subject of an important article in *The New Republic*. That he "could turn a vague desire to know what people think into a thriving business with clients including some of the wealthiest corporations in the world testifies to his skill as a salesman," wrote Stephen Chapman. "Caddell, with the help of dozens of other pollsters, has manufactured a spurious and largely useless commodity, dressed it up in the jargon of science and business, and parlayed a few glamorous clients into fame, power, and wealth. . . . His arrangement has the mark of genius: one day he labors to elect a liberal Democrat who will expand the control of the government over the big corporations, and the next he advises big corporations on how to manipulate public opinion to protect themselves against further extensions of this control. The more successful he is at the one, the more his help will be needed by the other. Somebody is being had, either the public or his clients. Pat Caddell insists it isn't the public."

A good example of how Caddell worked both sides of the street had previously been disclosed by Charles Mohr of *The New York*

Times. Mohr reported that in March 1976 Caddell's organization had furnished to Westinghouse, a member of the Atomic Industry Forum, a memorandum proposing a "Public Nuclear Acceptance Campaign." The purpose was to combat groups and individuals opposed to nuclear power development. The memorandum said that antinuclear forces were using the "mushroom cloud" and other symbols to foster the belief that nuclear power plants were unsafe. The "traditional" efforts of the industry to prove that nuclear power was safe had proved inadequate, the memo asserted, because most people didn't understand the technical arguments. "The industry needs to find levers with equal emotional intensity: massive unemployment, no growth, poor living standards, runaway costs, and foreign dominance," the memo went on.

At the same time, according to the *Times*, Caddell had been conducting a poll for the Science Institute for Public Information, an environmentalist group favoring the limiting of nuclear power development. As soon as officials of the public interest organization learned of the Westinghouse memorandum, they angrily canceled their contract with Caddell. And one official was quoted, "I have learned there is no ethical code for poll takers."

Despite all these revelations, Carter kept on defending his youthful pollster. "We chose him because he is the best," chimed in campaign manager Ham Jordan. Which is what Carter said about his running mate. Fritz Mondale, he insisted, was the "best" choice he could have made, noting that he agreed with the Minnesotan "on almost every major issue." Carter also went so far as to defend Mondale's action in sponsoring special tax legislation that would benefit Investors Diversified Services Inc., a Minneapolis-based financial service company. Although Carter had championed tax reform that would eliminate such special privileges as the one Mondale proposed, he did not think there was anything "illegal" or "improper" about giving a tax break to IDS. Carter felt, as he told a news conference in Plains, that the Senator was doing nothing more than any other representative or Governor would do to promote industry within his constituency. But, he added, he planned to discuss the matter with Mondale and said he had "no doubt" that his running mate would join him in his call for tax law revisions.

But few moralists were shocked. Nor was much concern expressed when, a week after the Convention, Carter turned up as guest of honor at a New York luncheon tendered by the kind of fat cats he had been excoriating for months, the same kind of "economic élite" who, he claimed, "never stood in line looking for a job." Here he was, the fellow who had said at Madison Square Garden that "too often, unholy, self-perpetuating alliances have been formed between money and politics," standing now in the elegant "21" Club before fifty blue-chip corporate and financial leaders, saying, "I will be a friend of business." The same Jimmy Carter who had been criticizing the export of American jobs abroad was saying, "I would not do anything to subvert or minimize foreign investment. . . . I am basically committed to . . . international trade." And he vowed (or seemed to vow) to help overcome the disastrous image problem dogging multinationals and Big Oil. "This will be an important responsibility of mine, and I won't let you down," he promised.

Carter had attended the luncheon at the suggestion of his old friend Charlie Kirbo, who was concerned about the candidate's relations with the business community. Some of Carter's aides thought the appearance a bad idea, contradicting the tone of the Populist-sounding speech he had made in accepting the nomination. *The New York Times* took a different tack: "While Mr. Carter's effort to demonstrate that he is a careful pragmatist, not a dogmatic ideologue, is welcome, he needs to recognize that among the most serious charges he faces are that he is vague in his policies, that he hedges when he is not vague, and that he tries to be all things to all people. On such major issues as tax reform, Americans have a right to know, in basic concept, what they are voting for or against, and should not have to wait for a year after the election to find out."

Only later, two years after the event took place at the "21" Club, was it to prove slightly embarrassing. It was then that the Federal Election Commission ordered Carter's campaign committee to repay the U.S. Treasury a sum of over $3,000 after ruling that the luncheon constituted an illegal contribution. Also fined were Seagram's liquor heir Edgar Bronfman and a Coca-Cola political committee. Auto magnate Henry Ford was not fined because, having been warned that his contribution to the luncheon might be illegal, he asked the Democratic National Committee for his money back. The purpose of the luncheon, of course, was to introduce prominent businessmen to the man who had just been nominated for President by the Democratic National Convention. And a man who, all polls indicated, was most likely to become the next President.

The polls indicated much more than that, in fact. They indicated that Carter had a lead over either Gerald Ford or Ronald Reagan—still slugging it out for the Republican nomination—which pollster Lou Harris described as "one of the most substantial ever recorded." The lead was indeed incredible. Carter ran 39 points over Ford (Carter 66; Ford 27) and 42 over Reagan (Carter 68; Reagan 26). Two weeks later, on August 1, George Gallup gave Carter a 33-point lead over Ford.

And the man from Plains thought he had it made. So much so that he almost forgot he had a campaign to run. He began to act as if he were already elected. Busloads of experts on the economy, foreign policy, and defense arrived at Plains, where Carter spent most of the summer. The candidate even brought in actor Robert Redford to discuss environmental concerns. And, as noted, Ralph Nader had been by for a well-publicized overnight stay, the visit causing concern particularly among Southern pols who considered the consumer advocate more a liability than a plus.

Other familiar figures were turning up in Plains to advise Carter on foreign policy. Which led *The New Republic* to review the men who had clustered in the pump house to tell Jimmy what was going on in the world. In an editorial titled "Trooping to Plains," the liberal magazine observed, "With few exceptions, the briefers in Plains and the Carter foreign and defense policy task forces are the old roll of the club—former Pentagon officials Cyrus Vance, Paul Nitze, Paul Warnke; State Department ex-bureaucrats like Charles Yost and Henry Owen; and what one observer aptly calls the 'hungry professors'—men such as Zbigniew Brzezinski and Richard Gardner of Columbia. . . . If there is one overriding characteristic shared by these homogeneous men of the establishment, it is how often, how long, and how unrepentently they have been wrong about international affairs. The Carter advisory group in large part reads like a class reunion of the early supporters of the Vietnam war. . . . The clique represented in Plains portends the same kind of bureaucratic disarray, secret closed government, and state thinking that plagued the Johnson Administration. . . ."

So cocksure was Carter that he would soon be residing in the White House that he made an unusual request of the Federal Election Commission. He told the FEC he would need additional funds in order to start planning the transition to his new Administration. And he asked the FEC whether some of the money expected to be arriving from private donors, unaware that the major candidates were being federally financed, couldn't be used for transition planning instead of being sent back.

Meanwhile, Carter had pointedly set up his headquarters in Atlanta, thus assuring that control of the campaign would remain in the hands of the Georgians who had engineered his nomination. Bob Strauss, whom Carter was now calling "the greatest party chairman I have ever known," remained in that post in Washington. But it wasn't the wily Texan who began calling the campaign shots; it was Ham Jordan, less experienced on the national scene. Like Carter, Jordan was euphoric over the pollsters' figures. They saw in them the possibility of duplicating Richard Nixon's unprecedented forty-nine-state landslide of 1972. "We're in too good a shape everywhere to start giving away states," Jordan told Bob Shogan of *The Los Angeles Times*.

In early August, before the Republican Convention was due to begin in Kansas City, Carter flew to New Hampshire, thus carrying out a pledge that he would return to the Granite State if he won the primary there. He had ordered a high-toned speech for a noon rally in Manchester on the "breakdown of the American family," replete with statistics on the huge divorce rate, illegitimacy, drug and alcohol abuse, and the like, an oration climaxed with the announcement that he had asked Washington attorney Joseph A. Califano, Jr., to serve as a special adviser on developing a "pro-family policy."

But in his introduction Carter lashed out at the "Nixon-Ford Administration" and accused it of governing by "vetoes and not vision . . . scandals and not stability or pride . . . rhetoric, not reason . . . an Administration of empty promises instead of progress and prosperity." And then he aimed at the race between Ford and Reagan: "We see an almost unbelievable spectacle in Washington. The President of the United States, deeply concerned by an ex-movie actor. We see him running all over the country for a handful of delegates, and neglecting the basic responsibilities of leadership." He did not suggest how else Ford could win the nomination. Nor did he allude to his own neglect of gubernatorial duties in launching his own covert campaign for the presidency.

The litany of complaint continued into the late afternoon, as he stood before a large crowd of Democrats who had paid ten dollars each to munch peanuts, have a drink, and listen to Carter at the Wayfarer Inn. Extolling the virtues of person-to-person campaigning of the kind he credited with his political success, Carter said it was important "to learn directly from those who feel the effect of unfair tax laws, of the lack of an energy policy, of a neglected foreign policy, of the disgrace of Watergate, of the embarrassment of the CIA revelations. . . ."

The campaign themes thus starkly stated, the Democratic nominee went on to suggest he knew what the Republicans would use as their theme. "As soon as the Republican Convention is over," he warned, "I predict there is going to be almost an unprecedented, vicious, personal attack on me" and on Mondale, out of "desperation." The Republican Party, he went on, was "going to be desperate and in desperation they will turn to personal attacks—mark my words." When pressed for harbingers of such evil, he cited "very strong statements" made by GOP Senator Bob Dole, which sent reporters scurrying to find out what the Kansan had been saying. All Dole, who was capable of much more, had said of the Georgian was that he was "a Southern-fried McGovern or Humphrey."

Carter's New Hampshire remarks were extraordinary, coming from a candidate billing himself as a champion of compassion and love; and they hardly augured well for the tone of the forthcoming campaign. Still, Carter was dismayed when the news of the day, as carried on television and in print, concentrated on his highly inflammatory remarks, generally ignoring his message on the American family. Just as dismayed was Ham Jordan, who in a memorandum urged Carter to desist from using the phrase "Nixon-Ford Administration." He said the phrase "suggests a very conscious effort on your part to equate Ford, the man, with Nixon, the man. This . . . will not wash with the American people, and I believe it will be generally interpreted as a personal attack on the integrity of Gerald Ford. When I watched you say that on the news recently, it sounded harsh and out of character for you. It certainly did not sound like a man who wanted to put Watergate behind us and unite the country."

But Carter ignored Jordan's admonition. Shortly after the Republicans selected Ford and Robert Dole as their nominees, Carter burst forth with a wide-ranging assault on points where he considered his opponents to be the weakest, including their Nixon legacy. While reiterating that he did not intend to exploit the Watergate scandal in the fall campaign, Carter insisted it was legitimate to link Nixon and Ford because there was "almost complete continuity" in policy under the two Republican Presidents. Of course, he wasn't suggesting that Ford was linked to the "crimes" of the Nixon Administration. Rather he was referring to "policies of the Nixon Administration in the domestic and foreign fields." But wasn't he linking Ford to a man who was "fairly unsavory?" Replied Carter, "It's not my fault that Nixon is unsavory."

A few days later, the candidate who had promised not to bring up Watergate reminded a Los Angeles audience that his opponent owed his job to Nixon by referring to Ford as an "appointed President," a term he had never used before. Invoking a neo-Populist theme, Carter declared, "It is time we had a President who will lead our nation and who will work with harmony with Congress for a change, with mutual respect for a change, out in the open for a change, so the working families of this country can be represented as well as the rich and the powerful and the special interest groups."*

In his prepared text, Carter also referred to people who "ride in limousines too long," but he struck this cheer line from his speech, explaining later that he thought it improper to mention

---

*Carter kept on referring to Ford as an "appointed President" during the campaign. But, strictly speaking, Ford was no more an "appointed President" than were Lyndon Johnson and Harry Truman. After all, Ford's elevation to the vice-presidency was weighed and approved by a Democratic Congress, aware that Nixon's days were numbered. By contrast, no congressional hearings were involved in the "appointment" of other vice-presidents who assumed the presidency. And it could be argued that no other vice-president was as carefully scrutinized as Ford. Carter's argument, therefore, was with Congress or with the Twenty-fifth Amendment.

the subject after the Secret Service had supplied him with a long, sleek black limousine for traveling around Los Angeles. Hereafter, he would ride only in regular cars, he said. And, if elected, he intended to curtail the use of limousines in Washington. Again recalling Nixon, he said, "I think this process reached a peak a few years ago, when we had a President who surrounded himself with people who knew everything about merchandising and manipulation and winning elections and nothing at all about the hopes and fears and dreams of average people."*

Of course, Carter said nothing about something even more non-Populist than Secret Service-driven Cadillacs—namely, his use of chartered jet planes. Arriving aboard one from Georgia, the candidate made certain that the cameras recorded him humbly carrying his own garment bag over his right shoulder as he deplaned. (The bag was quickly taken from him by an aide once the cameras were turned off; and most of Carter's luggage was processed in the usual way.) From the airport, the candidate was whisked off to the first event of the evening—a sumptuous Beverly Hills party thrown by Lew Wasserman, board chairman of the giant Music Corporation of America, and attended by many of the biggest names in movie moguldom.

After two hours of mingling with the moguls over caviar and lobster claws, Carter moved on to the Beverly Wilshire Hotel, where actor Warren Beatty was throwing a party for him in an eighth-floor suite. About fifty of Hollywood's trendy celebrities were gathered to meet their born-again Southern Baptist guest. Beatty, who usually performed such chores for more orthodox liberal candidates such as George McGovern, conceded the existence of a cultural gap. This meeting, Beatty said, should help blunt the religious issue in the campaign.

"If I came to Warren Beatty's party, it should help wipe out the

---

*True to his word, Carter ordered the Secret Service to provide him with a sedan for his campaigning. The sedan, necessarily super-protective and bullet-proofed, cost almost as much as the limousine. But, at least, Jimmy was able to keep the cheer line in his speech. The irony was that, despite Carter's implication, the White House used comparatively few limousines of the type the Georgian was attacking. According to an Associated Press dispatch, aside from special security vehicles, the records showed only fourteen large cars being used by the Executive branch. The reason was that during the 1974 energy crisis President Nixon slashed the use of big cars from 211 to a more modest level. Despite this disclosure, however, Carter kept on complaining about "big shots" riding "in limousines too long."

issue," joked Carter as he looked out over such luminaries as Diana Ross, George Segal, Peter Falk, Faye Dunaway, Neil Simon, Art Garfunkle, James Caan, Jon Voight, Alan Pakula, Hugh Hefner, George Peppard, and Dinah Shore. "It is a real thrill to meet the famous people here tonight," Carter went on. "I hope I don't get to know too much about you."

Carroll O'Connor, of "Archie Bunker" fame, then told the candidate of his distress over the mounting criticism of Secretary of State Kissinger's pursuit of détente, contending that Alexander Solzhenitsyn, around whom many opponents of détente had rallied, was becoming "a figure of propaganda for anti-Russian forces." Carter said he agreed with "almost everything" O'Connor said. "I think we ought to proceed aggressively with détente." But he added he didn't think Kissinger's words "have the force they used to"—which was considerably softer than the criticism he had made of the Secretary in the past. He said nothing about Solzhenitsyn.*

But he launched into a little sermon on how the poor and weak suffer as the rich and powerful, "who have good lawyers, who have lobbyists in the Capitol in Washington," organize for their own preservation. And he painted a bleak, heart-wrenching picture of rural Georgia. "In the county where I'm from," he said, "we don't have a doctor, a dentist, a pharmacist, a registered nurse, and people who live there who are very poor have no access to preventive health care. . . ."

"So I say," he went on, "public servants like me and Jerry Brown and others have a special responsibility to bypass the bigshots, including you and people like you and like I was, and make a concerted effort to understand people who are poor, black, speak a foreign language, who are not well educated, who are inarticulate, who are stymied. . . ."

The Tobacco Road routine apparently went over very well with a crowd described by Beatty as consisting of people sometimes

*On October 16, in a campaign appearance in Columbus, Ohio, Jimmy Carter accused President Ford of refusing to invite Solzhenitsyn to the White House because of pressure from "his Secretary of State and the Soviet Union." He added that when he goes to the White House in January, "I'm going to invite Alexander Solzhenitsyn to come by and see me." As yet, after two years in the White House, President Carter still hasn't met with the famed Russian writer.

regarded as "pinkos, leftists, and Commies." And it undoubtedly did produce an ecstasy of moral indignation. For these were people once described by Eugene Lyons as "swimming pool proletariat," who felt guilt over their own financial success.

But how accurate was Carter in his tear-jerking portrayal of rural Georgia? Not very, according to Kevin Phillips. The syndicated columnist noted that Plains, Georgia, lies in Sumter County. Not only did Sumter County have a hospital, twenty-two physicians, pharmacies, and registered nurses, but one James Earl Carter, Jr., served on the hospital authority there. What is more, Jimmy's mother, Miz Lillian, had been a registered nurse for years. By any of the usual criteria, in fact, medical care in Sumter County was normal for Georgia and not bad by most rural standards on a national basis.

"What was going on here?" wrote Jeffrey Hart. "Had Kevin Phillips caught Jimmy Carter telling an outright, needless, and easily detectable lie?"

Pondering this at *National Review*, Hart and his fellow editors decided there might be more to it than met the eye, and placed a call to Carter headquarters in Atlanta. Yes, there was an explanation. When Carter referred to "the county where I'm from," he didn't mean Sumter County, where he now lived, but adjacent Webster County, where he was reared.

And Webster County, a tiny entity with a population of 2,600 does not have any physicians, pharmacies, etc. But it is served by dozens of physicians located eight to twelve miles away in adjoining counties. Similarly, Webster County residents have to cross the county line to reach a pharmacy, though, in point of fact, pharmacies were not in short supply and not inaccessible.

"In view of these facts, Carter headquarters contended, you could not say that Carter was lying out in Hollywood," wrote Professor Hart. "Strictly speaking, I suppose he was not. Had Carter given that statement under oath, he might well have beaten a perjury charge. But the statement was certainly deceptive and the explanation given by his headquarters so ingenious as to constitute a different kind of outrage."

By the end of August, it seemed that Carter was off on a gaffe-a-week streak. There was, for example, the Wallace flap. What happened was that Carter was seeking to illustrate what he felt was low public regard for John Connally, at that time a possible running mate for Gerald Ford. In an interview published in *The New York Times*, Carter was quoted as saying that, in regard to public trust, "Maybe the only person in the country who has a lower rating in the polls than Connally is Governor George Wallace."

Carter then phoned Wallace to apologize for the remark. "I'm very sorry about any misunderstanding caused by this news report," Carter said in a statement after the telephone conversation. "Governor Wallace has agreed to campaign on my behalf during the general election. I repeated to him my statement of appreciation for the earlier endorsement and strong support of Governor Wallace which was so important to the Carter campaign after the last primary in June."*

A few days later came the Bush gaffe. In a speech before the American Bar Association convention in Atlanta, Carter accused the Nixon and Ford Administrations of using top jobs in regulatory agencies and elsewhere as "dumping grounds for unsuccessful candidates, faithful political partisans, out-of-favor White House aides, and representatives of special interests." Whom was the candidate talking about? According to a confidential staff memo, one of the defeated GOP candidates rewarded with a high office was George Bush, Director of the CIA. And the memo was shown to reporters shortly before Bush was due to arrive in Plains to brief Carter on national security matters. "It was a serious mistake on some staff member's part," said Carter as he praised Bush's abilities as CIA director.†

The gaffes continued. At the Iowa State Fair, Carter told a large audience of farm folk that, when elected, he would stop government embargoes on grain exports "once and for all." Not long after that, he told a reporter for *The Des Moines Register* that his words

---

*Carter also apologized to the Reverend Billy Graham, but not for anything he said. Rather he called the evangelist to apologize because one of his sons had declared publicly that Dr. Graham had purchased his doctorate for "five bucks."

---

†Another named among "out-of-favor White House aides" who obtained major posts was Alexander Haig, former chief of staff for President Nixon who occupied the post of Supreme Commander of the North Atlantic Treaty Organization. Significantly, Haig was kept on as Supreme Commander by President Carter.

may have been "too strong" in light of possible but unlikely disasters that would threaten hunger in the U.S. The stories the next day emphasized Carter's backing off from his original no-embargoes pledge. And it gave Bob Dole, the GOP vice-presidential candidate, who spoke at the fair that day, the opportunity to accuse Carter of willfully misleading farmers and again engaging in issue-juggling. At a news conference, Dole kept up the attack. "I don't know whether Jimmy Carter was a farmer or not. I know he inherited a big plantation down in Georgia. They made a great deal of money sharecropping, and I don't know if that's farming or not. That's when you let somebody else farm it and you take the profit."

Carter also appeared to be engaged in issue-juggling when he outlined his views on the heated abortion issue before six Roman Catholic bishops at the Mayflower Hotel in Washington. Ever since the Iowa primary, Carter had been the target of anti-abortion, Right-to-Life picketers and polls indicated he was in trouble with Catholic voters, long the backbone of the Democratic vote. Hence the meeting at the Mayflower. But, from the beginning, Carter was in trouble. Though he was personally opposed to abortion, he nevertheless would not support constitutional amendments prohibiting the practice. At the same time, he would not support the Democratic Party's own plank opposing citizen's efforts to obtain such anti-abortion amendments.

Carter's position was not good enough, and the bishops told him so. Finally, he indicated that he might sometime find some constitutional amendment he could support. But he would have to study the wording very carefully.

As he left the meeting, Carter told the clergy how much he enjoyed exchanging views and—using a phrase which startled his listeners—how much he hoped his relationship with them "will grow after this embryonic start."

Outside, Archbishop Joseph L. Bernardin, president of the bishop's conference, expressed "disappointment" in what Carter had to say. But, he added, "Governor Carter did tell us that if acceptable language could be found, he would support a constitutional amendment."

Did this signify a switch in Carter's position? No, he told reporters. What he meant to tell the bishops, he said, was that he did not intend to rule out something which he had not yet seen. Carter insisted he still was opposed to the anti-abortion amendments then being proposed. But once again Carter had enhanced his image as a "flip-flopper." Carter, commented Carl Rowan, "had better soon learn to live with the fact that neither Catholic, Protestant, agnostic, nor atheist will long respect" a candidate who plays wishy-washy on "important issues" like abortion. And New York's Terence Cardinal Cooke, among others, said he found it "hard to understand" how Carter "can say that he's personally opposed to abortion, but doesn't want to do anything about it."

Concerned about the erosion of support among Catholics, Carter undertook to do some fence-mending in a lengthy interview with the National Catholic News Service. In the interview, he underscored his disapproval of the strong pro-abortion plank of his party. He said it was "inappropriate" for the Democratic Party to discourage citizens from exercising their right to seek changes in the Constitution. Carter was corrected by the interviewer when he referred to his issues adviser, the Reverend Joseph Duffey, as a Catholic. Sure enough, the name sounded Irish to Carter, but Duffey had been ordained in the United Church of Christ and raised as a Southern Baptist.

At the same time, Carter sought to reassure the liberals by going before the American Legion convention in Seattle and bluntly stating that he would grant a "blanket pardon" to all Vietnam war resisters. The Legionnaires booed him, but the doubters in the left wing of his party were reassured. And, more important, perhaps, Carter momentarily was able to put down criticism that he always tailored his speeches to please his audiences. Nevertheless, Carter began to hear complaints from regular Democrats that he was going overboard with his newfound "liberalism."

All in all, August hadn't been a good month for Carter. If anything, the race between him and Ford had tightened. Gallup now showed Carter leading the President by thirteen points. Pat Caddell's polling showed Carter leading by even less. In a sense, the new figures—terrifying as they were to Carter's aides—proved a blessing. "It did wonders for the Carter campaign," said Caddell. "It brought everyone back from thinking about where their offices were going to be in the White House."

13

SHAFTING PRESIDENT FORD

TRADITIONALLY, DEMOCRATIC CANDIDATES HAD LAUNCHED their presidential campaigns addressing labor rallies in Detroit's Cadillac Square. But this Labor Day, Jimmy Carter pulled a switch. He kicked off his campaign in Warm Springs, Georgia, where Franklin Delano Roosevelt had spent his final days at the "Little White House." The reason, his aides explained, as if they had to, was to tie Jimmy in with the Democratic past, wrapping him in the aura of the Old Coalition. For Pat Caddell's poll information still indicated a further need to identify his candidate with the party's rank and file. There was another reason which was not mentioned publicly. Detroit's downtown district just was not safe. Roving gangs had been committing random acts of violence in the area. And the last thing Carter wanted was a kickoff marred by untoward incidents or a major display of police force—particularly in a city run by a Democratic mayor who had been an early Carter supporter.

Warm Springs was a lovely setting, and the day was beautiful. James Roosevelt introduced Carter, and FDR Jr. was also on the platform. Graham Jackson, the black navy veteran who was a favorite of FDR, played "Happy Days Are Here Again" on the accordion." In the audience were patients in wheelchairs. All that was missing, as Martin Schram noted, was James Farley and Fala.

In his speech, Carter took the offensive, waving the bloody shirt of Herbert Hoover with a missionary zeal, preaching Republican hellfire and Democratic salvation. He tried to suggest he was another Roosevelt, a bold man of action, close to the people, ready to restore "strength and hope" at a time "an afflicted nation" was crying out for forceful change. President Ford, he implied, was another Herbert Hoover. Hoover, too, was "an incumbent President, a decent and well-intentioned man who sincerely believed that there was nothing our government could or should do to attack the terrible economic and social ills of our nation." Moreover, Ford was a "timid" man, who "hides in his stateroom while the crew argues about who is to blame" for all the terrible things that have happened. Quoting the sign on Harry Truman's desk, "The buck stops here," he added, "There was never any doubt about who was captain of the ship. Now no one seems to be in charge. No one is responsible."

"During my lifetime," he went on, "from farm boy to nominee for President, I have always been close to the working families of this nation." And then in the line that got strong applause, he said, "I owe the special interests"—dramatic pause— "nothing. And I owe the people"—another dramatic pause— "everything."

Then the Man of the People flew off to Darlington, South Carolina, to attend the Southern 500 stock car classic. But when he heard Bob Dole was also going to be there, Carter was on the verge of canceling. He definitely wasn't going to be seen in the company of a mere vice-presidential candidate of the other party. Finally, almost at the last moment, a deal was struck. The two candidates would ride around the track in separate cars, then join each other in the VIP booth to watch the race. But Carter one-upped Dole. Instead of joining him in the booth, he pressed the flesh in the pits, promising he'd invite the drivers and their crews to the White House for dinner. And the crowds in the stands loved it. From the "people," Carter moved on to a Tara-like brick mansion in nearby Florence. There he mingled with beer distributors, tobacco plantation owners, well-to-do merchants, and local politicians and, standing on a Louis XIV chair, Carter said: "I'm a race car fan. I like to get in the infield. Rosalynn and I have been going to the car races since 1946. I kind of regard race car drivers as heroes."

All in all, it wasn't a bad beginning for the Carter campaign. But from then on, everything seemed to go downhill. The next morning at 7:40 A.M. Carter showed up at a subway station in Manhattan's Columbus Circle. But the only people there seemed to be photographers, dozens of them, busily snapping away. "Can't we find any real people?" the candidate asked plaintively. Congressman (later Mayor) Edward Koch, accompanying Carter, couldn't understand why the candidate's advance men had selected Columbus Circle. "Anybody who knows anything about New York knows this is not really a commuter stop," he told a newsman. "Especially not this early in the morning. They might start arriving here later (just before offices are to open), but nobody leaves for work from here. He should have been up at Eighty-sixth Street."

Carter's naïveté about New York again was demonstrated at Brooklyn College. In his prepared statement, he observed that "a healthy city neighborhood . . . is not so very different from the small town in Georgia where I grew up," with each having its "own special character." Noting he came from Plains, not "Americus, or Vienna, or Cordele," he added, "You come from Flatbush—and not Sunnyside, or Bay Ridge or Brooklyn Heights." This caused some bewilderment among the students who came from all parts of the city, including Sunnyside, Bay Ridge, and Brooklyn Heights.

But that was to prove the least of Carter's problems that morning. Out of the blue, Carter assailed Clarence Kelley, the Director of the FBI, for having permitted Bureau carpenters to construct $335 worth of drapery valances in his Washington apartment. The previous weekend, President Ford had given Kelley a vote of confidence with the proviso that he repay the government for any public costs involved in the work in his home. This Kelley said he would do.

Unable to leave the matter alone, Carter told the Brooklyn students that the FBI Director should "set an example" in fighting crime and "ought to be purer than Caesar's wife." At that stage, Carter professed to be reluctant to say whether he would have fired Kelley if he were President. But, pressed to the point, he replied, "Yes, based on what has been revealed." But, as the day progressed, Carter kept returning to the subject, evidently viewing Kelley's peccadilloes as essentially part of a continuum of Republican corruption. And the man who had previously said he would not raise Watergate as an issue began doing so.

In Philadelphia that day, he said that Kelley had been "caught with government employees using my and your tax money decorating his apartment. So President Ford had the Attorney General investigate it, and the Attorney General said he did it, and President Ford said, 'Well, let's let him stay where he is.'" There was no stopping Carter. "When people . . . see Richard Nixon cheating, lying, leaving the White House in disgrace, when they see the previous Attorney General violate the law and admit it," he went on, "when you see the head of the FBI break a little law and stay there, it gives everyone the idea that crime must be okay. If the big shots in Washington can get away with it, well, so can I."

Actually, it was difficult to ascertain from Carter's shifting positions whether, as President, he would fire Clarence Kelley. In fact, at one point he said, "I will cross that bridge when I come to it." The next day, Jim Wooten in *The New York Times* labeled the answer an "apparent contradiction" and Gerald Ford, talking to reporters at the White House, accused his opponent of flip-flopping. At the same time, the President accused Carter of having "a lack of compassion" because Kelley had accepted the valances at a time when his wife was dying of cancer. And, much to the amazement of even his own aides, Carter's response was that he could not be charged with lack of compassion because Director Kelley apparently "has found a new loved one." It was a cheap shot, labeled as such even by those in the media who made no secret of their pro-Carter sympathies.

"If the exchanges [between Carter and Ford] are a fair sample, the campaign is going to set a new level of muddiness and tastelessness," wrote Mary McGrory. ". . . Jimmy Carter had a chance to show something other than copybook morality, but he didn't. About the only thing he got out of the messy encounter was the chance to say he was sorry he got into it. He said it had diverted him from the main issues between him and Gerald Ford.

But it did something worse. It raised questions about his ability to ride the rapids of a national campaign, where it is important to demonstrate knowledge of the real issues. . . ."

Philadelphia had been a disaster for other reasons. Carter was supposed to meet with leaders of a community group to discuss housing, crime, and a shortage of mortage money in the slums of the City of Brotherly Love. And the meeting had been planned for Our Lady of Pompeii Church, but John Cardinal Krol said the church couldn't be used for the meeting unless abortion was added to the agenda. Whereupon the meeting was transferred to a nearby Lutheran church. The move wrecked Carter's plans, because he desperately wanted to appear in a Catholic church in a poor, urban neighborhood.

The abortion issue was now dogging Carter's every step. It was at the meeting at the Lutheran church, St. Simeon's, that Carter repeated his precisely waffled position that he abhorred abortion (nobody, he said, has sex with the goal of having an abortion), but he wouldn't support a pro-life constitutional amendment to do anything about it. And, he added, he didn't intend to change his position "even in an election year." Arriving at the Hilton Inn in Scranton that night, Carter found himself confronted with several hundred sign-waving demonstrators shouting, "Life! Life! Life!" It had not been a good day. And it was not to be a good week, either. Which Carter would acknowledge on his return to Plains for a weekend of recuperation and introspection. His big mistake, he told newsmen, was dragging out the business about Director Kelley. "It may have been better had I not got involved in [it] at all," he conceded. The media attention given it "kind of inter-rupted our week's main themes"—mainly his desire to identify with blue collar concerns.

The major bright spot in that dreary week was the welcome put on for Carter by Richard Daley. The Mayor had told reporters that the torchlight parade for Carter would be "the finest salute to a candidate ever given in the history of the city of Chicago." And it was indeed a grand parade, marred only by small bands of pro-life demonstrators waving banners in protest. And it was also a grand night for political orations. Daley's handpicked candidate for Governor, Michael Howlett, tore into his Republican opponent, James Thompson, as a "Nixon Republican" and an "opportunist" who was trying to reap a political harvest from the carcasses of "good men that he has destroyed." The "good men," needless to say, were Daley henchmen whom Thompson, as a federal prosecutor, had sent to the slammer on various charges involving corruption. All of which only served as a reminder of the fact that Daley was the very epitome of the political bossism that Carter had long claimed to loathe.

Howlett continued his assault on Thompson with rhetoric that embarrassed Carter's aides. For the rotund and quintessentially Irish pol was saying the kinds of things that Republicans were saying about Carter. Howlett warned about a man who "sounds like a Democrat when he talks to labor unions, a Republican when he talks to businessmen, and an independent when he talks to independents." And, incredibly, he wound up with, "We can't afford a rookie at the head of our government, because rookies make mistakes." Anyone, Howlett went on, "can make a nice speech." Or they can put on a fancy "Eastern media campaign." "But," shouted Howlett, "there is no substitute for experience." Recounting the incident, *The New York Times* reported that, "If not frozen, the face of Mr. Carter . . . did not seem joyful."

And then, after a mind-numbing speech by Daley himself, Carter was introduced. Everyone in Medinah Temple jumped to his feet, and the applause was deafening. Carter was pleased. So pleased, in fact, that he devoted several minutes in paying compliments to the Mayor, the boss of bosses, whom he described as "my very good friend." He recalled in detail the high vote totals Daley had managed to deliver for John Kennedy in 1960 and Lyndon Johnson four years later. And he told of the vote Daley had produced for Hubert Humphrey and George McGovern. Of course, Carter did not go into the unusual methods frequently employed by the Daley machine to jack up those totals and the fact that a goodly number of the Mayor's associates had served time for vote frauds.

"Mayor Daley is a man who never lets you down," Carter declared. "In good years and in bad, he makes a full effort for any candidate of the Democratic Party."

Carter had put in a hard day of campaigning, and he sounded tired. He began "winging" his speech without notes or text. He wandered rhetorically, plucking from memory excerpts from an old "basic speech" he used in the primary campaign. He began to talk about the need for preventive health care, and the crowd roared. He enjoyed good health as a farm boy, he said, because doctors tried to prevent childhood diseases. Suddenly, he called out their names— "Whooping cough! Cholera! Typhus! Typhoid! Diphtheria! Smallpox! Polio!" As he went through this somber catalog of illnesses, the enthusiasm of the boisterous crowd subsided. "The doctors," Carter told his baffled audience, "tried to immunize me against those diseases—and quite often they succeeded."

When all this was recounted in humorous fashion by David Broder in *The Washington Post*, rumors began to circulate in Democratic circles that Carter had cracked under the strain. According to Jules Witcover, checks were made into Carter's medical history for any evidence of psychiatric problems and, though none was found, the rumors continued to circulate well into the fall. "Such was the potency of a night's heavy exposure to Daleyism," wrote Witcover.

Questions were also raised about the propriety of some of Carter's allegations against his opponent. As a *New York Times* dispatch noted, the Democratic candidate "came close to accusing President Ford of misfeasance in office, or even malfeasance, suggesting that Mr. Ford is responsible for the 'wasting and stealing of billions of dollars' in the Medicaid program that offers health care assistance to the indigent." And, using his favorite phrase, he said President Ford's failure to take responsibility was "a national disgrace."

"A disgrace it is," commented *The Chicago Tribune*, "but it so happens that the administration of Medicaid is the responsibility of the state governments; the federal government only draws up the rules. So if Mr. Carter really wants to zero in on those who are responsible, he should name some of the governors in whose states the most notorious fraud has occurred—Governor Carey of New York, for example, and Governor Walker of Illinois. Both of them are Democrats; and so is the majority of Congress, which runs the District of Columbia—another hotbed of Medicaid fraud." The irony is, according to the *Tribune*, that it was Republican-led states like Michigan and North Carolina which had effectively combatted fraud. "We offer all this not as evidence that

Democrats invariably cause fraud in Medicaid or that Republicans invariably cure it, and certainly not in the expectation that Mr. Carter will aim his brickbats at fellow Democrats, but simply in the hope that he will avoid firing off his volleys without any aim at all."

In mid-September, there was another self-inflicted Carter wound. In an interview with the Associated Press, the Georgian seemed to say that he would raise income taxes for everybody earning over $14,000 a year. He said that as President, he would reform the income tax system "to shift a substantial increase toward those who have higher incomes" and reduce taxes for low- and middle-income families.

> Q.: What do you mean when you say "shift the burden?"
> CARTER: I don't know. I would take the mean or median level of income and anything above that would be higher and anything below that would be lower.
> Q.: The median family income today is somewhere around twelve thousand dollars. Somebody earning fifteen thousand dollars a year is not what people commonly think of as rich. . . .
> CARTER: I understand. I can't answer that question because I haven't gone into it. I don't know how to write the tax code in specific terms. It is just not possible to do that on a campaign trail. But I am committed to do it. . . .

Carter's seeming commitment to raise the taxes of all those above the median—about half the families in the U.S.—was spotted by White House staffer Jim Reichley, a former editor of *Fortune*. Reichley rushed the AP interview into Ron Nessen's office and almost immediately all White House resources were mobilized to take advantage of the apparent gaffe. Bob Dole, who happened to be meeting with Ford at the time, could hardly contain his glee. Meeting with newsmen on the front lawn, the vice-presidential nominee waved the AP copy at the TV cameras and declared, "I'm astounded to read here that [Carter] is going to raise taxes for half the American families, anyone above the median income. . . . I'm talking about families making between twelve thousand and fourteen thousand dollars. . . ." Nessen, meanwhile, called Carter's statement a "major blunder" similar to George McGovern's 1972 plan to give $1,000 to every American. The attack was blunted somewhat by the disclosure that the AP had inadvertently dropped the words "and middle-income" in publishing Carter's promise to reduce taxes for low- and middle-income families. But that still didn't invalidate the criticism of Carter's promise to raise taxes for everyone above the median level.

The issue clearly kept Carter on the defensive the next few days. Wherever he campaigned, he sought to explain away his latest gaffe.* He vigorously denied any intention to increase taxes for "the working people of our country in the lower- and middle-income groups." And on one occasion, he displayed four large volumes containing the U.S. Tax Code, telling his audience, "When you start to prepare your returns, how many of you have a battery of CPA's or lawyers to make sure that you get all the advantages of the windfalls that have been put in the regulations over the past fifty years?" Answering his own question, Carter said, "Very few of you, very few." And he added, "But there are those in this country who make a lot of money who pay practically no taxes."

Of course, Carter failed to tell his audience that he was one of those "very few" who took full advantage of loopholes that his CPA discovered in the nation's tax structure. In 1975, for example, he paid 12.8 percent of his $136,138 income, or $17,484, in federal taxes while President Ford paid more than 37 percent. Thus, Carter, who had been referring to the tax system as a "disgrace to the human race," took a $41,702 investment tax credit for the purchase of a new sheller for his peanut business. And Bob Dole couldn't help noting that Carter had been making "a nice little savings" on his own taxes while advocating tax reform. "The little man is going to be hard pressed to understand how one man, how Mr. Carter can take that off as a tax liability," said Dole, adding, "The 'common folks' out there he keeps talking about probably

---

*"I have a late score from the newsroom," Johnny Carson told his audience one night. "Jimmy Carter is ahead of Gerald Ford, two blunders to one." On another occasion, Carson said, "You know, the Carter-Ford election is going to be tough. It boils down to fear of the unknown versus fear of the known."

haven't had to pay $41,000 in tax for the past several years combined."

Carter retorted he was "not embarrassed" at all by the low percentage of taxes he paid. And, incredibly, he cited the tax break he received the past year for installation of a sheller as "illustrating vividly the need for tax reform." Which even some of the Democratic candidate's aides viewed as a prize example of Georgia-type *chutzpah*.

Carter plainly was worried. Worried, too, about the latest poll figures which showed an even tighter race ahead. It had been expected that Ford would go up in the polls and Carter down once the race got under way. But no one expected Carter to sink so far and Ford—without much campaigning—to rise so fast. Carter's lead throughout the country was now 49 to 38, according to Lou Harris. In most of the big industrial states like Pennsylvania, Ohio, Illinois and New York, Carter's lead was slender—43 to 40 percent with gadfly independent Eugene McCarthy taking 7 percent of the vote. In July, Harris had estimated McCarthy taking 10 percent. And most of his constituency consisted of blacks, liberals, and young voters fed up with Carter's "double-talk."

At first, the '76 McCarthy presidential campaign, his third in a row, was virtually ignored by the media. A fresh face in 1968, when he took on President Johnson on the war issue, he was now being treated as an eccentric, like fellow Minnesotan Harold Stassen. Then, as the polls showed him getting a sizable minority vote, the media became interested in his lonely crusade. After months of covering Carter, who smiled but rarely joked, newsmen seemed appreciative of an unprogrammed candidate with wit. Besides, McCarthy was a good quote. And Carter provided a good target. On *Meet the Press,* McCarthy said, "When Carter said only one voice can speak for the morality of the country, he's saying almost what Nixon said when Nixon said he was the moral leader of the country. Jimmy Carter isn't going to be my moral voice." Carter's language, he went on, was "on the edge of demagoguery." And the First Lady of Plains, Miz Lillian, was so angry with McCarthy that she said she wanted "to throw a cup of tea at him."

Officially, the Carter campaign professed not to be concerned about McCarthy. Even so, the Democratic Party officials were working overtime to keep his name off state ballots, the feeling being that votes for McCarthy would be at Carter's expense. Eventually, they were to succeed in the pivotal state of New York. Carter's concern over McCarthy was further demonstrated when his people organized a group of former McCarthy disciples to circulate a statement urging the party's left wing to ignore its erstwhile hero. Heading the group was Sam Brown, an antiwar activist who served as youth coordinator of McCarthy's 1968 campaign. "All McCarthy's doing now is helping to elect Ford," said Brown. "I don't believe his line about there being no difference between Ford and Carter."

McCarthy brushed off the criticism. As far as he was concerned, he said, Brown—the State Treasurer of Colorado—was "on the make." He predicted a big future for his former supporter in a Carter Administration. As for his being a "spoiler" candidate, as had been argued, McCarthy bristled, "Why am I the spoiler? Why aren't Ford and Carter spoiling it for me?"

Then came one of those unexpected events that explode in a campaign and almost derail it. Up to now, there had been a standing joke that the reason Ford could not be permitted out on the hustings was that he would surely shoot himself in the foot. Now, suddenly, it seemed as if Jimmy Carter had shot himself in both feet. And his weapon was an interview in *Playboy,* in which he used the words "screw" and "shack up" while making a candid, purposeless admission that, like other human beings, he harbors lustful thoughts. The interview was promoted on the cover in this fashion: "Now, the Real Jimmy Carter on Politics, Religion, the Press, and Sex in an Incredible *Playboy* Interview."

Incredible, indeed. So much so that when Hubert Humphrey heard about it in the Democratic cloakroom, off the Senate floor, he cracked, "Segretti did it. It had to be one of the dirty trick guys." It was indeed a dirty trick. But Carter played it on himself. And it was to result in intensive concern over Carter's judgment. It also led to rumblings that the Georgian was not all there. The reaction that most intrigued California pollster Mervin Field came from his sixteen-year-old Melanie. After she watched television news accounts of the *Playboy* interview, she asked, "Dad, is Jimmy Carter a weirdo?" And jazz trumpeter Al Hirt observed, "Jimmy Carter is weird like musicians are supposed to be weird, but I don't want anyone like me running the country."

Obviously, in agreeing to the interview, Carter had sought to convince *Playboy*'s presumably licentious subscribers that, because he strongly supported marital fidelity, he was far from being holier-than-thou. "We are taught not to judge other people," he said of his religious heritage. He said that the person who was "loyal to his wife" should not condemn others' sinfulness, even the "guy [who] screws a whole bunch of women."

"I try not to commit a deliberate sin," he went on. "I recognize that I'm going to do it anyhow, because I'm human and I'm tempted. And Christ set almost impossible standards for us. Christ said, 'I tell you that anyone who looks on a woman with lust in his heart has already committed adultery.'

"I've looked on a lot of women with lust. I've committed adultery in my heart many times. This is something that God recognizes I will do—and I have done it—and God forgives me for it. But that doesn't mean that I condemn someone who not only looks on a woman with lust but who leaves his wife and shacks up with somebody out of wedlock."

Another portion of the interview, ignored initially in the furor attending Carter's sex remarks, had the potential for serious political consequences. In the interview's final passage, Carter—described as clenching his fist and gesturing sharply—declared, "But I don't think I would ever take on the same frame of mind that Nixon or Johnson did—lying, cheating and distorting the truth."*

And Jimmy Carter sought to distort the truth. He tried to pretend that the most damaging portion of the interview—his defamation of Lyndon Johnson and his use of vulgarisms—was somebody else's doing, not his. "After the interview was over," he alleged, "there was a summary made—", and it was only in that post-interview summary—which Carter implied was done by a reporter betraying an off-the-record confidence—that those obscenities and the denunciation of LBJ occurred.

This was double-talk designed to place the blame on *Playboy* for the "summary." But under questioning, Carter soon retreated

---

*In his acceptance speech in Madison Square Garden, Carter had declared, "Ours is the party of a great-hearted Texan . . . who went on to do more than any other President . . . to advance the cause of human rights." And that "great-hearted Texan" was Lyndon Johnson.

from this explanation. At the same time, he and his aides were putting out the line that his use of obscenities was a slip, that "a salty word or two" was a "mistake" hardly worth noticing.

"That was untrue," wrote William Safire in *The New York Times*. "In reality, after Governor Jerry Brown had impressed the world with his *Playboy* interview in April, Governor Carter wanted to top him with that audience. His selection of *Playboy* and his conscious use of vulgarisms was a strategy to mollify all those worried about his ardent professions of piety."

But even as he kept contending that those vulgarisms were just "slips," Carter and his aides knew a bombshell was ticking away at *The New York Times*, whose Sunday magazine was about to publish an interview the candidate had given some weeks before to Norman Mailer. In the interview, Carter had again emphasized that, as President, he did not intend to tell people how to live their personal lives, adding, "I don't care if people say ----," and— as Mailer put it when the *Times* would not publish the word— "he actually said the famous four-letter word that the *Times* has not printed in the 125 years of its publishing life."

And, as Mailer noted, this was no slip— "it was, after all, not the easiest word to say to a stranger"—but spoken on the record "from the quiet decent demands of duty, as if he, too, had to present his credentials to that part of the 20th Century personified by his interviewer."

"Exactly," wrote Safire. "That is just what Mr. Carter was doing in *Playboy*, too—making friends by talking dirty. Just as he won Mr. Mailer's heart by using a four-letter word, Mr. Carter had hoped to win the heart of the *Playboy* audience by the use of a milder obscenity."

What was "weird"—to use Safire's description—about it all was the fact that while Carter and his aides were claiming the *Playboy* interview was only a "post-interview summary," they were aware that the Mailer interview was about to be published. In fact, Ham Jordan discussed the problem with several reporters the morning after the first Carter-Ford debate in Philadelphia. He made no secret of his concern that "the boss" was going to face a new flurry of criticism over his use of the ultimate obscenity.

It turned out Jordan didn't have to worry too much. The *Times* did make a minor reference to the forthcoming Carter obscenity, but on an inside page. And *The Washington Post,* which had reveled in publishing everything Richard Nixon had said in private, decided to ignore the whole business. As Jules Witcover informed Jordan, who had called him at his home, the *Post's* powers-that-be had concluded it wasn't worth the kind of coverage given the *Playboy* remarks. Jordan, needless to say, "seemed considerably relieved," according to Witcover.

Still hanging over Carter's head, however, was his gratuitous slap at Lyndon Johnson. True, he had telephoned Lady Bird Johnson to emphasize that he admired her husband—had spoken favorably of him elsewhere in the interview—and that he regretted "the implications that might be drawn" from linking LBJ with Nixon. But, for LBJ's widow, that wasn't good enough. Through an aide, she let it be known that she was still "distressed, hurt and perplexed." Meanwhile, Richard Nixon had phoned Lady Bird, expressing his dismay over the episode. And Lady Bird wondered whether Carter hadn't taken leave of his senses.

Another who wondered was the genial Texan who headed the Democratic National Committee, Bob Strauss. And Strauss, a close friend of the Johnson family, told Carter so as they were flying to Texas to campaign. Carter agreed he would have to do something to straighten out the mess. On arriving at Houston, he quickly walked over to a group of local reporters to reply to questions. Asked whether he had any regrets about the *Playboy* interview, Carter said the only thing he regretted was the misunderstanding of his remarks about LBJ.

He said that the post-interview "summary" had "unfortunately equated what I had said about President Johnson and President Nixon. . . . If any misrepresentation of what I feel about President Johnson caused Mrs. Johnson any discomfort or embarrassment, for that I am truly sorry. . . . My reference to Johnson was about the misleading of the American people; the lying and cheating part referred to President Nixon. And the unfortunate juxtaposition of these two names in the *Playboy* article grossly misrepresents the way I feel about him."

Sam Donaldson, the ABC correspondent, could hardly believe his ears. Was Carter claiming that *Playboy* was responsible for the "juxtaposition?" Finally, Carter conceded that the "juxtaposition" was his, not *Playboy*'s. Said he, "It was a mistake, and I have apologized for it."

And that, as far as he was concerned, was the end of it. But it wasn't. The national correspondents traveling with Carter were infuriated that the candidate had sought to mislead the Texas locals, then themselves. And they told Jody Powell so on the plane heading for California. Carter's press spokesman accused the correspondents of "nit-shitting," and accused them of "operating on a double standard, and I'm damn well sick and tired of it." He claimed that "everything Jimmy does is examined under a microscope and picked apart" while Ford "sits there hiding in the White House and gets off scot-free. We've tried to run an open campaign and look what we get. Why don't you go after Ford and smoke him out and make him answer questions? . . . Let me tell you right now, we don't have to do it this way any more. We can run a closed operation, too. We can cut off your access to the candidate."

Carter was also harried and frustrated. In San Diego that night, he summoned ten reporters to his motel room for an off-the-record, heart-to-heart conversation. Martin Schram, who was there and later wrote about it in his book *Running for President*, reported that "the essence of his opening remarks was that he realized that some problems had arisen between the reporters and himself and his staff, problems arising out of the Houston Airport press conference and problems concerning campaign coverage in general. Carter said that, after all, we were all in the campaign together, and he was sure we only wanted what was best for our country, and he'd asked us up to the room to see what advice we could give for how relations between the candidate, his staff, and the press could be improved."

If Schram was reporting faithfully—and the then *Newsday* correspondent is considered one of the best in the business—Carter's opening comments were indeed extraordinary. For he was suggesting that "what was best for our country" was linked to his political fortunes.

It was Schram who informed Carter it was not the media's job to advise candidates of either party; and Carter backed off, claiming his Houston remarks had been misunderstood. He denied any intention of seeking to mislead anyone. And, he said, it wasn't so much the print media but "the television coverage" that was "destroying us." (In a later interview, Carter admitted being so incensed with TV's coverage that, he said, "We were considering at one point sending either Jody or Jerry Rafshoon or Charles Kirbo or perhaps myself to meet with the executive officers of the three networks.")

Carter bitterly repeated Powell's lament about Ford being given a free ride while he was suffering political damage by being constantly accessible. But he was reminded that earlier he had stated it would "suit me fine" if Ford remained in the White House. After the discussion went on for about an hour, getting nowhere, Carter left. When news of the meeting leaked out, as it was bound to, it did Carter little good. His complaints contributed to the notion that, although he was still ahead in the polls, his campaign was in trouble and that he was uncertain about how to handle it.

Many liberals, for example, were annoyed by Carter's stressing of conservative themes in specific areas. These, he said, he invoked to offset the Republican portrait of him as a big-spending "ultraliberal." But the liberals were even more than annoyed by his remarks on the Supreme Court while campaigning in Oklahoma. In discussions with local officials, Carter had high praise for law enforcement rulings of the "Burger Court," dominated as it was by Nixon appointees. He said he favored "a shifting back toward the removal of technicalities which obviously prevent the conviction and punishment of those who are guilty." He also said he believed the high court was moving in "the proper direction" because for a time "it got so that sincere, honest, dedicated, competent law enforcement officers found it impossible to comply with all the technicalities . . . and obviously guilty people were released unpunished."

Expressions of disapproval came from American Civil Liberties Union quarters. Charles Morgan, Jr., an early Carter supporter, said he was "shocked" by the candidate's comments. And even Senator Mondale finally conceded there was a "difference in emphasis" between him and the presidential nominee over Carter's comment that the Supreme Court under Chief Justice

Earl Warren had gone "too far" in protecting the legal rights of defendants.

But casting even a greater shadow of gloom over the Carter camp was the fact that the Georgian hadn't done too well in his first "debate" with Gerald Ford. He hadn't been able to score a knockout against an opponent whom he considered an intellectual inferior. The Georgian had actually come to believe the liberal cartoonists who had pictured the President as somewhat of an oaf, out of his element in the Oval Office. Still, he wasn't willing to give Ford any edge. Which was why, among other things, Carter had insisted that the first confrontation be held in a "neutral" city, anywhere but Sodom-on-the-Potomac. His argument was that if the debate were scheduled in Washington the network TV cameras would surely focus on such visuals as Ford's "leaving the White House in a limousine." And that, said Jimmy, would be to Ford's advantage. Still it was a case of Carter crying wolf. For no one, either in the sponsoring group, the League of Women Voters, or in the Ford camp, had actually proposed Washington as the first site. "And in any case," as Vic Gold pointed out, "what more could Populist Jimmy ask to make his campaign theme than the Imperial President pictured arriving at the debate site in one of those fancy, black limousines."

Through his TV adviser, Carter demanded that the journalists who were to question the candidates should be instructed to address the President as "Mister Ford" instead of "Mister President" in order to assure complete equality to the Democratic candidate. Apparently this had aroused considerable concern and discussion within the Carter camp. Carter himself told newsmen he intended to call the President "Mister Ford." After all, he told astonished newsmen, Thomas Jefferson preferred to be called "Mister Jefferson." The negotiators, however, agreed to permit the questioners to address the candidates as they pleased.

Another Carter request that actually produced guffaws was the proposal that either Ford be required to stand in a depression on the stage or that Carter be permitted to stand on a stool in order to equalize their heights. Carter feared that Ford, being four inches taller, would look more "presidential."

Finally, after all the buildup and suspense, the "debate" took place at Philadelphia's Walnut Street Theater. And, to most everyone's surprise, Gerald Ford appeared to walk away with most of the honors. The surprise was that everyone expected Ford to act like a klutz. Which led one media observer to formulate the "counterklutzical theory." *Time's* Jess Cook, who thought Ford might have won because so little was expected of him, put it this way: "First you walk into your chopper door. Then you fall down the ramp of Air Force One. Before you even take office you arrange for the last Democratic President to suggest your inability to chew gum and do much of anything else. Then, when your opponent is all set up, you show up for a campaign debate, leaving your college football helmet at home, and play ninety minutes of *What's My Line?* without falling on your fanny. Viewers are impressed. You aren't an utter boob after all."

From the moment Ford appeared on stage, it was obvious that he had upstaged Carter. Tall, ramrod-straight, Ford was wearing a blue suit, quiet tie and—the murmurs could be heard in the audience—a *vest*. "He looked like a President," wrote Kandy Stroud. "Carter seemed to sense it. He tensed. When he shook hands with the President, he extended his arm stiffly, holding Ford as far away as possible. . . . Carter looked small and unimposing next to the massive, athletic President. What had seemed boyish only months ago now looked badly worn. The skin above his collar was wattled. . . . He seemed old and tired."

That Carter was jittery was also obvious. At first, he was unsteady and stumbled over words. He was choppy. He rambled. And he perspired. Nervously, he licked his lips. And he wove sentences too difficult to follow in their complexity and delivery. All this while his opponent exuded composure. Toward the end, he appeared to have recovered from a case of jangled nerves. And then he insisted that "Mister Ford" had not "except for avoiding another Watergate accomplished one single major program for this country." And he observed that "Mister Ford quite often puts forward a program just as a public relations stunt, and never tries to put it through the Congress by working with the Congress." Carter also criticized Ford's record of fifty-six vetoes in his two years in the White House as an example of "government by stalemate." To which Ford replied, "The Governor has played a little fast and loose with the facts about vetoes. The record shows that President Roosevelt vetoed on an average of fifty-five bills a year. President Truman vetoed on the average about thirty-eight bills a year. I understand that Governor Carter . . . vetoed between thirty-five and forty bills a year. My average in two years is twenty-six. But in the process of that we have saved nine billion dollars."

The next day, aware he had not done as well as he had hoped, Carter observed, "I think I was a little too reticent in being aggressive against the President." He vowed that, in the next debate, "I'll pick up where I left off. I'll be aggressive." Four days later, on September 27, Carter's worst suspicions were confirmed. A *New York Times-CBS* poll based on 1,167 telephone interviews indicated that Ford had won the debate. More significantly, Ford had cut Carter's lead roughly in half, led Carter among independent voters, and had taken an almost insurmountable lead in the West. "In a single month," wrote Patrick Buchanan, "[Carter] has managed to alter his image from that of a calm, competent, presidential figure to that of an unsure and erratic politician, about whom the nation is suddenly distrustful, suspicious, concerned." With only five weeks to go, the momentum was clearly against the Democratic candidate.

As Carter's campaign went into a nose dive in September, Ken Auletta reported in *The Village Voice* that many Democratic operatives were grumbling that the man they had pictured as "brilliant" in July was really a "lightweight," the candidate they thought was so "together" was really "unstable." In fact, wrote Auletta, there was a fair number of prominent Democrats who agreed with Republican Bob Dole that Jimmy Carter was a "flake."

And then, suddenly, the breaks began going Carter's way. There was the episode involving Earl Butz. The Secretary of Agriculture, who had been described by *The Wall Street Journal* as "pound for pound, the best man in the Cabinet," had unwisely responded to a question with a flippant slur on blacks. It was, he thought, a private conversation on a flight from Kansas City to Los Angeles. The Republican Convention was over and the Secretary was feeling quite good. Listening to the conversation was none other than the star of the Watergate hearings, John Wesley Dean III. Now writing for *Rolling Stone*, Dean reported what Butz had said in vivid detail, though without identifying him beyond his Cabinet membership. Several weeks later, the fat was in the fire when an NBC correspondent covering Carter in Plains called Ron Nessen and asked what President Ford thought of "the Butz thing." Butz' authorship of the offensive remark was about to break open and the White House was in a dither. Eventually, Butz was forced to pay for his indiscretion with the job he loved so much and in which he was so good. And Jimmy Carter, who was talking about love, compassion, and forgiveness, kicked Butz as he fell. Carter insisted that Ford should have fired him in disgrace. As far as he was concerned, he said, he "would not permit that kind of blatant racism to be expressed by anyone who served in my Administration."*

Carter, of course, was setting a new standard for hypocrisy. The very same issue of *Playboy* which published the now-famous interview described Brother Billy as an "incorrigible cracker who still uses the word 'nigger' when he's drinking with his old buddies at the gas station." And Brother Billy was managing Jimmy's multimillion-dollar peanut empire at the time. Yet no moves were made by Carter to get rid of a business partner given to uttering racial epithets.† Nor did he do anything about firing two of his "top staffers" who, according to Bill Safire in *The New York Times*,

---

*President Carter was to get his chance to practice what he preached in November 1978, when one of his appointees, Robert McKinney, head of the Federal Home Loan Bank Board, made an anti-Polish slur in a public speech. McKinney had told a Dallas audience that Pope John Paul II, the first Polish prelate, had performed his first miracle— "He found a lame man and left him blind." There was no White House reprimand, let alone a demand for McKinney's resignation.

---

†Nor did Carter, as President, evince any concern when his brother used the term "bastardized Jew" at a fund-raising dinner in Atlanta in December 1978. The occasion was a "roast" honoring Phil Niekro, the Atlanta Braves pitching star, who is of Polish descent. Billy told an audience of 1,200 people that he had not realized Niekro was a "Polack," but thought he was a "bastardized Jew." Jewish leaders were appalled. Stuart Lewengrub, of the Anti-Defamation League, wrote "an open letter" to Billy, reminding him that "it is highly questionable whether terms such as 'bastardized Jew' and 'Polack' are humorous, or appropriate" even in the context of a roast. And managing editor Vida Goldgar, in a signed editorial in *The Southern Isrealite*, said Billy's "latest remarks at a roast honoring one of the sports world's truly fine personalities were ill-conceived, grossly insensitive, and showed an utter disregard for any semblance of responsibility." When asked for his reaction, President Carter—who had been so sanctimonious about Earl Butz—made it clear he would not comment on controversies surrounding his brother. And there the story died. One wonders, however, how the story would have been treated had one of President Nixon's brothers been so intemperate.

were said "to have told racial jokes to reporters in wee-hour drinking sessions" and were living in fear "that their own off-color, off-the-record thigh-slappers will be revealed by practitioners of John Dean journalism."

Carter had also announced that his staff would bring a new moral tone to the White House. Yet, the same writer for *Playboy*, who spent four months traveling with the Carter team, also reported that "it becomes clear that Carter has not applied his concern with the Ten Commandments to the behavior of his staff. They are, at least some of them, as hard-drinking, fornicating, pot-smoking, free-thinking a group as has been seen in higher politics." Another view of the Elmer Gantry-like quality of the Carter campaign was provided by Kandy Stroud. Stroud had been seeking a television interview with the candidate, but was repeatedly turned down. "The trouble with you," explained a top Carter aide, "is you don't sleep with the right people. If you did, you'd have no trouble getting an interview." The aide told Stroud of one woman writer who, having succumbed to the charms of a Carter staffer, wound up with two hour-long interviews with the candidate himself in his Plains home.

Carter, meanwhile, could hardly contain his indignation when the press reported that Ford, as a Congressman, had accepted several golfing holidays at a New Jersey country club from William Whyte, chief Washington lobbyist of U.S. Steel. "I get so tired of this bullshit!" exclaimed Ford when he heard the charges. After all, he explained, he and Whyte had been close friends for a quarter of a century and, with their families, had often vacationed together.

Nevertheless, Carter attacked the golf outings, saying they represented everything he was opposed to in the nation's capital. "You can't expect any better from political leadership that has been bogged down in Washington for twenty-five or thirty years, drawing their advice, their counsel, their financial support from lobbyists and special interests," proclaimed Carter. "They go to the same restaurants, belong to the same clubs, play golf at the same golf clubs."

Carter's effort to link Ford to the lobbyists was ill advised. As *Washington Star* columnist Charles Bartlett pointed out, Carter's "best friend and *éminence grise*" was Charles Kirbo. "The Atlantan was his honorary chief of staff when he was Governor, but he was also the lawyer assigned to deal with the Georgia Legislature by a firm representing major corporations." At the same time, Carter's family business was tied tightly to the Southeastern Peanut Processors Association, a group lobbying fiercely to preserve a subsidy which cost the taxpayers $213 million a year. "Nothing was made of Kirbo," wrote Bartlett, "because he is respected as a decent, able man. Little has been made of the peanut lobby because it is an ordinary pressure group. Little would normally have been made of Ford's friendship with William Whyte of U.S. Steel, who has given the Washington community no reason to question his character and brains."

Still, Carter tried to use the Ford-Whyte connection to fill out his depiction of a capital mired in corrupt ways. But, as Bartlett also observed, Ford was "not the sort of person to whom casual mud will stick. When Carter castigates the 'mess in Washington,' he throws more aspersions on the Democrats who dominate Congress than on the President." And the Democrats who controlled Congress were themselves under fire in connection with the spreading scandal that became known as Koreagate. Directly involved was the Democratic leadership. Majority Leader Thomas P. "Tip" O'Neill had been the recipient of several lavish parties as well as gifts from Korean influence peddlers. And such leading lights as soon-to-be Majority Whip John Brademas conceded he had received $5,000 in campaign contributions from the same source. The significant thing was that candidate Carter said nary a word about any of this during the campaign.

Carter began cooling his rhetoric when it was also disclosed that, as Governor, he had accepted hospitality on several occasions at hunting lodges owned by companies that did business with the state of Georgia. Also disclosed was the fact that he had traveled on corporate airplanes owned by Lockheed and Coca-Cola. His explanation was that he had used those occasions to conduct official business and that he did not intend doing it again.

What Carter did not reveal at the time was the fact that he had, in the course of campaigning, also flown free aboard a plane owned by Bert Lance's National Bank of Georgia. Though denying any illegalities, the new President quickly reimbursed the bank $1,800 in personal and campaign funds.

(Nor did Carter reveal that he received $1,000 for his 1970 gubernatorial campaign from a lobbyist for the Gulf Oil Corporation. The lobbyist, Claude C. Wild, Jr., disclosed this fact in testimony before the Securities and Exchange Commission in April 1978. The SEC was looking into illegal corporate donations.)

Aside from the "great golf controversy," the media came up with another "biggie"—this time the allegation that Ford, while a member of Congress, had converted campaign contributions to personal use. And this, needless to say, was much more serious a charge than whether Ford had gone golfing at U.S. Steel's expense. Particularly when *The Wall Street Journal* reported the matter had become of interest to Special Watergate Prosecutor Charles Ruff, who had subpoenaed records of donations made by two maritime unions to Republican coffers in Ford's House district. That there was nothing to the allegation, however, was vouched for by none other than Leon Jaworski, the former Special Prosecutor, who told newsmen that he personally had looked into the same charges and had "found nothing that called for further investigation."

But Jaworski's comments were not good enough for Carter who called on the President to "tell the truth, the whole truth, and nothing but the truth," as if Ford was already on trial. And he kept repeating it, even though the President had flatly denied ever having converted contributions for private purposes. Carter was now doing his darndest to demonstrate that Ford was arm-in-arm with his predecessor who had left the White House in disgrace. He was saying such things as, "Gerald Ford has not changed the Nixon Administration" and "Richard Nixon had a secretive Administration . . . [and] Ford is less accessible than Nixon was at the depths of Watergate."

All of which caused *The Washington Star* to question whether Carter "really believes, as he implies, that the Ford presidency is a carbon copy of the Nixon presidency. Or whether he is merely unable to distinguish in fact (as well as for purposes of campaign talk) between continuities of policy, natural enough for two back-to-back Administrations of the same party, and continuities of criminal misbehavior of which, to our knowledge, none has been alleged. It would be well for Governor Carter to set these dubious propositions—whatever it is he's insinuating about Mr. Ford's links to Mr. Nixon—forthrightly before the public so that they may be analyzed and discussed. Together, of course, with his judgment and wisdom in offering the comparison."

None of which Jimmy Carter ever did. Of course, Carter could argue he never actually called Ford a crook. He only implied as much. At least, Ford thought so. And Ford grew to despise his opponent, barely concealing his feelings. At one point, the President told aides that Carter was little more "than a sanctimonious hypocrite," who had not learned to "play fair." And one can only surmise how Ford felt about the Special Prosecutor who permitted his probe to drag on through the crucial weeks of the campaign, causing no little embarrassment to the President, who was left twisting in the wind and barraged with press questions until just eighteen days before the election. On October 14, Charles Ruff announced that "the evidence developed during this investigation was not corroborative of the allegation on which it was predicated. . . . Accordingly, the matter has now been closed." In other words, there was nothing to the charges.*

Still, the role of the media in keeping the story alive in the headlines week after week, especially in the heat of a presidential contest, came in for criticism from *The New Republic*'s famed White House observer John Osborne. Osborne was particularly outraged by *The Washington Post*'s Woodward and Bernstein who, citing as their source "a supporter of the Jimmy Carter presidential campaign," had reported details from a supposedly secret Internal Revenue Service audit of Ford's tax returns from 1965 to 1972. And after the Associated Press and *The New York Times* had indicated that the investigation was over and that Ruff was about to clear the President, the Woodward-Bernstein team continued to fan the story, quoting Ruff on October 3 in such a manner as to imply that the AP and *Times* accounts were unfounded. Their article, front-page news in Washington and New

---

*Following the election, Ruff was named Deputy Inspector General for the Department of Health, Education, and Welfare. Confirmation was held up by Senator Dole, who suggested that Ruff was being rewarded by the Carter Administration for his activities as Special Prosecutor. Ruff adamantly denied this. And Dole adamantly denied he was "holding up" his nomination. The Kansas Senator maintained he was just trying to clear up "for the historical record . . . how the President of the United States can be investigated on the unsworn information of an anonymous informant, who the informant was, and why the case was handled in that fashion." Dole, who never got satisfactory answers, eventually let Ruff obtain his $47,500-a-year job.

York, was syndicated across the country. And Osborne, who was clearly disgusted with both Ruff and the celebrated Woodstein team, summed up his reaction as follows: "After weeks of principled pap from the Special Prosecutor's Office to the effect that he could not and would not comment upon any aspect of the matter, this gratuitous coöperation with Woodward and Bernstein to keep the story alive, facts or no facts, inclined me to vomit."

The Watergate connection was not dead, however. Just as the President was cleared by the Special Prosecutor, John Dean came up with a new allegation involving Ford. This time Dean leveled his charge on NBC's *Today* show as the opening shot of a promotion campaign to hustle a new book on his White House adventures, *Blind Ambition*. And his allegation was that Ford, while in Congress, had a role in the early stages of the Watergate coverup. Dean said the incidents occurred in the fall of 1972 when the White House was seeking to block a House Banking Committee investigation of Watergate by Chairman Wright Patman. In testifying about those incidents before the Senate Watergate Committee, Dean had never mentioned Ford was involved. But in his book, he identified Bill Timmons, head of the White House Congressional Liaison Office, as the White House contact with Ford. On the *Today* show, however, Dean said it was Timmons' assistant, Richard Cook, who had been the contact.

Both Timmons and Cook vociferously denied Dean's story.

As did Ford, who privately described Dean as "a low-down, no-good, son of a bitch, a sniveling bastard." And he was also outraged at NBC, which, though insisting it had not paid Dean a penny for his appearance on the *Today* show, neglected to disclose that the network had paid him $7,500 for an option on the television rights to his book, all in the highest traditions of checkbook journalism. Ford was told about this secret transaction by none other than Walter Cronkite of CBS, and the President asked Ron Nessen to "get that information out." But the press secretary, as he later reported, found a decided lack of media interest.

Though it stopped the Ford campaign in its tracks for a few days, what with NBC seeking to keep its investment alive, the Dean story was soon dropped. There had, of course, been the usual demands that Special Prosecutor Ruff look into the matter.

But they emanated from such unsurprising sources as Representatives Elizabeth Holtzman and John Conyers. This time, Ruff quickly ruled there were no grounds for such an investigation. And his predecessor, Leon Jaworski, questioned the timing of Dean's accusations. "What bothers me is why hold a matter of this kind for several years," Jaworski told an interviewer, "especially when the man is nominated for vice-president, succeeds to the presidency, and it's still withheld. And then, here shortly before the election, it comes out in connection with the sale of a book."

Other questions about the episode remained unanswered, according to Ron Nessen.* "For example: What role had the Carter campaign played in promoting the Dean allegations? Why did Associated Press stories on September 23 and 24, 1976, reporting Dean's charges against Ford, leaked from the book manuscript, appear under a Plains, Georgia, dateline? Why was the book's publication date, originally scheduled for January 1977, after the election, moved back to November and then October 1976, before the election?"

Also according to Nessen, the feeling grew in the White House, shared by the President, that the press was following a double standard, pursuing allegations against Ford far more vigorously than they did against Carter. And Carter had "successfully created an image for himself of the untainted outsider who would bring morality and honesty to Washington." For this, Nessen also blamed himself "for failing to prod or entice reporters into investigationg Carter's blemishes."

"One of the few efforts by the campaign organization," wrote Nessen, "to demonstrate that the pious Carter might not be so pure involved gossip that he once had a mistress. But attempts to persuade reporters to look into this rumor were done so heavy-handedly that they backfired: The news stories which resulted were about how the Ford campaign tried to pull a dirty trick by spreading suggestions that Carter had a mistress. The alleged mistress's name was Irene. The height of our ingenuity was an idea of campaign spokesman William Greener that a group of Ford

---

*From Nessen's book, *It Sure Looks Different from the Inside* (Chicago, Playboy Press, 1977). The book is a revealing look into the Ford White House and the GOP campaign waged against Jimmy Carter.

campaign workers should go to a Carter rally and serenade him with 'Goodnight, Irene.'"

Of course, a standard ploy of politicians is to blame the press when a campaign runs into trouble. So it was not unusual to find Ford and his associates moaning about the double standard of the press. But they were not all wrong. As philosopher-columnist Michael Novak had noted at the beginning of the campaign, "Most of the working journalists sympathize with Democrats; they reserve their best condescension for Republicans of the Right. Most have been letting Mr. Carter go unscathed. A piety the press could not stand in Richard Nixon or Ronald Reagan it accepts in Jimmy Carter. The oldest Southern magic (a thickening accent, tales of humble origins, family lore) has once again bewitched innocent Northern liberals abroad."

A few newspapers, most notably *The St. Louis Post-Dispatch,* *The Detroit News* and *The Christian Science Monitor,* did keep raising questions about Carter's background. *The Monitor,* for example, on October 19, 1976, urged the Democratic candidate to "step forth and respond to certain allegations surrounding his record." The *Monitor* said there was "growing evidence" that his 1970 gubernatorial campaign was linked to a series of "dirty tricks" against his opponent Carl Sanders. "A clarification of Mr. Carter's role and attitude in this matter would be helpful," said *The Monitor.* "Now that he has disclosed a list of corporate and business contributors to his gubernatorial campaign (following a TV interview question eight months ago) he would give added substance to his constant plea for more 'openness' in government by dealing publicly with the 'dirty tricks' charges as well."

But Carter never responded to such demands. Rather, he sought to keep his opponent on the defensive by dragging in Watergate (which he had said he would not do) in every conceivable way. Thus, in South Bend, he accused Ford of "stonewalling" the press and the public. "I remember under Richard Nixon the word 'stonewall,'" he said. Thus a classic case of guilt-by-association.

Ironically, the Carter campaign was hit soon afterward with a problem of its own that had Watergate overtones. This was the short-lived revelation that the Carter campaign manual advocated tricks and misrepresentations designed to enhance the campaign. Among the items suggested were such ploys as conducting voter surveys under the auspices of a phony polling firm, stalling a car in traffic to create a crowd just as Carter was arriving, and using a high spotlight over his head to create the illusion of a halo. In all, 111 pages of tricks of the type which got Nixon's men into trouble. In response, Jody Powell issued a statement expressing Carter's dismay over the manual, which the candidate claimed not to have read. Carter was further quoted as saying the material was "not in line with the way I want to see the campaign run" and would be ignored by his campaign aides.

Still, few of Carter's "dirty tricks," hyperbolic utterances, and outright misrepresentations were as damaging to Gerald Ford as what Gerald Ford did to himself in the second debate. The President, obviously getting fouled up in his own words, actually declared, "There is no Soviet domination of Eastern Europe, and there never will be under the Ford Administration." Obviously, what he meant to say was that the U.S. did not *accept* Soviet domination of Eastern Europe, which was what he had been briefed to say. But when given a chance to correct himself, Ford compounded his original gaffe by asserting he didn't "believe that the Poles consider themselves dominated by the Soviet Union."

This was the ultimate Polish joke, and, inexplicably, it took President Ford five days to finally admit it was a bad slip. Carter, meanwhile, could hardly be blamed for taking advantage of his opponent's startling liberation of Poland; but, as William F. Buckley shrewdly noted, the roles of the Democratic and Republican candidates had become "almost impossibly confused" because of the gaffe. "After all," wrote Buckley, "it is the Republicans who have traditionally done the most (however insufficient) to keep alive the hope of the liberation of Eastern Europe." On the other hand, the Democrats "tend to be associated with a foreign policy of permanent acquiescence in the colonization by the Communists of any part of the world. . . . A political party that, through Senator Frank Church and his committee, threatened congressional mutiny when the Executive tried to help Portugal and Italy stave off the Communists is not going to lie down for anything in Eastern Europe that tends to threaten their policy of appeasement at any cost."

That Ford was now on the defensive was obvious. Almost every ethnic group in the country was now berating the President. "But," as Mary McGrory observed, "Carter is never one to let well enough alone." Sensing that the competency issue had been rekindled, Carter went so far as to suggest that Ford had been "brainwashed" when he visited Poland the previous year. "I don't think he understood what was going on over there," Carter said. And, before a Polish group in Chicago, he declared, "It is time we had a President who will speak up for Eastern Europe." On another occasion he pronounced the Ford *faux pas* a "disgrace" and said he was "disgusted." But, as McGrory pointed out, "every American over the age of eight knew he was ecstatic. Mr. Compassion, who during the primaries declared his love for every soul within sound of his voice, was gloating."

All through the debates, Carter appeared to be four-square in favor of the usual contradictions: for husbandry and for plenty, against inflation and for public spending, against busing and against anything that would end busing, against abortion and against any impediment to abortion, for a reduced military budget and for an imposing military presence. Except he vociferously denied Ford's contention that he had ever advocated a $15 billion defense cut, implying the President had lied in so contending. But *The Savannah Morning News* of March 18, 1975, reported that Carter had advised a Rotary Club that "approximately $15 billion could be cut from the defense budget and not weaken this nation's military capability. . . ." And two days later, *The Los Angeles Times* reported Carter as saying in Beverly Hills that "he thinks the Ford defense budget for this year could be cut by about $15 billion without sacrificing national security." The conservative weekly, *Human Events*, checked with the *Times* reporter who wrote the story. The reporter, Ken Reich, said "there's no question" that Carter used the $15 billion figure. In fact, so pleased with his story were Carter's people that they used a portion of it in a campaign handout, Reich added. Concluded *Human Events*, "Jimmy Carter's been caught lying again."

"By deploying such code words as 'disgrace,' 'brainwashed,' and 'stonewall,'" commented Pat Buchanan, "Mr. Carter is suggesting to the American people that Gerald Ford is not only without intelligence but without integrity." And, on the other side of the political spectrum, Eric Sevareid commented on the *CBS Evening News*, "What has been going on since the last debate is a daily calculated effort by Jimmy Carter to discredit Mr. Ford, not just as a constitutional leader but as a man. It began with that debate in which Carter refused to call his opponent President Ford, which he is, though Ford repeatedly called the challenger Governor Carter, which he is not. The man who promised a government just as decent and loving as the American people, whatever that realistically means, is revealing another side of himself—an instinct for the delivered insult, the loaded phrase, and the broad innuendo . . . Carter . . . will have to pay attention to those who among his advisers are now telling him that his cutthroat tactics against Ford, whom most people still perceive as an honest man, have gone too far. What they are concerned about, obviously, is not injustice done to Ford, but the dangers this kind of attack will backfire on Carter. . . ."

In a post-election analysis, Carter himself conceded that he had aided his opponent by attacking him unmercifully for his Polish blunder. "If I had let them just stew in the misstatement on Eastern Europe, rather than push the issue," he said, "I would have been better off. The polls showed that the people thought I was being strident."

In their third debate, it soon became obvious that Carter had decided to take the high road. He apologized for unidentified "mistakes" of his campaign and even managed to address his opponent as "President Ford" instead of "Mister Ford." Moreover, he vowed that in the limited time left in the campaign he intended to focus on the issues and not on the character of his opponent—whom he at one point conceded to be a "good and decent man."

But during this confrontation in Williamsburg, Virginia, Carter made what Joseph Kraft (one of the interrogators) described in his column as "a far more damaging blunder" than Ford's misstatement about Eastern Europe, but one that went "virtually unnoticed." Carter had asserted that, as President, he would not send U.S. troops into Yugoslavia to counter a Soviet attack in the wake of President Tito's eventual death. Ford declared firmly that "it's unwise for a President to signal in advance what options he might exercise if any international problem arose." He recalled that Secretary of State Dean Acheson had drawn a U.S. defense perimeter in 1950 that did not include South Korea and suggested that it could well have invited North Korea to invade.

In outlining his position, Carter had made reference to two of his prestigious advisers—former Ambassador Averell Harriman and James Schlesinger, whom Ford had ousted as Defense Secretary. A follow-up question disclosed that neither Harriman nor Schlesinger had approved Carter's Yugoslav position. "Neither did any of the other distinguished men on Carter's list of foreign policy advisers," noted Kraft. "But though there was involved a serious policy matter—not a correctable error of fact such as President Ford made—the commentators of television and press have remained mute, inglorious Miltons."

Though Carter claimed he would take the high road for the rest of the campaign, his message obviously did not reach his running mate. In the final week of the campaign, Mondale kept dragging out Watergate. Repeatedly, Mondale accused Ford and Dole of defending Nixon "right up to the dying moments of the Nixon Administration," even though Nixon's position was indefensible. The Minnesota Senator's renewal of the Watergate issue, after he had laid off it for a month, immediately raised questions about whether he was acting out of desperation in the final days of the campaign.

Six days before the election, Herbert Hafif, the former cochairman of the Carter National Steering Committee, took out an ad in *The Los Angeles Times* to deliver "a personal warning about Jimmy Carter." Hafif, who had also served as the California finance chairman of the Carter campaign, wrote, "I am a Democrat, and I would like to see a Democratic President, but I am now convinced that it would be a disaster if that Democratic President was Jimmy Carter. The reason is not because he has promised all things to all people, nor is it because I witnessed such things as his private scheming to get farmers' money in California, only to see his change of position to get the farm worker vote after the primary, but rather . . . because, independent of character flaws, the man is simply not capable by experience or ability to be President. . . ."

Hafif claimed that when evidences of "staff racism and intolerance" were brought to the candidate's attention, "Carter's response was to get rid of the messengers. . . . Hidden behind the smiles and hang-loose joking of the small Carter team is the fact that it is a team experienced only in campaigning with no higher goal, save getting their man the presidency. . . . In short, this country is not being asked to elect a Democratic President but to elect another Imperial President who will promise anything to get elected, but whose words stand in stark contrast to his records and actions."

It was a bombshell of an ad, and Ford headquarters expected it to create great excitement in the political community. But, perhaps because it came so late in the campaign, it was virtually ignored by the national press. At any rate, to give Hafif's views greater circulation, the Ford campaign paid for full-page repro-ductions of his ad in forty newspapers, including *The New York Times*. But they appeared the day before the election and stirred little attention. The campaign, for better or worse, was over.

Somehow, commented Roger Mudd, in summing up the campaign on the *CBS Evening News*, most voters had the feeling that they had been "vaguely cheated." Caustically, Mudd placed the blame for a "vapid and egocentric" campaign squarely on the candidates. Carter, he said, had "condemned" the campaign to an "issueless status" by making trust and integrity his main themes. Ford then met his challenger on that battleground, all of which made for a depressing and banal campaign. Whether that was the way it really was all through those fall months could, of course, be argued.

What could not be argued was the fact that neither of the candidates had aroused much passion. Carter, particularly, did not stir partisan juices the way Roosevelt, Truman, Kennedy, John-son, and Humphrey did in their respective battles. Liberal intellectuals, who played prominent roles in previous Democratic contests, sat pretty much on their hands in 1976. As Henry Steele Commager, professor of history at Amherst College and a man old enough to have voted in thirteen presidential elections, put it, "The intellectuals are not very ardently attracted to Mr. Carter. But they have nowhere else to go."

"They'll vote for him, and more or less grudgingly support him," observed Norman Podhoretz, editor of *Commentary*. Still there were some intellectuals—curiously further on the left—who appeared genuinely enthusiastic about Carter. Among them was Norman Mailer, who had written that effusive profile of the candidate for *The New York Times Magazine*. Along with Irving Howe, Lillian Hellman, Bernard Malamud, Philip Roth, Robert Coles, Robert Penn Warren, and Susan Sontag, Mailer had signed a pro-Carter advertisement initiated by William Phillips, editor of *Partisan Review*. At the same time, James Reston complained that Carter's Atlanta staff had fended off "old Democratic loyalists like Kenneth Galbraith with mimeographed rejections of offers for help." Still, Reston was no longer referring to Carter as "Wee Jimmy." The pundit's references to the candidate were now uniformly deferential.

Not so deferential was Reston's more conservative *Times* colleague, Bill Safire, who had this to say the day before the election: "The Carter campaign appeared to be managed by Chicken Little, starting off to the right, lurching to the left, veering back right as the sky seemed to fall. He started off as the enemy of the Establishment and wound up its supplicant, mass-producing puddings without themes, dragging in Nixon the way a Nixon would drag in a Nixon. The candidate was left wrung out and fearful, his support ebbing, his only hope the election would be held in time."

And so, finally, in the bicentennial year of 1976, the American people went to the polls. Not all who were entitled to vote, however, did so. Just 54.4 percent of the 150 million eligible, the lowest election turnout since Truman edged Dewey in 1948. Carter won the electoral vote 297 to 241, the popular vote 40.8 million to Ford's 39.1 million. Ford carried four of the eight biggest states. But he needed five or six. Had Ford carried New York with its 41 electoral votes, he would have won the election. But he lost the Empire State by 289,000 votes. And though New York Republicans were prepared to demand the impoundment of all the voting machines because of suspected irregularities, the White House decided the Democrats couldn't have pilfered all those votes. What really was decisive in New York was the success of regular Democrats in keeping Gene McCarthy's name off the ballot. For, undoubtedly, McCarthy would have been able to siphon off a fairly large number of votes from Carter and thus, conceivably, have helped Ford carry New York.

Still, all the what-might-have-beens did not matter any more. James Earl Carter— "please call me Jimmy"—was now the President-elect, the about-to-be-inaugurated Leader of the Free World. It was a close election, and various ethnic groups began putting in their claims of having "elected" him. Blacks, for example, demanded most of the credit, though Gallup's data indicated that Carter received a slightly lesser proportion of their vote than did McGovern in 1972 or Humphrey in 1968. Likewise, the Jews claimed credit. As did organized labor, with perhaps somewhat greater justification. And, as Richard M. Scammon and Ben J. Wattenberg, leading analysts of pollsters' findings, observed, "In a sense they are *all* correct. Carter could not have won *without* their support. But that is the very nature of a close election. A close election is close. . . . But saying 'you couldn't have won *without* us' is not quite the same as saying 'you won *because* of us.' It may be said that the latter claim can properly be made by a group that not only provides a margin of difference, but votes *away from traditional patterns* to provide the margin of difference."*

There was "one most obvious major group of voters who can lay claim to that formula for 1976," wrote Scammon and Wattenberg. "That grouping is 'The South.'" The South is an area where recent Democratic presidential candidates had been running worst. And Carter narrowly carried the South, the most conservative part of the nation, largely because of regional loyalties—much as John F. Kennedy carried Catholic areas in 1960. The percentage of Southern blacks voting Democratic has been much higher than Southern whites—but it remained constant in 1976. Where the big change came was among the white Southerners. Had they not switched to Carter in large numbers, he would not have won. "The most conservative part of the country voted for the more liberal candidate," Scammon and Wattenberg went on. Obviously, many white Southerners voted for Carter because he was a

*From the article "Jimmy Carter's Problem," by Scammon and Wattenberg, in *Public Opinion*, March/April 1978.

Southerner—and, in spite of their ideological leanings. "With all ·
that extra help, Carter managed to carry the South narrowly.
Slightly more than half of the white Southerners still voted *against*
him." And, outside of the Old Confederacy, Gerald Ford carried
the nation in both popular and electoral votes.

That the election had left the new Administration with certain
"weaknesses" was reported in a secret memorandum to the
President-elect by pollster Pat Caddell. These were:

(1) Carter is still viewed as inexperienced.

(2) He is viewed as an individual who often flip-flops on issues
and positions—a situation that we must be careful of, given the
way the realities of government may force seeming changes in
campaign positions.

(3) Carter was also viewed during the election as a person who
"overpromised." There was considerable skepticism about many of
his proposals.

(4) Most important, of course, is the general sense that Carter is
a "risk" as President. Because he is an "unknown," whose actions
and behavior can only be discerned when he is finally in office,
many voters worry.

For this, Carter blamed the press, or at least part of it. In an
extraordinary seventy-five-minute meeting with the writing
press—a session closed to the electronic media—the President-
elect said some tough things about the television coverage of his
campaign, calling it a "crippling thing" and suggesting that the
networks' nightly news had given Ford a free ride while emphasizing his errors. "Every time I made a mistake, it was in the news,"
he said, "and Mr. Ford's news was that he came into the Rose
Garden and signed a bill. He was in charge of things—very
authoritative, very sure of himself, no problems, no squabbles, no
mistakes."

In political parlance, Jimmy Carter was acting like a "sore
winner."

"What baffled me all fall," self-styled "good Democrat" John
Roche wrote the following spring, "was how, in a year when,
seemingly, Benedict Arnold running on the Democratic ticket
could walk away from Jerry Ford, Carter almost managed to lose
the presidency. Believe me that was some trick. . . . What almost

put Ford back in the White House was an increasing perception among the electorate that Carter wasn't acting—he began to spook people."

It was a perception that was to haunt Jimmy Carter all through his presidency.

14
THE NEW SPIRIT

SHORTLY AFTER THE ELECTION, THE PRESIDENT-ELECT TOLD Barbara Walters that blue jeans were his "normal attire" and that he expected to go about the White House wearing them while his wife went around upstairs in her bathrobe. Carter also told Walters that he expected, as President, to carry his own garment bags: "I don't want to lose them, in the first place; and it's just part of my nature to do my own physical work."

The idea of a President of the United States worrying about losing his bags was, of course, preposterous. But carrying his luggage was part of the image that Carter still sought to project even now that he was elected. Thus, while visiting overnight in Washington prior to the Inauguration, he was pictured carrying his bags up the steps of Blair House. The staff of the nation's number-one guest house had been advised by his aides that that's the way Carter wanted it.*

---

*One social observer, Betty Beale of *The Washington Star*, thought Carter's luggage habits just too much. In her column, she bluntly advised the President-elect to stop "posturing as a common man."

The Carters had come to Washington at President Ford's invitation to discuss the transition. They had planned to walk across Pennsylvania Avenue to the White House. But the White House wanted them to drive over from Blair House. This became a matter for considerable negotiation. Finally, the White House won out, after Ron Nessen argued that any walk by the President-elect and his wife would dominate the news coverage and detract from the primary purpose of the Ford-Carter meeting—namely, to project the get-together as a symbol of national unity and the orderly transfer of power.

In keeping with the just-plain-folks image he was cultivating, the President-elect also made clear that what he wanted was a "people's Inauguration." And Bardyl Tirana, who organized the Inaugural jubilee, said, "We're trying to give Mr. Carter what he wants—a simple, modest, inexpensive Inauguration that will involve all the 215 million people in this country. . . ." But the festivities turned out to be anything but simple. Lasting five days, they included fireworks, dances, concerts, scriptural readings by the President's sister, horse shows, symphonies, puppet shows, and a special eighteen-car train from Plains—the Peanut Special. Nor were the festivities inexpensive. They ended up costing nearly $3.5 million.

As Carter got off the plane in Washington that cold day in January, he carried his bags again, but the transformation had begun. That night at the Kennedy Center, the audience—in evening dress—stood to applaud the Carter family, Jimmy in a black tuxedo and ruffled shirt, Rosalynn in a long red skirt and black blouse, and Amy in a red jumper. Shortly after they settled into the plush seats of the presidential box, the nationally televised two-and-a-half hour New Spirit Inaugural Concert began. Leonard Bernstein conducted the National Symphony Orchestra and James Dickey read a new poem, describing Carter as a mythic hero drawing strength from a walk in the Georgia countryside. John Wayne was there, too, drawling, "I am considered a member of the opposition—the loyal opposition, accent the loyal, I'd have it no other way." Carter acknowledged the "Duke" by throwing a highball salute.

For his swearing-in, Carter sought to set the tone for his new

Administration by wearing a business suit, forsaking the traditional morning coat and top hat. And he took the oath of office in the name of plain "Jimmy," instead of his baptismal name, James Earl Carter, Jr. His Inaugural speech was a curious blend of high-campaign oratory (delivered in singsong cadence) and a Christian sort of identification of the people with spirituality (while avoiding the concept of people being the mystical body of Christ). His best line was the very first he uttered, "For myself and our nation, I want to thank my predecessor for all he has done to heal our land." It obviously constituted an apologetic gesture to an opponent whom he and his running mate had savaged all through the electoral campaign.

But the rest of the speech was quickly forgotten. What was remembered on that cold, crisp, clear day was the fact that the newly inaugurated President walked down Pennsylvania Avenue toward the White House. The walk was not as spontaneous as it had seemed on television; it had been well planned in advance with the Secret Service. Four years before, following his second Inaugural, Nixon himself had thought of walking, but the Secret Service had objected. There were too many antiwar protesters around. Carter did not have any such problem. The angry protesters who plagued Nixon were mute. Carter was fortunate in that the nation he took over was in pretty good shape. No depression, world war, Korea, recession, assassination, Vietnam, or Watergate confronted him. This may not have been the way Carter painted the state of the union during the campaign; but that's the way things actually were. And the mood of the Inauguration reflected hope rather than despair, though Carter's speech could hardly be described as inspiring. Opinions naturally were mixed about the new President. And while most observers said, in effect, he seemed like a nice man, youthful R. Emmett Tyrrell, Jr., editor-in-chief of the *Alternative* (now *The American Spectator*), let it be known that "few pols have ever been more banal, more tedious, and more stupendously uninteresting" than Carter, whom he dubbed "a grinning dunce." Of course, at the time, Tyrrell's was a lonely voice.

Black tie was optional at the seven Inaugural Night parties— known as "balls" in pre-Populist days—and the program noted carefully the folksy qualities of the various Carters and their offspring. Beer bottle in hand, Billy was heard complaining that John Wayne, a proud right-winger, had no place in the Carter doings. Which sounded funny coming from someone who had made no secret of his admiration of George Wallace, another honored guest at the Inaugural ceremonies. The nation's new First Brother may have had ample belly and country ways, but Billy arrived in Washington by chartered jet, and the family's peanut operations were worth far more than peanuts. Even the jaded in the capital city were impressed. Billy Carter was a robust fellow, not a lout. What really was annoying Billy, moreover, was the way folks back home were "commercializing" on his brother's election. "My only regret about Jimmy being elected is that I wished he had lived in Atlanta," he had told an interviewer. "Plains has gone straight to hell. I went to a meeting the other night of landowners and property owners. I was the only one voting against commercialization. I'm the only person in this whole town who isn't selling peanuts to tourists. I really regret what's happening in Plains." Of course, Billy was to take advantage of his brother's new station in more lucrative ways. And he didn't sell himself for peanuts, either.

Not all was aw-shucks country chic, however. Some of the new President's more affluent friends, 250 of them and many from Georgia, gathered at the Sulgrave Club for one of the more elegant of the week's parties, a black tie affair hosted by Atlanta attorney Philip H. Alston, Jr., Carter's later choice for Ambassador to Australia. Carter and his family had vacationed often at the Alstons' Sea Island plantation. Among the guests at the Sulgrave Club party were Reynolds Tobacco heir Smith Bagley and his wife, Vicki, described by *Time* as "potential pacesetters in a new Washington social order centered on moneyed and well-connected Southerners." Another guest was the new Budget Director, Bert Lance, a giant of a man who, unlike his leader, couldn't have cared less about projecting an image of humility. Lance had arrived in a black Cadillac bearing specially ordered license plates: BERT on the front bumper, LANCE on the rear.

Nevertheless, an image was being etched by the incoming Administration. "We have a remarkable man," wrote veteran White House observer Nick Thimmesch, "a one-time peanut farmer (now a millionaire), insisting on simplicity, leading by evoking spirituality and walking among the people to make the bond." No longer were bands to play the traditional ruffles and flourishes and "Hail to the Chief" when he arrived. Carter considered these just too regal for a people's President. And, carrying de-imperialization to his White House staff, he barred his senior aides from using governmental limousines except for official business. Henceforth, outside working hours, staffers would have to depend on cabs or their own cars. This also was supposed to apply to Bert Lance. But the President's genial banker buddy couldn't have cared less. He was using his own formidable chauffeur-driven vehicle wherever he went, hardly in keeping with the Populist image of the new Administration. And he and wife LaBelle managed to find an expensive house in Georgetown. Even Jody Powell, for all his down-home style, got himself digs on Foxhall Road, only three blocks from the property that Nelson Rockefeller had put on the market for $8 million. Jody could afford the rent, however. For he was making more money than he ever had in his youthful life—$56,000 a year, which was more than double his campaign salary.

Jody wasn't the only one doing well under Carter. The Populist President made sure that others of his senior staff—Zbigniew Brzezinski, Jack H. Watson, Jr., Ham Jordan, Stu Eizenstat, Midge Costanza (who earned $15,000 as a Rochester city councilperson)—also received $56,000, a leap of $11,200 above what their jobs had paid in previous administrations. But the White House insisted that the twenty-five percent increase in salaries was actually an example of government economy, because the President could have given his aides another $1,500, which he hadn't done. A press release claimed great "savings" for the taxpayers. And the President said, "I don't have any apology to make."

Junior staffers were taking home pretty hefty paychecks, too. All were under thirty-five years of age. And all were making more than $40,000 a year. Most had received what amounted to 400 percent pay raises since going on the federal payroll. Typical was Rick Hutcheson, the staff secretary who, at the tender age of twenty-five, was pulling down a cool $42,500. His job was to monitor the flow of paper in and out of the Oval Office. Later in the year, he and others making less than $47,500 were awarded a raise of 7.05 percent. This boost for 321 White House employees, at a total annual cost of $550,000, went unpublicized for five weeks. Only when reporters made inquiries were the pay raises confirmed. In former Administrations, this would have been called news management.

Also embarrassing were news stories about how Carter's White House was actually larger than that of his predecessor. And this after Carter had charged that the White House had become bloated under Nixon and had remained so under Ford. And he promised to make drastic reductions. On taking office, Carter ordered a thirty percent, across-the-board reduction in the size of the staff, a figure he apparently pulled out of thin air. Two months later, the staff had grown by thirty percent—from 510 under Ford to 665 under Carter. The main reason, aides said sheepishly, was the enormous increase in mail and phone calls.

But the President did request proposals for trimming the bureaucracy, particularly the 13,500 lawyers on the federal payroll. Citing his own experience as a businessman, he complained that because they didn't have too much to do, these lawyers spent their time dreaming up unnecessary regulations requiring "oceans of paperwork" by businessmen and local officials. At the same time, the President did order the sale of the presidential yacht Sequoia and did get rid of some of the twenty-nine presidential planes. But the latter move was more sleight of hand than real savings, for the planes were always available anyway from the Air Force. Likewise, Carter contemplated closing Camp David when he took office, but he quickly decided that the rustic paradise in the Catoctin Mountains was one adjunct of the imperial presidency worth saving.

One campaign assurance he did live up to was the family decision to send Amy to a public school. The decision ended months of speculation as to whether the First Family would somehow find an excuse to register Amy in one of the capital's pale-faced private schools, as most other affluent families did with their children.

Adequately protected by the Secret Service, nine-year-old Amy began attending Stevens Elementary, five blocks from the White House. Amy's enrollment was milked by the White House publicity apparatus for all it was worth. For that reason, it was somewhat surprising when the news broke in June 1978 that Amy would be transferring out of Stevens a year earlier than expected. Predictably, the White House sought to downplay the move. "This is the logical time to put Amy in middle school so that she will be settled for the next few years," explained Mary Hoyt, Mrs. Carter's press secretary. The new school was the fifty-one percent white Hardy Middle School on Foxhall Road in Nelson Rockefeller's old neighborhood. So exclusive was this area that when Rockefeller wanted to sell his estate to a developer, nearby residents complained bitterly that the $250,000 homes which were contemplated. would "run down the neighborhood." Hardy also was unusual in that it moves its pupils ahead as quickly as they are able to advance, regardless of age or grade level. "Few would take issue with the Carters' desire that their daughter get the advantage of such schooling," commented *Human Events*. "But . . . not all parents are fortunate enough to be able to send their children to a public school that satisfies them."

Much of Carter's first few months as President was largely devoted to symbolic acts. And this at the suggestion of his personal pollster, Pat Caddell, who, in a secret memorandum prepared during the interregnum, also advised the President-elect on the need for "a series of small promises and projects accomplished quickly that provide evidence that longer-term goals will also be realized."

Caddell focused on the merits of what can only be described as charismatic inertia. "The old cliché about mistaking style for substance usually works in reverse in politics," he declared. "Too many good people have been defeated because they tried to substitute substance for style; they forgot to give the public the kind of visible signals that it needs to understand what is happening." He proceeded to indicate in Hegelian-Marxist terms that since neither the "thesis" nor the "antithesis" would provide any political mileage, the thing to do was wait for a new "synthesis," smiling all the while.

"To borrow from the philosophy of science," Caddell advised the President-elect, "we desperately need an ideological 'paradigm' to replace the 'free market capitalist model' that we don't really want. American society does not need another 'patch-up' job; it needs some kind of direction. . . . Our most successful primary opponent, Jerry Brown, was successful because he was able to present an ideology that fitted no tradition in a rhetorical style that was refreshing to voters."

Caddell also recommended a number of cosmetic ventures— "stylistic approaches," he dubbed them—as standby measures while Carter waited for Hegel's world spirit to manifest itself. Among other things, he urged "fireside chats," "town meetings" as well as "question periods"—all designed to "build a sense of personal intimacy with the people." The first order of business was to make a good impression on a skeptical electorate, he went on. First impressions are everything, and so the first ninety days had to be devoted to selling Carter to the people.

So it began right away, on Inauguration Day, with the Carter walk, and it continued relentlessly—the fireside chat on television, with carefully rigged town meetings and overnight stays with local folks, the cardigan sweaters and sixty-five-degree thermostats, the dial-a-President radio show with Walter Cronkite at the helm, and on and on. And when the Man of the People began abandoning some of the "frills" that go with the presidency, Pat Caddell—who, incidentally, was not personally averse to enjoying the life style of an eminently successful pollster—must have been in ecstasy.

After ninety days, Caddell looked around and found things good. Carter had risen twenty points in the polls, from fifty-one on Election Day to seventy-one percent. Even when Carter got into substance—orchestrating a weeklong hoopla in Congress and over television about an all-too-familiar energy package ("the moral equivalent of war")*—his popularity held, with an incredible eighty-nine percent finding Carter "sincere in his desire to become closer to the people." Said Caddell, "He's convinced people he's in charge and he knows what he's doing."

For a Democratic President, Carter did appear to take some unusual positions. Having promised during his campaign to provide aid to the cities, the President risked at least the

---

*Said Frank Zarb, energy chief in the Ford Administration: "It all looks so familiar. I can't get into a fight with anybody. I don't see how I can be critical, because so far I haven't seen anything new. It's the same program."

appearance of inconsistency in telling New York City that he would not agree to an extension of Washington's commitment to underwrite its municipal loans. (Later he modified that position.) Then he proceeded to notify the "knowledge industry" that he intended to drastically reduce federal funding of education; to offend AFL-CIO president George Meany by his talk of reviving wage-price guidelines on a "voluntary" basis; to permit Attorney General Griffin Bell—whom the civil rights activists considered guilty of "racism" until proven innocent—to remark that recent Supreme Court decisions appeared to favor those opposed to school busing. Carter, moreover, informed the Governors of the parched Western states that he felt compelled to reduce funds for irrigation and power development.

It was obvious whom Carter was trying to please. As described in the Caddell memo, the prime targets of Carter's politics were "the college-educated, white-collar, middle and upper-middle income voting groups," among whom "there was tremendous suspicion of Carter . . . as a traditional Democrat." According to Caddell, "this is the largest rising group in the population. It must be attracted in significant numbers if Democrats are to be successful in the future. These are voters who are often, however, cautious on the questions of increased taxes, spending, and particularly inflation, an issue which mobilizes this group in a conservative fashion."

None of which sat too well with the Democratic leadership in Congress. At an extraordinary White House meeting of the President and the leaders, Speaker of the House Tip O'Neill told Carter that the Administration seemed to have forgotten the Democrats' traditional role as the party of the have-nots. To begin with, the O'Neill-Carter relationship had not started off promisingly. For months, O'Neill had endured what he regarded as "oafishness" on the part of certain staffers in the White House, at one point muttering darkly about someone named "Hannibal Jerkin" who was close to the President. O'Neill hadn't forgotten how he was treated by "Jerkin" when he complained about getting Inaugural seats in the last row of the second balcony at the Kennedy Center. Ham Jordan had even offered to rebate $299 of the $300 O'Neill had paid for the tickets. "They looked on me as a Boston Irish politician," said O'Neill. "They didn't pay any attention to me. The President said he was going to the people on his programs and I said, 'Lookit, this isn't the Georgia Legislature.'" Carter himself seemed to go out of his way to disconcert the Speaker. The first two Massachusetts appointments in his new Administration went to a card-carrying Republican, Elliot Richardson, and a recent convert from the GOP, Evan Dobelle.

Still, O'Neill came to Carter's defense in May 1977, after George McGovern had bitterly accused the President of abandoning campaign promises and party principle out of fear of big business and a preoccupation with his image. In a speech to the Americans for Democratic Action, the South Dakota Democrat declared that "in reviewing economic policy this spring, it sometimes seems difficult to remember who won last fall." Responding, O'Neill said it was "very unfair to make judgments when Carter's only been President 100 days. There hasn't been any elected President since 1932 [who] passed one piece of major legislation in his first 100 days." Privately, however, according to James Wieghart of *The New York Daily News*, the Speaker was railing "about Carter's obsession with a balanced budget and abandonment of liberal programs that have always been the heart of the Democratic platform—public works jobs, more aid for the cities, and expanded federal health insurance."

In foreign policy, the new President appeared to be signaling that he truly believed in the efficacy of sweet reason and Christian pieties in the governance of global passions. And this was all to the liking of liberals who were drawn to Carter by campaign positions which some critics had labeled as "McGovernism without McGovern." The President appeared intent on proving that he meant what he said during the campaign about international arms control, as witness the brusqueness with which he canceled President Ford's order—admittedly delivered in the heat of electoral combat—that concussion bombs be provided the Israelis. Meanwhile, he continued in his headlong rush to SALT II, dropping B-1 bombers, cruise missiles, MX mobile missiles, Minuteman IIIs, and $2.75 billion in defense money in his pursuit of a nuclear deal with Moscow. And his nominations of people like Ted Sorensen and Paul Warnke to high positions were signals to the liberals that he stood with them, at least in foreign policy.

Contradictory as his programs may have appeared at the time, they fell in line with Caddell's recommendations. In his memo dated December 10, 1976, the pollster had urged the President-elect to "devise a context" for his new Administration "that is neither traditionally liberal nor traditionally conservative"—rather, "one that cuts across traditional ideology." However, Caddell added that "trying to be 'liberal' on some issues and conservative on others is not likely to result in a new coalition, but will appear as an attempt to play both sides of the issue. . . . What we require is not stew, composed of bits and pieces of old policies, but a fundamentally new ideology."

All of which sounded like Carter had a Machiavelli hiding in the Oval Office, particularly when Caddell's updated version of *The Prince* came to light after some anti-intellectual-in-residence leaked the fifty-six-page document to the press in the spring of 1977. The leak caused consternation in the higher echelons of the Carter Administration. Obviously, its disclosure was aimed at embarrassing Caddell, who apparently had some enemies in the White House. For there were those who believed that the youthful pollster, representing major corporations and Arab nations, was not a salutary influence on the President. The leak recalled the embarrassments of the Nixon people when supposedly confidential documents began finding their way into the hands of hostile newsmen.*

The Caddell memo explained a great deal as to what the new President was up to. It also showed, among other things, that Carter's inner circle had anticipated—and, indeed, relied on—opposition from the liberal left as one of the basic forces shaping Carter's political strategy. "To be frank," the pollster had written, "Jimmy Carter is not particularly popular with major elements of the Democratic Party, whether it be activists, the Congress, labor leaders, or the political 'bosses.' Each of these groups presents potential problems in a primary situation. Each must be carefully watched and to the extent possible pacified over the next four

---

*Purely by coincidence I ran into Caddell in the elevator of a New York hotel the day after portions of his memo were published in *The New York Times*. When I asked the pollster just how they got out, he said, "That's what I would like to know." "Well," I responded, "when Mr. Carter brings in the 'plumbers' to find out, make sure they don't botch the job as they did under Nixon." Caddell obviously didn't think my effort at humor was funny. He grimaced, said nothing, and disappeared into the streets of Manhattan.

years so we do not experience a party splitting primary situation. Given the realities of the country, I think it's fair to say that more of the opposition to Carter programs will come from Democrats than from Republicans."

While denigrating "traditional liberals" as being as "antiquated and anachronistic" as "conservative Republicans," Caddell warned that "because of their representation in the establishment, the media, and in politics, they have a weight in public affairs far greater than their numbers. . . . This wing is composed of individuals such as Ted Kennedy, George McGovern, and Mo Udall. For these people, there is little risk in challenging an incumbent President coupled with an overwhelming desire to do so. There are already rumblings from Senator Kennedy—privately—that he senses problems with Governor Carter. . . . He and others may develop a mind set that enables them to build up seemingly rational arguments for opposing the President's policies and even instigating political opposition."

Also representing a threat to Carter's future was the Congress, whose "new leadership . . . is likely to be more aggressive and assertive than past leadership. . . . While they intend to coöperate, they are anxious to be independent. Their recent years of opposition has done nothing for their willingness to coöperate with the Executive Branch." Another threat lay in the Young Turks, the youthful Senators and Governors risen to power since 1972, who were elected "because they speak to different concerns of the American public than their older colleagues. . . . They are not wedded to political tradition or to political protocol. They are, on the whole, articulate and politically ambitious. They represent the coming generation of power, and if not handled properly, they may want to exercise their right to challenge quickly." The group included Gary Hart, Dick Clark, Joe Biden, Jay Rockefeller, Don Riegle, "and, of course, Jerry Brown—who must be viewed as the single largest threat on the horizon within the Democratic Party. He speaks well, has a new definition of American politics, and is shrewd and ambitious to boot, and he is already beginning to test the water."

The Republican Party seemed to Caddell to be "bent on self-destruction" and, he advised Carter, "we have an opportunity to co-opt many of their issues and to take away large chunks of their normal [vote] by the right actions in government."

"Unfortunately," he added, "it is those same actions that are likely to cause rumblings from the left of the Democratic Party."

Caddell also recommended the identifying and co-opting of "the people who might help staff opposing presidential campaigns. One of the best ways, I think, to limit the potential opposition in the future is to remove from the job market as many of those with the experience and talent in presidential politics as can be accommodated." And this is precisely what Carter did. He co-opted the aides and allies of potential Democratic opponents by hiring and hiding them in the catacombs of the bureaucracy. And, as we shall see, he practically deflowered the New Left by placing its leading lights in second- and third-level Administration jobs.

For his major appointments, Carter had gone to more traditional Establishment sources—the world of big business, corporate law firms, and the Trilateral Commission. And several of his more important Cabinet appointments had been second-echelon officials under President Kennedy. Which led one wit to observe that Carter had chosen the "junior varsity" from the New Frontier, only now they had gotten starting positions. In view of the Vietnam involvement of some of his appointees, another wit suggested that Carter's campaign slogan be changed to "Why not the best—and the brightest?"

In a long, bitter piece in *The Washington Post*, William Greider noted that "Carter has brought back the 'whiz kids' from [Robert] McNamara's Pentagon to run the government. What shall we call them? The 'whiz men?'" These were the men who had been in government "when the big lies were told in the sixties" about Vietnam. "None of them spoke up, at least not so they could be heard by the public. Will anyone believe them now that they are back in government, running Carter's foreign policy and defense strategy? It is a dangerous legacy this new President has embraced."

"Moreover," Greider went on, "Carter has chosen his team, with few exceptions, from a very small universe of Americans. Most of them know each other well, because they have often met in corporate boardrooms, doing business, serving government.

The public squabbling over adequate representation for women and blacks has obscured this reality—corporate America is the best represented of all. If this is Carter's idea of Populism, what on earth would élitism be like?"

For his top foreign policy advisers, Carter reached into the Trilateral Commission to select Cyrus R. Vance as his Secretary of State and Zbigniew Brzezinski as his National Security Adviser, Henry Kissinger's old White House job. Their appointments apparently came as a surprise only to Hamilton Jordan, who had been quoted in *Playboy* as saying he would quit if such Establishment characters as Vance and Brzezinski were named. Obviously, Jordan had been influenced by what Carter had been saying while seeking the presidency. On February 17, 1976, for example, the candidate couldn't have made it clearer: "I can tell you that there is a major and fundamental issue taking shape in this election year. That issue is the division between the 'insiders' and the 'outsiders.'. . . The people of this country know from bitter experience that we are not going to get these changes merely by shifting around the same group of insiders. . . . The insiders have had their chance, and they have not delivered. And their time has run out. The time has come for the great majority of Americans—those who have for too long been on the outside looking in—to have a President who will turn the government of this country inside out."

Cy Vance was hardly a "new face." A lawyer in a prestigious Wall Street firm, he had served in the Kennedy and Johnson Administrations. And, for a time, he had also served JFK's brother-in-law by organizing a Sargent Shriver for President Committee to work in the 1976 primaries. Though not a leading architect of the Kennedy-Johnson policy in Vietnam which eventually led to disaster, he was—in the words of William Greider—more like one of the "senior draftsmen and cheerleaders." As Deputy Secretary of Defense under McNamara, Vance claimed in August 1964 that the Gulf of Tonkin incident was an unprovoked attack by the North Vietnamese, requiring retaliatory bombing raids. "The United States is prepared to take any action which will be required by the circumstances," Vance had declared, "but we hope that the firmness of the action which we have taken will indicate to the Communists that it would be unwise for them to take any further aggressive acts." All of which made Vance known for "his careful organization loyalty and lack of independent opinion," according to former NSC staffer Roger Morris, writing in *Harper's*. "Afterward, the same values helped make him a successful corporate lawyer and pliant director of the Rockefeller Foundation, Pan Am, IBM, and *The New York Times* in the Nixon interregnum. At sixty, his life is marked by no cause, issue, or question save his own advancement and acceptability."

Likewise, Carter's National Security Adviser Brzezinski had been known as a "hawk," defending the war and its purposes at academic gatherings. Though he later became known as an advocate of a negotiated settlement and a mild critic of Nixon's war policy, his deepest scorn was reserved for the "self-flagellating intellectuals" who were so noisily against the war. Brzezinski was often compared with Kissinger. In fact, he was called "Carter's Kissinger." But there was little love lost between the two European-born advisers, both of whose patrons, incidentally, were Rockefellers. In fact, a cynic might have noted that the transition in foreign affairs was not so much from Ford to Carter as from Nelson to David. However, Brzezinski differed strongly with Kissinger on the question of Euro-Communism. Kissinger felt "the advent of Communism in major European countries is likely to produce a sequence of events in which other European countries will also be tempted to move in the same direction." Brzezinski responded, "It doesn't do us any good to go around talking loudly and carrying a weeping willow. Hectoring the West Europeans about the Communist threat simply makes the Communists more popular."

Named Secretary of Defense was another retread from McNamara's stable, Harold Brown. As LBJ's Air Force Secretary, Brown was a leading advocate of Vietnam bombing. During the Nixon years, he was president of the California Institute of Technology and served part time as a technical adviser at the SALT talks. He also sat on the boards of several companies (including *The Los Angeles Times* and, with Vance, IBM) and was a Trilateralist. Probably his greatest attraction for Carter was the fact that he represented a compromise choice as between James

Schlesinger, whom the hardliners were urging for the Pentagon post, and Paul Warnke, a McGovern adviser who was the favorite of the "doves."

As his Secretary of Health, Education and Welfare, Carter selected Joseph A. Califano, Jr. A highly paid corporate lawyer (his Washington practice brought him over $500,000 in 1976 alone), Califano, like Vance and Brown, had worked for McNamara's Defense Department. From the Pentagon, he went to the White House. As legislative counsel, he orchestrated LBJ's domestic programs and legislation. And he also defended the war. In 1965, he accepted a petition supporting the war from students and faculty at American University. "Of course," he said in 1965, "we recognize the right to dissent. That's what our boys in Vietnam are fighting for. But this shows that the overwhelming majority of American college students and the American public stand fully behind the President in his policy in Vietnam." In 1967, following the Detroit riot, Califano was assigned to monitor potential domestic hot spots for the White House. Previously, he had been involved in Operation Mongoose, the Robert F. Kennedy-directed covert operation designed to bring down Fidel Castro by any means, fair or foul. For Carter, Califano had another significant qualification—he and partner Edward Bennett Williams were lawyers for *The Washington Post*.

After analyzing Carter's Cabinet, Roger Morris, the former member of the NSC and various Senate staffs, concluded that the eleven senior officials selected by the new President had "about seventy cumulative years on the public payroll, some thirty corporate directorships, and an average 1976 income of $211,000."

"Ironically," Morris wrote in *Harper's*, "what most distinguishes Jimmy Carter's 'outsiders' from that [Nixon] GOP regime of privilege and power is that present Cabinet members are individually and collectively far wealthier. . . . Like their predecessors for the past three decades, the ranking advisers to Jimmy Carter are hardly the best and the brightest from among a large and generously gifted population. (Indeed, counting their collective debacles from the LBJ era as well as the pedestrian quality of their other performances, they may even be worse and duller than usual.) They are just the most available, and often the least exceptionable, from among a class of institutional survivors. . . . In many ways, these people are precisely the opposite of the classic capitalist. In place of boldness, risk and innovation, they prize routine, safety, and acceptability. . . .

"What is worse about the present regime, as distinct from its Republican forerunners, is that there has been so much pretense—and so much apparent public credulity—that it is something else. . . ."

Carter did not have clear sailing on all his appointments. Opposition quickly surfaced when the President-elect announced his choice of Theodore C. Sorensen to become Director of Central Intelligence. Sorensen, of course, had been counsel to President Kennedy and his most gifted speechwriter. He had maintained close ties to the Kennedy family and, following Chappaquiddick, had rushed to Hyannisport to advise the beleaguered Ted Kennedy what to tell the public about that distressing affair. And this, as *The Washington Post* conjectured, may well have led to his undoing. For, as the *Post* editorialized, following the collapse of his nomination, Sorensen "is identified in the minds of many— ourselves included— not only with devoted service but also with discriminating allegiance—personal loyalty beyond the bounds of public duty—to the President he served and to his brothers. . . . It is hard to say out loud; certainly it is hard to say so in a chamber of the U.S. Senate. We got the impression, nonetheless, that a substantial majority was unwilling to entrust some of the most sensitive and secret responsibilities of government to a man whose judgment many of them privately question. . . ."

There were, of course, other reasons for the opposition. "It is not clear," the *Post* had also editorialized, "how [Sorensen's] background would help prepare him to preside over the U.S. Government's espionage agency." There also had been mutterings about Sorensen's youthful effort to obtain noncombatant status in the draft. And then, just before the Senate Select Committee on Intelligence was to hold hearings on the nomination, most of its members were shocked to learn that Sorensen had filed affidavits in the 1973 Pentagon Papers case involving Dan Ellsberg, conceding that he had taken seven cartons of classified documents from the White House in February 1964 for use in writing his book *Kennedy*. And just as shocking was the revelation that he had later claimed $232,000 in tax deductions for donating those very documents to the John F. Kennedy Library. (The Internal Revenue Service reduced the appraised value to $89,000.)

To such liberal Democrats as Joseph Biden of Delaware, Adlai E. Stevenson of Illinois, and Daniel K. Inouye of Hawaii, Sorensen's admissions were, in Biden's words, "political dynamite." Adding to their concern were quotations taken from *Watchmen in the Night*, a 1975 book Sorensen had written on presidential "accountability" after Watergate. In that tome, Sorensen had declared, "The greatest danger to our national security interests lies in the excessive use of secrecy by the executive branch. . . . Why not start erring on the side of overdisclosure instead of overconcealment." The possibility of a CIA director's overdisclosing rather than overconcealing did not sit too well with most members of the Senate Intelligence Committee. Meanwhile, Democratic Senator Robert B. Morgan of North Carolina raised the objection that as an intimate of JFK Sorensen "was in a position to know or should have known" about intelligence operations, including the assassination attempts on Fidel Castro, but had insisted in Senate testimony in 1975 that he had not known.

By now, the opposition had developed into what one Carter adviser called a "firestorm." And when the Intelligence Committee hearings opened, three days before the Inauguration of the new President, Sorensen abruptly withdrew his nomination. "It is now clear," he told a surprised committee, "that a substantial portion of the United States Senate and the intelligence community is not yet ready to accept as Director of Central Intelligence an outsider who believes as I believe." Not since the Republican-controlled Senate of 1925 rejected President Coolidge's nomination of Charles B. Warren as Attorney General had a President been rebuffed by a Congress controlled by his own party. For Jimmy Carter, it constituted his first major setback in his dealings with Congress, an omen of things to come.

Nevertheless, it was obvious that Carter did not want to take on the Senate on the sensitive subject of "national security." And he particularly didn't want to have blood on the floor during Inaugural Week. Moreover, he was involved in a battle over Griffin Bell, whom he had named as Attorney General. A lifelong friend of Carter, Bell was also a law partner of Jimmy's top adviser,

Charlie Kirbo. In fact, it was Bell who had introduced Kirbo to Carter. A member of the Atlanta establishment, Bell had worked on both the Kennedy and Carter presidential campaigns. In 1961, he was named by JFK to the Court of Appeals and served for fifteen years, quitting because of the heavy caseload and low pay. He had been, almost all his peers conceded, an excellent jurist, knowledgeable about the law and temperate in his decisions.

Yet Carter immediately had trouble with Bell's nomination. In the first place, all through the campaign Carter had promised to remove the Attorney General from politics, contending that it was "a disgrace" that during Watergate the public had come to believe "the Attorney General was not fair enough and objective enough and nonpolitical enough to pursue the enforcement of the law." Yet, when he had the opportunity to practice what he preached, Carter selected a trusted friend to be the nation's number-one law officer.

Bell came under bitter attack for other reasons. Though he had built a generally moderate record on the bench, some civil rights activists didn't think that was good enough. They complained about his membership in Atlanta's pre-eminent "social" clubs—the Capital City and the Piedmont Driving Club—both noted for their segregationist ways. Another issue was Judge Bell's letter of support of President Nixon's nomination of fellow Fifth Circuit Judge G. Harrold Carswell for the Supreme Court—a nomination rejected by the U.S. Senate. Also criticized was Judge Bell's ruling upholding the State Legislature's decision not to seat black Representative-elect Julian Bond because of his antiwar views (a ruling overturned by the Supreme Court). And then in the late fifties, it seems, Bell had served for a time as legal aide to Governor Vandiver, who was looking for loopholes in the Supreme Court desegregation decisions.

For five days, Bell endured intensive grilling by the Senate Judiciary Committee. The irony was that it was liberal Republicans who kept asking the tough questions. By and large, conservative Republicans were on Bell's side. Bell's nomination eventually was approved by a 75 to 21 vote, with sixteen of the "no" votes coming from liberal Republicans. The majority of liberal Democrats, who had so vigorously battled Nixon's Supreme Court nominations of Carswell and Clement F. Haynsworth, Jr., now were supporting Bell. And, of all people, it was Senator Birch Bayh, the Hoosier Democrat who had led the successful campaigns against Nixon's Southern choices, who acted as floor manager for the nomination. As James Flug, a former aide to Senator Ted Kennedy, said, "If Bell was a Nixon nominee, we would have beaten him."

Another familiar face to whom Carter turned was Paul C. Warnke, selected to be director of the Arms Control and Disarmament Agency (ACDA) and chief U.S. arms negotiator with the Soviet Union. And that appointment, too, aroused considerable controversy. For Warnke, as Assistant Defense Secretary under LJB, possessed "dovish" views, had been the principle adviser to George McGovern on national security issues during the 1972 campaign, and had argued ever since in behalf of what his critics alleged was unilateral disarmament. In his confirmation testimony, Warnke acknowledged that he had opposed the B-1 bomber, the Trident submarine, the mobile ICBM, and the XM tank, and had advocated a cutback in U.S. tactical nuclear weapons in Germany from 7,000 to 1,000.

When asked about the USSR's dramatic strides forward in nuclear power and the Kremlin's view that, in the future, the Soviets would be in a position to fight and win a nuclear war, Warnke responded, "In my view, this kind of thinking is on a level of abstraction which is unrealistic. It seems to me that instead of talking in these terms, which would indulge what I regard as the primitive aspects of Soviet nuclear doctrine, we ought to be trying to educate them into the real world of strategic nuclear weapons, which is that nobody could possibly win."

Taking strong issue with Warnke was Harvard Professor Richard Pipes, an expert on Soviet strategy. In *Commentary*, he wrote, "On what grounds does he, a Washington lawyer, presume to 'educate' the Soviet general staff composed of professional soldiers who thirty years ago defeated the Wehrmacht—and, of all things, about the 'real world of strategic nuclear weapons' of which they happen to possess a considerably larger arsenal than we? Why does he consider them children who ought to be 'indulged'? And why does he chastise for what he regards as 'primitive' and unrealistic strategic doctrine, not those who hold it, namely the Soviet military, but Americans who worry about it?"

Under fire, Warnke drew strong praise from Carter as a man whose qualifications in the field were unequalled. "I know Mr. Warnke very well," he said. "I have met with him several times to discuss his attitude on disarmament matters. I have complete confidence in him. . . . His views are well considered by me. I have accepted them. I think when the members of the Senate consider what Mr. Warnke stands for, he will be approved overwhelmingly."

The members of the Senate did consider Warnke's views. And the opposition led by Scoop Jackson produced a surprisingly large vote—40—against his nomination. Though Warnke was confirmed (and not with the overwhelming approval Carter had predicted), the size of the opposition vote provided a warning to the new President that he did not have carte blanche to make any deal he wanted in the new SALT talks with Moscow.

Despite the warning, Warnke remained true to his principles. Within weeks, he abolished the disarmament agency's Verification and Analysis Bureau, the group which sought to determine whether the Soviets were violating existing arms agreements. At his confirmation hearings, Warnke had been asked under oath about reports of such a "purge" in the agency. Warnke replied firmly there was "no substance" to those reports. In fact, seeking to ingratiate himself with skeptical Senators, he said, "An agreement which is not verifiable is worse than no agreement." The following month saw the end of the Verification Bureau. In addition, numerous hardline professionals were told to resign or find jobs elsewhere, to make room—as Bill Safire reported— "for men who won't make waves when U.S. strategic interests are conceded away."

Other such congenial types were now to be found throughout the Carter bureaucracy. At the State Department, for example, Anthony Lake had been named director of the Policy Planning Staff. A former aide on Henry Kissinger's NSC staff, Lake had resigned after President Nixon approved the 1970 "incursion" into Cambodia.

Others who now labored in Foggy Bottom included Trilateralist Richard Holbrooke, named Assistant Secretary for East Asian and Pacific Affairs; Richard Moose, out of the Senate Foreign Relations Committee, named Assistant Secretary for African Affairs; and

Leslie Gelb, director of the Bureau of Politico-Military Affairs. (As a *New York Times* diplomatic correspondent, Gelb had been helpful to the Carter campaign by publicizing a supposedly confidential document attesting to the decline in U.S. prestige abroad during the Ford years.) Writing in *New America,* the Social Democrat journal, Martin Taussig described the Carter foreign policy advisers in these words: "Holbrooke, Lake, Moose, Gelb . . . are committed softline ideologues. . . . They contribute regularly, and sometimes jointly, to *Foreign Policy,* the out-of-office instrument of the post-Vietnam Democratic softline establishment. In combinàtion, they are likely to constitute the most potent force in a department otherwise staffed by bland career diplomats or people without foreign policy experience. Indeed, it seems likely that the State Department team was shaped more by them than by anyone else."

Not surprisingly, George McGovern was happy about the new foreign policy team. He was quoted as saying that most of the people selected by Vance and Carter were "excellent, quite close to those I would have made myself." Not surprisingly, either, was the dismay voiced by Ben Wattenberg, the adviser to Scoop Jackson, as to the great number of "professional neutralists" assembled by the Carter Administration. Noting that *The Wall Street Journal* had complained that Carter "seemed to be giving us George McGovern's State Department," Wattenberg said that he and "like-minded Democrats . . . do not want to stand by while our party is wrongly and inaccurately described as a party of mush and weakness."

Those "like-minded Democrats" also viewed with alarm the mixed assortment of professional outsiders—environmentalists, political dissidents, *pro bono publico* lawyers, consumerists, and militant feminists—who were brought into the new Administration. All this by way of "co-opting" the personnel of potential opponents, as Pat Caddell had suggested in his memo.

Probably the most visible of the scores of anti-Establishment figures employed by the new Administration was Sam Brown, who led the mass antiwar demonstrations in Washington during the Nixon years. Having moved to Denver to dabble in Colorado politics, Brown later won election as State Treasurer. Brown also dabbled in national politics by. vigorously opposing the maverick candidacy of Gene McCarthy, arguing that a vote for his former hero was, in effect, a vote for Jerry Ford. Brown thus did a great deal to establish Carter's legitimacy among left-leaning Democrats.

Among Carter's first acts upon assuming his heavy burdens was to call Brown to offer him the directorship of ACTION, the federal agency that oversees such voluntary organizations as the Peace Corps and its domestic cousin, VISTA. Brown and his "close friend and companion" Alison Teal had just returned from an overnight visit in Aspen with Dr. Hunter Thompson, the Gonzo journalist, when Jimmy called. "I couldn't believe it was the President," Alison recalled. "He wanted to know what Sam was wearing. Now, I thought that was very curious. Sam said jeans. But he said that when he talks to businessmen he wears three-piece suits. Why offend with style when you can offend with substance, he says."

Obviously, Brown didn't offend the President when he agreed to come to Washington. But he did offend a few diehards among his friends who felt Sam was being taken on to protect the President's very weak left flank. Carter's eclectic taste in personnel was demonstrated at the swearing-in ceremony. In fact, it was a joint swearing-in. Besides Brown, there was Max Cleland, the new head of the Veterans Administration, a triple-amputee from Vietnam, in his wheelchair. "I don't think we could have two more startling contrasts among young men," Carter smiled, saying the obvious. But it was one means of assuring more traditional citizens that he believed in balance.

"Some of my friends say everyone's been co-opted," Brown said later. "It's not a mark of failure, but success. We've got a whole collection of movement people here. . . . That's the genius of the system."

And Brown wasn't kidding. He loaded his domain with people from various activist groups. Where once they had been out on the streets protesting policy, they were now on the inside, ensconced in high-paying jobs. Typical were Marge Tabankin, the head of VISTA, who on her return from North Vietnam in 1972 had helped host a "war crimes" press conference; and John Lewis, now associate director of ACTION, who was arrested more than forty times in connection with civil rights activities. And Brown himself remained true to the traditions which brought him to prominence. This led to a rebuke from none other than Henry Kissinger.

In a colloquy with Pat Moynihan on America's failure of nerve, in *Public Opinion*, the former Secretary of State singled out Brown as symptomatic of the sickness within society:

> KISSINGER: What I have difficulty understanding is the "relish" with which some Americans greeted our humiliation in Southeast Asia. When I see, for example, the head of ACTION going to a meeting where the North Vietnamese Ambassador, upon joining the UN, castigates the United States, and this American official says, "This is the proudest day of my life. This is what we've been working for all these years," that raises to me really profound questions about the fundamental motivation from the beginning.
>
> MOYNIHAN: That scene where the Vietcong flag was flown from the Peace Corps headquarters took place during a demonstration which that particular man organized.
>
> KISSINGER: Exactly.

The meeting which Brown attended took place at the Beacon Theater in Manhattan. That meeting, Eric Sevareid declared, was arranged by "that part of the antiwar movement which was not antiwar at all; it was anti the American role in the war and pro-Hanoi." The CBS commentator said there was a great deal of difference between "Americans who wanted the U.S. out of the war because they thought it was unwinnable . . . and the Americans who wanted Hanoi to win. Most of those in the New York theater were not celebrating peace. They were celebrating the triumph of Communist totalitarianism, which is what they had always been working for in the guise of a peace movement."

Criticism of Brown also came from such varied sources as Mary McGrory, Jack Anderson, and Patrick Buchanan. Always thinking of those glorious Kennedy days, Ms. McGrory complained that Brown had not given the Carter Administration "a much-needed touch of Camelot. He was expected to rouse college youth from its new apathy. It hasn't worked out quite that way." Anderson, more recently, claimed that after two years in the post Brown had "become an authoritarian martinet who brooks no interference from his subordinates." Anderson also reported that Brown and his cronies "have been trying to apply the anti-Establishment idealism of their New Left days to the complicated task of administering multimillion-dollar social programs. The result has been chaos . . . [and] the squandering of taxpayers' money. . . ." Buchanan was irate because Brown had conceded that the Peace Corps had shelled out taxpayers' money to subsidize abortions for its volunteers. "Is this what Jack Kennedy had in mind when he established the Peace Corps?" asked Buchanan. "That taxpayers should be shelling out 50 grand a year to execute the unborn children of upper-middle-class bimbos whose idea of bringing the blessings of Western civilization to the Third World is to take a tumble in the hay with the local witch doctor?"

Despite the extraordinary criticism, Sam Brown retained his clout with the President. This was demonstrated late in 1978 when he got into a public feud with Howard psychologist Carolyn Payton, the first black director of the Peace Corps. At the time of her appointment, Dr. Payton said the Corps had been "a white, middle-class adventure" for most of its volunteers. She was determined, she said, to recruit more members of minority groups and to "tap the great reservoir of interest in Africa among black Americans." Brown had other ideas. According to *The New York Times,* he wanted to reopen contacts with such Marxist-run nations as Vietnam, Angola, and Mozambique. He also spoke of a "reverse Peace Corps" in which Third World nations would send volunteers to work in American ghettoes. Neither idea seemed plausible to Dr. Payton, who said so to Brown's face. And that meant she had to go. Brown got Carter to accept Dr. Payton's resignation. It was, as Jack Anderson later wrote, a "monumentally mishandled affair," one that gave "credence to charges that Brown simply was not up to the job Carter had given him."

Another appointee who proved to be a "pain in the ass" to the President, as a top aide so eloquently phrased it (long before the disclosure of Carter's hemorrhoids) was Margaret "Midge" Costanza, the upstate New Yorker named as Carter's special assistant for public liaison, the job held under Nixon by Charles Colson. Her specific job was to serve as the White House link to women, ethnics, handicapped, civil rights groups, minorities, senior citizens, young people, and religious organizations—to lead an effort, she said, "to reach those traditionally powerless and to balance that with a continuing access for groups who've always had entree."

At forty-four, Midge was the only woman and the only non-Georgian besides Brzezinski on the President's senior staff. And her office was just down the hall from the President's, a few steps away from the Vice-President's, and a stone's throw from those of Jody Powell and Ham Jordan. Before long, Jody and Ham were wishing she were somewhere else. She was quickly involved in controversy. For example, she held a three-hour rap session with gay activists in her office, and that caused a minor uproar in the West Wing. And in one astonishing innovation, she convened a gathering of women who worked in the Carter Administration to protest publicly the President's opposition to government-financed abortion. There could be no doubt that Carter was nettled by what his aides considered lack of loyalty to the occupant of the Oval Office. When asked if her critics in the Administration were aiming at her, she replied, "Naw, if they were, they'd have failed that, just like they fail at everything else they aim for."

Also upsetting was the disclosure that Midge had enlisted Vice-President Mondale for a $500-a-ticket cocktail party in New York to help wipe out some old campaign debts from her unsuccessful 1974 congressional race in Rochester. The party was a success. It raised more than $21,000—$17,000 of it to repay Midge herself—but she neglected to report the details to the Federal Election Commission. Midge, who earned about $12,000 a year more than Henry Kissinger in his heyday at the Nixon White House, even decided to pay herself back for a $150 contribution she had made to a New York friend. "I'm not a wealthy woman," she told Walter Pincus of *The Washington Post*. "That $150 was something I could not afford personally." As for the $3,400 remaining in surplus funds, Ms. Costanza said she was thinking of handing it over to her administrative assistant as soon as the latter could work up a bill for past services to Costanza campaigns.

What all this amounted to, as Pat Buchanan noted, was "naked exploitation of high office for personal benefit. If Chuck Colson, after being named Mr. Nixon's liaison man, had held a fund raiser to pay off his old campaign debts or campaign contributions, his body would still be swinging from a lamp post in Lafayette Square." And attorney Alan B. Morrison, director of Ralph Nader's Public Citizen Litigation Group, observed, "Rightly or wrongly, the impression is that a high government official, earning well over $50,000 a year, invited people with business pending before the government to give her money to help with her financial problems. . . . Costanza . . . has plainly transgressed the bounds of proper conduct. . . ." Eventually, the Federal Election Commission fined Costanza $500 for failing to file a report on the funds raised at the party.

The irony of all this, too, was the fact that Costanza was the first—and only—White House staffer to call on the embattled Bert Lance, Carter's good friend, to resign as Director of the Budget. That, probably more than anything else, was to lead to her downfall. "I think she sealed her fate when she said Bert Lance ought to resign," another White House woman told James Wooten of *The New York Times*. "That's a blood test, you know. Loyalty is the primary currency here. . . ."

It took months before it finally dawned on Costanza she wasn't wanted around the White House. In May 1978, her area of responsibility was narrowed to women's issues, and she lost virtually her entire staff. She was forced to move to a tiny office in the basement. She was repeatedly ignored, snubbed, and humiliated. In July, she was bumped from appearing on ABC's *Good Morning, America*. The order came from Jerry Rafshoon, and the ostensible reason was to give more time to her co-star, Mr. Excitement himself, Stu Eizenstat, the President's domestic adviser.

That was the final straw, and on August 1 she submitted her resignation, which the President accepted with "regret." And Costanza said she still thought highly of Carter, though she referred to other White House aides as having been "recruited from under rocks." But she approved the appointment of her successor, Sarah Weddington, another feminist, but one less raucous.

"In a sense, of course," commented *The Washington Star*, "Midge Costanza had to go because Andrew Young has to stay. Or at least somebody up there thinks Andrew Young has to stay. An

Administration bent on demonstrating unity and the firmness of a leader's hand on the tiller can afford only so much public contradiction from its own. One *enfant terrible* to a family."

And the reason Young had to stay—despite the numerous embarrassments he had caused the Carter Administration, far more consequential than anything Costanza had done— was simple. President Carter had good reason to believe that if he ever dumped his Ambassador to the United Nations the nation's black leadership would never forgive him. And, more important, that would cost Carter at the polls. This was what the Congressional Black Caucus pretty much said after numerous demands had been made for Young's departure from the national stage. Congressman Parren J. Mitchell, who headed the group in the House of Representatives, put it that "in the event something untoward should happen to Andy Young, the black community will walk away from the Carter Administration." And Mitchell predicted that blacks would be willing to pay the price of their defection: "Admittedly, when we have sat out elections before, terrible things have happened. Witness Richard Nixon. But we survived Richard Nixon."

Arousing considerable furor was Young's remark to *Le Matin*, a Socialist newspaper in Paris, comparing Soviet dissidents to American civil rights campaigners and saying that there were "hundreds, perhaps thousands of political prisoners in the United States." He himself, he claimed, had been such a prisoner for participating in civil rights demonstrations in Atlanta.* And commenting on the scheduled meeting between Secretary Vance and Mrs. Anatoly Scharansky, wife of a dissident on trial in Moscow on espionage charges, Young urged that the situation of the dissidents should not be overdramatized, adding, "Mrs. Scharansky does not dictate U.S. policy."

Vance was described as "grimly angered" by Young's remarks. Indeed, they cast a shadow over Carter's visit at the Bonn economic summit, raising the question of whether Carter was really master of his household. After all, Carter had made human rights in the Soviet Union a major issue. He had, for example,

---

*Young had been arrested in the late sixties for obstructing a garbage cleanup in a garbage collectors strike. He was released in less than twenty-four hours. There had been as much political oppression involved in Young's arrest as there would have been in his receiving a traffic ticket.

written a personal letter to Soviet dissident Andrei Sakharov early in his Administration. And his various utterances on the subject had provoked anger in the Kremlin. Now his own Ambassador had undercut him by referring to mythical "political prisoners" in the U.S. As *National Review* put it so succinctly, "Jimmy Carter is now the first American President to send diplomatic protests to his own Ambassador."

Carter had seized upon the human rights issue as a means of countering the Congressional hardliners who had so embarrassed him in combating the Warnke and Sorensen nominations. The President realized that their strength could well prevent a new arms treaty with the Kremlin. As Ham Jordan put it so frankly to Bob Shogan, "He feels that human rights is something that can bind our people together. And in terms of the SALT talks, it provides a good argument against those who later on might accuse him of being soft on the Commies, to be able to point back to an experience where he was really tough on the Soviet Union." Jordan said that the timing of the human rights campaign, so early in the Carter presidency, was just right. "In politics, just as in personal relations, first impressions are very important. One of the first impressions that the American people have of their new President is that he's been tough with the Soviets on human rights. So when he comes back to sell us a SALT treaty, and he says it's good and it's fair and it protects our country, there will be some evidence for believing him."

One can only deduce from Jordan's remarks that human rights was not really a primary concern to the President. It was only a means of getting something else accomplished, namely a SALT II agreement. And this was the thinking in the Oval Office which Ambassador Young may well have been reflecting when he rambled so confusedly about political prisoners. And, needless to say, the Kremlin seized on the Ambassador's rhetoric as being "noteworthy, since it comes from a member of the Cabinet and therefore signifies an official admission that political persecution is widespread in the United States." Of course, Young's latest attack of what *The Washington Star* labeled *yakkita inepta* had gone too far. And there were calls for his dismissal from members of both parties. Senate Majority Leader Robert Byrd, for example, put it this way: "If Andrew Young makes another irresponsible statement that fits into this pattern of bad judgment, I think he should go." And former Secretary Kissinger said that Young should either keep his private opinions to himself and "learn discipline" or resign from his post.

Young made it clear he didn't intend to quit. Far from it. In effect, he dared the President to ask for his resignation. "Predictably, Carter won't do it," wrote Max Lerner in *The New York Post*, "because Young has a constituency, both in America and the Third World. Hard as it was for Carter to fire Bert Lance, it was a picnic compared to the risks involved in firing Young."

On September 30,1978, after the controversy had cooled, the President of the United States addressed 4,000 people at a dinner sponsored by the Congressional Black Caucus and praised the much-criticized Andrew Young as "a man who's not afraid to speak out when he sees something wrong."

That brought the diners to their feet. And they were back up again, applauding, when the President said, "I don't know of any one in the Administration of Jimmy Carter who has done more for our country throughout the world than Andy Young."

"Even if you hadn't stood up for that," Carter went on, "I was going to tell you that as long as I am President and Andy Young is willing to stay there, he'll be the United States Ambassador."

But, at least, he no longer referred to Andy as a "national treasure."

15

IT DIDN'T STOP WITH WATERGATE

ON OCTOBER 25, 1978, BILLY CARTER EMERGED FROM A WIN-
dowless basement room of the Forsythe Street Federal Courthouse in Atlanta and announced to newsmen that he had invoked
the Fifth Amendment several times while appearing before a
grand jury investigating the tangled financial affairs of Bert Lance,
President Carter's closest friend and longtime personal banker.

The President didn't think the matter important enough to
comment upon. After all, as Chief Executive, he had other, more
important things to worry about. China, the Middle East, Iran,
inflation, etc. Why should he wallow in such trivia as his brother's
affairs?

And Carter got away with it; something that never would have
happened to Richard Nixon, had one of his brothers taken the
Fifth Amendment. That extraordinary fact surely would have
dominated news coverage for weeks on end. But stories on the
Atlanta grand jury investigation involving Bert Lance and Billy
Carter were generally buried in the back pages, if used at all.
There was little of the feverish investigative reporting that marked
the Watergate era. And it was not for lack of material. For, from
the beginning, the Carter years were replete with questionable

activities which cast a dark shadow over the holier-than-thou image of a candidate who had run as a political Sir Galahad, *sans peur et sans reproche*.

He was in office barely six months when the gilt began to tarnish badly. The man who claimed to be above politics, purer than pure, turned out to be no better than other mundane politicians, no more virtuous than anybody else. Except, in the main, the others were less hypocritical.

There was the matter of free rides in Bert Lance's airplane. Actually, it was a plane owned by Lance's National Bank of Georgia, and it was an "oversight" that Carter had never reimbursed the bank for five campaign trips. Now, when the facts emerged, Carter announced he would repay the costs, half in leftover campaign funds, half from Carter's personal funds. The Federal Election Commission took no action. "It is a small matter," commented James J. Kilpatrick, "but it stands in glaring contrast to the FEC's relentless prosecution of other candidates who fell into trivial violations of election laws."

Then there were the trips to Annapolis which were never made. Instead, as it turned out, various Carter aides had falsified travel vouchers in order to dip into transition funds. In effect, the staffers had helped themselves to interest-free, pre-Christmas loans from public funds. The story was broken by columnists Robert Walters and Martha Angle, but it created little excitement.

What happened was this: shortly after the November 2 election, the General Services Administration created an account in the name of the Carter/Mondale Transition Group and credited it with $2,000,000. Soon vouchers began to flow into the GSA—for air travel, office supplies, and the like. All these were routinely paid. Then, toward the middle of December, a sharp-eyed administrative assistant, Rosa Keatts, noticed that numerous members of the Carter/Mondale Group had taken trips to Annapolis. For example: Mary Finch Hoyt, Mrs. Carter's press secretary, had received a $300 advance for a ten-day trip to that beautiful city. This was debited to "Carter Family Support." Timothy Kraft, listed as Carter's appointments secretary, got $300 for his projected trip to Annapolis. Barry Jagoda, Carter's TV adviser, dipped into the till for $300 for a similar purpose. In all, seventy-five staffers drew

$73,500 for more than 600 trips to Annapolis—and none of the trips was ever made. The advances were regarded by Carter's people as personal loans until their first federal paychecks arrived. The Annapolis device was a "cover" for bookkeeping purposes. All the "loans" were eventually repaid, and the Justice Department dropped the matter.

"Very well," commented Kilpatrick. "It is perhaps no big thing. But we may vividly recall Jimmy Carter's high, shrill rectitude in the matter of Clarence Kelley, FBI Director, who unthinkingly accepted a piddling bit of carpentry from overzealous FBI associates. Mr. Carter wanted him fired. And just the other day, Mr. Carter sounded off piously on the sins of Mr. Nixon. Mr. Carter is holier in these matters than anyone on earth. Where was the reverend gentleman when his transition team was borrowing public funds on bogus vouchers?

"And where are my ferocious colleagues of the Washington press? Shall we speculate on how they would have seized upon this deception if it had occurred under Mr. Nixon? Or shall we, in charity, dismiss the matter as just one of those curious things that happen in our town?"

A more important story was one involving Robert Vesco, the fugitive financier who was wanted on five felony charges. This was the same Vesco, who, by contributing $200,000 to the 1972 Nixon campaign, had hoped—but failed—to get the Justice Department to drop its case against him.

Shortly after Carter's election, Vesco tried again. According to the court depositions, he met in Costa Rica with three Georgians. They were attorney Fred Bartlett and businessmen Jerry Dorminey and R.L. Herring. What Vesco proposed was this: If the Carter Administration would promise him leniency, he would arrange for several Latin American countries under his "control" to work more closely with the United States. Back in the U.S., Bartlett conveyed the offer to Secretary of State-designate Vance, who turned it down.

But Vesco's emissaries didn't stop trying. Herring then made an arrangement with a Georgia real estate lawyer, William Spencer Lee IV, a Carter campaign manager in 1976 and a boyhood buddy of Ham Jordan. For a $10,000 retainer and a promise of $1 million more, Lee agreed to carry Vesco's case to Jordan and other White House aides. Meanwhile, Vesco told Herring and Dorminey that he would arrange for them to receive nearly $10 million in stock if they made the White House connection. Writing in *Barron's*, Alan Abelson noted how dramatically the episode pointed up the "alarming rate at which inflation is rising. In 1972, when Mr. Vesco solicited similar favors from the Administration then in power, he felt that $200,000 was enough to turn the trick. Five years later, the price had risen to $10 million. Pure and simply, the cost of bribery is getting out of hand."

From then on, the story gets even murkier. Though Jordan played tennis and went partying with Lee several times during the following months, the White House aide insisted that at no time did they discuss Vesco. But Lee did discuss Vesco with another old Georgia friend, Richard Harden, who was a Special Assistant to the President. "We bounced it back and forth, and he advised me not to contact Hamilton Jordan," Lee recalled. "The next morning, I got up and called Herring and told him I could not contact Hamilton, that he was too close a friend."

But Lee and two others did meet with Charlie Kirbo on January 17, 1977. The Atlanta lawyer did hear them out for about ten minutes and then cut them short. At first, Kirbo told reporters, "Nobody had ever talked to me about Vesco." Later, he said his date book reflected that a meeting had taken place, but that he couldn't recall the session itself or any mention of Vesco. But as Anthony Marro noted in *The Washington Star*, Kirbo's statement was puzzling. For it suggested that "three Georgians, one with close ties to the Carter group," were able to walk into Kirbo's office three days before the Inauguration to "lay out a plan to cut a deal between the new Administration and the world's best-known fugitive," and yet this meeting "made such a small impression on him that he can't recall it now."

"A despicable lie," was the way Ham Jordan characterized a charge of his involvement in this scheme; at a White House press conference, he insisted he had not been contacted by the SEC "or any other investigative agency." But one month before, it was later disclosed, the President's chief political adviser had been interrogated by the FBI about this very matter.

Likewise, the versions given by others raised questions about their reactions to the approaches that were made. For example, Jordan insisted that Harden had never told him about Lee's plan to aid Vesco. Yet Harden, the White House later admitted, told Carter himself about the plan. Why Harden should tell Carter but not Jordan seemed peculiar. And it also raised questions as to why it was not officially disclosed that the President had been told until after it became known that an affidavit wrung from Lee by the SEC would be made public. In that affidavit, Lee swore under oath that Harden had told him the President had been informed.

Moreover, no one at the White House or the Justice Department was able to explain why Carter, while meeting with Harden on the Vesco matter, would write in longhand to Attorney General Bell, saying, "Please see Spencer Lee from Albany when he requests an appointment." The terse note was signed "J.C."

The White House explanation was that the President wanted to make sure that any other dealings concerning Vesco were brought to the attention of the Justice Department. If that were the case, then why didn't the President's note make mention of Vesco and the fix attempt? In fact, the note on its face could be read as suggesting that Carter thought Bell should hear what Lee had to say. And, finally, since the President knew that Spencer Lee had approached Harden with a $1 million influence-peddling scheme, why did he reward Lee, soon afterward, with an appointment to a panel selecting the Fifth Circuit Court of Appeals judge?

Most incredible of all was what 'happened to the President's handwritten note. Though it apparently was logged in at the Attorney General's office, Bell said he had never seen it. Somehow it got lost in a file and was never brought to the A.G.'s attention. Moreover, and most importantly, according to White House apologists, nothing was done for Vesco by the Carter Administration. But, as Bill Safire noted, "that is irrelevant: Nothing was done for Vesco by John Mitchell or Maurice Stans, either—and they suffered through a long trial. What is relevant is that a potential conspiracy to defraud the U.S. Government and obstruct justice reached the President, and that he did not carry out his duty to order an investigation."

And that, supposedly, was one of the major lessons of Watergate. Failure of President Nixon to act in a similar situation dominated his impeachment proceedings. There was another

similarity. "Since the influence-peddling scheme came to light,"
Safire observed, "the Carter men have been acting the way the
Nixon men used to act in those halcyon days of 1973."

Late in November 1978, it was disclosed that a federal grand
jury had begun probing the new Vesco affair. The Justice
Department said that FBI agents were planning to question the
President, along with other individuals named in the case. But
complicating the search for the truth was what White House aides
called Carter's lack of independent recollection of the entire
episode. The man who promised never to lie to the American
people said he had no idea why he wrote that note to his Attorney
General. And there were no presidential tapes to jog his memory.
Still, as *The Christian Science Monitor* observed, "it seems
beyond belief that a man who has so vehemently castigated 'big
shot crooks' would do any favors for a Vesco. By the same token,
one would have expected the Carter White House to have taken
more of a lead in investigating the matter and disclosing the facts,
instead of coming out with things step by step in response to the
press. The Vesco efforts to influence the government were such a
hot potato for the Nixon Administration that the Carter Administration should have seen all sorts of red flags attached to even the
hint of any subsequent efforts by Vesco representatives. The
White House has reportedly acknowledged that the situation was
awkward in that questions arose as to why Mr. Carter did not tell
Attorney General Bell about the Vesco episode 19 months ago or
call for an investigation of it then."

The only investigation inspired by the White House was one
conducted by Charlie Kirbo. And the subject was Jack Anderson,
whose columns on the Vesco matter had so agitated the White
House. "I've got a good case against him," Kirbo told *The Atlanta
Journal-Constitution*. "I have yet to decide what to do with it."
But, despite his close association with the President, Kirbo was
not a government official. Which led to some questioning as to
what right a private citizen had to investigate anyone, particularly
a Carter critic. If anything, Anderson commented, the situation
was beginning to smell of the days when self-styled "plumbers"
were probing White House enemies. Except this time most of the
media, so concerned about excesses of the Nixon White House,

remained silent. As Safire noted, "Some lapdogs among the White House news hounds . . . tut-tutted at the investigative columnist for being 'irresponsible,'" after he had clarified one portion of his story.

The manner in which Kirbo conducted his investigation was rather startling, too. On October 1, 1978, the Atlanta lawyer interviewed the wife of R.L. Herring, the Georgia man who admitted he was in on a scheme to fix the Vesco indictments. Kirbo had hired a private plane to go to Albany, Georgia, for the meeting with Cindy Herring. Kirbo had arranged the meeting through Tina Harden, sister-in-law of White House aide Richard Harden. What Kirbo didn't know was that Mrs. Herring had concealed a tape recorder in her purse.

"I'm just an ordinary south Georgia cracker you're talking to," Kirbo told her, "and I feel sorry for you. . . ."

Then the President's confidant said it was a "mistake" for her "to trust everybody."

"You need to really have a lawyer to talk with you and help you to analyze it," Kirbo went on. "I think it would be a mistake for you to put too much trust in me, 'cause I'm trying to protect my reputation. I think you've got some misplaced trust in Jack Anderson. And it's a mistake to be too open with the FBI. Because they've got another thing they're working on."

Kirbo at first denied telling the woman not to be "too open" with the FBI. But Kirbo refreshed his recollection when he learned that a recording existed of the conversation. And, as Fred Graham reported on the *CBS Evening News,* since "Kirbo is appointed by President Carter to investigate things for the Justice Department from time to time . . . there are some raised eyebrows here about his advice to a witness not to be 'open' with the FBI." One was left to wonder whether he had given similar advice to the President and the President's men when they were questioned about the Vesco affair by the FBI.

Meanwhile, another—but lesser—scandal involving a Georgia connection erupted at the White House. This one concerned William Milliken, identified as an unpaid adviser to Mrs. Carter on urban problems. So close was he to the family that he sometimes spent nights at the White House. Now, it turned out, Milliken had interceded with federal housing officials in behalf of a wealthy Johnstown, Pennsylvania, developer seeking a $15.5 million federal grant. In return, Milliken received a $10,000 contribution for his private, federally assisted project to aid ghetto youngsters.

"I was just trying to help Johnstown," Milliken said. "I made a mistake in judgment. . . . I'm just not used to this arena."

Jody Powell told newsmen that the matter was being investigated by White House counsel Robert J. Lipshutz. But he declined to admit that Milliken used an office on the fourth floor of the adjacent Executive Office Building for his "Action in Schools Program," which received $2.7 million in federal assistance after the President wrote a letter to several departments praising it.

Milliken, who had met Governor Carter through Dr. Peter Bourne, was most appreciative. He put the President's son, Chip, to work at $26,500 a year. And one of Chip's jobs was to accompany Milliken on fund-raising visits to corporation officials. Asked whether such activity was proper for a President's son, Milliken replied, "I can't be God. I can't figure all that out." After *The Washington Monthly* suggested there was a connection between Chip's job and federal assistance, the President's son resigned and went back to work for the Democratic National Committee.

Following the inquiry by counsel Lipshutz, Powell announced that "questions of propriety" had been raised by the Milliken case. He also announced that Milliken would no longer use EOB office space. Despite the "appearance of impropriety," Powell said that the White House inquiry had turned up nothing to contradict Milliken's description of his intervention for the developer as "a mistake in judgment" that was "done innocently." Asked if the White House had considered asking Milliken to return the $10,000, Powell said that "would strike me as a little harsh." He said nothing had turned up in the Lipshutz investigation that "indicated any violation of the law."

Whenever tough problems arose which required especially careful handling, the President turned to his longtime political guru, Charlie Kirbo. For example, he asked the Atlanta lawyer to monitor various investigations being conducted into the huge graft scandal at the General Services Administration. Attorney General Bell, obviously miffed, said firmly that his former law partner would have "no role" in the Justice Department's investigations, no access to information derived from criminal probes, and no involvement in any prosecutions. Kirbo's role, the White House now hastened to explain, would be to counsel GSA Administrator Jay Solomon on the nonprosecutorial aspects of cleaning up the federal housekeeping agency.

"For one thing," commented *The Washington Post*, "Mr. Kirbo has no standing in the chain of command; he is not officially accountable to anybody. So it was hardly surprising that his appearance on the scene immediately sparked concerns about possible White House interference with the current investigations of alleged bribes, kick-backs and other crimes. Mr. Carter evidently did not anticipate how quickly the specter of Watergate-type obstructions of justice can still arise. Such fears may be entirely unfounded; at least so far, nobody has suggested that the Carter White House has any wrongdoing at GSA to cover up. But the principle involved is sound in any case. There is no proper place in a criminal investigation for an unofficial White House overseer—especially one who, no matter how close to the President, is still a private citizen and a lawyer with corporate clients who do business with GSA."

The major internal investigation of the scandal-plagued GSA was being conducted by Special Counsel Vincent Alto. As a result of his work, probing what Alto called "the biggest money scandal in the history of the federal government," his superior, Jay Solomon, decided to get rid of Robert Griffin, the second-in-command of the agency, which spends $5 billion a year to provide federal bureaucrats with office space, supplies, and housekeeping services. News accounts explained that Solomon felt powerless to make fundamental changes in the GSA as long as Griffin continued to pull the strings from his entrenched position in the agency.

The problem went to the Oval Office, and President Carter agreed that Griffin had to be forced to resign or be fired. He was fired, the official reason said to be a personality conflict with

Solomon. But, several months later, *Time* reported that a memorandum prepared by Alto had raised questions about Griffin's conduct at the GSA. The memo claimed that Griffin had sought to undermine efforts to crack down on corruption within the agency and had harassed a GSA employee who would not go along.

The problem didn't end with Griffin's dismissal. Instead, it was intensified. For Griffin, as the White House was aware, was a close friend of Thomas P. "Tip" O'Neill. In fact, "Tip" had tried to convince the President to appoint Griffin as head of the GSA only a year before. Which explains why the Speaker of the House reacted angrily to Griffin's ouster, denouncing the "cruel" and "shabby treatment" that his buddy received from the White House as "one of the worst things I have ever seen." O'Neill's tantrum didn't end there. He announced that Carter's congressional liaison man, Frank Moore, was never to darken his doorway again. "I want you to stay the hell out of this office," he told the startled presidential aide.

Carter was shaken by the barrage of vituperation emanating from O'Neill. Knowing he must defer to the powerful Speaker, lest he risk defeat on important legislation, the President acted quickly to heal the rift. As *The Washington Post* noted editorially, the President had "let himself be bullied" into assigning the Vice-President—no less—to find the ousted Griffin a new, comparably well-paying job. Demonstrating an inordinate talent for such major assignments, Mondale soon came up with a post befitting Griffin's qualifications. And, thus, Carter—the man who campaigned in behalf of cutting bureaucratic fat and streamlining the White House—announced he was creating a new job for Griffin. The Speaker's pal was to become an assistant to Robert Strauss, then anti-inflation czar, whose reaction to this good fortune was not immediately disclosed. "The affair," commented James R. Dickenson in *The Washington Star*, "has the distinct aroma of the good old pre-Civil Service reform days, the late 19th Century 'Great Barbeque' era of the patronage spoilsmen."

Griffin, at least, was pleased. "I'm terribly grateful," he said. And so he should have been—with a $50,000-a-year sinecure. Meanwhile, the Speaker and Moore were speaking again. "We've shaken hands, and we're friends again," said O'Neill. And the President was off to suburban Virginia to sell the merits of his Civil

Service reform proposals to government workers.

But the story was not over. On December 18, 1978, Jack Anderson reported that a Justice Department task force was "cautiously investigating" Griffin's conduct as the "power behind the scenes" at GSA. The columnist also reported that Jay Solomon had complained to Senator Lawton Chiles that Griffin was using his White House influence to sabotage the GSA probes. But Chiles, the Florida Democrat heading the Senate investigation of the GSA scandals, reported back he could find no evidence of White House interference. Solomon remained unconvinced. A few months later, Solomon's worst fears were confirmed. The White House asked for his resignation.

In challenging the President, O'Neill had operated from a position of strength. In that summer of 1978, he was well aware of Carter's political weakness. And he took advantage of it. O'Neill was feeling his oats for other reasons. Earlier in the year, he had successfully weathered a minor storm after *The New York Times* published a lengthy report on the Speaker's finances. The front-page story said that some of his business dealings had raised questions of conflict of interest and his candor. The story, written by Wendell Rawls, Jr., noted that *The Boston Herald American*, the Boston television station WBZ-TV, and O'Neill's Republican opponent, William Barnstead, had raised questions about the propriety of some loans which O'Neill had obtained. The *Times'* inquiry, Rawls reported, "produced no evidence of illegality, but it did find understatements of holdings and conflicting information in financial documents, and it raised many questions about Mr. O'Neill's role in certain transactions. It also offered insight into how politicians can operate away from the spotlight on Capitol Hill, where the Speaker last year became the most vocal and forceful advocate of higher standards of ethics for Congressmen, including stronger provisions for financial disclosure."

Still, the well-documented charges made little impact, since, as the *Times* itself noted, "most voters and politicians believe that Mr. O'Neill is being judged in the light of post-Watergate morality for things that were done according to pre-Watergate standards."

The irony, of course, was that O'Neill had obtained considerable publicity for his role in promoting the Nixon impeachment hearings. In fact, the Bostonian became the hero of a bestselling book by Jimmy Breslin on the subject, *How the Good Guys Finally Won*. When the *Times*, in its investigative report, noted that O'Neill had a piece of a nursing home, the irreverent Alexander Cockburn of the *Village Voice* was moved to suggest a title for a new Breslin book: *How the Good Guys Finally Won a Nursing Home Contract*.

The Herald American later disclosed that O'Neill was a partner in the nursing home during the life of a Small Business Administration loan. This, according to the Boston paper, seemed to violate a federal law which bars a Congressman from being a partner in a business at any time during the life of a federal contract. The article also reported that SBA investigators who had looked into the matter had sent the findings to the Justice Department, where they appeared to have gotten lost.

O'Neill was far more concerned about charges linking him with Korean influence peddlers. There was a lot of sound and fury involving the Speaker and other Democratic bigwigs; but most of it came to naught. Very early in the Justice Department investigation, Mary McGrory noted that its probing into what had become known as "Koreagate" was "proceeding at the pace of the U.S. Postal Service. Attorney General Bell appears to share President Carter's unwillingness to expose Democratic members of Congress to revelations of wrongdoing, at least in public."

Fearing that cover-ups were in the works, the Republican congressional leaders, Senator Howard Baker of Tennessee and Congressman John Rhodes of Arizona, wrote to the President asking that a special prosecutor be named to direct the Koreagate probe. Not for five weeks did Carter reply to the letter, and only after Philip Lacovara resigned as Special Counsel from the House Ethics Committee, alleging that it had been impossible for him to direct a full and complete investigation.

Carter's reply to the GOP leaders, dated July 18, 1977, was that naming a Watergate-style special prosecutor "would be inappropriate and unwarranted and would probably impede the investigation." Carter said that the investigation, which had begun two years previously, had proceeded to where "potential prosecutions have been identified and, in several cases, the evidence gathering process is nearly completed."

The President's decision hardly quieted the matter. Indeed, demands for a special prosecutor grew even louder, with Common

Cause joining the Republicans in insisting on a full-scale independent investigation. Mary McGrory, too, blessed the idea: "You don't have to be a Republican to think a Special Prosecutor for the Korean scandal might be a good idea. Just because John Connally is for it is no longer sufficient reason to be against it." Appearing in Chicago, Connally said, "You're talking about dozens of members of Congress involved in millions of dollars of payoffs, and there's not been much news on it. They were the first to proclaim loudly during Watergate that no one should investigate themselves. Now Congress itself is involved in a major scandal, but says it can handle it. If they can cover it up, they're going to cover it up."

As the clamor increased, the Democratic leadership decided, however reluctantly, that something had to be done to restore public confidence. Speaker O'Neill, smarting from an ABC report that he had pressured the ethics panel into slowing its probe, called former Special Prosecutor Leon Jaworski to take over the congressional probe. And Jaworski, the Media Hero of Watergate, was to announce that he believed that approximately "two dozen" members of the House were guilty of unethical behavior—some serious enough to warrant expulsion. Previously, *The New York Times* reported that 115 former and present members of Congress were implicated in the scandal.

With Democrat Jaworski at the helm, the Korean story began losing steam. The problem, observed Charles B. Seib, ombudsman for *The Washington Post,* was "one that besets much of investigative reporting today, at least on the national level: a lack of official follow-through.

"The Watergate story had a major ingredient that is missing today. Since the folks in trouble were Republicans, the Democrats who controlled Congress were happy to take a handoff from the press and run with it. Today the situation is different. The partakers of Korean kindness were mostly Democrats, and Democrats not only still control Congress but they control the White House as well. The unsurprising result is official foot-dragging and confusion."

For a time, things did get kind of tense in the committee room. For one thing, Speaker O'Neill made it clear he was extraordinarily sensitive to being questioned about the $8,000 in parties and gifts he received from Tongsun Park. So sensitive was he, in fact, that when cartoonist Garry Trudeau, creator of the Doonesbury comic strip, urged readers to write O'Neill about the Korean funds, one of O'Neill's top aides leaned on the Universal Press Syndicate to suppress the strip. Which the syndicate refused to do.

O'Neill, needless to say, was not questioned in open hearings. His "interrogation" took place behind closed doors and was conducted by Jaworski staff members, wearing kid gloves, with only one House member present. O'Neill was asked about a lengthy document found by federal investigators in Tongsun Park's Washington home which, written in Korean, suggested that O'Neill had solicited funds and favors for himself and other Democratic Congressmen. Like Park, O'Neill insisted it was a forgery. (Which led one cynic to observe that Chuck Colson could not write in Korean.) But, as *The Boston Globe*, generally friendly to the Speaker, editorialized, the document had "some intrinsic credibility" and raised "serious questions."

Those "serious questions" were never answered. Instead, O'Neill was exonerated of wrongdoing, even though a staff report of the Ethics Committee did say he acted with "questionable propriety" in accepting Korean largesse. Also exonerated was Majority Whip John Brademas, the Hoosier Democrat who conceded he had taken nearly $3,000 in Korean money. In the end, the committee voted to censure only one sitting Congressman—Edward Roybal, for repeatedly lying under oath—and to reprimand two other California Democrats: Charles H. Wilson and John J. McFall. But when the matter came before the full House, the Congressmen voted 219-170 to reject the motion to censure Roybal and agreed to reprimand him instead. Concurrently, the Ethics Committee concluded that only two— dead—Senators, Hubert Humphrey and John McClellan, took illegal contributions from the Koreans; and that even they probably acted unwittingly. Only two Americans were actually to be indicted as a result of the Korea probe and they were *former* Democratic Congressmen, Richard Hanna of California and Otto Passman of Louisiana. And Hanna commented bitterly, after being sentenced, that despite all the sound and fury over Koreagate, he would be the only lawmaker to serve time. And he was right.

Which led William Safire to observe, "Devotees of successful criminal cover-ups doff their hats reverently to Speaker O'Neill, who quietly limited the scope of the probe; to Benjamin R. Civiletti of President Carter's Department of Political Justice, who won powerful friends on the Hill in his botching of the investigation; to Special Counsel Leon Jaworski, king of press clips, who just did not have the gumption to go after the key witness who could have put thirteen of our most powerful Congressmen behind bars."

What all this meant was that Democratic politicians generally don't like to investigate other Democratic politicians—even in a Washington dominated by a President who had promised repeatedly that he would go after "big shot crooks" and clean out corruption. Yet Carter said nary a word about Koreagate, though he had been extremely loquacious about Watergate. But that involved Republicans. And they were fair game.

A good example of how the "buddy system" still operated in Carter's Washington was provided by the case of Senator Birch Bayh, who had become a liberal household word by engineering the rejection of Clement F. Haynsworth as Nixon's appointee to the Supreme Court on the grounds that the U.S. appellate judge from South Carolina had been insensitive to the highest standards of ethics.

In 1977, Bayh had gotten a taste of his own medicine. Newspaper reports linked him to Tongsun Park. When asked to explain by the Senate Ethics Committee, the Hoosier Democrat responded with an undated letter denying all.

"At no time," Bayh insisted in the letter, a copy of which went to the Justice Department, "did he [Tongsun Park] offer me any money, honorary degrees, trips to Korea, or any of the numerous items we've all read about in the newspaper."

It turned out that Bayh had suffered a lapse of memory. For when shown documents, canceled checks, and sworn testimony by others while he himself was under oath, Bayh's memory was refreshed. Referring to himself as a "pumpkinhead," Bayh said he should have "chosen different words" in his letter.

Bayh failed to convince his colleagues. Among the Ethics Committee's conclusions: "Senator Bayh's undated letter of July 1977 . . . was wrong in that Tongsun Park had given a party in

Senator Bayh's honor, costing Mr. Park about $3,800. The Senator invited a substantial portion of the guests." Even more seriously, the Committee noted that either Bayh or an aide accepted $1,000 from an associate of Tongsun Park in the Senator's office. Federal law prohibits accepting campaign contributions on government property, but—as William Safire noted on October 20, 1978— "nobody's holding his breath for 'Baltimore Ben' Civiletti at the Justice Department to prosecute a Democratic Senator."

Two and a half months later, Deputy Attorney General Civiletti announced that the Justice Department had ended its investigation of Bayh and was planning no action against him. Asked if that meant that Bayh had been cleared of any wrongdoing, Civiletti repeated that the case had been "closed without any action." Which meant Bayh was home free.

The Justice Department had a far greater problem with the case of Bert Lance, who was forced to resign as Director of Management and Budget following sensational Senate hearings into his bewildering practices as a banker in Georgia. But Bert was more than just another bureaucrat in a jam. He was a presidential crony. And he had been banker for the Carter family's peanut business. In fact, when Lance headed the National Bank of Georgia, the Carters ran up their loans to $4.7 million, thus becoming the NBG's biggest borrower.

Lance "was the first person that I thought about when I was finally sure that I would be elected President," Carter told Jack Anderson late in 1977. "I wanted him in a major department that had a profound influence on the rest of the government. . . . I chose Bert for that job, and I have no reason to think that I made the improper choice."

What was to prove most embarrassing for Carter was his appointment of Lance despite previous investigations of him by the Comptroller, the Justice Department, and the U.S. Attorney in Atlanta. Among other things, Lance had been under federal investigation for possible criminal violations in connection with overdrawing on campaign accounts during his 1974 race for Governor. And an FBI agent assigned to an embezzlement case involving an official at the Calhoun First National Bank, of which Lance was still chairman of the board, discovered what he described as a "pattern" of other overdrafts on the personal accounts of Lance, his wife LaBelle, and other bank officials and relatives.

On the eve of Lance's White House appointment, the U.S. Attorney in Atlanta dropped the Justice Department investigation, and the Comptroller's Office in Atlanta canceled a disciplinary action against the Calhoun bank. And the day after the U.S. Attorney's action, December 3, 1976, Jimmy Carter announced his choice of Bert Lance on nationwide television. In doing so, the President-elect failed to inform the public of the two federal investigations into Lance's affairs. And this was a politician who had promised the American people to be honest with them. And, as was noted by Bill Safire, who was to win the Pulitzer Prize for breaking open the Lance affair, "once the decision was made to allow the Lance train to leave the station in November 1976, nearly everything that flowed from that decision was inexorable." Safire, who had served as a speechwriter in the Nixon White House, added, "Once a cover-up strategy is decided upon, the subsequent tactical decisions are choices between greater and lesser mistakes. . . ." Or, as Jimmy Carter himself had observed, "The Watergate tragedy . . . showed that concealment of a mistake or impropriety can be more serious in some instances than the impropriety itself. I think the main thing is a complete openness of any sort of relationship where a conflict of interest might be involved."

At first the Bert Lance affair was little more than a minor personal crisis for the Georgia banker. But, before it was over, as Haynes Johnson and George Lardner, Jr., described it in *The Washington Post*, it shook "the foundations of the Carter presidency, struck at the core of his pledges, raised questions about his judgment and standards, laid bare weaknesses in his inner circle of advisers, stirred partisan discord, aroused passions against the press, shamed the Senate and the U.S. investigatory processes, and once again [had] drawn the nation through a period of presidential crisis."

The crisis had come gradually. On July 12, 1977, the President had sent a seemingly routine letter to the Senate Government Affairs Committee, headed by Senator Ribicoff, reporting that his budget director had a problem. And the problem "has placed an undue financial burden on Mr. Lance." Would it be possible for the committee to modify an earlier agreement under which Lance had promised to sell his Georgia bank stock by the end of the year? Of course it was possible, and Senator Ribicoff asked Senators Proxmire and Brooke, both of the Banking Committee, to meet with Lance to work out the details.

Then they were all "blindsided," as Safire, who did the blindsiding, later put it. His column of July 21 charged that Lance had received a "sweetheart loan" of $3.4 million from the First National Bank of Chicago on terms so favorable that the main collateral could only be Lance's proximity to the President. At that point in time, to exume a phrase from another era, nothing had yet surfaced about overdrafts or curiously terminated criminal investigations. And Bert Lance, given the opportunity to respond to the charges, acquitted himself well. So well, in fact, that Ribicoff for a time believed that Lance was the victim of a press "smear." He was to change his mind quickly.

And what changed his mind was a report by the new Comptroller of the Currency John Heimann, who had launched his own investigation into allegations that Lance "may have committed infractions of laws or regulations relating to national banks." And while the Heimann report did not indict Lance, it did not unequivocally absolve him either. As for Ribicoff, the most important part of the report was the stack of exhibits and records that pointed to a wide variety of improper and perhaps illegal activities. Ribicoff felt Lance was in trouble, deep trouble. "I felt his going was inevitable," he said.

But that wasn't the way the 403-page report was read at the White House. On the afternoon of August 18, Carter choppered down from Camp David to be with Lance at a celebratory press conference. "Bert Lance enjoys my complete confidence and support," the President said. Then he embraced his friend and uttered those immortal words, "Bert, I'm proud of you." Up in Boston the next day, a beaming Vice-President Mondale announced that the Comptroller's report "vindicates Mr. Lance from any allegations of illegality. Bert Lance is a valued and central part of this Administration. . . . I have absolutely no doubt about his honesty and integrity." The Vice-President then said happily, "The difficulties are behind us."

It kept getting worse. Each new disclosure of Lance's affairs, public and private, raised new doubts about his fitness to remain in office. "Mr. Lance," *The Washington Post* editorialized, "can now perform only one useful service for the President and that is to resign." And why the President insisted on keeping him on, despite all the painful revelations, was puzzling. This was, after all, the same man who as a candidate had said he would fire the FBI Director for accepting a window valance made in the FBI carpentry shop. By now, too, it had become clear that Lance had dominated a mini-empire, built largely on borrowed credit, with loans often obtained through false promises and misleading financial statements. All of which was hardly in keeping with the code unveiled with such fanfare the previous January: "It will be the policy of the Carter-Mondale Administration to appoint . . . only persons of high ability who will carry out their official duties without fear or favor and with an equal hand, unfettered by any actual or apparent conflicts of interest."

Then it was disclosed that Jody Powell had been peddling gossip about Senator Charles Percy, the Illinois Republican who with Ribicoff had advised Carter that Lance's goose was cooked. Powell had called Loye W. Miller, the Washington bureau chief of *The Chicago Sun-Times,* and suggested he look into some derogatory information about Percy. It turned out that the information was without foundation and was cut from whole cloth. Powell, who was forced to apologize to Percy, later put the blame on *The Sun-Times* for violating a confidence. "Powell has served neither himself nor the President," commented *The Washington Star.* "His desperate flailing as point man for the Lance defense has damaged his credibility as spokesman for the Administration. And, along with the actions of others in the Administration, it has helped pull down public confidence in the Carter White House."

Finally, on September 21, 1977, it was over. Or appeared to be over. "I accept Bert's resignation with the greatest sense of regret and sorrow—," a near-tearful President told a news conference. "He is close to me and always will be."

Lance remained close to Carter. He continued to visit the White House, staying overnight occasionally. He retained a highly prized token of his former office—black diplomatic passport X-000065, which lent credence to his assertions that he was "a special envoy of the President." With Lance now a freewheeling broker for foreign investors, the document had become a controversial symbol of his continuing ties with the President. "Lance's insistence on retaining his special passport is important for other reasons," commented *The Philadelphia Inquirer*. "It symbolically demonstrates what has been reported in recent weeks: Mr. Lance continues to receive special treatment and access at the White House. . . . If Mr. Carter is simply trying to be loyal to an old friend, his intentions are admirable but misplaced. As President, Mr. Carter's loyalty is to the American people."

All of which prompted Bill Safire to ask these questions: "Why, knowing the unfavorable publicity it would cause, did the White House order the Passport Office to let private citizen Bert Lance keep his black, special-privilege diplomatic passport? Why is it so important for Mr. Lance, now selling his bank stock to Arabs and desperate for cash, to be able to travel in and out of the country with the assurance that his baggage will not be searched?"

Lance's troubles accelerated. In February 1978, Financial General Bankshares, Inc., filed a civil suit alleging that Lance and others had secretly conspired to take control of the $2.2 billion Washington-based bank holding company. Then, exactly one month later, the SEC charged Lance and nine others, including four influential Arabs, with violating securities laws in connection with their recent purchase of stock in Financial General. The next day, a federal court ordered Lance and his nine associates to clarify their relationship with the bank, and four of them, not including Lance, were called on to pay financial penalties.

Soon afterward, the SEC and the Comptroller of the Currency accused Lance of fraud, deceit, and misrepresentation that bordered on criminality. In an unusual joint civil complaint, the two regulatory agencies alleged that the President's close friend had falsified his net worth in bank loan applications and to Senate investigators during his confirmation hearings; had signed the names of relatives to inaccurate financial statements; had doctored bank records; and authorized for himself and his family large overdrafts not extended to other bank customers. Lance did not deny the charges; nor did he admit guilt. Rather, he pledged that he would not violate the same securities laws again.

Meanwhile, it was disclosed that Lance had turned in his diplomatic passport.

But for the President, Lance was still a walking time bomb. A federal grand jury in Atlanta was investigating Lance's curious financial practices. This was the same grand jury which had heard Billy Carter invoke the Fifth Amendment several times. The First Brother declined to answer certain questions, on the ground that his answers might subject him to criminal prosecution. And the questions had to do with the $4.7 million in loans made by Lance's bank to the Carter family's peanut business. One loan amounted to $1 million for business improvements, but without proper collateral. It developed that the improvements cost about $700,000, leaving a goodly sum for undisclosed business—or political—investment. Suddenly, it became more understandable why it was such a wrench for the President to fire his great and good friend from the Office of Management and Budget.

Billy Carter emerged from the grand jury hearings to denounce the investigation as "a vicious thing by the Republican and Yankee press to get Bert Lance." The press conspiracy charge was not new: previously, Lance said of the intense media coverage of his new Arab partners, "I don't know whether all the hurrah stems from the great Jewish ownership of the press or not." (Lance later withdrew that comment, saying, "I've tried always to speak without prejudice. . . .")

Whether, in taking the Fifth Amendment, Billy Carter had consulted with his brother, the President, was not immediately known. But his brother was the majority stockholder of the family business at the time of the suspicious transactions. And, as Bill Safire reported in January 1979, "We do know that President Carter has resolutely refused to make public the 1976 tax return and balance sheet of the family business, on the grounds that it would invade his brother's privacy.

"If nothing criminal took place, why all the stonewalling? It would clear the air to ask the President at an open press conference if (a) he approved his brother-partner's taking the Fifth, (b) if he used any money borrowed from the warehouse for political purposes, or (c) if he will make public his business tax returns and balance sheets."

Safire also noted that "the unconscionable foot-dragging" on the part of the Justice Department "may not help Mr. Lance, but it serves a purpose: Election reform laws have a three-year statute of limitations, and the clock is running out on any 1976 Carter violations." Still, the Lance affair, as Jack Anderson reported, "could develop into a nasty campaign issue in 1980, particularly for a President who fought his way into the White House with such a great clanking of the crusader's armor. . . ."

The clanking of the crusader's armor sounded very tinny in January 1978 when it developed that the Carter Administration had fired a Republican U.S. Attorney who had been investigating corruption in Pennsylvania. At a press conference on January 12, Carter declared:

"I have recently learned about the United States Attorney named [David] Marston. This is one of hundreds of United States Attorneys in the country and *I was not familiar with the case until it became highly publicized*. The Attorney General is handling the investigation of the replacement for Mr. Marston . . . and *I've not interfered at all*. . . . We have encouraged . . . the Democratic members of Congress not to be involved in trying to influence the Attorney General about who should be the new United States Attorney there. *I've not discussed this case with the Attorney General*."

Marston was not just one of hundreds of U.S. Attorneys. There were actually ninety-four and during the campaign, Carter had pledged to select them "strictly on the basis of merit without any consideration of political aspects or influence." More importantly, Carter, further along in the same press conference, all but conceded that he had not been entirely truthful. He was indeed "familiar" with the case before it became public. Back in November, he finally acknowledged, he had taken a call from Democratic Representative Joshua Eilberg, who had urged him to get rid of Marston. And he had also "interfered," for he "discussed" the matter with—and ordered—Attorney General Bell to "expedite" Marston's ouster. But the President denied knowing that Eilberg was being investigated by Marston and insisted that Marston's successor would be chosen "on merit" and would be a "superb person."

So from protestations of virtual ignorance and non-interference, Carter progressed, under newsmen's prodding, to an acknowledgement that he had been approached by a Congressman and had expedited the "process." Thus, in one fell swoop, Carter seemed to turn his campaign pledge to appoint U.S. Attorneys on the basis of merit into political cant. And this was made even more emphatic when his Attorney General announced that Marston would be replaced for strictly political reasons. "We have two parties in this country," Griffin Bell said. "The 'in' party right now happens to be the Democrats. They can get in to complain probably faster than the other party right now. That's the system we have. So there are a lot of complaints about Mr. Marston. They say we ought to have a Democrat as United States Attorney in Philadelphia."

The Marston controversy had actually begun on January 8, 1978, when *The Philadelphia Inquirer* ran a front-page story disclosing that Bell had secretly set up a selection panel of five lawyers to propose a replacement for Marston. Thirty-five-year-old Marston, after being appointed by President Ford, had been putting all sorts of local officials behind bars, both Democrats and Republicans. In his eighteen months on the job, he successfully prosecuted two key Democratic leaders on corruption charges: State Representative Herbert Fineman, a former Speaker of the House, and former State Senator Henry J. Cianfrani. He had also bagged the former Republican Chairman of Chester County, and had been looking into the activities of Joshua Eilberg and another Democratic lawmaker from Pennsylvania, Daniel Flood.

Under the headline, "Carter Administration Cripples the Foes of Graft," the *Inquirer* on January 10 editorially declared, "The Administration of President Carter, through the actions of Attorney General Bell, has struck a crippling blow to investigation of political corruption in Eastern Pennsylvania. . . . In doing that, Mr. Bell, in effect, has allied the U.S. Justice Department and the Carter Administration with the forces of government by graft and those forces' classic self-preservation weapon: to punish or to remove anyone who effectively combats political corruption."

Carter's press conference and subsequent efforts at "clarification" of what he said did not aid the President's cause. Liberal and conservative newspapers across the country heatedly denounced Carter's performance. Perhaps the most eloquent was *The New York Times*, which entitled its January 29 lead editorial,

For the Sake of the Presidency: "As Jimmy Carter once brilliantly perceived— 'I shall never lie to you'—the American people want their President back on the pedestal of authority and dignity. After a decade of Vietnam and Watergate, they want to be liberated from suspicion and cynicism; they want the presidency rescued from its recent corrosion. They cringe at the spectacle of reporters questioning every presidential phrase for evasion or inaccuracy. They abhor the idea of investigators taking affidavits from a President and Attorney General to deny an obstruction of justice. They do not want to hear, even from a party that hungers for political restitution, the chant of 'what did he know and when did he know it.' Yet here we are, again. First Lance, now Marston."

"Whatever you attribute these various shortcomings to—naïveté, bad briefings, dissembling, or caving in to congressional pressure," remarked *The Washington Post,* "the picture is not pretty. The implication is there that the President and the Attorney General have been a part—wittingly or not—of an attempt to cover up a Democratic scandal in Philadelphia."

"So Mr. Carter has a problem," commented *The Wall Street Journal,* "The experiences of American Presidents in the not-too-distant past, including Mr. Carter's own experience in the Lance affair, suggest his best bet for handling it. He had better come forward, sooner rather than later, and admit that he has made a mistake."

Admitting a mistake was the last thing Carter had in mind. At a press conference on January 30, the President defended his involvement in Marston's ouster as "a routine matter" quite compatible with his campaign promise to remove politics from the Justice Department. "If it occurred now, I would do the same," he said, referring to his request to Bell to "expedite" the removal of Marston.

And the President also denied there was any conflict between his statement at his January 12 press conference that he knew nothing about a Justice Department investigation of Eilberg and his subsequent statement to a Justice Department lawyer that he had been told of the inquiry just before starting that same meeting with reporters.

The lawyer, Michael Shaheen, was investigating the allegation that Carter, by ordering Marston's dismissal at the behest of a

Democratic Congressman under official inquiry, may have been involved in an obstruction of justice, the same charge levelled against Richard Nixon in the Watergate cover-up. And, to no one's surprise, the Shaheen report (rhymes, as Bill Safire noted, with "Dean report") fully exonerated the President and his Attorney General of any suggestion of obstruction of justice. "This intrepid self-investigation consisted solely of collecting sworn statements from eleven Justice officials plus the President (whose statement was not sworn—he doesn't spend his weekends at Camp Affidavit)," wrote Safire. "The 'Shaheen report' is an unconscionable whitewash of the man at the top, deliberately avoiding the normal process of investigating conspiracies by using the FBI and a grand jury. That this matter is not being investigated by a Special Prosecutor and a grand jury is a scandal in itself. . . . One might think that the lawyers in the Justice Department, and the aides at the White House, after the Watergate experience, would know enough to avoid even inadvertently joining in a possible felony, or at least to do so with some finesse.

"But they never learn. To see that justice is done, it's now up to the Senate Judiciary Committee. . . ."

But the Senate Judiciary Committee was under the control of Democrats, who made it clear from the outset they were not interested in further embarrassing a Democratic President. So, when its hearings were concluded, a staff report concluded that there was no "cover-up" by the Administration of the Eilberg investigation. But Committee Republicans charged that the report was misleading and contained outright falsehoods. The Republicans, led by Senator Malcolm Wallop of Wyoming, questioned, for example, the report's contention that no investigation of Eilberg was under way when the Congressman telephoned the President to urge Marston's dismissal. The evidence developed by the committee showed exactly the opposite: that the FBI had opened a file on Eilberg and had agents in the field asking about him, probably triggering the panicked call to Carter to fire his tormentor. The record was replete with direct conflicts—under oath—among top officials in the U.S. Government.

And there the Marston affair ended. Thanks again to Democratic control of Congress, Jimmy Carter did not need to suffer the indignities suffered by a Nixon who, when he got into a jam, was faced with a legislature—controlled by the opposition—out to get him. As Carter's Attorney General had stated, "The 'in' party right now happens to be the Democrats."

That the "in" party takes care of its own was also demonstrated in the case of the British-born psychiatrist Peter G. Bourne, Special Assistant to the President and Director of the White House Office of Drug Abuse Policy. Dr. Bourne, long a Carter family friend and one of those who claimed to have much to do with convincing Carter to seek the presidency, also—according to *Newsweek*—played "an ad hoc role as family doctor to the Georgians dating to statehouse days in Atlanta—source of routine medication . . . and, in those days, as one old hand remembered, 'something to make you sleep or help keep you awake' in high-stress political situations."

On July 11, 1978, a young woman named Toby Long attempted to fill a prescription for fifteen quaaludes at a drug store in a Virginia hamlet twenty-five miles from Washington. Nicknamed the "heroin for lovers," quaaludes had become notorious because of their abuse by the acid rock generation. By chance, a state pharmacy inspector was in the store, and she decided to verify the prescription. On discovering that the telephone number on the doctor's prescription had been disconnected, the inspector called the police. When the police learned the name on the prescription was fictitious, they arrested Long.

The case became more than routine when the police learned that the phony prescription had been written by Dr. Bourne. They questioned Bourne twice, and, because of his White House position, they notified the U.S. Attorney's office in Washington. On July 14, Jody Powell received a call from the Justice Department. The press secretary, who was with the President in West Germany, was told that Bourne had a "problem" involving a prescription. He didn't think the matter was serious.

It became serious only when on July 19, following the presidential party's return from Europe, *The Washington Post* blew the whistle on Bourne with the headline, "Carter Aide Signed Fake Quaalude Prescription." At first, Carter's aides agreed to let Bourne try to ride out the controversy. And Bourne agreed to take a leave of absence while continuing to draw his $51,000-a-year salary. At the same time, he released a statement to the press in which he declared that what he had done was "neither legally nor morally wrong." About that contention, however, there immediately was strong dispute.

And the question remained as to why Bourne had used a fictitious name in the first place. His explanation was that the prescription was for one of his aides, Ellen Metsky, twenty-five, who was suffering from insomnia, and that he had used a pseudonym to protect her privacy.

On the morning of July 20, Jack Anderson disclosed that Bourne had used cocaine at a party given the previous December by the National Organization for the Reform of Marijuana Laws (NORML), a lobbying group that advocates the repeal of penalties for smoking pot. Though Bourne denied the Anderson report, *Time* confirmed it: "The party was held in a renovated town house in central Washington. At one point, according to some of the guests, Bourne went into a bedroom, sniffed some coke through a rolled-up dollar bill, and smoked some marijuana."

That the President's chief drug abuse adviser was now being accused of abusing the drug laws himself was just too much for the White House. Besides, Carter was due to appear that evening at a televised press conference, the President's first on prime time. Bourne's hours were numbered; but he did not know it. Then, unexpectedly, Bourne was called by his lawyer, Charles "Chuck" Morgan, who had been in touch with Carter's aides. And by midafternoon, a tearful Bourne was composing a farewell letter to Jimmy Carter.

In his letter, the man whom Carter had once described as "one of the best personal friends I have in the world," told the President he regarded himself as having become "an instrument through which others attempt to bring disfavor to you." Then, in a valedictory interview with James Wooten of *The New York Times*,

Bourne got in a dig at his former colleagues by reporting that there was "a high incidence" of marijuana and "occasional" cocaine use among members of the White House staff. He also said that at the NORML party "about half the White House staff was there that night, looking—well, looking as though they belonged."

Jody Powell was properly indignant. The press secretary said the President sternly disapproved of such drug use. And, he himself didn't "have any knowledge of anyone on the White House staff who has ever used cocaine or marijuana."

"Ho, ho," commented Alexander Cockburn and James Ridgeway in *The Village Voice*. "We hope Jody does not ever have to submit to a lie detector test on that one. In campaign days, the coke-snorting among some of Carter's highest aides was a byword among the press corps (many of whom merely hoped to share the occasional snort themselves, the price of cocaine being beyond their usually modest salaries). . . .

Confirmation of the shared drug experiences between White House aides and members of the press came from Dr. Hunter Thompson. Interviewed by Ron Rosenbaum in the September 1978 issue of *High Times* (the magazine for drug fanciers), the Gonzo journalist told of his experiences on the 1976 campaign trail:

> THOMPSON: What we're talking about here is a new generation of highly competent professional political operatives and also a new generation of hot-rod political journalists who are extremely serious and competitive during the day, but who happened to share a few dark and questionable tastes that could only be mutually indulged late at night in absolute privacy. . . . It was true that for the first time there was a sort of midnight drug underground that included a few ranking staff people . . . along with some of the most serious blue-chip press people. . . . Hell, it was a fantastic luxury to be able to get together at night with a few bottles of Wild Turkey or Chivas Regal . . . yeah, and also a bag of ripe Colombian tops and a gram or two of the powder . . . in '76 we were able—

because there were enough of us—to establish a sort of midnight-to-dawn truce that transcended all the daytime headline gibberish, and I think it helped all of us to get a better grip on what we were really doing. I could illustrate this point a lot better by getting into names and specific situations, but I can't do that now for the same reason I couldn't get into it during the campaign. . . .

ROSENBAUM: . . . since we're talking about drug use during the '76 campaign, it's obvious we're talking about some people who are now in the White House, right?

THOMPSON: Well . . . some of them, yes. . . . Let's see how thin a wire we can walk here without getting ourselves locked up. . . . Anyway, yeah, we're talking about at least a few people in the White House inner circle. . . .

ROSENBAUM: The inner circle of Carter's people are serious drug users?

THOMPSON: Wait a minute. I didn't say that. For one thing, a term like *serious users* has a very weird and menacing connotation: and, for another, we were talking about a *few people* from almost *everybody's* staff. Across the board. . . . Not junkies or freaks, but people who were just as comfortable with weed, booze, or coke as we are— and we're not weird, are we? Hell no, we're just over-worked professionals who need to relax now and then, have a bit of the whoop and giggle, right?

Which helps explain why, when *The New York Times'* Wooten was asking him about drug use in the White House, an unnamed "high official" in one of Carter's "executive agencies" said, almost incredulously, "I can't believe you're asking me these questions." But, as columnist Michael Novak noted, "An Administration worried about the three-martini lunch might begin to worry about the tax-free $100 snort of cocaine in a few of its own offices. An Administration pretending to be populist might wish to examine its chic, corrupt élite."

But, from the beginning, there was no intention to do any such thing. Every law enforcement agency in the Carter Administration was busy making sure that the Bourne affair would fall between the cracks of the legal system.

The announcement of Bourne's resignation came just four hours before Carter held his news conference. And an obviously upset Carter sought to deflect the matter by stating he did not intend to "answer questions on the subject." But he was only partly successful.

Fifteen minutes into the session, former CBS correspondent Daniel Schorr—now a columnist for *The Des Moines Register* Syndicate—rose to challenge the unprecedented censorship:

"Mr. President, I hope that this doesn't fall within the area of legal issues that you prefer not to discuss tonight, but the health of the President himself has always been a matter of great concern to the country. Can you say whether any of the prescriptions that were signed by Dr. Bourne were for substances that went either to you or members of your family?"

The President replied obliquely, "Dr. Bourne has never given me any treatments of any kind." Since Carter ignored the reference to other members of his family, Schorr pressed on: "None of those substances went to your—." "No, sir," Carter interrupted, hurrying to the next questioner. Later, he refused flatly to answer a question from ABC's Sam Donaldson on whether he agreed with Bourne's statement that the attacks on him were really attacks on the President. "I would prefer not to answer that question," said the President.

The President did warn his minions several days later that if they wanted to break the law by using illicit drugs they should seek jobs elsewhere. And then, while electioneering in tobacco country, he made a joke about it when he said that HEW Secretary Joe Califano thought it time for the White House staff to smoke something "regular."

As the perceptive Meg Greenfield observed in *Newsweek*, "a lot of people around Jimmy Carter . . . refuse to acknowledge the obligations that go with their power and position, almost as if by this refusal they could retain the wonderfully burden-free state that went with being 'outsiders.' But politically speaking, there is something approaching the suicidal in this attitude. And there sits Jimmy Carter in the White House, Mr. Morality himself, having to answer questions over the first nineteen months about his close associates' entanglements with the quest for dough, the use of drugs, boozing, whoop-de-doo and blabber-mouthing. An open Administration, they called it. I think he had better close it down, if he can, at least in its chaotic, permissive aspects. The carelessness may be keeping those around him 'young,' but it is aging Jimmy Carter plenty fast."

On August 21, 1978, what Bill Safire had predicted a month before came to pass—Dr. Bourne, the *Times* columnist had written, "will neither be missed nor prosecuted." Both Virginia and U.S. prosecutors announced they had decided not to charge Bourne for writing a false name on a prescription. Paul Ebert, the Democratic prosecutor in Prince William County, said that since Bourne had written the prescription in Washington, he "has not violated the laws of the Commonwealth of Virginia." It would have been a different matter had Bourne written the prescription in Virginia. Then he would have violated the law, Ebert said. A spokesman for the U.S. Attorney's Office in Washington said, "We originally deferred to Virginia authorities to decide whether to prosecute or not in this case. They've made their decision, and as far as this office is concerned, that's the end of the matter."

All of which, commented columnist Les Kinsolving, "should be welcome news to every pusher in D.C. For all they have to do now is forge drug prescriptions in Washington and cross the Potomac to begin the buying. . . ." And, *The Christian Science Monitor,* in an unusually impassioned editorial, suggested that the Bourne case had "become symbolic of lapsed integrity at the top. And, whatever the proper legal judgment on his admitted deceit may be, the nation needs a sense that the full legal process has been pursued—and that the Administration *cares* about pursuing it. . . . If Americans cannot expect concern for an uncompromising sense of ethics in the White House, where can they expect it? . . . The Bourne case cannot be left in legal limbo between Pennsylvania Avenue and Prince William County."

But that's precisely where it was left. Which did not sit too well with some career Justice Department attorneys. As one told columnist Michael Novak, "Here is a President who can lecture lawyers about equal justice for the downtrodden and the big shots. A ghetto kid caught with a small amount of marijuana can go to jail, but his own drug adviser—a federal official—escapes without even a federal investigation. If a President wants to crack down on big shots, he can begin right in his own office."

But the Carter Administration was apparently determined to stonewall the scandal in the hope that the American people would be either forgetful or unconcerned. And the White House succeeded in so doing. Bourne became a barely remembered figure out of the past. But he remained on good terms with the President, and met with him several times after his resignation. They both agreed it was "not timely" for Bourne to return to the Administration.

Still, the White House remained accident prone. Its inhabitants seemed unable to learn the lessons of recent history. During the 1978 election campaign, for example, two senior members of President Carter's political family purveyed what Rowland Evans and Robert Novak described as "malicious and untrue gossip" about a prominent Republican. According to the columnists, the slander was transmitted by "one of Carter's hard-boiled aides" and, more surprisingly, by "gentlemanly" John White, the President's handpicked Democratic National Chairman.

The slander was that the Republican politician was homosexual.

"After considerable checking," wrote the columnists, "we can now report that the rumor comes as close to being disprovable as any personal slander ever is." Whether the politician in question "runs for President, the Senate, or the House," they went on, "the vicious canard has no place on the political scene. That is probably also true of homosexual rumors whispered about other prominent politicians, rumors that not only do gross injustice to their victims but also demean and pollute democratic government."

The irony was that Donald Segretti, a Republican prankster in 1972, was convicted for handing out a few leaflets in Florida that contained sexual innuendoes (not homosexual) about Hubert Humphrey and Henry Jackson. After spending several months in jail, Segretti personally apologized to the two Senators.

But there were no immediate apologies forthcoming from Chairman White and the President's top political aide. Carter himself said nothing.

As for the media, there seemed to be little interest in the kind of story which, had it involved Nixon's cohorts, undoubtedly would have been pursued with a fanatical devotion to the "pursuit of the truth."

Obviously, if it didn't *start* with Watergate, it didn't *stop* with Watergate, either.

16
"MASSIVE APPLAUSE THROUGHOUT THE NATION"

ONLY HOURS BEFORE HE ANNOUNCED THAT FULL DIPLOMATIC relations would be established with Communist China, President Carter met with congressional leaders in the White House. In the midst of the briefing, the President was informed that an important telephone hookup had been arranged.

The President explained he wanted to soften the shock of ending the twenty-three-year-old mutual defense pact with Taiwan. The telephone call was to connect him with the leaders of a small island nation in Asia whose security long depended on the American defense umbrella. After all, he said, that was the least he could do for old friends.

But the old friends were not the Taiwanese. The call was to the Japanese.

There was no call to the Taiwanese.

The fact was the Taiwanese were treated like outcasts. Their Ambassador to the U.S., James C. H. Shen, was informed of the unilateral American decision only a short time before the President went on national television. And within days, the U.S.-educated Shen was on his way home. The official amenities were few. The State Department's third-ranking officer was at Dulles

Airport to say goodbye. There was no phone call from the President, nor a visit from the Secretary of State. Whether a sense of shame pervaded the highest councils of government was doubtful. There was too much joy over the normalization of relations with China—at a time when Jimmy Carter badly needed a foreign policy spectacular. For, wherever one looked at the globe, things were going bad for the U.S. And full relations with the People's Republic were just what was needed to stir up the adrenalin. After all, look what the original breakthrough had done for President Nixon on the eve of his 1972 re-election effort.

No wonder, then, that Jimmy Carter played the announcement for all it was worth. With a great sense of drama, the White House had asked the three networks for time during which the President would address the nation on an undisclosed subject. And after his eight-minute speech, Carter leaned back in his chair, unaware the microphone had not been turned off. With a touch of smugness, the President remarked almost to himself, "Massive applause . . . throughout the nation."

The applause was far from universal. Opposition to the "betrayal" of Taiwan was quickly expressed by such diverse voices as George Meany and Barry Goldwater. And, of all people, John B. Oakes, former senior editor of *The New York Times*, argued that "by taking the action he has now taken in the way he has taken it, President Carter has seriously undermined American pretensions to be the moral leader of the world and an exemplar of constancy and faithfulness to our friends."

Around the globe, apprehensions were expressed about the durability of agreements with Americans. The Israelis, for example, were absolutely dismayed. Long dependent on the U.S. for their security, the Israelis had been having problems with a President who was seeking to convince them to accept an Egyptian-approved formula for a peace treaty between the two countries.

Also giving concern to the Israelis (and, for that matter, the Egyptians) was the extraordinary episode involving Billy Carter and the Libyans. Here was the brother of the President welcoming to Georgia a group of officials from one of the most outspokenly anti-Israel of the Arab countries and a frequent bankroller of terrorist groups pledged, among other things, to assassinate such moderate Arab leaders as Egypt's Sadat. And Billy was saying such things as, "The Libyans are the best friends I've ever made in my life." This on the basis of an eight-day visit Billy had made to Libya the previous fall. Who had arranged the trip and for what purpose was not immediately disclosed. And now, he said, he was repaying the hospitality of his Libyan hosts. Moreover, he claimed, his participation in the Libyan mission to the U.S. had been cleared in writing by the State Department, and, he added, he had informed his brother of the forthcoming visit during the Christmas holidays when the President was in Plains.

Billy's antics had aroused concern even as he awaited the arrival of the Libyans at the Atlanta airport. At one point, he stepped from the limousine and, in the presence of an Arab diplomat, reporters and others, proceeded to urinate al fresco on the concrete. From then on, everything began to go downward. Insisting that the U.S. ought to end its hostility toward the oil-rich North African regime, Billy said, "There's a hell of a lot more Arabians than there is Jews." Asked about Libya's support of Palestinian guerrillas who have engaged in bombings and skyjackings, the First Brother said, "The Jewish media tears up the Arab countries full time, as you well know."

No longer were Billy's buffoonish activities a subject for bemused editorial tolerance. As word of Billy's anti-Semitic mouthings spread north, editors took a new look at the First Brother's antics. Billy wasn't "funny now," declared *The Philadelphia Inquirer*. "He's becoming a menace." A bit more tolerantly, *The Baltimore Sun* said, "Not even a President should be required to repudiate his own brother in public, however crude and contemptible the brother may be."

The President, of course, did not immediately repudiate his brother. In fact, he didn't even reproach him. When asked to explain why by NBC's John Chancellor, the President said, "We love each other, but any attempt that I might make to control Billy's words or actions would not be successful at all." In fact, he added, "it would be counterproductive."

The President's kid-gloves treatment of his brother bewildered many people. None more so than Bill Safire, who wondered whether Billy wasn't blackmailing the President. Recalling that Billy had taken the Fifth Amendment, Safire asked, "What information, potentially incriminating to himself or his family, is Billy Carter concealing from the Lance grand jury?"

The episode could not have come at a worse time for the President for another reason. Carter had been having stormy relations with portions of the Jewish community over his pressuring of Israel to sign a peace treaty with Egypt.

And it came at a time when Carter appeared to be facing disaster in Iran, the oil-rich linchpin of U.S. security in the Middle East. There was also personal embarrassment for the President in the collapse of Shah Mohammed Reza Pahlevi. The President had flown to Tehran to celebrate the arrival of the year 1978 with the Iranian ruler. The Shah, then at the peak of his power and ambition, was host at a lavish state dinner at the palace for the President, Secretary Vance, and their wives. And Carter said he had timed his visit for that night because he had asked Rosalynn with whom she wished to celebrate New Year's Eve. And Rosalynn had responded, "Above all others, I think, with the Shah and Empress Farah." Then, toasting the Shah, Carter said:

"Iran, because of the great leadership of the Shah, is an island of stability in one of the more troubled areas of the world. This is a great tribute to you, Your Majesty, and to your leadership and to the respect and admiration and love which your people give to you."

Continuing with words that were to come back to haunt him, the President talked of the commitment which he and the Shah shared for "the cause of human rights," adding, "We have no other nation on earth who is closer to us in planning for our mutual military security. We have no other with whom we have closer consultation on regional problems that concern us both. And there is no leader with whom I have a deeper sense of personal gratitude and personal friendship."

Within a year, Iran teetered on the brink of civil war, and the Shah was desperately seeking to save his peacock throne. The liberalization which Carter had urged upon the Shah had backfired. A strange combination of Moslem fundamentalists (seeking an Islamic Republic) and left-wing militants (seeking a People's Republic) had seized on the new freedoms to take to the streets and, for all intents and purposes, had literally crippled the nation.

Examining Carter's role in the midst of the Iranian crisis, Henry

Trewhitt, the diplomatic correspondent of *The Baltimore Sun*, wrote on January 7, 1979, "Mr. Carter now is being tested . . . to determine his will, his flexibility, and his instincts under pressure. Very little has worked for him so far. . . . Iran above all is the test of the moment. . . . For if Iran slips from the influence of the West, the world will hold Carter responsible, rightly or wrongly, for a geopolitical disaster of the first magnitude and treat him accordingly."

Carter, Trewhitt went on, is a "local and regional politician with no global experience. . . . He is squeamish—his detractors say naïve—about the use of power. But the larger point is that he is the first President to be elected since World War II with full awareness and indeed a commitment that the United States, rightly or wrongly, no longer will act with the boldness of his predecessors."

Carter appeared genuinely perplexed by the dramatic turn of events in Iran. And, almost by instinct, he and his national security advisers faulted the CIA for failing to warn of the internal opposition to the Shah. And when asked whether he thought the Shah would prevail, the President—in somewhat less than ringing, Churchillian tones—replied, "I don't know. I hope so. This is something that is in the hands of the people of Iran. We have never had any intention, and don't have any intention, of trying to intercede in the internal political affairs of Iran." Once again, the President had talked without thinking. Within hours, both the White House and the State Department issued statemen's reaffirming U.S. support of the Shah in his increasingly threatened position. Jody Powell declared that the President was "very concerned about the erroneous interpretations" of his remarks.

Finally, after a warning from Leonid Brezhnev not to interfere in Iran, Carter ordered an American task force, led by the carrier *Constellation*, to leave the Philippines for a show-the-flag visit in the Persian Gulf. The hawks thought they had won the day, but not for long. For then the doves, led by Fritz Mondale, turned the President around, arguing that such a show of support might alienate whoever followed the Shah into power. "There, churning around in circles in the South China Sea, half a world away from trouble," noted Bill Safire, "is the symbol of the Carter Administration's Iranian policy, the first example of no-boat gunboat diplomacy. We showed a naked flagpole." Carter's irresolution, needless to say, was not lost on Moscow.

Nor was it lost on many of Europe's statesmen who traditionally looked to Washington for leadership. And their feelings were verbalized at an off-the-record dinner given by the Aspen Institute's Robert Anderson (board chairman of Atlantic Richfield) in London in December 1978. They were summed up by former British Prime Minister Harold Macmillan: "Things are as bad for the West as they could possibly be, and they are getting worse. The Europeans have to deal with the weakest American Administration in my lifetime."

That one of the West's most revered elder statesmen could dub his stewardship of the Free World as "the weakest American Administration in my lifetime" stung Carter. It stung so much that when he flew off to the January 1979 summit meeting in sun-drenched Guadeloupe, the President was resolved to demonstrate to his British, French, and West German counterparts that he was not the weakling they thought he was. "As U.S. sources told it," *Newsweek* reported, "Carter gave the allies some discreet but firm talk. Annoyed by complaints of weak U.S. leadership, Carter chided the Europeans, especially the West Germans, for wavering in the face of Soviet pressure." But the main reason for the "wavering" was West German Chancellor Helmut Schmidt's lack of confidence in Carter's leadership and resolve to stand up to the Soviet Union. None of which was assuaged in the wake of the resignation as NATO Commander in Europe of General Alexander M. Haig, Jr., who made no secret of his concern over Carter's soft-line approach to the SALT talks, Soviet military buildups in Eastern Europe, and Communist incursions in Africa and Central Asia.

And all this after the highly (perhaps overly) publicized Carter summit with Israel's Begin and Egypt's Sadat at Camp David. After thirteen days on the mountaintop, a delirious national press set out to canonize the President as the greatest peacemaker of all time. Of course, the press had adequate help from the President himself in coming to that conclusion. After doing "some of his own bragging," as John Osborne put it in *The New Republic,* he let some of his minions—Vance, Brzezinski, Jordan, Powell, and several midlevel officials—tell the story of how "a tireless President, frustrated at times and . . . close to giving up" managed to get those two Levantine characters to agree to what was billed as "a framework for peace." The term "framework" was a novelty in diplomatic encounters. It delimits a certain portion of space, but does not define what—specifically—was to occupy that space. What the labors at Camp David brought forth, therefore, was an agenda for subsequent discussion. Carter, Sadat, and Begin had negotiated an agreement to negotiate.

But that's not what the euphoric White House was stressing as the President continued to revel in unaccustomed adulation. And wherever he went that fall, the President managed to get in references to "the remarkable results of Camp David"—even before the results were in.

And, instead of letting Begin and Sadat work out their remaining differences at their own speed, Carter insisted on a peace settlement—one that would be signed and delivered in his presence at, of all places, Mount Sinai—by December 17, 1978. But it was not to be. And Carter was described by aides as "livid" at Begin for being "intransigent." All Begin wanted was to make certain that his tiny nation's security would not be threatened by hastily signed agreements. Carter called this "quibbling" over "technicalities" and "legalisms." But to Israel, surrounded by nations pledged to drive her people into the sea, it was not "quibbling." It was a matter of life and death. Begin, particularly, had not forgotten U.S. promises to South Vietnam and that tiny nation's fall in 1975. Begin had no intention, his aides said, of becoming a liquor store owner in Orange County like South Vietnam's former Vice-President Nguyen Cao Ky.

More to the point, Begin—whose memory had been tempered by years of servitude in the Soviet Arctic Gulag—had not forgotten Carter's original proposal in late 1977 that the USSR be brought back into a position of power (and disruption) in all future Mideast negotiations. Carter had also insisted that the PLO be made the centerpiece of a "comprehensive" peace plan in one single framework. That would have provided the militant Palestinians with a veto over any Israeli-Egyptian settlement.

Sadat, too, had been flabbergasted by Carter's proposal that the Russians be involved in a renewed Geneva Conference. After all, Sadat had just kicked them out of his country. Now Carter was suggesting they again have a say over Egypt's destiny. No wonder, then, that Sadat grabbed a plane and flew to Israel to begin talks with the Israelis. At first, Carter seemed put out by the historic meeting in Jerusalem of the two ancient foes, Sadat and Begin. His Administration continued to call for a "comprehensive" conference including the PLO and the Soviet Union, a posture scarcely designed to bolster the Sadat-Begin initiative. A cartoon in the November 22, 1977 *Christian Science Monitor* told the story better than words. It showed a forsaken Jimmy Carter twiddling his thumbs and staring at a phone that does not ring. At his knees are newspapers with headlines proclaiming the exclusion of the U.S. from the Begin-Sadat talks.

In the weeks following the Sadat visit to Jerusalem, Carter could not resist getting involved. Getting involved to such a point that confusion reigned. Just before taking off on his world trip in the dying days of 1977—a trip which, in retrospect, made no sense—the President reacted to a complicated set of peace proposals from Begin so positively as to "disappoint" and "embarrass" Sadat. In an effort at damage control, an unscheduled stop in Egypt was announced, denied, announced again, and then duly took place. Following that hurried January 4, 1978, visit to Sadat, the President announced, in effect, he had been converted to the Egyptian point of view. That, at least, was the implication of his remark that his views and those of the Egyptian leader were "identical."

All of which prompted the usually placid *Washington Star* to suggest that the President was talking too much. "One would think that at this delicate stage of negotiations . . . Mr. Carter would avoid saying anything capable of being stretched into an endorsement of the negotiating position of either party. . . . The President and his gray eminence, Mr. Brzezinski (whom we guess to be that oft-quoted blabbermouth of a 'senior official' in the Carter entourage) seem unable to resist kibbitzing over the shoulders of the negotiators and upstaging the principals. To do it not once, not twice, but practically every day is recklessly self-indulgent. It tends to reinforce the suspicion that Mr. Carter, well-meaning as he may be, is also inept."

In effect, the Camp David accords constituted a de facto repudiation of Carter's previous demands for a comprehensive settlement and an endorsement of Henry Kissinger's step-by-step approach, first conceived by President Nixon. And they also constituted a repudiation of Carter's previous advocacy of what he called "open diplomacy." All through the campaign, he had scorned the Kissinger approach. "Under the Nixon and Ford Administrations," he said, "there . . . evolved a kind of secretive, 'lone-ranger' foreign policy—a one-man policy of international adventure. A foreign policy based on secrecy inherently has to be closely guarded and amoral, and we have had to forgo openness, consultation, and a constant adherence to fundamental principles and high moral standards."

The "lone ranger" got in his licks following Camp David. "Every Administration," said Kissinger, "has come in and said, 'We're going to change the world.' This one came in and said, 'We created the world.'"

As the weeks passed into months without a peace treaty, the glow of Camp David began to dim. And Carter was almost beside himself. He went public and berated Israel, expressing frustration over how every point in dispute with Egypt had to go "to the Prime Minister and to the Cabinet" for resolution. Of course, Carter had no such problem with Egypt. For Egypt was not a democracy.

"The U.S. has not of late played the role of honest broker; we have instead *sponsored* Egypt's new demands," commented *The Washington Star* on December 17, 1978. "Perhaps the American role stems from the disconcerting realization that President Sadat expected more than was thought from U.S. 'full partnership.' But what has resulted is a feeling in Israel that the U.S. is playing favorites, and the two nations are farther from a peace treaty than they were a few weeks ago."

Carter had hoped to achieve a triple crown in foreign policy by the end of 1978. But he failed to get Egypt and Israel to sign a peace pact. And he was unable to push through an agreement on strategic arms limitation with the Soviet Union. He did establish normal relations with mainland China. But he tarnished that act by double-crossing Taiwan. "We gave all and got nothing," said George Bush, former chief of the U.S. mission to Peking. "In acquiescing to China's three demands, with no apparent guarantee of a Taiwan solution, we are simply diminishing U.S. credibility around the world." Moreover, the deed had been done while Congress was away on Christmas holiday. The President had not consulted that eminent body or, for that matter, the American people, as he had repeatedly promised to do on foreign policy during the campaign. "Perhaps Professor Schlesinger will write a new book called *Son of the Imperial Presidency*," commented William F. Buckley.

Except for China, for which critics alleged the price was too high, none of the other foreign policy extravaganzas Carter had in mind worked. The President had obviously thought that playing the "China card" would also induce Moscow into a hurry-up signing of SALT II. But Brezhnev, even after the White House had trumpeted a breakthrough, said "nyet." Meanwhile, Saudi Arabia, upset by U.S. inability to do anything about events in Iran, was unable or unwilling to hold down a hefty OPEC price increase.

On the eve of the meeting in Guadaloupe, James Reston reported that no longer was Western Europe's major complaint, as it was in the early 1970s, that the U.S. was taking too strong and dominant a lead in the NATO alliance. Now, Reston reported from Paris, the complaint is "just the opposite: that Washington is too indecisive, too capricious, amateurish, and unpredictable."

"The criticism," Reston went on, "is directed primarily at President Carter, whose character and motives are generally admired, but whose policies are seen here as improvised and inconsistent, without careful prior analysis of their probable consequences. . . . [For] the first time since World War II, I've been hearing doubts in Europe about the capacity of the United States to manage its own economy, and even about its will and ability to defend Europe and the rest of the free world. . . . The fact that such things are even discussed in official quarters is something new and significant."

And questions persisted about Carter personally, particularly after his astonishing performance while visiting Mexico on a goodwill mission in February 1979. Perhaps too much was made of it, but the President's clumsy jest about having been afflicted with "Montezuma's revenge" on a previous visit made him look like a country bumpkin telling an off-color joke. The supposed jest caused only a titter of embarrassed laughter in the audience. Mrs.

Carter was reported to have thrust her hands over her face to hide her shock. And the President appeared mindless that his jest smacked of the very sort of superiority and chauvinism that Mexico's President José Lopez Portillo had been deploring in his more measured public remarks.

Back in Washington the joke was that the President must have employed a new speechwriter—his brother Billy. And some critics wondered whether Carter couldn't be described as "Nixon's revenge."

The tasteless Mexican episode occurred after a day of horrors in other parts of the globe. An American Ambassador was killed in Afghanistan, a land recently seized by pro-Soviet elements. And the United States Embassy in Tehran was seized for a time by the same kind of elements. In Mexico, meanwhile, President Carter was forced to endure a tongue lashing by President Lopez Portillo. And the Chinese, despite all of Washington's entreaties, launched an invasion of Vietnam as punishment for capturing much of Cambodia.

More than ever the United States was beginning to look like the "pitiful, helpless giant" which President Nixon had once warned that the nation was becoming. And no one looked more pitiful and helpless than a President whose major experience in foreign policy, until his election, was to attend occasional conferences of the Trilateral Commission at fancy resorts in Europe and Japan.

Among those who had accompanied President Carter to Guadeloupe was Hamilton Jordan. But he spent most of his "working vacation" out of sight. He had a typewriter installed in his cottage, and, according to aides, was working on a new memorandum for Carter: one proposing strategy to be employed by the President for re-election in 1980. What the memo contained was not immediately revealed but, according to usually well-informed sources, Jordan proposed that the President "toughen up his act."

Which the President proceeded to do on his return from Guadeloupe. The "new" Carter ordered Bella Abzug's dismissal as cochairperson of the National Advisory Committee on Women after, according to the White House, "Mrs. Abzug attempted to lecture the President on the duties of the committee and its role in serving the needs of its constituents."

Earlier, he had made a peace of sorts with George Meany during a ninety-minute meeting with the aging labor leader in the Oval Office. But, in talking with newsmen afterward, Meany stopped short of saying he was "happy" with the President. Nevertheless, they had "cleared up the question of our relations and communication." Previously, Meany had criticized the President for not doing enough for labor. He had also attacked the decision to recognize China, saying it was a sellout of Taiwan and warning that it would weaken U.S. credibility. In an act of pique, the President had let it be known that Meany would not be reappointed as a director of COMSAT—the Communications Satellite Corporation. In response, Lane Kirkland, Meany's heir apparent, felt obliged to resign all his presidential appointments. Rarely in the history of the labor movement have its leaders been forced to deal with a President (particularly one who was elected with their support), who sought to exact such petty revenge for imagined slights.

Aside from personality, the labor people were annoyed with Carter for hauling down the flag of "more jobs, new social programs" and running up the banner of "less inflation, cut back old programs." As Meany said angrily, "Carter is the most conservative President since Calvin Coolidge." That was not exactly accurate. For, as Marshall Loeb noted in a *Time* essay, Carter on taking office had "attempted to meet the demands of every constituency of the old Democratic coalition, and practically everybody else as well. He gave in to—or actively encouraged—increases in the minimum wage, Social Security benefits, farm subsidies, civil service pensions, grants to states, and a plethora of other payouts. He acceded to tariff increases or stricter import limits on sugar and steel, TV sets, CB radios, and other products, thus sheltering domestic producers from competition and enabling them to get theirs—by raising prices."

Which meant inflation, the rate of which doubled in the two years Carter was in office.

Following passage of Proposition 13 in California, Carter decided to change his tune. As he barnstormed through the country, promoting Democratic candidates in the fall of 1978, he sounded a conservative line reminiscent—as Fred Barnes reported in *The Washington Star*— "of the rhetoric of his Republican predecessor, Gerald Ford." In a *New York Times* dispatch, headlined *Carter Pre-Empts Republican Issues,* Terence Smith reported that the President had "hammered away at themes usually associated more with moderate Republicanism than with liberal Democratic politics. He drew the strongest applause with his promises to bolster the dollar abroad, control inflation, and trim the federal budget deficit."

At a rally in Sacramento, Carter said he had come to salute "one of our nation's greatest Governors—my friend and your Governor, Jerry Brown." Brown, who had beaten Carter in five primaries in 1976 and had been making noises about taking him on again in 1980, had introduced the President without noticeable enthusiasm. During his set speech, described by John Osborne, as "a skillful blend of fact and exaggeration, never to the point of outright deception," Carter noticed signs reading, "No to Proposition 6." The proposition was a proposal to bar homosexuals from teaching in public schools. Finishing his speech, Carter—once again unaware that the microphone had not been turned off—turned to Brown and asked whether he should say something about it. Brown said it was perfectly safe for him to do so, since both Ronald Reagan and Gerald Ford were opposed to the proposal. Racing back to the microphone, the President declared, "I also want to ask everybody to vote against Proposition 6. Everybody go to work. Let's win, let's win!" All of which, reported Osborne, made for a great deal of chortling on the part of the newsmen, some of whom cracked jokes about "Jimmy's profile in courage."

At the halfway mark of his term, it seemed Jimmy Carter was still learning how to be President. Though he had promised competence, efficiency and strong leadership, he had yet to deliver on any of these. Rather the early Carter years were marked by extraordinary confusion and ineptitude. His long and difficult apprenticeship appeared to be continuing. Among the people there seemed to be a huge emotional void about the President. He was neither loved nor hated, neither greatly admired nor deeply distrusted. "Rather," as *The Baltimore Sun* perceptively noted on January 21, 1979, "he is regarded as a fairly smart and enterprising politician who finds himself in a job that would daunt the most extraordinary of men, of which he is not. He lacks the fiery commitment that excites loyalty or the intellectual reach that can make sense out of swirling events. The result is an apparent sense of drift and make-do. This may be more a reflection on our times than on the President but politics demands of a great President that he rise above his times. Mr. Carter has not done so."

Nor was he able to resolve the question in people's minds about the kind of man he really was. After two years in office, he remained as much an enigma as when he first marched down Pennsylvania Avenue into the White House.

In fact, it could be said he was even more of an enigma.

A Personal Note

Talking to the President briefly at a White House reception shortly before Christmas 1978, I could see how bone-tired he was, as he shook hands with dozens of guests. The "young man," who had been pictured in those *Why Not the Best?* posters no longer looked youthful. He now had deep lines etched in his face and shadows under his eyes. And, even though he knew that this book was in the works, he could not have been nicer. "It's a great honor to have you in this house, Mr. Lasky," he said.

The next day, it was announced that he was suffering from a painful anal affliction.

SOURCES

CHAPTER 1

Time essay: July 17, 1978; Carter mountaintop meeting: Helen Thomas, UPI, *Baltimore News American*, Apr. 23, 1978; Goldwater remark: *Chicago Tribune*, Oct. 16, 1977; candidate Carter on India: *The Presidential Campaign 1976, Vol. 1*, Jimmy Carter (Washington, D.C., U.S. Government Printing Office, 1978), p. 817; Sen. Jackson on "abulia": Mary McGrory, *Washington Star*, Mar. 19, 1978; Panetta in *Washington Post:* Apr. 10, 1978; Lou Harris polls and quotation: *Human Events*, July 22, 1978; *Economist* quoted: Apr. 22, 1978; Reston in N.Y. *Times: ibid.;* Kilpatrick quoted: *Washington Star*, July 18, 1978; Flora Lewis quoted in N.Y. *Times:* July 17, 1978; Patrick Anderson quoted: "Peanut Farmer for President," *The New York Times Magazine*, Dec. 14, 1975; Carter interview in Plains: Vermont Royster, *Wall Street Journal*, Mar. 15, 1978; Kraft quoted: *National Review*, Feb. 3, 1978.

CHAPTER 2

Reg Murphy interview, San Francisco, Feb. 3, 1978; Murphy in *Newsweek:* July 19, 1976; Kristofferson song quoted: *ibid.;* Carter on childhood hardships: *Why Not the Best?* (N.Y., Bantam, 1976), pp. 7-8; *"I'll Never Lie to You,"* Jimmy *Carter in His Own Words*, ed. Robert Turner (N.Y., Ballantine, 1976), p. 14; *Athens Daily News* quoted: June 18, 1970; Lillian Carter quoted: *New York Post*, May 21, 1976; *People*, July 19, 1976; Jimmy on black neighbors: *Why Not the Best?, op. cit.*, p. 37; Miz Lillian a "nigger" lover: *Time*, Mar. 8, 1970; Jimmy on parents: *Why Not the Best?, op. cit.*, p. 13; Miz Lillian on "nigger" at church: James Wooten, *Dasher: The Roots and The Rising of Jimmy Carter* (N.Y.,

Summit, 1978), p. 86; Prof. Goodwyn quoted: *The New York Times* (Op-Ed Page), Nov. 6, 1977; Tom Watson background: Josephine Mellichamp, *Senators from Georgia* (Huntsville, Ala., Strode Publishers, 1976), pp. 218-223; Nathaniel Weyl, *The Jew in American Politics* (New Rochelle, N.Y., Arlington House, 1965), pp. 87-92; C. Vann Woodward, *Tom Watson, Agrarian Rebel* (N.Y., Macmillan, 1938), p. 486; Carter on Watson helping grandfather: *The Presidential Campaign 1976, op. cit.*, p. 212; uncle named Tom Watson Gordy: Hugh Carter, as told to Frances Spatz Leighton, *Cousin Beedie and Cousin Hot* (Englewood Cliffs, N.J., Prentice-Hall, 1978), p. 197; *U.S. News & World Report* interview: Sept. 13, 1976; *The Presidential Campaign 1976, op. cit.*, pp. 734-735; "Jewish influence": *Washington Post*, May 16, 1978; Carter on fighting spirit: Bob Cohn, *Athens (Ga.) Daily News*, June 18, 1970; Carter on "prom parties" and N.Y. trip: *ibid.*, June 19, 1970; Carter on Naval Academy: *Why Not the Best?, op. cit.*, pp. 42-46; U.S. Naval Academy yearbook: *The Lucky Bag*, 1947; Carter on sea duty: *Why Not the Best?, op. cit.*, p. 50; Carter on Rickover: *The Presidential Campaign 1976, op. cit.*, pp. 64-65; Nordan in *Atlanta Journal* quoted: Feb. 8, 1976; Carter "served in two wars": James Wooten, *Dasher, op. cit.*, pp. 147-148.

CHAPTER 3
Carter on leaving Navy: interviewed by Bill Moyers, PBS, May 6, 1976, transcript in *The Presidential Campaign 1976, op. cit.*, p. 164; Miz Lillian on Rosalynn: Hugh Carter, *Cousin Beedie and Cousin Hot, op. cit.*, pp. 65-66; Carter interviewed by Bill Moyers: *op. cit.*; deciding where to live in Plains: James Wooten, *Dasher, op. cit.*, p. 217; Carter peanut business: *Why Not the Best?, op. cit.*, p. 71; Jim Merrimer, *Atlanta Constitution*, May 31, 1976; Hugh Carter, *Cousin Beedie and Cousin Hot op. cit.*, p. 91; Carter running for state representative: *Why not the Best. op. cit.*, p. 87; Carter on black/white school inequities: *Why Not the Best?, op. cit.*, pp. 72-73; Neil Maxwell, *Wall Street Journal*, March 25, 1976; Miz Lillian on Jimmy's boredom: James Wooten, *Dasher, op. cit.*, p. 241; running for State Senate: *Why Not the Best?, op. cit.*, pp. 88-95; Carter in State Senate: *ibid.*, p. 98; Reg Murphy quoted: *Newsweek*, July 19, 1976; Reinhold Niebuhr quoted: *Why Not the Best?, op. cit.*, p. 106; Carter vote on integration: *St. Louis Post-Dispatch*, May 23, 1976; Carter on hodgepodge education laws: *Why Not the Best?, op. cit.*, p. 100; Senator Zorn quoted in *Constitution: St. Louis Post-Dispatch, op. cit.*; Senator Johnson's bills: *ibid.*; Calloway quoted: interview, June 1, 1978; Carter on Calloway: *Why Not the Best?, op. cit.*, p. 110; Carter a Russell Democrat: *Atlanta Journal*, Apr. 18, 1966; Carter no longer a Russell Democrat: *Atlanta Constitution*, July 13, 1966; *Constitution* writer quoted: Sam Hopkins, *Atlanta Constitution*, July 20, 1966; another *Constitution* writer quoted: Bruce Galphin, *Atlanta Constitution*, Aug. 26, 1966; Troutman described: *Atlanta Constitution*, July 20, 1966; campaign schedule: *Atlanta Constitution*, Aug. 26, 1966; *Nation* writer on campaign: John Dennis, "Jimmy Carter's Fierce Campaign," *The Nation*, May 17, 1975; Galphin quoted: *Atlanta Constitution*, July 2, 1966; Carter on arrest of Carmichael:

Atlanta Constitution, Sept. 10, 1966; *U.S. News & World Report* quoted: Sept. 26, 1966; Carter quoted on state of mind after defeat: Moyers interview, *The Presidential Campaign 1976, op. cit.,* p. 176; Quinn interview, *Washington Post,* Mar. 28, 1976; Stapleton quoted: James David Barber, "On Nixon, Ford, and Carter," *The Washington Monthly,* April 1977; Carter on walk with Stapleton: *Time,* Oct. 4, 1976; Carter on preacher's question: Moyers interview, *The Presidential Campaign 1976, op. cit.,* p. 176; Carter on "conversion experience": *Washington Post,* Mar. 21, 1976; Anderson quotes Carter: *Washington Post,* Nov. 19, 1977; timing of Amy's birth: *Washington Post,* Mar. 28, 1976; Carter on loser: *Why Not the Best?, op. cit.,* p. 112.

CHAPTER 4

Carter on work 1966-70: *Why Not the Best?, op. cit.,* p. 112; Billy Graham quoted: David Kucharsky, *The Man from Plains* (N.Y., Harper & Row, 1976), p. 42; Carter did not doubt winning: *Why Not the Best?, op. cit.,* p. 114; Reg Murphy quoted: *Newsweek,* July 19, 1976; Carter on his campaign organization: *Why Not the Best? op cit.,* p. 114; Carter memo on Sanders: Bill Shipp, *Atlanta Constitution,* Nov. 8, 1970; Hamilton poll: *ibid.;* and Bill Shipp, *Atlanta Constitution,* Nov. 11, 1970; Carter on his campaign: *Why Not the Best?, op. cit.,* 115-116; Carter commercial on Sanders: James M. Perry, *National Observer,* Apr. 5, 1971; Carter announced his candidacy: Reg Murphy, *Atlanta Constitution,* Apr. 4, 1970; peanuts symbol: *Atlanta Journal,* Aug. 16, 1970; Carter campaign off and running: Bill Shipp, *Atlanta Constitution,* Apr. 11, 1970; Sanders on cufflinks: *Atlanta Constitution,* Aug. 29, 1970; Carter billboard: Bill Shipp, *Atlanta Constitution,* Nov. 11, 1970; Shipp on Carter TV spot: *Atlanta Constitution,* July 21, 1970; Carter's links to big shots: Nicholas Horrock, *The New York Times,* May 26 and 27, 1976; *Atlanta Constitution,* Aug. 27, 1970; Phil Stanford quoted: *Columbia Journalism Review,* July/Aug. 1976; Gambrell quoted in N.Y. *Times:* May 27, 1976; 1970 financial records made public: *The New York Times,* Oct. 22, 1976; other contributors: Nicholas Horrock, *op. cit.;* Carter on tying Sanders to big shots: *Why Not the Best?, op. cit.,* pp. 115-116; Carter on Sanders-Humphrey: Phil Stanford, "Carter," Capitol Hill News Bureau (Wash., D.C.), 1976; Carter on Sanders got rich in government: *ibid.; Valdosta Daily Times,* June 14, 1970; Carter on Sanders' use of inside information: *News-Press,* June 10, 1970; AP, *Valdosta Daily Times,* June 16, 1970; Stoner challenge: *Valdosta Daily Times,* June 14, 1970; Carter bombshell on Sanders: *Atlanta Constitution,* Aug. 25, 1970; Carter "proof" against Sanders: Steven Brill, "Jimmy Carter's Pathetic Lies," *Harper's,* March 1976; AP, *Gwinnett Daily News,* Sept. 3, 1970; AP, *Washington Star,* Mar. 13, 1978.

CHAPTER 5

Others in '70 race: Hal Gulliver and Reg Murphy, *The Southern Strategy* (N.Y., Scribner's, 1971), pp. 176-178; Bill Shipp quoted: *Atlanta Constitution,* July 14, 1970; Carter now a conservative: *Atlanta Constitution,* Aug. 28, 1970; Steven Brill, *Harper's, op. cit.;* Carter quoted in *Atlanta Journal:* July 27, 1971;

Carter on support from Wallace to NAACP: *Atlanta Journal/Constitution*, June 21, 1970; Bill Shipp quoted: *Atlanta Constitution*, Nov. 8-11, 1970; Carter on blacks' reaction: *Newsweek*, Mar. 8, 1976; Pope on "nigger campaign": *Washington Post*, Mar. 7, 1976; Sanders photo with black ballplayer: Hal Gulliver and Reg Murphy, *The Southern Strategy, op. cit.,* pp. 184-185; Bill Shipp, *Atlanta Constitution*, June 11, 1970; Abernathy interviewed by Phil Stanford: "Carter," *op. cit.;* Abernathy interviewed by George Lardner Jr.: *Washington Post*, Mar. 7, 1976; Dorothy Wood interview: Phil Stanford, "Carter," *op. cit.;* Shipp interview: *ibid.;* Pope interview: *ibid.;* Murphy on Carter's leaflet: interview, San Francisco, June 22, 1978; other "fact sheets" and leaflets: *Atlanta Magazine,* December 1970; Black Concern Committee pamphlet: *Atlanta Constitution*, July 14, 1970; Carter reaction to pamphlet: *ibid.;* Segretti comparison: *Westmore News (N.Y.C.),* July 29, 1976; C.B. King's radio ads: Steven Brill, *Harper's, op. cit.;* Phil Stanford, "Carter," *op. cit.;* Abernathy interviewed by Hallas: Clark Hallas, Detroit News, Mar. 7, 1976; Wood and Smith confirmations: *ibid.;* C.B. King on his radio ads: *ibid.;* Wood comment: *ibid.;* Abernathy interview by Phil Gailey: *Miami Herald,* Feb. 23, 1976; Carter on Atlanta papers: *Why Not the Best?, op. cit.,* pp. 116-117; Murphy comments: interview, San Francisco, Feb. 3, 1978; Pope quoted by Bill Shipp: *Atlanta Constitution*, Nov. 11, 1970; Carter on Sanders' airplane number: *Athens (Ga.) Herald,* June 28, 1970; Carter's use of racism: *The New York Times,* Sept. 10, 1970; *Atlanta Constitution*, Sept. 3, 1970; Carter ties self to Maddox: *Atlanta Journal,* Aug. 14, 1970; *Columbus (Ga.) Ledger,* Oct. 7 and 27, 1970; Atlanta phone-in show: *Atlanta Constitution*, Sept. 3, 1970; Carter links self to Wallace: *Washington Post*, Mar. 7, 1976; *Atlanta Constitution*, Aug. 26, 1970; Carter speech at Lions Club: Phil Stanford, "Carter," *op. cit.;* Griffin meeting with Wallace: *Washington Post*, Mar. 7, 1976; Sanders on Wallace: *Atlanta Constitution*, Nov. 11, 1970; Vandiver letter of support: *Athens Herald,* Aug. 16, 1970; poll of Wallace voters: *Savannah Morning News,* Sept. 15, 1970; primary results: *Atlanta Constitution*, Sept. 10, 1970; AP, *Jacksonville Times-Union,* Sept. 13, 1970; Sanders press conference: *Albany (Ga.) Herald,* Sept. 12, 1970; *Atlanta Magazine,* December 1970; Carter reaction: *Atlanta Constitution*, Sept. 22, 1970; Carter on debate: *Atlanta Magazine, op. cit.; Atlanta Journal,* Sept. 18, 1970; *Atlanta Constitution*, Sept. 22, 1970; Carter attack on press: *Athens Herald,* June 28, 1970; *Atlanta Constitution*, Sept. 22, 1970; Billy Carter quoted: *Atlanta Journal,* Sept. 17, 1970; Carter's tenants' houses: AP dispatch, Sept. 17, 1970; Carter reaction: *Atlanta Constitution*, Sept. 19, 1970; Sanders leaflet: undated; Carter-Harris meeting: *Atlanta Constitution*, Sept. 15, 1970; *Savannah Morning News,* Sept. 15, 1970; Carter would not reappoint Harris: *Augusta Courier,* Oct. 5, 1970; Maddox-Carter relationship: *Columbus Ledger,* Oct. 7 and 27, 1970; Leslie Wheeler, *Jimmy Who?* (Woodbury, N.Y., Barron's, 1976), p. 59; Harris summary of campaign: *Augusta Courier,* Oct. 5, 1970; Carter commanding lead over Suit: Hal Gulliver and Reg Murphy, *The Southern Strategy, op. cit.,* pp. 193-194; Carter on "shoot to kill": UPI, *Savannah Morning News,* Oct. 27, 1970; Carter on Nixon-Agnew and Maddox: *ibid.;* Nixon-Agnew visits: Hal Gulliver and Reg Murphy, *op. cit.,* p. 194; Jordan on calling Carter

"Governor": James Wooten, *Dasher, op. cit.*, p. 295; Carter quoted on campaign tactics: Howard Norton and Bob Slosser, *The Miracle of Jimmy Carter* (Plainfield, N.J., Logos International, 1976), p. 48; Lardner in *Washington Post:* Mar. 7, 1976.

CHAPTER 6

"Camelot Down South": *Atlanta Constitution*, Jan. 13, 1971; Inaugural parties: Bill Shipp, *Atlanta Constitution*, Jan. 3 and 11, 1971; Diane Stepp, *Atlanta Constitution*, Jan. 12, 1971; Hugh Merrill, *Atlanta Journal*, Jan. 13, 1971; Celestine Sibley, *Atlanta Constitution*, Jan. 13, 1971; Yolande Gwinn, *Atlanta Journal*, Jan. 13, 1971; Carolyn McCullough, *Atlanta Constitution*, Jan. 13, 1971; swearing-in and speech: Hal Gulliver, *Atlanta Constitution*, Jan. 11, 1971; Bill Shipp, *Atlanta Constitution*, Jan. 13, 1971; (text) *Atlanta Constitution*, Jan. 13, 1971; Miz Lillian-Rosalynn disagreement: Hugh Carter, *Cousin Beedie and Cousin Hot, op. cit.*, p. 185; *Time's* editors impressed: Bruce Galphin, *Atlanta Magazine*, July 1971; Shipp quoted: *Atlanta Constitution*, Apr. 16, 1971; Nixon on Calley episode: Richard Nixon, *RN, The Memoirs of Richard Nixon* (N.Y., Grosset & Dunlap, 1978), pp. 499-500; *The New York Times* dispatch quoted: May 21, 1976; Carter news conference re Calley: *Atlanta Constitution*, Apr. 2, 1971; Carter change on war and Calley: *The New York Times*, May 21, 1976; Shipp on Democratic Governors meeting: *Atlanta Constitution*, June 22, 1971; Rev. Hope quoted: UPI, *Atlanta Constitution*, Oct. 9, 1972; Carter praised by *Atlanta Journal;* July 15, 1973; Carter on Supreme Court busing decision: *Atlanta Constitution*, May 4, 1971; Carter praised Wallace: *Atlanta Journal*, Aug. 16, 1971; Carter urged parent protest but not defiance of law: *Atlanta Constitution*, Aug. 31, 1971; *Los Angeles Times*, Sept. 7, 1971; Carter on presidential candidates' views on busing: *Washington Star*, Nov. 8, 1971; *Arkansas Gazette* on Carter's views: Nov. 10, 1971; Carter support of busing amendment: AP, *Atlanta Constitution*, Feb. 17, 1972; Carter reverse on busing amendment: *Madison (Wis.) Capitol Times*, Mar. 29, 1976; *Arkansas Gazette* quoted: Feb. 24, 1972; *Newsweek*, Mar. 6, 1972; Carter introduced Wallace: *Atlanta Constitution*, Feb. 24 and 25, 1972; Carter speech at Peace Officers Assn.: *Atlanta Constitution*, May 27, 1971; Carter statement to Maddox: *Los Angeles Times*, Mar. 29, 1976; legislators quoted in N.Y. *Times:* May 17, 1976; Reg Murphy on Carter tantrums: *Atlanta Constitution*, Feb. 15, 1971; *Newsweek*, July 19, 1976; Carter criticism of press: *Atlanta Constitution*, June 19, 1971; Carter on reorganization: *The New York Times*, May 17, 1976; other views on reorganization: *Atlanta Constitution*, Feb. 16, 1976; Phil Stanford, "Carter," *op. cit.; Newark (N.J.) Star Ledger*, June 13, 1976; *Washington Post*, Feb. 28, 1976, and Apr. 11, 1977; Tom Murphy quoted: *The New York Times*, May 17, 1976; NEA dispatch by Tom Tiede, Feb. 10, 1976; Lardner quoted: *Washington Post*, Feb. 28, 1976; Human Resources Dept.: State-of-the-State Message, *Atlanta Constitution*, Jan. 15, 1974; Georgia Dept. of Audits & Accounts, Dept. of Human Resources, year ended June 30, 1974; Busbee reorganization of Human Resources: Handbook of Georgia State Agencies (Georgia Institute of Government, University of Georgia, 1975); speech, Georgia

Municipal Assn. Convention, Jekyll Island, Ga., June 21, 1976; Carter on zero-based budget: speech, Virginia Municipal League, Norfolk, Va., Sept. 19, 1973; *Why Not the Best?*, *op. cit.*, p. 132; growth of employees and budget: *Washington Post*, Feb. 28, 1976; Georgia Dept. of Audits & Accounts, Report of the State Auditor of Georgia, Salary Supplement, year ended June 30, 1971 and June 30, 1974; Carter on federal reorganization in '76; *Washington Post*, Mar. 15, 1976; *Wall Street Journal*, May 13, 1976; Culver Kidd episode: Bill Shipp, *Atlanta Journal/Constitution*, Mar. 25, 1978; *Washington Post*, Apr. 15, 1978; Prentice Palmer, *Atlanta Journal*, Apr. 18 and 19, 1978; *Washington Star*, Apr. 16 and 22, 1978; *The New York Times*, Apr. 20, 1978; *Newsweek* May 1, 1978.

CHAPTER 7

Associate quoted in N.Y. *Times:* May 17, 1976; Carter critical of presidential contenders: *Newsweek*, Mar. 8, 1976; James Wooten, *Dasher*, *op. cit.*, pp. 315-316; Shipp quoted: *Atlanta Constitution*, Apr. 22, 1971; Carter preferences quoted in *Constitution:* Apr. 27, 1971; Governor's Club luncheon: *Atlanta Constitution*, Sept. 2, 1971; Carter adds Wallace: *Atlanta Constitution*, Nov. 5, 1971; Wallace quoted: *Arkansas Gazette*, Nov. 23, 1971; Carter quoted on V.P.: *ibid.*; Askew trumpeted: *The New York Times Magazine*, Mar. 5, 1972; Carter view of McGovern: AP, *Birmingham News*, May 11, 1972; Carter on stop-McGovern: Ken Bode, "How to Stop a Frontrunner," *New Republic*, June 5, 1976; Gambrell proposes Carter: *Atlanta Constitution*, May 26, 1972; Carter on McGovern rules: *ibid.*; Carter challenges McGovern on issues: *ibid.*; Carter denies stop-McGovern stand: *The New York Times*, June 5, 1971; Carter-McGovern meeting: interview, Frank Mankiewicz, Aug. 8, 1978; Wallace expected Carter backing: *Miami Herald*, Feb. 23, 1976; speech missing from Archives: Steven Brill, *Harper's*, *op. cit.*; Jody Powell response: press release, Feb. 2, 1976; Wallace interviewed by Drew: Elizabeth Drew, *American Journal, the Events of 1976* (N.Y., Random House, 1976), pp. 123-127; Julian Bond criticism of Carter: Julian Bond, "Why I Don't Support Jimmy Carter," *The Nation*, Apr. 17, 1976; Carter willing to be on McGovern ticket: Kandy Stroud, *How Jimmy Won* (N.Y., Morrow, 1977), p. 208; Jules Witcover, *Marathon, The Pursuit of the Presidency 1972-1976* (N.Y., Viking, 1977), p. 106; Young presented Carter name: *Washington Post*, Apr. 23, 1976; Julian Bond, *The Nation*, *op. cit.*; Rafshoon-Caddell meeting: Jules Witcover, *Marathon, op. cit.*, pp. 106-107; Caddell on Carter's chances: Kandy Stroud, *How Jimmy Won, op. cit.*, p. 191; Carter quoted on Eagleton: *Kansas City Times*, July 14, 1972; Rafshoon quoted by Stroud: Kandy Stroud, *How Jimmy Won, op. cit.*, p. 208; Bourne on Carter view of Muskie: *ibid.*, p. 22-23; Bourne memo: *ibid.*, pp. 23-24; McGovern-Eagleton episode: Theodore H. White, *The Making of the President 1972* (N.Y., Atheneum, 1973), pp. 204-206; Bond quoted in *Constitution:* Aug. 1, 1972; Carter quoted after McGovern-Wallace meeting: UPI dispatch, Aug. 4, 1972; Carter meeting with aides: Martin Schram, *Running for President, A Journal of the Carter Campaign* (N.Y., Pocketbooks, 1977), pp. 58-59; Rafshoon memo: *ibid.*, pp. 59-60; Jordan memo: *ibid.*, pp. 62-69; Jules

Witcover, *Marathon*, *op. cit.*, pp. 111-115; *Newsweek*, May 10, 1976; Garry Wills quoted: *Atlantic*, June 1976.

CHAPTER 8

Patrick quoted: *Atlanta Constitution*, July 13, 1973; Carter on tone: *Atlanta Constitution*, Nov. 30, 1972; Carter support for Strauss: *Atlanta Constitution*, Nov. 30, Dec. 9 and 10, 1972; *Kansas City Star*, Dec. 3, 1972; *Orlando Sentinel*, Dec. 7, 1972; Gilligan quoted: *Cleveland Plain Dealer*, Apr. 29, 1973; Osborne in *New Republic:* reprinted in *Washington Star*, Jan. 2, 1978; Brill's article in *Harper's:* March 1976; Carter attacks Nixon: *Atlanta Constitution*, Jan. 19 and 20, 1973; Carter family at Nixon Inaugural: Hugh Carter, *Cousin Beedie and Cousin Hot*, *op. cit.*, pp. 132-133; Carter on Rafshoon contract: *Atlanta Constitution*, Apr. 14, 1976; removal of stumps controversy: *Atlanta Constitution*, Jan. 27, 1971; Jan. 15 and 16, July 6, 1973; National Press Club speech: *Washington Post*, Feb. 11, 1973; *Atlanta Constitution*, Feb. 10, 1973; Jules Witcover, *Marathon*, *op. cit.*, p. 115; Ziegler quoted: *Atlanta Constitution*, Mar. 1, 1973; vanden Heuvel quoted: *Village Voice*, Feb. 9, 1976; Carter support of Agnew: *Washington Post*, July 6, 1976; Maddox view: *Atlanta Constitution*, June 18, 1971; *Meet the Press* transcript: *The Presidential Campaign 1976*, *op. cit.*, pp. 293-294; gifts from corporations: *The New York Times*, Apr. 1, 1976; *Atlanta Constitution*, Apr. 4, May 25 and 29, 1972; *Village Voice*, Apr. 5 and Oct. 11, 1976; Coke connection: *Newsweek*, Feb. 7, 1977; *Parade* on trip to Israel: Aug. 28, 1977; Trilateral Commission: *Why Not the Best?*, *op. cit.*, pp. 145-146; *Washington Post*, June 19, 1978; *Playboy* quote: November 1976; Carter-Strauss meeting: Jules Witcover, *Marathon*, *op. cit.*, p. 117; John Osborne, *op. cit.*; Jordan to DNC: James Wooten, *Dasher*, *op. cit.*, p. 339; *New York Daily News*, Sept. 17, 1976; John Osborne, *op. cit.*; Carter thought of Talmadge seat: *New York Daily News*, *op. cit.*; Grimes article: republished in *Los Angeles Times*, July 29, 1976; Carter's secret poll episode: *Atlanta Constitution*, June 28, Nov. 30, Dec. 5 and 8, 1973; *Atlanta Journal*, Nov. 29 and Dec. 5, 1973; King. Sr., on Lance: *Atlanta Constitution*, Aug. 7, 1974; Howell campaign: *Washington Post*, Nov. 1, 1973; Jordan-Carter denials: *Atlanta Constitution*, July 20 and Aug. 30, 1973; Carter on Mondale and self: *The Atlanta Journal and Constitution Magazine*, Apr. 28, 1974; Schram quoted: *Running for President*, *op. cit.*, p. 70; Nixon techniques: *National Journal*, Nov. 29, 1975; Carter on Watergate in spring 1973; Clayton Fritchey, *Washington Post*, May 20, 1973; Robert Shogan, *Promises to Keep, Carter's First 100 Days* (N.Y., Crowell, 1977), p. 35; Strauss realization: John Osborne, *op. cit.*; Martin Schram, *Running for President*, *op. cit.*, p. 70; Carter and Strauss at Governors Conference: Robert Shogan, *Promises to Keep*, *op. cit.*, pp. 23-24; Carter's statements on Nixon: *Atlanta Constitution*, Apr. 15, 1974; Carter on Nixon guilty: *Atlanta Constitution*, June 3, 1974; Carter on Nixon resignation: *Atlanta Constitution*, Aug. 9, 1974; Carter on Ford's energy policy: *The Presidential Campaign 1976*, *op. cit.*, pp. 653-656; Carter on oil companies: *Atlanta Constitution*, July 31, 1974; Carter attacks on Nixon-Connally: *Atlanta Constitution*, June 1, 1973; Billy Carter's gas shipments:

St. Petersburg Times dispatch republished in *Washington Star*, Feb. 27, 1978; Jack Anderson, *Washington Post*, July 22, 1978.

CHAPTER 9

Thompson-Carter meet: Hunter S. Thompson, "Fear and Loathing on the Campaign Trail '76," *Rolling Stone*, June 3, 1976; Vic Gold quoted: Vic Gold, *PR as in President* (Garden City, N.Y., Doubleday, 1977), p. 86; Carter interview in *Playboy:* November 1976; Carter-Dylan meeting: Robert Sam Anson, *New Times*, Sept. 3, 1976; Carter interview by Sally Quinn: *Washington Post*, Mar. 28, 1976; Denver-Carter meeting: James Wooten, *Dasher, op. cit.*, p. 365; Carter-Walden friendship: Robert Sam Anson, *New Times, op. cit.;* Jordan memo re Wallace-Kennedy: Jules Witcover, *Marathon, op. cit.*, pp. 132-138; Carter "running" quote in *Los Angeles Times:* June 27, 1976; Carter-O'Neill conversation: Martin Schram, *Running for President, op. cit.*, p. 71; Carter announces for President: *The Presidential Campaign 1976, op. cit.*, pp. 3-10; Carter speech at Atlanta rally: *ibid.*, pp. 11-13; *Newsweek* quoted: Dec. 23, 1974; plan to win: *Time*, Oct. 4, 1976; K. Reich, *Los Angeles Times, op. cit.; Washington Post*, May 9, 1976; letter to friends: *The Presidential Campaign 1976, op. cit.*, pp. 1-2; *National Journal* quoted: Nov. 29, 1975; Reston in N.Y. *Times:* Feb. 7, 1975; Stroud in *New York:* Mar. 24, 1975; Tuck in *Playboy:* March 1976; Anderson in *The New York Times Magazine:* Dec. 14, 1975; Carter on harpsichord music: *Washington Post*, May 9, 1976; Carter on stock car racing: *Washington Post*, Mar. 28, 1976; *Playboy* interview: November 1976; Walden help: Robert Sam Anson, *New Times, op. cit.;* Witcover quoted: *Marathon, op. cit.*, p. 258; Askew on Carter: Martin Schram, *Running for President, op. cit.*, p. 94; Julian Bond quoted: James Wooten, *Dasher, op. cit.*, p. 338; Powell on local media: Jules Witcover, *Marathon, op. cit.*, pp. 195-196; Kraft trick on *Register* poll: *ibid.*, p. 201; Tom Wicker, *Washington Star*, Oct. 29, 1975; Iowa caucuses results: Jules Witcover, *Marathon, op. cit.*, pp. 213-214; Carter appeal in Iowa: *Time*, Dec. 1, 1975; abortion issue in Iowa: Jules Witcover, *Marathon, op. cit.*, pp. 206-207; Carter-Humphrey potshots: *Newsweek*, Feb. 2, 1976; Mississippi results: Jules Witcover, *Marathon, op. cit.*, p. 215; New Hampshire primary: *ibid.*, p. 228; Caddell on "trust thing": James Wooten, *Dasher, op. cit.*, pp. 355-356; Broder column: *Washington Post*, Jan. 18, 1976; Carter-Loeb meeting: James Wooten, *Dasher, op. cit.*, p. 358; Carter letter on right-to-work: Jules Witcover, *Marathon, op. cit.*, pp. 235-236; Prof. Patterson's paper: "Press Coverage . . . in Presidential Primaries: The 1976 Democratic Race," Annual Meeting of the American Political Science Assn., 1977, Washington, D.C.; Carter on Governors' coolness: *Washington Post*, July 7, 1976; Carter on attack on liberalism: *Time*, Feb. 2, 1976.

CHAPTER 10

Evans and Novak column: *Washington Post*, Jan. 8, 1976; Kraft column: *Washington Post*, Jan. 14, 1976; *Time* questions Carter advisers: Feb. 2, 1976; *Village Voice* on N. Korea incident: Jan. 12, 1976; Carter on scrutiny: *Newsweek*, Mar. 8, 1976; Carter on too much attention: Jules Witcover, *Marathon, op. cit.*,

p. 226; *Harper's* article by Brill: March 1976; reaction to Brill article: *Time*, Feb. 16, 1976; Lewis Lapham, *Harper's*, May 1976; Jack Germond, *Washington Star*, Feb. 4, 1976; Kandy Stroud, *How Jimmy Won*, *op. cit.*, p. 98; Henry A. Grunwald, *Time*, Mar. 8, 1976; *Enquirer* puffery: *The Washington Post Magazine*, Aug. 6, 1978; Carter's UFO experience: Tom Tiede (NEA), *Milwaukee Journal*, Feb. 8, 1978; *New York*, Mar. 6, 1978; Carter on home mortgages: *Boston Globe*, Feb. 26, 1976; Jules Witcover, *Marathon*, *op. cit.*, pp. 245-246; Carter attacks critics: *ibid.*, p. 247; Udall and McGovern aide strike back: *Time*, Mar. 8, 1976; Powell-Udall disagree: Kandy Stroud, *How Jimmy Won*, *op. cit.*, p. 259; Caddell-Carter on Jackson: Jules Witcover, *Marathon*, *op. cit.*, p. 248; Clephas quoted by Stroud: *How Jimmy Won*, *op. cit.*, p. 260; Weaver on Carter-Jackson votes: Paul Weaver, "Captives of Melodrama," *The New York Times Magazine*, Aug. 29, 1976; Carter critical of *Globe*: *Boston Globe*, Mar. 3, 1976; Carter snappish with press: Martin Schram, *Running for President*, *op. cit.*, p. 84; Reeves on Florida primary: *New York*, Mar. 22, 1976; Schram quoted: *Running for President*, *op. cit.*, pp. 89-90; Carter on Jackson: *ibid.*, p. 85; Jules Witcover, *Marathon*, *op. cit.*, p. 257; Florida election results: *The New York Times*, Mar. 10, 1976; Jenkins quoted: Richard Reeves, *Convention* (N.Y., Harcourt Brace Jovanovich, 1977), p. 46; Kraft quoted: Tom Bethall, "Anybody But Broder: Our Stop-the-Columnists Movement," *Washington Monthly*, July/Aug. 1976; Illinois primary: *The New York Times*, Mar. 17, 1976; Stapleton help: Martin Schram, *Running for President*, *op. cit.*, pp. 98-100; *Meet the Press* transcript: *The Presidential Campaign 1976*, *op. cit.*, pp. 296-297; Carter on religion for votes: Martin Schram, *Running for President*, *op. cit.*, p. 105; Reeves article: *New York*, Mar. 22, 1976; Bremer ghost: Jules Witcover, *Marathon*, *op. cit.*, pp. 273, 279; Carter-Humphrey attacks: Elizabeth Drew, *American Journal, The Events of 1976*, *op. cit.*, pp. 139-140; Carter-Bond attacks: *ibid.*, p. 140; *Washington Star*, Mar. 29, 1978; Wisconsin results: Martin Schram, *Running for President*, *op. cit.*, p. 132; Jules Witcover, *Marathon*, *op. cit.*, pp. 285-286; New York primary: *ibid.*, pp. 294-295; Prof. Robinson in *Public Opinion*: May/June 1978; "ethnic purity" remark: *New York Daily News*, Apr. 2, 1976; Jules Witcover, *Marathon*, *op. cit.*, pp. 302-309; Martin Schram, *Running for President*, *op. cit.*, pp. 135-137; *Philadelphia Inquirer*, Apr. 12, 1976; Carter-King, Sr., meeting: Jules Witcover, *Marathon*, *op. cit.*, pp. 307-308; Dr. Allen's opinion: Kandy Stroud, *How Jimmy Won*, *op. cit.*, pp. 171-172; Shrum episode: *ibid.*, pp. 291-294; Martin Schram, *Running for President*, *op. cit.*, pp. 157-160; Jules Witcover, *Marathon*, *op. cit.*, pp. 319-326; *Washington Post*, May 3, 1976; Mary McGrory, *Washington Star*, May 3, 1976; Robert Scheer, *Playboy*, November 1976; Young reaction: *Village Voice*, June 28, 1976.

CHAPTER 11
Carter on "beating" Humphrey: *Washington Post*, Nov. 4, 1976; Kirbo on Humphrey: *The New York Times*, July 14, 1976; Church and Brown defeat Carter: Martin Schram, *Running for President*, *op. cit.*, pp. 157-163; Jules Witcover, *Marathon*, *op. cit.*, pp. 333-337; Vic Gold on Brown: *PR as in President*, *op. cit.*, p. 163; Carter relations with Georgetown: *Washington Post*,

Mar. 17, 1976; *Newsweek,* Mar. 29, 1976; *Time,* Mar. 29, 1976; Bayh endorsement: Elizabeth Drew, *American Journal, The Events of 1976, op. cit.,* p. 174;
Udall in Michigan: *New Republic,* May 29, 1976; Martin Schram, *op. cit.,* pp.
164-165; Kennedy remark: *The New York Times,* May 26, 1976; Nordan quoted:
Washington Post, May 29, 1976; Carter attacks critics: *ibid.;* Martin Schram, *op.
cit.,* p. 176; Carter testy: *National Journal,* May 29, 1976; *Boston Globe,* Mar.
30, 1976; *National Observer,* Apr. 3, 1976; Carter "enemies" list in press: *The
Atlantic,* July 1976; Carter vindictiveness: Evans & Novak, *Washington Post,*
June 3, 1976; *The New York Times,* May 30 and July 1, 1976; Buchanan quoted:
New York Daily News, June 3, 1976; Anderson background: Martin Schram,
Running for President, op. cit., pp. 170-172; *Wall Street Journal* article by A.
Hunt: May 13, 1976; Carter in Beverly Hills: Evans & Novak, *Washington Post,*
May 25, 1976; Martin Schram, *op. cit.,* p. 263; Carter on Ambassadors: *Inquiry,*
Nov. 21, 1977; *Face the Nation* transcript, *The Presidential Campaign 1976, op.
cit.,* pp. 99-108; Daley on Ohio primary: Jules Witcover, *Marathon, op. cit.,* pp.
349-350; Len O'Connor, *Requiem, The Decline and Demise of Mayor Daley and
His Era* (Chicago, Contemporary Books, 1977), pp. 71-72; *New York Times-CBS*
survey: *The New York Times,* June 9, 1976; Carter promise to Wallace: *Time,*
June 21, 1976; Humphrey on Carter organization: *Washington Post,* July 3, 1976;
Shields quoted in *Times:* July 12, 1976; Brown criticism: *Newsweek,* June 21,
1976; *Time,* June 21, 1976; Cloud in *Time:* June 21, 1976; Hart column:
Columbus Dispatch, July 12, 1976; Carter-Strauss relations: Evans & Novak,
Washington Post, May 11, 1976; *The New York Times,* July 7, 1976; Governors
Mandel and Lucey line up: *ibid.;* Convention site selection: Richard Reeves,
Convention, op. cit., p. 32; Complete analysis of week's proceedings: Richard
Reeves, *Convention, op. cit.;* Buckley quoted: *Washington Star,* July 16, 1976;
Rolling Stone party: *Washington Star,* July 18, 1976; *National Review Bulletin,*
Aug. 13, 1976; Mott quoted: *Washington Post,* July 17, 1976; Walters-Rafshoon
conversation: *Washington Post,* July 15, 1976; *National Review* on "Imperial
Presidency": Aug. 26, 1976; Stein in *Wall Street Journal:* July 19, 1976; Carter-
Rodino meeting: Martin Schram, *Running for President, op. cit.,* p. 231; Glenn
tax returns: *The Presidential Campaign 1976, op. cit.,* pp. 315-316; Rep. Jordan
on Carter: *Wall Street Journal,* July 13, 1976; Mondale chosen VP: Richard
Reeves, *Convention, op. cit.,* pp. 17-18; Jules Witcover, *Marathon,* p. 367;
liberal reaction: *Washington Post,* July 20, 1976; *New Times,* Sept. 3, 1976;
Mondale as "Mr. Busing": *The New York Times,* July 25, 1976; Carter press
conference on choice of Mondale: *The Presidential Campaign 1976, op. cit.,* pp.
324-329; press conference on airplane: Kandy Stroud, *How Jimmy Won, op. cit.,*
pp. 329-330; Rafshoon on Carter failings: *Richmond News-Leader,* July 15, 1976.

CHAPTER 12
Mondale speech: Richard Reeves, *Convention, op. cit.,* p. 195; Carter
acceptance speech: *The Presidential Campaign 1976, op. cit.,* p. 349; Buchanan
quoted: *New York Daily News,* July 27, 1976; Carter interview by Hearst: *The
Presidential Campaign 1976, op. cit.,* p. 440; Reeves on Carter convention
bugging: *Convention, op. cit.,* pp. 68-72; *The New York Times,* Dec. 6, 1976;

Rather interview of Reeves: transcript, *Who's Who*, Vol. 1, Broadcast 17, as broadcast on CBS-TV network, June 5, 1977; Caddell on Saudi payroll: William Safire, *The New York Times*, July 22, 1976; *Washington Star*, July 20, 1976; *New Republic* on Caddell: Nov. 25, 1976; Caddell nuclear business: *The New York Times*, Aug. 2, 1976; Mondale-IDS connection: *Washington Post*, July 21, 1976; *The New York Times*, July 21, 1976; Carter at "21": *Washington Post*, July 23, 1976; *Chicago Tribune*, July 28, 1976; *Wall Street Journal*, July 23, 1976; *Village Voice*, Aug. 2, 1976; *The New York Times*, July 26, 1976; FEC ordered repayment: UPI, *Washington Post*, July 14, 1978; Carter lead in Harris Poll: Martin Schram, *Running for President*, *op. cit.*, p. 244; *New Republic* on foreign policy advisers: Aug. 21 and 28, 1976; Carter requests transition funds: *Wall Street Journal*, July 19, 1976; campaign headquarters: Jules Witcover, *op. cit.*, p. 516; Jordan quoted by Shogan: Robert Shogan, *Promises to Keep, Carter's First 100 Days*, *op. cit.*, p. 49; New Hampshire speech: *The Presidential Campaign 1976*, *op. cit.*, pp. 462-465; *Washington Star*, Aug. 4, 1976; Carter attack on Republicans: *The New York Times*, Aug. 4, 1976; Carter dismay at reaction: Martin Schram, *op. cit.*, pp. 248-249; Carter on Nixon-Ford link: *Washington Post*, Aug. 2, 1976; Carter attack on Ford "appointed" and limousines: *Washington Post*, Aug. 24, 1976; footnote on campaign sedan: AP, *Washington Post*, Aug. 25, 1976; Beverly Hills parties: Kandy Stroud, *How Jimmy Won*, *op. cit.*, pp. 337-341; Jules Witcover, *Marathon*, *op. cit.*, p. 525; Phillips criticism of Carter on rural Georgia: Jeffrey Hart, *Baltimore News-American*, Sept. 19, 1976; Wallace attack and apology by Carter: *Washington Post*, Aug. 8, 1976; Bush gaffe: *Washington Post*, Aug. 13, 1976; embargoes gaffe: *Washington Post*, Aug. 29, 1976; *Washington Star*, Aug. 27, 1976; abortion problem: Martin Schram, *op. cit.*, pp. 251-252; Carl Rowan, *Washington Star*, Sept. 8, 1976; *Washington Post*, Aug. 13, 1976; Caddell on polls: Martin Schram, *op. cit.*, p. 266.

CHAPTER 13

Campaign kickoff: Martin Schram, *Running for President*, *op. cit.*, pp. 302-304; Vic Gold, *PR as in President*, *op. cit.*, p. 206; *New York Daily News*, Sept. 7, 1976; *The Presidential Campaign 1976*, *op. cit.*, *pp. 701-705; stock car races:* Martin Schram, *op. cit.*, pp. 304-305; Kandy Stroud, *How Jimmy Won*, *op. cit.*, *p. 346;* Carter at Columbus Circle: Martin Schram, *op. cit;* p. 306; Carter speech at Brooklyn College: *The Presidential Campaign 1976*, *op. cit.*, pp. 705-708; Carter attacks FBI Director: *Washington Star*, Sept. 8, 1976; Jules Witcover, *Marathon*, *op. cit.*, pp. 547-548; McGrory criticism: *Washington Star*, Sept. 14, 1976; place of Philadelphia meeting changed: *National Observer*, Sept. 18, 1976; *Washington Star*, Sept. 8, 1976; dragging out Kelley a mistake: Jules Witcover, *op. cit.*, pp. 552-553; Daley-Carter in Chicago: Len O'Connor, *Requiem*, *op. cit.*, pp. 144-146; *The New York Times*, Sept. 13, 1976; Martin Schram, *op. cit.*, p. 312; Jules Witcover, *op. cit.*, p. 552; Carter criticism of Ford on Medicaid: *The New York Times*, Sept. 11, 1976; *Chicago Tribune*, Sept. 21, 1976; AP interview on taxes: *The Presidential Campaign 1976*, *op. cit.*, p. 764; Ron Nessen, *It Sure Looks Different from the Inside* (Chicago, Playboy, 1978), pp. 255-256; Victor Lasky, NANA, Nov. 1, 1978; *Washington Post*, Sept. 20,

1976; Carter's taxes: *Washington Post*, Sept. 4, 1976; McCarthy campaign: Martin Schram, *op. cit.*, pp. 317-318; *(Meet the Press)* as quoted in *National Review Bulletin*, Sept. 7, 1976; *Wall Street Journal*, Oct. 22, 1976; *New York Post*, Oct. 14, 1976; *Playboy* interview: November 1976; reaction to *Playboy* interview: *Time*, Oct. 4, 1976; *The New York Times*, Sept. 30, 1976; *Washington Star*, Sept. 23 and 25, 1976; Jules Witcover, *op. cit.*, pp. 561-583; Martin Schram, *op. cit.*, pp. 332-343; Al Hirt on Carter: *Time*, Nov. 1, 1976; Safire on *Playboy* interview: *The New York Times*, Sept. 30, 1976; Carter meeting with press in San Diego: Martin Schram, *op. cit.*, pp. 343-344; Carter on Supreme Court: *Washington Post*, Sept. 14 and 15, 1976; *Washington Star*, Sept. 30, 1976; *The New York Times*, Sept. 30, 1976; preparations for first debate: Vic Gold, *PR as in President*, *op. cit.*, p. 217; Ron Nessen, *op. cit.*, p. 259; first debate: *Time*, Oct. 4, 1976; Kandy Stroud, *op. cit.*, pp. 360-372; Buchanan quoted: *New York Daily News*, Sept. 5, 1976; Auletta quoted: *Village Voice*, Oct. 11, 1976; Butz incident: Jules Witcover, *op. cit.*, pp. 590-592; Martin Schram, *op. cit.*, pp. 346-347, Ron Nessen, *op. cit.*, pp. 280-281; Billy Carter's racial slurs: *Playboy*, November 1976; (footnote) *The Jewish Weekly* (Wash., D.C.), Dec. 28, 1978; Safire on staffer racial jokes: *The New York Times*, Oct. 1, 1976; Stroud told how to get interview: Kandy Stroud, *op. cit.*, p. 272; Ford-lobbyist flap: Jules Witcover, *op. cit.*, p. 584; Ron Nessen, *op. cit.*, pp. 286-287; Bartlett quoted: *Washington Star*, Sept. 7, 1976; Gulf lobbyist gave money to Carter: AP, *Baltimore Sun*, June 3, 1978; allegation that Ford misused contribution: Jules Witcover, *op. cit.*, pp. 584-588; *Washington Star*, Oct. 12, 1976; Ron Nessen, *op. cit.*, pp. 291-292; Ruff nomination: *Washington Star*, Sept. 23, 1977; criticism of Woodstein by Osborne: *Human Events*, Oct. 23, 1976; John Dean accusation against Ford: Ron Nessen, *op. cit.*, pp. 296-298; AP, *Los Angeles Times*, Oct. 14, 1976; Michael Novak quoted: *Washington Star*, Sept. 5, 1976; Carter attack on Ford as "stonewalling": *Washington Star*, Oct. 11, 1976; Carter campaign manual: *Dossier*, February 1977; *Washington Star*, Oct. 11, 1976; second debate: Ron Nessen, *op. cit.*, pp. 268-269; William Buckley, Jr., *Washington Star*, Oct. 15, 1976; Carter overkill on Polish remark: Mary McGrory, *Chicago Tribune*, Oct. 20, 1976; *Washington Star*, Oct. 11, 1976; Carter contradictions: *Human Events*, Oct. 23, 1976; Buchanan on code words: *New York Daily News*, Oct. 14, 1976; Sevareid quoted: as reported in *Washington Post*, Oct. 14, 1976; Carter postelection analysis: Jules Witcover, *op. cit.*, pp. 644-645; third debate: *Washington Post*, Oct. 23, 1976; *Time*, Nov. 1, 1976; Joe Kraft, *Washington Post*, Oct. 26, 1976; Mondale on Watergate: *Washington Star*, Oct. 28, 1976; *Washington Post*, Oct. 31, 1976; Hafif ad: republished in *The New York Times*, Nov. 1, 1976; Ron Nessen, *op. cit.*, pp. 308-309; Mudd summary: *The New York Times*, Nov. 1, 1976; liberals reaction to campaign: *Washington Post*, Nov. 23, 1976; Safire on campaign: *The New York Times*, Nov. 1, 1976; Caddell memo: Patrick H. Caddell, "Initial Working Paper on Political Strategy," Dec. 10, 1976; Carter criticism of TV coverage: *New York Daily News*, Nov. 8, 1976.

CHAPTER 14

Carter carrying his luggage: Betty Beale, *Washington Star*, Nov. 24, 1976; Nessen on visit to White House: *It Sure Looks Different from the Inside, op. cit.*, pp. 322-323; Inauguration: *Time*, Jan. 31, 1977; *National Review Bulletin*, Feb. 11, 1977; Robert Shogan, *Promises to Keep, op. cit.*, pp. 100-109; Nicholas Thimmesch, column, Jan. 22, 1977; Tyrrell criticism of Carter: as quoted in *Time*, Mar. 7, 1977; Billy Carter on others "commercializing" on brother's election: *Washington Star*, Nov. 14, 1976; staff salaries increased: *The New York Times*, Mar. 24 and Nov. 15, 1977; *Washington Star*, June 22, 1977; *Human Events*, Nov. 26, 1977; staff size increased: *Washington Post*, Mar. 31, 1977; *Washington Star*, Apr. 16 and June 17, 1977; Amy's public schools: *Human Events*, July 1, 1978; *Washington Post*, June 16, 1978; *Washington Star*, Nov. 29, 1976; Caddell memo: Patrick H. Caddell, "Initial Working Paper on Political Strategy," Dec. 10, 1976; Caddell pleased after ninety days: *The Trib* (N.Y.), June 27, 1977; O'Neill-Carter relationship: Nicholas Thimmesch, column, Feb. 20, 1978; Mary McGrory, *Washington Star*, Dec. 11, 1977; O'Neill defense of Carter: AP, *The New York Times*, May 9, 1977; Wieghart quoted: *New York Daily News*, May 13, 1977; Greider in *Washington Post*, Dec. 26, 1976; Carter on "insiders" and "outsiders": as quoted by Roger Morris, *Harper's*, October 1977; Greider on Vance: *op. cit.*; Morris quoted: *Harper's*, October 1977; Brzezinski background: Greider, *op. cit.*; Kissinger-Brzezinski differ: *Newsweek*, Apr. 26, 1976; Harold Brown background: Robert Shogan, *Promises to Keep, op. cit.*, p. 86; Greider, *op. cit.*; Califano background: Greider, *op. cit.*; Roger Morris, *Harper's*, *op. cit.*; Sorensen nomination: Mary McGrory, *Washington Star*, Jan. 18, 1977; *Washington Post*, Jan. 18, 1977; *The New York Times*, Jan. 17, 1977; Evans & Novak, *Washington Post*, Jan. 17, 1977; *Human Events*, Jan. 22, 1977; Robert Shogan, *op. cit.*, pp. 91-93; Bell nomination: *ibid.*, pp. 88-91; *Newsweek*, Dec. 27, 1976; Warnke nomination: *Human Events*, Nov. 11, 1978; Robert Shogan, *op. cit.*, pp. 216-218; Prof. Pipes in *Commentary*: as quoted in *Human Events*, *op. cit.*; Warnke verification opinion and action: William Safire, *The New York Times*, Apr. 21, 1977; Taussig on Carter advisers: as quoted in *Human Events*, Nov. 11, 1978; McGovern and Wattenberg on foreign policy team: Robert Shogan, *op. cit.*, p. 217; Sam Brown background: *Washington Post Magazine*, Feb. 5, 1978; Mary McGrory, *Washington Star*, Feb. 19, 1978; *Newsweek*, Jan. 2, 1978; Patrick Buchanan, *Human Events*, July 22, 1978; Jack Anderson, *Washington Post*, Dec. 14, 1978; Sevareid on antiwar people: as quoted in *Human Events*, Oct. 8, 1977; Costanza in the White House: *The New York Times*, July 4, 1978; *Newsweek*, Nov. 7, 1977; *Washington Post*, July 26, 1978; criticism of Costanza fund-raising: Patrick Buchanan, *Washington Weekly*, Nov. 25, 1977; *Washington Post*, Oct. 20, 1977; Costanza on Lance: James Wooten, *The New York Times*, July 4, 1978; Costanza office moved: *Baltimore Sun*, Aug. 2, 1978; *Washington Star* comment: Aug. 3, 1978; Why Young must stay: *Washington Post*, Oct. 1, 1978; *Wall Street Journal*, July 24, 1978; *National Review* comment: Aug. 4, 1978; Jordan quoted by Shogan: Robert Shogan, *op. cit.*, pp. 219-220; *Washington Star* on "yakkita inepta": July 14, 1978; Lerner in *New York Post*: July 17, 1978; Carter at Congressional Black Caucus dinner: *Washington Post*, Oct. 1, 1978.

CHAPTER 15

Billy Carter took Fifth Amendment: UPI, *Washington Star*, Oct. 26, 1978; FEC criticized by Kilpatrick: *Washington Star*, Aug. 27, 1977; Carter staff falsified travel vouchers: *ibid.; Human Events*, May 28, 1977; AP, *Miami Herald*, Dec. 30, 1977; Vesco-Carter connection: *Newsweek*, Sept. 25, 1978; *Time*, Oct. 2, 1978; Abelson on inflation: *Barron's*, Sept. 18, 1978; Marro quoted in *Washington Star:* Sept. 25, 1978; Carter note to Bell: *Washington Post*, Sept 20, 1978; William Safire, *Washington Star*, Sept. 26 and 29, 1978; *Christian Science Monitor* on Vesco matter: Sept. 28, 1978; Kirbo investigates Jack Anderson: Jack Anderson, *Washington Post*, Oct. 27, 1978; *Atlanta Journal/Constitution*, Oct. 8, 1978; *Washington Post*, Oct. 9, 1978; Kirbo-Herring conversation: *Washington Post*, Nov. 5, 1978; *CBS Evening News*, Oct. 19, 1978; Milliken-Carter connection: *Washington Star*, May 3, 1978; *Washington Monthly*, June 1978; *Baltimore Sun*, Sept. 26, 1978; *Washington Post*, Sept. 21 and 26, 1978; Kirbo to monitor GSA investigation: *Washington Post*, Sept. 8, 1978; *Washington Post* comment: Sept. 15, 1978; GSA firing of Griffin: *Time*, Sept. 25, 1978; Martin Schram, *Washington Post*, Aug. 10, 1978; *The New York Times*, July 29, Aug. 3 and 4, 1978; James Dickinson, *Washington Star*, Aug. 14, 1978; *Washington Post*, July 31 and Aug. 11, 1978; Anderson on Griffin sabotage: *Washington Post*, Dec. 18, 1978; O'Neill's finances: *The New York Times*, Apr. 9, 1978; *Village Voice*, Apr. 17, 1978; *Boston Herald American*, as quoted by UPI, *Washington Post*, Oct. 24, 1978; other criticisms of Koreagate investigation: *Washington Post*, July 19, 1977; William Safire, *The New York Times*, June 22 and July 20, 1978; *Washington Post*, July 14 and Oct. 14, 1978; O'Neill wanted to suppress comic strip: *Los Angeles Times* dispatch in *Philadelphia Inquirer*, June 22, 1978; Safire on cover-up heroes: *The New York Times*, July 20, 1978; Bayh-Koreagate connection: William Safire, *Washington Star*, Oct. 20, 1978; Civiletti closed Bayh case: *Washington Post*, Jan. 6, 1979; Lance-Carter connection: Jack Anderson, *Washington Post*, Dec. 5, 1978; William Safire, *The New York Times*, July 21 and Aug. 11, 1977; *Newsweek*, Aug. 15 and 29, 1977; editorial, *The New York Times*, Aug. 21, 1977; editorial, *Washington Post*, Sept. 8, 1977; *Washington Star*, Sept. 14, 1977; *Time*, Sept. 19, 1977; Haynes Johnson and George Lardner, Jr., *Washington Post*, Sept. 25, 1977, and Sept. 21, 1978; William Safire, *The New York Times Magazine*, Oct. 16, 1977; *The New York Times*, Apr. 27, 1978; Mondale on Lance vindication: AP, *Washington Post*, Aug. 20, 1977; *Washington Star* comment: Sept. 15, 1977; *Philadelphia Inquirer* comment: Dec. 5, 1977; Safire on Lance passport: *The New York Times*, Dec. 12, 1977; SEC charges Lance: *The New York Times*, Apr. 27, 1978; Billy Carter denounces press: *The New York Times*, Nov. 6, 1978; Lance attacks Jews and press: *Washington Post*, Aug. 10, 1978; Safire on Billy and President refuse to make tax returns public: *The New York Times*, Jan. 8, 1979; Anderson on Lance as 1980 issue: *Washington Post*, Dec. 5, 1978; Marston affair: *Philadelphia Inquirer*, editorials, Jan. 10 and Feb. 1; Jan. 11, 1978; *The New York Times*, Jan. 13, 23, 25, 26 (editorial), 29 (editorial), 31; Apr. 2, 26, and 27, 1978; William Safire, *The New York Times*, Jan. 23 and 26, 1978, and "The Philadelphia Story," *The New York Times Magazine*, Feb. 19, 1978; *Washington Post*, Jan. 14

(editorial), 27, 31, Mar. 8, 10 (editorial), and Apr. 25, 1978; *Washington Star,* Jan. 16 (editorial); Mary McGrory, Jan. 17; James J. Kilpatrick, Feb. 11, 1978; *Human Events,* Jan. 28 and Feb. 4, 1978; James A. Wechsler, *New York Post,* Jan. 19, 1978; T.D Schellhardt, *Wall Street Journal,* Jan. 18, 1978; *The Register* (Calif.), Feb. 2, 1978; *Boston Globe* editorial, Feb. 1, 1978; *Time,* Mar. 6, 1978; Walter Karp, *Politicks & Other Human Interests,* Mar. 14, 1978; Bourne affair: *Washington Post,* July 20, 21 (editorial); Meg Greenfield, July 26, Charles B. Seib, July 26; Aug. 22, 1978; *The New York Times,* (Wooten), July 22; William Safire, July 24, 1978; *Washington Star,* July 19, 23; Mary McGrory, July 21 and 25; Michael Novak, Aug. 2, 13, and 23; William Safire, Sept. 11, 1978; *Baltimore Sun,* July 21 and 22, 1978; *Christian Science Monitor* (editorials), July 24 and Aug. 23, 1978; *Atlanta Journal/Constitution,* July 23, 1978; *Baltimore News Amerivan,* July 23, 1978; *Human Events,* July 29, 1978; Cockburn & Ridgeway, *Village Voice,* July 31, 1978; *Boston Globe,* Aug. 6, 1978; Nicholas von Hoffman, *Philadelphia Inquirer,* Aug. 5, 1978; Les Kinsolving, *Washington Weekly,* Aug. 31, 1978; *Newsweek,* Jan. 15, 1979; White and Carter aide slander Republican: Evans & Novak, *Washington Post,* Dec. 29, 1978.

CHAPTER 16

Carter meeting with congressional leaders: *Chicago Tribune,* Dec. 24, 1978; Carter speech on China and remark afterward: *Newsweek,* Dec. 25, 1978; Oakes in *The New York Times:* Dec. 29, 1978; Billy Carter and Libyans: *New York Daily News,* Jan. 12, 1979; *The New York Times,* Jan. 12, 1979; *Washington Post,* Jan. 11 and 12, 1979; *Washington Star,* Jan. 11, 1979; *Baltimore Sun,* Jan. 12, 1979; William Safire, *The New York Times,* Jan. 15, 1979; Carter-Shah relations: AP, *New York Daily News,* Dec. 31, 1978; James Wieghart, *New York Daily News,* Jan. 3, 1979; Victor Lasky (NANA), *Washington Weekly Globe,* Jan. 4, 1979; Constellation orders: *The New York Times,* Jan. 3, 1979; William Safire, *The New York Times,* Jan. 4, 1979; Macmillan quoted: Evans & Novak, *Washington Post,* Jan. 1, 1979; Guadeloupe meeting: *Newsweek,* Jan. 15, 1979; Osborne on Camp David meeting: *New Republic,* Sept. 30, 1978; Carter-Begin relations: James Reston, *The New York Times,* Dec. 10, 1978; *Washington Post,* Dec. 15, 1978; Sadat view: editorial, *Wall Street Journal,* Sept. 19, 1978; Carter involved in Israeli-Egyptian problem: *Washington Post,* Jan. 4 and 5, 1978; *The New York Times,* Jan. 4 and 5, 1978; *Washington Star,* comment: Jan. 5, 1978; Carter on secret diplomacy: as quoted by William F. Buckley, Jr., *Washington Star,* Sept. 24, 1978; Kissinger quoted: *Washington Star,* Nov. 2, 1978; Carter blames Israel: *Washington Post,* Dec. 15, 1978; Bush quoted: *National Review,* Jan. 5, 1979; Buckley comment: *Washington Star,* Dec. 24, 1978; Reston on European view of Carter: *The New York Times,* Dec. 29, 1978; H. Jordan in Guadeloupe: *Newsweek,* Jan. 15, 1979; Abzug firing: *The New York Times,* Jan. 13, 1979; Meany meeting: *ibid.;* Carter-Meany relations: as quoted in *Citizens for Republic Newsletter,* Nov. 15, 1978; Barnes on Carter campaign rhetoric: *Washington Star,* Oct. 22, 1978; Smith in *N.Y. Times:* Nov. 6, 1978; Osborne on Carter campaigning with Brown: *New Republic,* Nov. 18, 1978.

INDEX

418